An

AUTOBIOGRAPHY

of

JACK LONDON

An

AUTOBIOGRAPHY

of

JACK LONDON

Edited and Introduced by

Stephen Brennan

SKYHORSE PUBLISHING

Skyhorse Publishing books may be purchased in bulk at special discounts for sales promotion, corporate gifts, fund-raising, or educational purposes. Special editions can also be created to specifications. For details, contact the Special Sales Department, Skyh orse Publishing, 307 West 36th Street, 11th Floor, New York, NY 10018 or info@skyhorsepublishing.com.

www.skyhorsepublishing.com

10 9 8 7 6 5 4 3 2 1

Library of Congress Cataloging-in-Publication Data

London, Jack, 1876-1916.
An autobiography of Jack London / Jack London, Stephen Brennan (editor).
p. cm.
ISBN 978-1-62087-364-9 (alk. paper)
1. London, Jack, 1876-1916. 2. Authors, American--20th century--Biography.
I. Brennan, Stephen Vincent. II. Title.
PS3523.O46Z46 2013
813'.52--dc23
[B]

2012034937

Printed in the United States of America

Contents

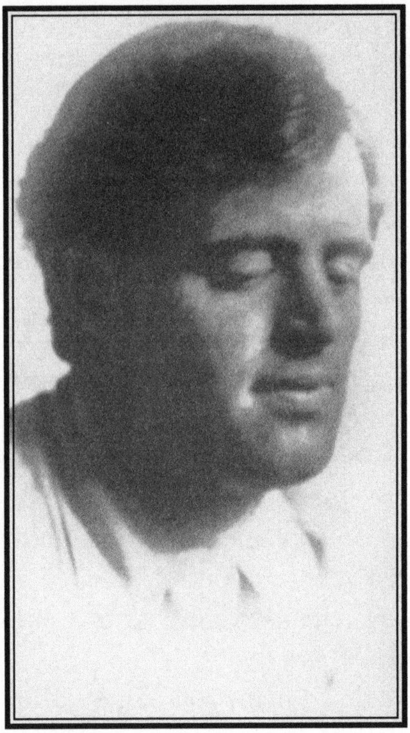

Introduction

"We live in an age when men treat art as if it were meant to be a form of autobiography."

—Oscar Wilde

The art or practice of autobiography—that is, writing about one's self—has been going on since folk first took up sticks to scratch their names in the mold. The practice of calling this scribbled self-publication an *autobiography*, is of a more recent origin. The word itself doesn't appear in English until the late 1700, when some wag famously judged it too "pedantic" for general use, and even today the word retains a faintly sophistical air. But eventually a whole literary genre grew up around the idea that one could—perhaps even should—write one's own biography, that is, practice autobiography.

We know the impulse well enough. Which of us has not, at one time or another, experienced an almost overwhelming compulsion to tell his or her own story, to get it out and get it down on paper? *I was there and I saw all, and this and that occurred, and this is how I felt about it, and how I feel about it now.*

If one accepts a holistic take on the genre—that is, that autobiography comes in many forms—one recognizes an array of sub-genres. There are the diarists and composers of memoir, tell-all, and true-confessions. Even formal journalism is sometimes practiced as a true-life adventure story—depending on the point of view. Thus the journal-keepers of an earlier time became the journalists of a later age. Fact is, if you insert yourself into, or are already an actor in, the story you are telling, you are writing autobiography. Sorry, but that's how it is.

And of course there *are* many reasons to sit down and write one's own story.

Brag is one of them. *Look at all I've accomplished! Ain't I swell?* Or, one may purpose apology. Autobiography in ancient times was called *apologia*—translated "confession," mea culpa. This may be regarded as telling a tale—cautionary or otherwise—on one's self. Or one can write defensively, like an old general attempting to explain or excuse old slaughters; or aggressively, to hurt or wound, to settle old scores, to spin. Or one may write for the sheer pleasure, or pain, of conjuring and confronting—perhaps re-configuring—old memories, absent friends, heartbreaks.

Implicit in most autobiography is the desire to be remembered, and to be remembered aright—whatever *aright* might mean. Mark Twain said somewhere that he wished to write his own biography, so he "could rely on getting in all the facts."

The facts of Jack London's life are not in doubt. He was born John Chaney, in San Francisco in 1876, to an unwed mother by the name of Flora Wellman and a father, W. H. Chaney, whom Jack was never to know. By and by Flora (a music teacher and sometimes

spiritualist) married up with John London a hard-working, quiet man, with two daughters. One of these girls, Eliza, is said to have acted as little Jack's mother surrogate. They remained close all of Jack's life. The family lodged in various places in the Bay area, but soon settled in Oakland. There they lived what we might today call a *middle-class*—what they called a *working-class*—life. Either way, theirs was not the abject poverty London was to later suggest. The boy attended school in Oakland, was an indifferent student, and often a truant, routinely slipping away for a day's ramble down on the city's waterfront. Here first, at a young age, Jack learned to drink. Not, as he was later to assert, for the drink itself, for the "jingle," but more for the company of other men and boys, their acceptance and fellowship. By his early teens Jack was ditching school, almost all the time. But, quite amazingly, he had by this time discovered the Oakland Public Library, and in particular the librarian, Ina Coolbrith (she was later to become the first Poet Laureate of the State of California) who loaned the boy books, and guided his course of reading. By night Jack sailed his own small boat, and *oyster-pirated* in the rich shell beds of the Bay, usually managing to elude the harbor patrol. Eventually his little sloop became damaged, and Jack turned around and worked for the State Fishing Patrol, doing his best to thwart other oyster pirates. But soon he had enough of this and signed aboard a sealing schooner bound for the islands in the seal-rich northern Pacific. This experience was to inspire his later fictional masterpiece *The Sea Wolf.* When he returned home, the States were in severe recession owing to the financial panic of 1893. Jack tried his hand at a couple of back-breaking jobs, but quickly gave them up and hit the road, beginning his life as a "tramp." As the expression went, he joined "Kelly's Army," an informal association of thousands of unemployed, determined to march on Washington.

These hobo adventures, riding rails, looking for work, begging for food, and ducking the railroad company "bulls," he was to later chronicle in his memoir *The Road.* In 1894 Jack served a thirty-day sentence for vagrancy, in the Erie County Penitentiary, in Buffalo NY. This time, returning home, he set himself to get an education, completing his high school work and publishing his first short story, *"Typhoon Off the Coast of Japan,"* in the school's magazine.

In 1896 he attended Berkeley College, but quit after the first year. In 1897 he joined the gold rush and took passage to the Klondike. This time in Alaska was to furnish Jack London with inspiration for many short stories, and for his two most famous works: *The Call of the Wild* and *White Fang.* Again returning to Oakland, he set himself to becoming a published author. By 1900, Jack's twenty-fourth year,

he was doing very well indeed, selling his tales of adventure to several of the big magazines. In this year Jack married Bessie Maddern, with whom he was to have two daughters, but their marriage ended after four years. In 1905 he married Charmian Kittredge. He called her his "mate-woman," and their marriage was to last the rest of his life. *The Call of the Wild* had been published in 1903 and became an instant best-seller. Jack London has been a best-seller every year since—that's over one hundred years. Which other American author can we say the same of? Mark Twain perhaps. By 1913 he was the best-paid, most famous, most widely read American author in the world. In his short writing life—only sixteen years—he wrote twenty-five novels, dozens and dozens of short stories, plays, and essays. Today he is recognized as a forerunner of such literary giants as Ernest Hemingway, John Steinbeck, and Jack Kerouac.

Jack London was also an adventurer, journalist, celebrity, polemicist, and drunk. And it was the drink that got him in the end, John Barleycorn. He died at his ranch of uremia, or kidney failure, very likely brought on by an acute alcoholic condition. He was forty years old.

An Autobiography of Jack London is composed of excerpts of three works: *The Road* (1907), *The Cruise of the Snark* (1911), and *John Barleycorn* (1913). I have retained the variant punctuation and spelling of the originals.

Stephen Brennan
West Cornwall, CT

Part One
The Road

Chapter 1
Confession

There is a woman in the state of Nevada to whom I once lied continuously, consistently, and shamelessly, for the matter of a couple of hours. I don't want to apologize to her. Far be it from me. But I do want to explain. Unfortunately, I do not know her name, much less her present address. If her eyes should chance upon these lines, I hope she will write to me.

It was in Reno, Nevada, in the summer of 1892. Also, it was fair-time, and the town was filled with petty crooks and tin-horns, to say nothing of a vast and hungry horde of hoboes. It was the hungry hoboes that made the town a "hungry" town. They "battered" the back doors of the homes of the citizens until the back doors became unresponsive.

A hard town for "scoffings," was what the hoboes called it at that time. I know that I missed many a meal, in spite of the fact that I could "throw my feet" with the next one when it came to "slamming a gate" for a "poke-out" or a "set-down," or hitting for a "light piece" on the street. Why, I was so hard put in that town, one day, that I gave the porter the slip and invaded the private car of some itinerant millionnaire. The train started as I made the platform, and I headed for the aforesaid millionnaire with the porter one jump behind and reaching for me. It was a dead heat, for I reached the millionnaire at the same instant that the porter reached me. I had no time for formalities. "Gimme a quarter to eat on," I blurted out. And as I live, that millionnaire dipped into his pocket and gave me . . . just . . . precisely . . . a quarter. It is my conviction that he was so flabbergasted that he obeyed automatically, and it has been a matter of keen regret ever since, on my part, that I didn't ask him for a dollar. I know that I'd have got it. I swung off the platform of that private car with the porter manoeuvring to kick me in the face. He missed me. One is at a terrible disadvantage when trying to swing off the lowest step of a car and not break his neck on the right of way, with, at the same time, an irate Ethiopian on the platform above trying to land him in the face with a number eleven. But I got the quarter! I got it!

But to return to the woman to whom I so shamelessly lied. It was in the evening of my last day in Reno. I had been out to the race-track watching the ponies run, and had missed my dinner (*i.e.* the mid-day meal). I was hungry, and, furthermore, a committee of public safety had just been organized to rid the town of just such hungry mortals as I. Already a lot of my brother hoboes had been gathered in by John Law, and I could hear the sunny valleys of California calling to me over the cold crests of the Sierras. Two acts remained for me to perform before I shook the dust of Reno from my feet. One was to catch the blind baggage on the westbound overland that night. The other was first to get something to eat. Even youth will hesitate at an all-night ride, on an empty stomach, outside a train that is tearing the atmosphere through the snow-sheds, tunnels, and eternal snows of heaven-aspiring mountains.

But that something to eat was a hard proposition. I was "turned down" at a dozen houses. Sometimes I received insulting remarks and was informed of the barred domicile that should be mine if I had my just deserts. The worst of it was that such assertions were only too true. That was why I was pulling west that night. John Law was abroad in the town, seeking eagerly for the hungry and homeless, for by such was his barred domicile tenanted.

At other houses the doors were slammed in my face, cutting short my politely and humbly couched request for something to eat. At one house they did not open the door. I stood on the porch and knocked, and they looked out at me through the window. They even held one sturdy little boy aloft so that he could see over the shoulders of his elders the tramp who wasn't going to get anything to eat at their house.

It began to look as if I should be compelled to go to the very poor for my food. The very poor constitute the last sure recourse of the hungry tramp. The very poor can always be depended upon. They never turn away the hungry. Time and again, all over the United States, have I been refused food by the big house on the hill; and always have I received food from the little shack down by the creek or marsh, with its broken windows stuffed with rags and its tired-faced mother broken with labor. Oh, you charity-mongers! Go to the poor and learn, for the poor alone are the charitable. They neither give nor withhold from their excess. They have no excess. They give, and they withhold never, from what they need for themselves, and very often from what they cruelly need for themselves. A bone to the dog is not charity. Charity is the bone shared with the dog when you are just as hungry as the dog.

There was one house in particular where I was turned down that evening. The porch windows opened on the dining room, and through them I saw a man eating pie—a big meat-pie. I stood in the open door, and while he talked with me, he went on eating. He was prosperous, and out of his prosperity had been bred resentment against his less fortunate brothers.

He cut short my request for something to eat, snapping out, "I don't believe you want to work."

Now this was irrelevant. I hadn't said anything about work. The topic of conversation I had introduced was "food." In fact, I didn't want to work. I wanted to take the westbound overland that night.

"You wouldn't work if you had a chance," he bullied.

I glanced at his meek-faced wife, and knew that but for the presence of this Cerberus I'd have a whack at that meat-pie myself. But Cerberus sopped himself in the pie, and I saw that I must placate him if I were to get a share of it. So I sighed to myself and accepted his work-morality.

"Of course I want work," I bluffed.

"Don't believe it," he snorted.

"Try me," I answered, warming to the bluff.

"All right," he said. "Come to the corner of blank and blank streets"—(I have forgotten the address)—"to-morrow morning. You know where that burned building is, and I'll put you to work tossing bricks."

"All right, sir; I'll be there."

He grunted and went on eating. I waited. After a couple of minutes he looked up with an I-thought-you-were-gone expression on his face, and demanded:—

"Well?"

"I . . . I am waiting for something to eat," I said gently.

"I knew you wouldn't work!" he roared.

He was right, of course; but his conclusion must have been reached by mind-reading, for his logic wouldn't bear it out. But the beggar at the door must be humble, so I accepted his logic as I had accepted his morality.

"You see, I am now hungry," I said still gently. "To-morrow morning I shall be hungrier. Think how hungry I shall be when I have tossed bricks all day without anything to eat. Now if you will give me something to eat, I'll be in great shape for those bricks."

He gravely considered my plea, at the same time going on eating, while his wife nearly trembled into propitiatory speech, but refrained.

"I'll tell you what I'll do," he said between mouthfuls. "You come to work to-morrow, and in the middle of the day I'll advance you enough for your dinner. That will show whether you are in earnest or not."

"In the meantime—" I began; but he interrupted.

"If I gave you something to eat now, I'd never see you again. Oh, I know your kind. Look at me. I owe no man. I have never descended so low as to ask any one for food. I have always earned my food. The trouble with you is that you are idle and dissolute. I can see it in your face. I have worked and been honest. I have made myself what I am. And you can do the same, if you work and are honest."

"Like you?" I queried.

Alas, no ray of humor had ever penetrated the sombre work-sodden soul of that man.

"Yes, like me," he answered.

"All of us?" I queried.

"Yes, all of you," he answered, conviction vibrating in his voice.

"But if we all became like you," I said, "allow me to point out that there'd be nobody to toss bricks for you."

I swear there was a flicker of a smile in his wife's eye. As for him, he was aghast—but whether at the awful possibility of a reformed humanity that would not enable him to get anybody to toss bricks for him, or at my impudence, I shall never know.

"I'll not waste words on you," he roared. "Get out of here, you ungrateful whelp!"

I scraped my feet to advertise my intention of going, and queried: "And I don't get anything to eat?"

He arose suddenly to his feet. He was a large man. I was a stranger in a strange land, and John Law was looking for me. I went away hurriedly. "But why ungrateful?" I asked myself as I slammed his gate. "What in the dickens did he give me to be ungrateful about?" I looked back. I could still see him through the window. He had returned to his pie.

By this time I had lost heart. I passed many houses by without venturing up to them. All houses looked alike, and none looked "good." After walking half a dozen blocks I shook off my despondency and gathered my "nerve." This begging for food was all a game, and if I didn't like the cards, I could always call for a new deal. I made up my mind to tackle the next house. I approached it in the deepening twilight, going around to the kitchen door.

I knocked softly, and when I saw the kind face of the middle-aged woman who answered, as by inspiration came to me the "story" I was to tell. For know that upon his ability to tell a good story depends the success of the beggar. First of all, and on the instant, the beggar must "size up" his victim. After that, he must tell a story that will appeal to the peculiar personality and temperament of that particular victim. And right here arises the great difficulty: in the instant that he is sizing up the victim he must begin his story. Not a minute is allowed for preparation. As in a lightning flash he must divine the nature of the victim and conceive a tale that will hit home. The successful hobo must be an artist. He must create spontaneously and instantaneously—and not upon a theme selected from the plenitude of his own imagination, but upon the theme he reads in the face of the person who opens the door, be it man, woman, or child, sweet or crabbed, generous or miserly, good-natured or cantankerous, Jew or Gentile, black or white, race-prejudiced or brotherly, provincial or universal, or whatever else it may be. I have often thought that to this training of my tramp days is due much of my success as a story-writer. In order to get the food whereby I lived, I was compelled to tell tales that rang true. At the back door, out of inexorable necessity, is developed the convincingness and sincerity laid down by all authorities on the art of the short-story. Also, I quite believe it was my tramp-apprenticeship that made a realist out of me. Realism constitutes the only goods one can exchange at the kitchen door for grub.

After all, art is only consummate artfulness, and artfulness saves many a "story." I remember lying in a police station at Winnipeg, Manitoba. I was bound west over the Canadian Pacific. Of course, the police wanted my story, and I gave it to them—on the spur of the moment. They were landlubbers, in the heart of the continent, and what better story for them than a sea story? They could never trip me up on that. And so I told a tearful tale of my life on the hell-ship *Glenmore*. (I had once seen the *Glenmore* lying at anchor in San Francisco Bay.)

I was an English apprentice, I said. And they said that I didn't talk like an English boy. It was up to me to create on the instant. I had been born and reared in the United States. On the death of my parents, I had been sent to England to my grandparents. It was they who had apprenticed me on the *Glenmore*. I hope the captain of the *Glenmore* will forgive me, for I gave him a character that night in the Winnipeg police station. Such cruelty! Such brutality! Such diabolical ingenuity of torture! It explained why I had deserted the *Glenmore* at Montreal.

But why was I in the middle of Canada going west, when my grandparents lived in England? Promptly I created a married sister who lived in California. She would take care of me. I developed at length her loving nature. But they were not done with me, those hard-hearted policemen. I had joined the *Glenmore* in England; in the two years that had elapsed before my desertion at Montreal, what had the *Glenmore* done and where had she been? And thereat I took those landlubbers around the world with me. Buffeted by pounding seas and stung with flying spray, they fought a typhoon with me off the coast of Japan. They loaded and unloaded cargo with me in all the ports of the Seven Seas. I took them to India, and Rangoon, and China, and had them hammer ice with me around the Horn and at last come to moorings at Montreal.

And then they said to wait a moment, and one policeman went forth into the night while I warmed myself at the stove, all the while racking my brains for the trap they were going to spring on me.

I groaned to myself when I saw him come in the door at the heels of the policeman. No gypsy prank had thrust those tiny hoops of gold through the ears; no prairie winds had beaten that skin into wrinkled leather; nor had snow-drift and mountain-slope put in his walk that reminiscent roll. And in those eyes, when they looked at me, I saw the unmistakable sun-wash of the sea. Here was a theme, alas! With half a dozen policemen to watch me read—I who had never sailed the China seas, nor been around the Horn, nor looked with my eyes upon India and Rangoon.

I was desperate. Disaster stalked before me incarnate in the form of that gold-ear-ringed, weather-beaten son of the sea. Who was he? What was he? I must solve him ere he solved me. I must take a new orientation, or else those wicked policemen would orientate me to a cell, a police court, and more cells. If he questioned me first, before I knew how much he knew, I was lost.

But did I betray my desperate plight to those lynx-eyed guardians of the public welfare of Winnipeg? Not I. I met that aged sailorman glad-eyed and beaming, with all the simulated relief at deliverance that a drowning man would display on finding a life-preserver in his last despairing clutch. Here was a man who understood and who would verify my true story to the faces of those sleuth-hounds who did not understand, or, at least, such was what I endeavored to play-act. I seized upon him; I volleyed him with questions about himself. Before my judges I would prove the character of my savior before he saved me.

He was a kindly sailorman—an "easy mark." The policemen grew impatient while I questioned him. At last one of them told me to shut up. I shut up; but while I remained shut up, I was busy creating, busy sketching the scenario of the next act. I had learned enough to go on with. He was a Frenchman. He had sailed always on French merchant vessels, with the one exception of a voyage on a "lime-juicer." And last of all—blessed fact!—he had not been on the sea for twenty years.

The policeman urged him on to examine me.

"You called in at Rangoon?" he queried.

I nodded. "We put our third mate ashore there. Fever."

If he had asked me what kind of fever, I should have answered, "Enteric," though for the life of me I didn't know what enteric was. But he didn't ask me. Instead, his next question was:—

"And how is Rangoon?"

"All right. It rained a whole lot when we were there."

"Did you get shore-leave?"

"Sure," I answered. "Three of us apprentices went ashore together."

"Do you remember the temple?"

"Which temple?" I parried.

"The big one, at the top of the stairway."

If I remembered that temple, I knew I'd have to describe it. The gulf yawned for me.

I shook my head.

"You can see it from all over the harbor," he informed me. "You don't need shore-leave to see that temple."

I never loathed a temple so in my life. But I fixed that particular temple at Rangoon.

"You can't see it from the harbor," I contradicted. "You can't see it from the town. You can't see it from the top of the stairway. Because—" I paused for the effect. "Because there isn't any temple there."

"But I saw it with my own eyes!" he cried.

"That was in—?" I queried.

"Seventy-one."

"It was destroyed in the great earthquake of 1887," I explained. "It was very old."

There was a pause. He was busy reconstructing in his old eyes the youthful vision of that fair temple by the sea.

"The stairway is still there," I aided him. "You can see it from all over the harbor. And you remember that little island on the right-hand side coming into the harbor?" I guess there must have been one there (I was prepared to shift it over to the left-hand side), for he nodded. "Gone," I said. "Seven fathoms of water there now."

I had gained a moment for breath. While he pondered on time's changes, I prepared the finishing touches of my story.

"You remember the custom-house at Bombay?"

He remembered it.

"Burned to the ground," I announced.

"Do you remember Jim Wan?" he came back at me.

"Dead," I said; but who the devil Jim Wan was I hadn't the slightest idea.

I was on thin ice again.

"Do you remember Billy Harper, at Shanghai?" I queried back at him quickly.

That aged sailorman worked hard to recollect, but the Billy Harper of my imagination was beyond his faded memory.

"Of course you remember Billy Harper," I insisted. "Everybody knows him. He's been there forty years. Well, he's still there, that's all."

And then the miracle happened. The sailorman remembered Billy Harper. Perhaps there was a Billy Harper, and perhaps he had been in Shanghai for forty years and was still there; but it was news to me.

For fully half an hour longer, the sailorman and I talked on in similar fashion. In the end he told the policemen that I was what I represented myself to be, and after a night's lodging and a breakfast I was released to wander on westward to my married sister in San Francisco.

But to return to the woman in Reno who opened her door to me in the deepening twilight. At the first glimpse of her kindly face I took my cue. I became a sweet, innocent, unfortunate lad. I couldn't speak. I opened my mouth and closed it again. Never in my life before had I asked any one for food. My embarrassment was painful, extreme. I was ashamed. I, who looked upon begging as a delightful whimsicality, thumbed myself over into a true son of Mrs. Grundy, burdened with all her bourgeois morality. Only the harsh pangs of the belly-need could compel me to do so degraded and ignoble a thing as beg for food. And into my face I strove to throw all the wan wistfulness of famished and ingenuous youth unused to mendicancy.

"You are hungry, my poor boy," she said.

I had made her speak first.

I nodded my head and gulped.

"It is the first time I have ever . . . asked," I faltered.

"Come right in." The door swung open. "We have already finished eating, but the fire is burning and I can get something up for you."

She looked at me closely when she got me into the light.

"I wish my boy were as healthy and strong as you," she said. "But he is not strong. He sometimes falls down. He just fell down this afternoon and hurt himself badly, the poor dear."

She mothered him with her voice, with an ineffable tenderness in it that I yearned to appropriate. I glanced at him. He sat across the table, slender and pale, his head swathed in bandages. He did not move, but his eyes, bright in the lamplight, were fixed upon me in a steady and wondering stare.

"Just like my poor father," I said. "He had the falling sickness. Some kind of vertigo. It puzzled the doctors. They never could make out what was the matter with him."

"He is dead?" she queried gently, setting before me half a dozen soft-boiled eggs.

"Dead," I gulped. "Two weeks ago. I was with him when it happened. We were crossing the street together. He fell right down. He was never conscious again. They carried him into a drug-store. He died there."

And thereat I developed the pitiful tale of my father—how, after my mother's death, he and I had gone to San Francisco from the ranch; how his pension (he was an old soldier), and the little other money he had, was not enough; and how he had tried book-canvassing. Also, I narrated my own woes during the few days after his death that I had spent alone and forlorn on the streets of San Francisco. While that good woman warmed up biscuits, fried bacon, and cooked more eggs, and while I kept pace with her in taking care of all that she placed before me, I enlarged the picture of that poor orphan boy and filled in the details. I became that poor boy. I believed in him as I believed in the beautiful eggs I was devouring. I could have wept for myself. I know the tears did get into my voice at times. It was very effective.

In fact, with every touch I added to the picture, that kind soul gave me something also. She made up a lunch for me to carry away. She put in many boiled eggs, pepper and salt, and other things, and a big apple. She provided me with three pairs of thick red woollen socks. She gave me clean handkerchiefs and other things which I have since forgotten. And all the time she cooked more and more and I ate more and more. I gorged like a savage; but then it was a far cry across the Sierras on a blind baggage, and I knew not when nor where I should find my next meal. And all the while, like a death's-head at the feast, silent and motionless, her own unfortunate boy sat and stared at me across the table. I suppose I represented to him mystery, and romance, and adventure—all that was denied the feeble flicker of life that was in him. And yet I could not forbear, once or twice, from wondering if he saw through me down to the bottom of my mendacious heart.

"But where are you going to?" she asked me.

"Salt Lake City," said I. "I have a sister there—a married sister." (I debated if I should make a Mormon out of her, and decided against it.) "Her husband is a plumber—a contracting plumber."

Now I knew that contracting plumbers were usually credited with making lots of money. But I had spoken. It was up to me to qualify.

"They would have sent me the money for my fare if I had asked for it," I explained, "but they have had sickness and business troubles. His partner cheated him. And so I wouldn't write for the money. I knew I could make my way there somehow. I let them think I had enough to get me to Salt Lake City. She is lovely, and so kind. She was always kind to me. I guess I'll go into the shop and learn the trade. She has two daughters. They are younger than I. One is only a baby."

Of all my married sisters that I have distributed among the cities of the United States, that Salt Lake sister is my favorite. She is quite real, too. When I tell about her, I can see her, and her two little girls, and her plumber husband. She is a large, motherly woman, just verging on beneficent stoutness—the kind, you know, that always cooks nice things and that never gets angry. She is a brunette. Her husband is a quiet, easy-going fellow. Sometimes I almost know him quite well. And who knows but some day I may meet him? If that aged sailorman could remember Billy Harper, I see no reason why I should not some day meet the husband of my sister who lives in Salt Lake City.

On the other hand, I have a feeling of certitude within me that I shall never meet in the flesh my many parents and grandparents—you see, I invariably killed them off. Heart disease was my favorite way of getting rid of my mother, though on occasion I did away with her by means of consumption, pneumonia, and typhoid fever. It is true, as the Winnipeg policemen will attest, that I have grandparents living in England; but that was a long time ago and it is a fair assumption that they are dead by now. At any rate, they have never written to me.

I hope that woman in Reno will read these lines and forgive me my gracelessness and unveracity. I do not apologize, for I am unashamed. It was youth, delight in life, zest for experience, that brought me to her door. It did me good. It taught me the intrinsic kindliness of human nature. I hope it did her good. Anyway, she may get a good laugh out of it now that she learns the real inwardness of the situation.

To her my story was "true." She believed in me and all my family, and she was filled with solicitude for the dangerous journey I must make ere I won to Salt Lake City. This solicitude nearly brought me to grief. Just as I was leaving, my arms full of lunch and my pockets bulging with fat woollen socks, she bethought herself of a nephew, or uncle, or relative of some sort, who was in the railway mail service, and who, moreover, would come through that night on the very train on which I was going to steal my ride. The very thing! She would take me down to the depot, tell him my story, and get him to hide me in the mail car. Thus, without danger or hardship, I would be carried straight through to Ogden. Salt Lake City was only a few miles farther on. My heart sank. She grew excited as she developed the plan and with my sinking heart I had to feign unbounded gladness and enthusiasm at this solution of my difficulties.

Solution! Why I was bound west that night, and here was I being trapped into going east. It *was* a trap, and I hadn't the heart to tell her that it was all a miserable lie. And while I made believe that I was delighted, I was busy cudgelling my brains for some way to escape. But there was no way. She would see me into the mail-car—she said so herself—and then that mail-clerk relative of hers would carry me to Ogden. And then I would have to beat my way back over all those hundreds of miles of desert.

But luck was with me that night. Just about the time she was getting ready to put on her bonnet and accompany me, she discovered that she had made a mistake. Her mail-clerk relative was not scheduled to come through that night. His run had been changed. He would not come through until two nights afterward. I was saved, for of course my boundless youth would never permit me to wait those two days. I optimistically assured her that I'd get to Salt Lake City quicker if I started immediately, and I departed with her blessings and best wishes ringing in my ears.

But those woollen socks were great. I know. I wore a pair of them that night on the blind baggage of the overland, and that overland went west.

Chapter 2
Holding Her Down

Barring accidents, a good hobo, with youth and agility, can hold a train down despite all the efforts of the train-crew to "ditch" him—given, of course, night-time as an essential condition. When such a hobo, under such conditions, makes up his mind that he is going to hold her down, either he does hold her down, or chance trips him up. There is no legitimate way, short of murder, whereby the train-crew can ditch him. That train-crews have not stopped short of murder is a current belief in the tramp world. Not having had that particular experience in my tramp days I cannot vouch for it personally.

But this I have heard of the "bad" roads. When a tramp has "gone underneath," on the rods, and the train is in motion, there is apparently no way of dislodging him until the train stops. The tramp, snugly ensconced inside the truck, with the four wheels and all the framework around him, has the "cinch" on the crew—or so he thinks, until some day he rides the rods on a bad road. A bad road is usually one on which a short time previously one or several trainmen have been killed by tramps. Heaven pity the tramp who is caught "underneath" on such a road—for caught he is, though the train be going sixty miles an hour.

The "shack" (brakeman) takes a coupling-pin and a length of bell-cord to the platform in front of the truck in which the tramp is riding. The shack fastens the coupling-pin to the bell-cord, drops the former down between the platforms, and pays out the latter. The coupling-pin strikes the ties between the rails, rebounds against the bottom of the car, and again strikes the ties. The shack plays it back and forth, now to this side, now to the other, lets it out a bit and hauls it in a bit, giving his weapon opportunity for every variety of impact and rebound. Every blow of that flying coupling-pin is freighted with death, and at sixty miles an hour it beats a veritable tattoo of death. The next day the remains of that tramp are gathered up along the right of way, and a line in the local paper mentions the unknown man, undoubtedly a tramp, assumably drunk, who had probably fallen asleep on the track.

As a characteristic illustration of how a capable hobo can hold her down, I am minded to give the following experience. I was in Ottawa, bound west over the Canadian Pacific. Three thousand miles of that road stretched before me; it was the fall of the year, and I had to cross Manitoba and the Rocky Mountains. I could expect "crimpy" weather, and every moment of delay increased the frigid hardships of the journey. Furthermore, I was disgusted. The distance between Montreal and Ottawa is one hundred and twenty miles. I ought to know, for I had just come over it and it had taken me six days. By mistake I had missed the main line and come over a small "jerk" with only two locals a day on it. And during these six days I had lived on dry crusts, and not enough of them, begged from the French peasants.

Furthermore, my disgust had been heightened by the one day I had spent in Ottawa trying to get an outfit of clothing for my long journey. Let me put it on record right here that Ottawa, with one exception, is the hardest town in the United States and Canada to beg clothes in; the one exception is Washington, D.C. The latter fair city is the limit. I spent two weeks there trying to beg a pair of shoes, and then had to go on to Jersey City before I got them.

But to return to Ottawa. At eight sharp in the morning I started out after clothes. I worked energetically all day. I swear I walked forty miles. I interviewed the housewives of a thousand homes. I did not even knock off work for dinner. And at six in the after-noon, after ten hours of unremitting and depressing toil, I was still shy one shirt, while the pair of trousers I had managed to acquire was tight and, moreover, was showing all the signs of an early disintegration.

At six I quit work and headed for the railroad yards, expecting to pick up something to eat on the way. But my hard luck was still with me. I was refused food at house after house. Then I got a "hand-out." My spirits soared, for it was the largest hand-out I had ever seen in a long and varied experience. It was a parcel wrapped in newspapers and as big as a mature suit-case. I hurried to a vacant lot and opened it. First, I saw cake, then more cake, all kinds and makes of cake, and then some. It was all cake. No bread and butter with thick firm slices of meat between—nothing but cake; and I who of all things abhorred cake most! In another age and clime they sat down by the waters of Babylon and wept. And in a vacant lot in Canada's proud capital, I, too, sat down and wept . . . over a mountain of cake. As one looks upon the face of his dead son, so looked I upon that multitudinous pastry. I suppose I was an ungrateful tramp, for I refused to partake of the bounteousness of the house that had had a party the night before. Evidently the guests hadn't liked cake either.

That cake marked the crisis in my fortunes. Than it nothing could be worse; therefore things must begin to mend. And they did. At the very next house I was given a "set-down." Now a "set-down" is the height of bliss. One is taken inside, very often is given a chance to wash, and is then "set-down" at a table. Tramps love to throw their legs under a table. The house was large and comfortable, in the midst of spacious grounds and fine trees, and sat well back from the street. They had just finished eating, and I was taken right into the dining room—in itself a most unusual happening, for the tramp who is lucky enough to win a set-down usually receives it in the kitchen. A grizzled and gracious Englishman, his matronly wife, and a beautiful young Frenchwoman talked with me while I ate.

I wonder if that beautiful young Frenchwoman would remember, at this late day, the laugh I gave her when I uttered the barbaric phrase, "two-bits." You see, I was trying delicately to hit them for a "light piece." That was how the sum of money came to be mentioned. "What?" she said. "Two-bits," said I. Her mouth was twitching as she again said, "What?" "Two-bits," said I. Whereat she burst into laughter. "Won't you repeat it?" she said, when she had regained control of herself. "Two-bits," said I. And once more she rippled into uncontrollable silvery laughter. "I beg your pardon," said she; "but what . . . what was it you said?" "Two-bits," said I; "is there anything wrong about it?" "Not that I know of," she gurgled between gasps; "but what does it mean?" I explained, but I do not remember now whether or not I got that two-bits out of her; but I have often wondered since as to which of us was the provincial.

When I arrived at the depot, I found, much to my disgust, a bunch of at least twenty tramps that were waiting to ride out the blind baggages of the overland. Now two or three tramps on the blind baggage are all right. They are inconspicuous. But a score! That meant trouble. No train-crew would ever let all of us ride.

May as well explain here what a blind baggage is. Some mail-cars are built without doors in the ends; hence, such a car is "blind." The mail-cars that possess end doors, have those doors always locked.

Suppose, after the train has started, that a tramp gets on to the platform of one of these blind cars. There is no door, or the door is locked. No conductor or brakeman can get to him to collect fare or throw him off. It is clear that the tramp is safe until the next time the train stops. Then he must get off, run ahead in the darkness, and when the train pulls by, jump on to the blind again. But there are ways and ways, as you shall see.

When the train pulled out, those twenty tramps swarmed upon the three blinds. Some climbed on before the train had run a car-length. They were awkward dubs, and I saw their speedy finish. Of course, the train-crew was "on," and at the first stop the trouble began. I jumped off and ran forward along the track. I noticed that I was accompanied by a number of the tramps. They evidently knew their business. When one is beating an overland, he must always keep well ahead of the train at the stops. I ran ahead, and as I ran, one by one those that accompanied me dropped out. This dropping out was the measure of their skill and nerve in boarding a train.

For this is the way it works. When the train starts, the shack rides out the blind. There is no way for him to get back into the train proper except by jumping off the blind and catching a platform where the car-ends are not "blind." When the train is going as fast as the shack cares to risk, he therefore jumps off the blind, lets several cars go by, and gets on to the train. So it is up to the tramp to run so far ahead that before the blind is opposite him the shack will have already vacated it.

I dropped the last tramp by about fifty feet, and waited. The train started. I saw the lantern of the shack on the first blind. He was riding her out. And I saw the dubs stand forlornly by the track as the blind went by. They made no attempt to get on. They were beaten by their own inefficiency at the very start. After them, in the line-up, came the tramps that knew a little something about the game. They let the first blind, occupied by the shack, go by, and jumped on the second and third blinds. Of course, the shack jumped off the first and on to the second as it went by, and scrambled around there, throwing off the men who had boarded it. But the point is, that I was so far ahead that when the first blind came opposite me, the shack had already left it and was tangled up with the tramps on the second blind. A half dozen of the more skilful tramps, who had run far enough ahead, made the first blind, too.

At the next stop, as we ran forward along the track, I counted but fifteen of us. Five had been ditched. The weeding-out process had begun nobly, and it continued station by station. Now we were fourteen, now twelve, now eleven, now nine, now eight. It reminded me of the ten little niggers of the nursery rhyme. I was resolved that I should be the last little nigger of all. And why not? Was I not blessed with strength, agility, and youth? (I was eighteen, and in perfect condition.) And didn't I have my "nerve" with me? And furthermore, was I not a tramp-royal? Were not these other tramps mere dubs and "gay-cats" and amateurs alongside of me? If I weren't the last little nigger, I might as well quit the game and get a job on an alfalfa farm somewhere.

By the time our number had been reduced to four, the whole train-crew had become interested. From then on it was a contest of skill and wits, with the odds in favor of the crew. One by one the three other survivors turned up missing, until I alone remained. My, but I was proud of myself! No Croesus was ever prouder of his first million. I was holding her down in spite of two brakemen, a conductor, a fireman, and an engineer.

And here are a few samples of the way I held her down. Out ahead, in the darkness,—so far ahead that the shack riding out the blind must perforce get off before it reaches me,—I get on. Very well. I am good for another station. When that station is reached, I dart ahead again to repeat the manoeuvre. The train pulls out. I watch her coming. There is no light of a lantern on the blind. Has the crew abandoned the fight? I do not know. One never knows, and one must be prepared every moment for anything. As the first blind comes opposite me, and I run to leap aboard, I strain my eyes to see if the shack is on the platform. For all I know he may be there, with his lantern doused, and even as I spring upon the steps that lantern may smash down upon my head. I ought to know. I have been hit by lanterns two or three times.

But no, the first blind is empty. The train is gathering speed. I am safe for another station. But am I? I feel the train slacken speed. On the instant I am alert. A manoeuvre is being executed against me, and I do not know what it is. I try to watch on both sides at once, not forgetting to keep track of the tender in front of me. From any one, or all, of these three directions, I may be assailed.

Ah, there it comes. The shack has ridden out the engine. My first warning is when his feet strike the steps of the right-hand side of the blind. Like a flash I am off the blind to the left and running ahead past the engine. I lose myself in the darkness. The situation is where it has been ever since the train left Ottawa. I am ahead, and the train must come past me if it is to proceed on its journey. I have as good a chance as ever for boarding her.

I watch carefully. I see a lantern come forward to the engine, and I do not see it go back from the engine. It must therefore be still on the engine, and it is a fair assumption that attached to the handle of that lantern is a shack. That shack was lazy, or else he would have put out his lantern instead of trying to shield it as he came forward. The train pulls out. The first blind is empty, and I gain it. As before the train slackens, the shack from the engine boards the blind from one side, and I go off the other side and run forward.

As I wait in the darkness I am conscious of a big thrill of pride. The overland has stopped twice for me—for me, a poor hobo on the bum. I alone have twice stopped the overland with its many passengers and coaches, its government mail, and its two thousand steam horses straining in the engine. And I weigh only one hundred and sixty pounds, and I haven't a five-cent piece in my pocket!

Again I see the lantern come forward to the engine. But this time it comes conspicuously. A bit too conspicuously to suit me, and I wonder what is up. At any rate I have something else to be afraid of than the shack on the engine. The train pulls by. Just in time, before I make my spring, I see the dark form of a shack, without a lantern, on the first blind. I let it go by, and prepare to board the second blind. But the shack on the first blind has jumped off and is at my heels. Also, I have a fleeting glimpse of the lantern of the shack who rode out the engine. He has jumped off, and now both shacks are on the ground on the same side with me. The next moment the second blind comes by and I am aboard it. But I do not linger. I have figured out my countermove. As I dash across the platform I hear the impact of the shack's feet against the steps as he boards. I jump off the other side and run forward with the train. My plan is to run forward and get on the first blind. It is nip and tuck, for the train is gathering speed. Also, the shack is behind me and running after me. I guess I am the better sprinter, for I make the first blind. I stand on the steps and watch my pursuer. He is only about ten feet back and running hard; but now the train has approximated his own speed, and, relative to me, he is standing still. I encourage him, hold out my hand to him; but he explodes in a mighty oath, gives up and makes the train several cars back.

The train is speeding along, and I am still chuckling to myself, when, without warning, a spray of water strikes me. The fireman is playing the hose on me from the engine. I step forward from the car-platform to the rear of the tender, where I am sheltered under the overhang. The water flies harmlessly over my head. My fingers itch to climb up on the tender and lam that fireman with a chunk of coal; but I know if I do that, I'll be massacred by him and the engineer, and I refrain.

At the next stop I am off and ahead in the darkness. This time, when the train pulls out, both shacks are on the first blind. I divine their game. They have blocked the repetition of my previous play. I cannot again take the second blind, cross over, and run forward to the first. As soon as the first blind passes and I do not get on, they swing off, one on each side of the train. I board the second blind, and as I do so I know that a moment later, simultaneously, those two shacks will arrive on both sides of me. It is like a trap. Both ways are blocked. Yet there is another way out, and that way is up.

So I do not wait for my pursuers to arrive. I climb upon the upright ironwork of the platform and stand upon the wheel of the hand-brake. This has taken up the moment of grace and I hear the shacks strike the steps on either side. I don't stop to look. I raise my arms overhead until my hands rest against the down-curving ends of the roofs of the two cars. One hand, of course, is on the curved roof of one car, the other hand on the curved roof of the other car.

By this time both shacks are coming up the steps. I know it, though I am too busy to see them. All this is happening in the space of only several seconds. I make a spring with my legs and "muscle" myself up with my arms. As I draw up my legs, both shacks reach for me and clutch empty air. I know this, for I look down and see them. Also I hear them swear.

I am now in a precarious position, riding the ends of the down-curving roofs of two cars at the same time. With a quick, tense movement, I transfer both legs to the curve of one roof and both hands to the curve of the other roof. Then, gripping the edge of that curving roof, I climb over the curve to the level roof above, where I sit down to catch my breath, holding on the while to a ventilator that projects above the surface. I am on top of the train—on the "decks," as the tramps call it, and this process I have described is by them called "decking her." And let me say right here that only a young and vigorous tramp is able to deck a passenger train, and also, that the young and vigorous tramp must have his nerve with him as well.

The train goes on gathering speed, and I know I am safe until the next stop—but only until the next stop. If I remain on the roof after the train stops, I know those shacks will fusillade me with rocks. A healthy shack can "dewdrop" a pretty heavy chunk of stone on top of a car—say anywhere from five to twenty pounds. On the other hand, the chances are large that at the next stop the shacks will be waiting for me to descend at the place I climbed up. It is up to me to climb down at some other platform.

Registering a fervent hope that there are no tunnels in the next half mile, I rise to my feet and walk down the train half a dozen cars. And let me say that one must leave timidity behind him on such a *passear.* The roofs of passenger coaches are not made for midnight promenades. And if any one thinks they are, let me advise him to try it. Just let him walk along the roof of a jolting, lurching car, with nothing to hold on to but the black and empty air, and when he comes to the down-curving end of the roof, all wet and slippery with dew, let him accelerate his speed so as to step across to the next roof, down-curving and wet and slippery.

Believe me, he will learn whether his heart is weak or his head is giddy.

As the train slows down for a stop, half a dozen platforms from where I had decked her I come down. No one is on the platform. When the train comes to a standstill, I slip off to the ground. Ahead, and between me and the engine, are two moving lanterns. The shacks are looking for me on the roofs of the cars. I note that the car beside which I am standing is a "four-wheeler"—by which is meant that it has only four wheels to each truck. (When you go underneath on the rods, be sure to avoid the "six-wheelers,"—they lead to disasters.)

I duck under the train and make for the rods, and I can tell you I am mighty glad that the train is standing still. It is the first time I have ever gone underneath on the Canadian Pacific, and the internal arrangements are new to me. I try to crawl over the top of the truck, between the truck and the bottom of the car. But the space is not large enough for me to squeeze through. This is new to me. Down in the United States I am accustomed to going underneath on rapidly moving trains, seizing a gunnel and swinging my feet under to the brake-beam, and from there crawling over the top of the truck and down inside the truck to a seat on the cross-rod.

Feeling with my hands in the darkness, I learn that there is room between the brake-beam and the ground. It is a tight squeeze. I have to lie flat and worm my way through. Once inside the truck, I take my seat on the rod and wonder what the shacks are thinking has become of me. The train gets under way. They have given me up at last.

But have they? At the very next stop, I see a lantern thrust under the next truck to mine at the other end of the car. They are searching the rods for me. I must make my get-away pretty lively. I crawl on my stomach under the brake-beam. They see me and run for me, but I crawl on hands and knees across the rail on the opposite side and gain my feet. Then away I go for the head of the train. I run past the engine and hide in the sheltering darkness. It is the same old situation. I am ahead of the train, and the train must go past me.

The train pulls out. There is a lantern on the first blind. I lie low, and see the peering shack go by. But there is also a lantern on the second blind. That shack spots me and calls to the shack who has gone past on the first blind. Both jump off. Never mind, I'll take the third blind and deck her. But heavens, there is a lantern on the third blind, too. It is the conductor. I let it go by. At any rate I have now the full train-crew in front of me. I turn and run back in the opposite direction to what the train is going. I look over my shoulder. All three lanterns are on the ground and wobbling along in pursuit. I sprint. Half the train has gone by, and it is going quite fast, when I spring aboard. I know that the two shacks and the conductor will arrive like ravening wolves in about two seconds. I spring upon the wheel of the hand-brake, get my hands on the curved ends of the roofs, and muscle myself up to the decks; while my disappointed pursuers, clustering on the platform beneath like dogs that have treed a cat, howl curses up at me and say unsocial things about my ancestors.

But what does that matter? It is five to one, including the engineer and fireman, and the majesty of the law and the might of a great corporation are behind them, and I am beating them out. I am too far down the train, and I run ahead over the roofs of the coaches until I am over the fifth or sixth platform from the engine. I peer down cautiously. A shack is on that platform. That he has caught sight of me, I know from the way he makes a swift sneak inside the car; and I know, also, that he is waiting inside the door, all ready to pounce out on me when I climb down. But I make believe that I don't know, and I remain there to encourage him in his error. I do not see him, yet I know that he opens the door once and peeps up to assure himself that I am still there.

The train slows down for a station. I dangle my legs down in a tentative way. The train stops. My legs are still dangling. I hear the door unlatch softly. He is all ready for me. Suddenly I spring up and run forward over the roof. This is right over his head, where he lurks inside the door. The train is standing still; the night is quiet, and I take care to make plenty of noise on the metal roof with my feet. I don't know, but my assumption is that he is now running forward to catch me as I descend at the next platform. But I don't descend there. Halfway along the roof of the coach, I turn, retrace my way softly and quickly to the platform both the shack and I have just abandoned. The coast is clear. I descend to the ground on the off-side of the train and hide in the darkness. Not a soul has seen me.

I go over to the fence, at the edge of the right of way, and watch. Ah, ha! What's that? I see a lantern on top of the train, moving along from front to rear. They think I haven't come down, and they are searching the roofs for me. And better than that—on the ground on each side of the train, moving abreast with the lantern on top, are two other lanterns. It is a rabbit-drive, and I am the rabbit. When the shack on top flushes me, the ones on each side will nab me. I roll a cigarette and watch the procession go by. Once past me, I am safe to proceed to the front of the train. She pulls out, and I make the front blind without opposition. But before she is fully under way and just as I am lighting my cigarette, I am aware that the fireman has climbed over the coal to the back of the tender and is down at me. I am filled with apprehension. From his position he can mash me to a jelly with lumps of coal. Instead of which he addresses me, and I note with relief the admiration in his voice.

"You son-of-a-gun," is what he says.

It is a high compliment, and I thrill as a schoolboy thrills on receiving a reward of merit.

"Say," I call up to him, "don't you play the hose on me any more."

"All right," he answers, and goes back to his work.

I have made friends with the engine, but the shacks are still looking for me. At the next stop, the shacks ride out all three blinds, and as before, I let them go by and deck in the middle of the train. The crew is on its mettle by now, and the train stops. The shacks are going to ditch me or know the reason why. Three times the mighty overland stops for me at that station, and each time I elude the shacks and make the decks. But it is hopeless, for they have finally come to an understanding of the situation. I have taught them that they cannot guard the train from me. They must do something else.

And they do it. When the train stops that last time, they take after me hot-footed. Ah, I see their game. They are trying to run me down. At first they herd me back toward the rear of the train. I know my peril. Once to the rear of the train, it will pull out with me left behind. I double, and twist, and turn, dodge through my pursuers, and gain the front of the train. One shack still hangs on after me. All right, I'll give him the run of his life, for my wind is good. I run straight ahead along the track. It doesn't matter. If he chases me ten miles, he'll nevertheless have to catch the train, and I can board her at any speed that he can.

So I run on, keeping just comfortably ahead of him and straining my eyes in the gloom for cattle-guards and switches that may bring me to grief. Alas! I strain my eyes too far ahead, and trip over something just under my feet, I know not what, some little thing, and go down to earth in a long, stumbling fall. The next moment I am on my feet, but the shack has me by the collar. I do not struggle. I am busy with breathing deeply and with sizing him up. He is narrow-shouldered, and I have at least thirty pounds the better of him in weight. Besides, he is just as tired as I am, and if he tries to slug me, I'll teach him a few things.

But he doesn't try to slug me, and that problem is settled. Instead, he starts to lead me back toward the train, and another possible problem arises. I see the lanterns of the conductor and the other shack. We are approaching them. Not for nothing have I made the acquaintance of the New York police. Not for nothing, in box-cars, by water-tanks, and in prison-cells, have I listened to bloody tales of man-handling. What if these three men are about to man-handle me? Heaven knows I have given them provocation enough. I think quickly. We are drawing nearer and nearer to the other two train-men. I line up the stomach and the jaw of my captor, and plan the right and left I'll give him at the first sign of trouble.

Pshaw! I know another trick I'd like to work on him, and I almost regret that I did not do it at the moment I was captured. I could make him sick, what of his clutch on my collar. His fingers, tight-gripping, are buried inside my collar. My coat is tightly buttoned. Did you ever see a tourniquet? Well, this is one. All I have to do is to duck my head under his arm and begin to twist. I must twist rapidly—very rapidly. I know how to do it; twisting in a violent, jerky way, ducking my head under his arm with each revolution. Before he knows it, those detaining fingers of his will be detained. He will be unable to withdraw them. It is a powerful leverage. Twenty seconds after I have started revolving, the blood will be bursting out of his finger-ends, the delicate tendons will be rupturing, and all the muscles and nerves will be mashing and crushing together in a shrieking mass. Try it sometime when somebody has you by the collar. But be quick—quick as lightning. Also, be sure to hug yourself while you are revolving—hug your face with your left arm and your abdomen with your right. You see, the other fellow might try to stop you with a punch from his free arm. It would be a good idea, too, to revolve away from that free arm rather than toward it. A punch going is never so bad as a punch coming.

That shack will never know how near he was to being made very, very sick. All that saves him is that it is not in their plan to manhandle me. When we draw near enough, he calls out that he has me, and they signal the train to come on. The engine passes us, and the three blinds. After that, the conductor and the other shack swing aboard. But still my captor holds on to me. I see the plan. He is going to hold me until the rear of the train goes by. Then he will hop on, and I shall be left behind—ditched.

But the train has pulled out fast, the engineer trying to make up for lost time. Also, it is a long train. It is going very lively, and I know the shack is measuring its speed with apprehension.

"Think you can make it?" I query innocently.

He releases my collar, makes a quick run, and swings aboard. A number of coaches are yet to pass by. He knows it, and remains on the steps, his head poked out and watching me. In that moment my next move comes to me. I'll make the last platform. I know she's going fast and faster, but I'll only get a roll in the dirt if I fail, and the optimism of youth is mine. I do not give myself away. I stand with a dejected droop of shoulder, advertising that I have abandoned hope. But at the same time I am feeling with my feet the good gravel. It is perfect footing. Also I am watching the poked-out head of the shack. I see it withdrawn. He is confident that the train is going too fast for me ever to make it.

And the train *is* going fast—faster than any train I have ever tackled. As the last coach comes by I sprint in the same direction with it. It is a swift, short sprint. I cannot hope to equal the speed of the train, but I can reduce the difference of our speed to the minimum, and, hence, reduce the shock of impact, when I leap on board. In the fleeting instant of darkness I do not see the iron hand-rail of the last platform; nor is there time for me to locate it. I reach for where I think it ought to be, and at the same instant my feet leave the ground. It is all in the toss. The next moment I may be rolling in the gravel with broken ribs, or arms, or head. But my fingers grip the hand-hold, there is a jerk on my arms that slightly pivots my body, and my feet land on the steps with sharp violence.

I sit down, feeling very proud of myself. In all my hoboing it is the best bit of train-jumping I have done. I know that late at night one is always good for several stations on the last platform, but I do not care to trust myself at the rear of the train. At the first stop I run forward on the off-side of the train, pass the Pullmans, and duck under and take a rod under a day-coach. At the next stop I run forward again and take another rod.

I am now comparatively safe. The shacks think I am ditched. But the long day and the strenuous night are beginning to tell on me. Also, it is not so windy nor cold underneath, and I begin to doze. This will never do. Sleep on the rods spells death, so I crawl out at a station and go forward to the second blind. Here I can lie down and sleep; and here I do sleep—how long I do not know—for I am awakened by a lantern thrust into my face. The two shacks are staring at me. I scramble up on the defensive, wondering as to which one is going to make the first "pass" at me. But slugging is far from their minds.

"I thought you was ditched," says the shack who had held me by the collar.

"If you hadn't let go of me when you did, you'd have been ditched along with me," I answer.

"How's that?" he asks.

"I'd have gone into a clinch with you, that's all," is my reply.

They hold a consultation, and their verdict is summed up in:—

"Well, I guess you can ride, Bo. There's no use trying to keep you off."

And they go away and leave me in peace to the end of their division.

I have given the foregoing as a sample of what "holding her down" means. Of course, I have selected a fortunate night out of my experiences, and said nothing of the nights—and many of them—when I was tripped up by accident and ditched.

In conclusion, I want to tell of what happened when I reached the end of the division. On single-track, transcontinental lines, the freight trains wait at the divisions and follow out after the passenger trains. When the division was reached, I left my train, and looked for the freight that would pull out behind it. I found the freight, made up on a side-track and waiting. I climbed into a box-car half full of coal and lay down. In no time I was asleep.

I was awakened by the sliding open of the door. Day was just dawning, cold and gray, and the freight had not yet started. A "con" (conductor) was poking his head inside the door.

"Get out of that, you blankety-blank-blank!" he roared at me.

I got, and outside I watched him go down the line inspecting every car in the train. When he got out of sight I thought to myself that he would never think I'd have the nerve to climb back into the very car out of which he had fired me. So back I climbed and lay down again.

Now that con's mental processes must have been paralleling, mine, for he reasoned that it was the very thing I would do. For back he came and fired me out.

Now, surely, I reasoned, he will never dream that I'd do it a third time. Back I went, into the very same car. But I decided to make sure. Only one side-door could be opened. The other side-door was nailed up. Beginning at the top of the coal, I dug a hole alongside of that door and lay down in it. I heard the other door open. The con climbed up and looked in over the top of the coal. He couldn't see me. He called to me to get out. I tried to fool him by remaining quiet. But when he began tossing chunks of coal into the hole on top of me, I gave up and for the third time was fired out. Also, he informed me in warm terms of what would happen to me if he caught me in there again.

I changed my tactics. When a man is paralleling your mental processes, ditch him. Abruptly break off your line of reasoning, and go off on a new line. This I did. I hid between some cars on an adjacent side-track, and watched. Sure enough, that con came back again to the car. He opened the door, he climbed up, he called, he threw coal into the hole I had made. He even crawled over the coal and looked into the hole. That satisfied him. Five minutes later the freight was pulling out, and he was not in sight. I ran alongside the car, pulled the door open, and climbed in. He never looked for me again, and I rode that coal-car precisely one thousand and twenty-two miles, sleeping most of the time and getting out at divisions (where the freights always stop for an hour or so) to beg my food. And at the end of the thousand and twenty-two miles I lost that car through a happy incident. I got a "set-down," and the tramp doesn't live who won't miss a train for a set-down any time.

Chapter 3
Pictures

> "What do it matter where or 'ow we die,
> So long as we've our 'ealth to watch it all?"
> —*Sestina of the Tramp-Royal*

Perhaps the greatest charm of tramp-life is the absence of monotony. In Hobo Land the face of life is protean—an ever changing phantasmagoria, where the impossible happens and the unexpected jumps out of the bushes at every turn of the road. The hobo never knows what is going to happen the next moment;

hence, he lives only in the present moment. He has learned the futility of telic endeavor, and knows the delight of drifting along with the whimsicalities of Chance.

Often I think over my tramp days, and ever I marvel at the swift succession of pictures that flash up in my memory. It matters not where I begin to think; any day of all the days is a day apart, with a record of swift-moving pictures all its own. For instance, I remember a sunny summer morning in Harrisburg, Pennsylvania, and immediately comes to my mind the auspicious beginning of the day—a "set-down" with two maiden ladies, and not in their kitchen, but in their dining room, with them beside me at the table. We ate eggs, out of egg-cups! It was the first time I had ever seen egg-cups, or heard of egg-cups! I was a bit awkward at first, I'll confess; but I was hungry and unabashed. I mastered the egg-cup, and I mastered the eggs in a way that made those two maiden ladies sit up.

Why, they ate like a couple of canaries, dabbling with the one egg each they took, and nibbling at tiny wafers of toast. Life was low in their bodies; their blood ran thin; and they had slept warm all night. I had been out all night, consuming much fuel of my body to keep warm, beating my way down from a place called Emporium, in the northern part of the state. Wafers of toast! Out of sight! But each wafer was no more than a mouthful to me—nay, no more than a bite. It is tedious to have to reach for another piece of toast each bite when one is potential with many bites.

When I was a very little lad, I had a very little dog called Punch. I saw to his feeding myself. Someone in the household had shot a lot of ducks, and we had a fine meat dinner. When I had finished, I prepared Punch's dinner—a large plateful of bones and tidbits. I went outside to give it to him. Now it happened that a visitor had ridden over from a neighboring ranch, and with him had come a Newfoundland dog as big as a calf. I set the plate on the ground. Punch wagged his tail and began. He had before him a blissful half—hour at least. There was a sudden rush. Punch was brushed aside like a straw in the path of a cyclone, and that Newfoundland swooped down upon the plate. In spite of his huge maw he must have been trained to quick lunches, for, in the fleeting instant before he received the kick in the ribs I aimed at him, he completely engulfed the contents of the plate. He swept it clean. One last lingering lick of his tongue removed even the grease stains.

As that big Newfoundland behaved at the plate of my dog Punch, so behaved I at the table of those two maiden ladies of Harrisburg. I swept it bare. I didn't break anything, but I cleaned out the eggs and the toast and the coffee. The servant brought more, but I kept her busy, and ever she brought more and more. The coffee was delicious, but it needn't have been served in such tiny cups. What time had I to eat when it took all my time to prepare the many cups of coffee for drinking?

At any rate, it gave my tongue time to wag. Those two maiden ladies, with their pink-and-white complexions and gray curls, had never looked upon the bright face of adventure. As the "'Tramp-Royal" would have it, they had worked all their lives "on one same shift." Into the sweet scents and narrow confines of their uneventful existence I brought the large airs of the world, freighted with the lusty smells of sweat and strife, and with the tangs and odors of strange lands and soils. And right well I scratched their soft palms with the callous on my own palms—the half-inch horn that comes of pull-and-haul of rope and long and arduous hours of caressing shovel-handles. This I did, not merely in the braggadocio of youth, but to prove, by toil performed, the claim I had upon their charity.

Ah, I can see them now, those dear, sweet ladies, just as I sat at their breakfast table twelve years ago, discoursing upon the way of my feet in the world, brushing aside their kindly counsel as a real devilish fellow should, and thrilling them, not alone with my own adventures, but with the adventures of all the other fellows with whom I had rubbed shoulders and exchanged confidences. I appropriated them all, the adventures of the other fellows, I mean; and if those maiden ladies had been less trustful and guileless, they could have tangled me up beautifully in my chronology. Well, well, and what of it? It was fair exchange. For their many cups of coffee, and eggs, and bites of toast, I gave full value. Right royally I gave them entertainment. My coming to sit at their table was their adventure, and adventure is beyond price anyway.

Coming along the street, after parting from the maiden ladies, I gathered in a newspaper from the doorway of some late-riser, and in a grassy park lay down to get in touch with the last twenty-four hours of the world. There, in the park, I met a fellow-hobo who told me his life-story and who wrestled with me to join the United States Army. He had given in to the recruiting officer and was just about to join, and he couldn't see why I shouldn't join with him. He had been a member of Coxey's Army in the march to Washington several months before, and that seemed to have given him a taste for army life. I, too, was a veteran, for had I not been a private in Company L of the Second Division of Kelly's Industrial Army?—said Company L being commonly known as the "Nevada push." But my army experience had had the opposite effect on me; so I left that hobo to go his way to the dogs of war, while I "threw my feet" for dinner.

This duty performed, I started to walk across the bridge over the Susquehanna to the west shore. I forget the name of the railroad that ran down that side, but while lying in the grass in the morning the idea had come to me to go to Baltimore; so to Baltimore I was going on that railroad, whatever its name was. It was a warm afternoon, and part way across the bridge I came to a lot of fellows who were in swimming off one of the piers. Off went my clothes and in went I. The water was fine; but when I came out and dressed, I found I had been robbed. Someone had gone through my clothes. Now I leave it to you if being robbed isn't in itself adventure enough for one day. I have known men who have been robbed and who have talked all the rest of their lives about it. True, the thief that went through my clothes didn't get much—some thirty or forty cents in nickels and pennies, and my tobacco and cigarette papers; but it was all I had, which is more than most men can be robbed of, for they have something left at home, while I had no home. It was a pretty tough gang in swimming there. I sized up, and knew better than to squeal. So I begged "the makings," and I could have sworn it was one of my own papers I rolled the tobacco in.

Then on across the bridge I hiked to the west shore. Here ran the railroad I was after. No station was in sight. How to catch a freight without walking to a station was the problem. I noticed that the track came up a steep grade, culminating at the point where I had tapped it, and I knew that a heavy freight couldn't pull up there any too lively. But how lively? On the opposite side of the track rose a high bank. On the edge, at the top, I saw a man's head sticking up from the grass. Perhaps he knew how fast the freights took the grade, and when the next one went south. I called out my questions to him, and he motioned to me to come up.

I obeyed, and when I reached the top, I found four other men lying in the grass with him. I took in the scene and knew them for what they were—American gypsies. In the open space that extended back among the trees from the edge of the bank were several nondescript wagons. Ragged, half-naked children swarmed over the camp, though I noticed that they took care not to come near and bother the men-folk. Several lean, unbeautiful, and toil-degraded women were pottering about with camp-chores, and one I noticed who sat by herself on the seat of one of the wagons, her head drooped forward, her knees drawn up to her chin and clasped limply by her arms. She did not look happy. She looked as if she did not care for anything—in this I was wrong, for later I was to learn that there was something for which she did care. The full measure of human suffering was in her face, and, in addition, there was the tragic expression of incapacity for further suffering. Nothing could hurt any more, was what her face seemed to portray; but in this, too, I was wrong.

I lay in the grass on the edge of the steep and talked with the men-folk. We were kin—brothers. I was the American hobo, and they were the American gypsy. I knew enough of their argot for conversation, and they knew enough of mine. There were two more in their gang, who were across the river "mushing" in Harrisburg. A "musher" is an itinerant fakir. This word is not to be confounded with the Klondike "musher," though the origin of both terms may be the same; namely, the corruption of the French *marche ons*, to march, to walk, to "mush." The particular graft of the two mushers who had crossed the river was umbrella-mending; but what real graft lay behind their umbrella-mending, I was not told, nor would it have been polite to ask.

It was a glorious day. Not a breath of wind was stirring, and we basked in the shimmering warmth of the sun. From everywhere arose the drowsy hum of insects, and the balmy air was filled with scents of the sweet earth and the green growing things. We were too lazy to do more than mumble on in intermittent conversation. And then, all abruptly, the peace and quietude was jarred awry by man.

Two bare-legged boys of eight or nine in some minor way broke some rule of the camp—what it was I did not know; and a man who lay beside me suddenly sat up and called to them. He was chief of the tribe, a man with narrow forehead and narrow-slitted eyes, whose thin lips and twisted sardonic features explained why the two boys jumped and tensed like startled deer at the sound of his voice. The alertness of fear was in their faces, and they turned, in a panic, to run. He called to them to come back, and one boy lagged behind reluctantly, his meagre little frame portraying in pantomime the struggle within him between fear and reason. He wanted to come back. His intelligence and past experience told him that to come back was a lesser evil than to run on; but lesser evil that it was, it was great enough to put wings to his fear and urge his feet to flight.

Still he lagged and struggled until he reached the shelter of the trees, where he halted. The chief of the tribe did not pursue. He sauntered over to a wagon and picked up a heavy whip. Then he came back to the centre of the open space and stood still. He did not speak. He made no gestures. He was the Law, pitiless and omnipotent. He merely stood there and waited. And I knew, and all knew, and the two boys in the shelter of the trees knew, for what he waited.

The boy who had lagged slowly came back. His face was stamped with quivering resolution. He did not falter. He had made up his mind to take his punishment. And mark you, the punishment was not for the original offence, but for the offence of running away. And in this, that tribal chieftain but behaved as behaves the exalted society in which he lived. We punish our criminals, and when they escape and run away, we bring them back and add to their punishment.

Straight up to the chief the boy came, halting at the proper distance for the swing of the lash. The whip hissed through the air, and I caught myself with a start of surprise at the weight of the blow. The thin little leg was so very thin and little. The flesh showed white where the lash had curled and bitten, and then, where the white had shown, sprang up the savage welt, with here and there along its length little scarlet oozings where the skin had broken. Again the whip swung, and the boy's whole body winced in anticipation of the blow, though he did not move from the spot. His will held good. A second welt sprang up, and a third. It was not until the fourth landed that the boy screamed. Also, he could no longer stand still, and from then on, blow after blow, he danced up and down in his anguish, screaming; but he did not attempt to run away. If his involuntary dancing took him beyond the reach of the whip, he danced back into range again. And when it was all over—a dozen blows—he went away, whimpering and squealing, among the wagons.

The chief stood still and waited. The second boy came out from the trees. But he did not come straight. He came like a cringing dog, obsessed by little panics that made him turn and dart away for half a dozen steps. But always he turned and came back, circling nearer and nearer to the man, whimpering, making inarticulate animal-noises in his throat. I saw that he never looked at the man. His eyes always were fixed upon the whip, and in his eyes was a terror that made me sick—the frantic terror of an inconceivably maltreated child. I have seen strong men dropping right and left out of battle and squirming in their death-throes, I have seen them by scores blown into the air by bursting shells and their bodies torn asunder; believe me, the witnessing was as merrymaking and laughter and song to me in comparison with the way the sight of that poor child affected me.

The whipping began. The whipping of the first boy was as play compared with this one. In no time the blood was running down his thin little legs. He danced and squirmed and doubled up till it seemed almost that he was some grotesque marionette operated by strings. I say "seemed," for his screaming gave the lie to the seeming and stamped it with reality. His shrieks were shrill and piercing;

within them no hoarse notes, but only the thin sexlessness of the voice of a child. The time came when the boy could stand it no more. Reason fled, and he tried to run away. But now the man followed up, curbing his flight, herding him with blows back always into the open space.

Then came interruption. I heard a wild smothered cry. The woman who sat in the wagon seat had got out and was running to interfere. She sprang between the man and boy.

"You want some, eh?" said he with the whip. "All right, then."

He swung the whip upon her. Her skirts were long, so he did not try for her legs. He drove the lash for her face, which she shielded as best she could with her hands and forearms, drooping her head forward between her lean shoulders, and on the lean shoulders and arms receiving the blows. Heroic mother! She knew just what she was doing. The boy, still shrieking, was making his get-away to the wagons.

And all the while the four men lay beside me and watched and made no move. Nor did I move, and without shame I say it; though my reason was compelled to struggle hard against my natural impulse to rise up and interfere. I knew life. Of what use to the woman, or to me, would be my being beaten to death by five men there on the bank of the Susquehanna? I once saw a man hanged, and though my whole soul cried protest, my mouth cried not. Had it cried, I should most likely have had my skull crushed by the butt of a revolver, for it was the law that the man should hang. And here, in this gypsy group, it was the law that the woman should be whipped.

Even so, the reason in both cases that I did not interfere was not that it was the law, but that the law was stronger than I. Had it not been for those four men beside me in the grass, right gladly would I have waded into the man with the whip. And, barring the accident of the landing on me with a knife or a club in the hands of some of the various women of the camp, I am confident that I should have beaten him into a mess. But the four men *were* beside me in the grass. They made their law stronger than I.

Oh, believe me, I did my own suffering. I had seen women beaten before, often, but never had I seen such a beating as this. Her dress across the shoulders was cut into shreds. One blow that had passed her guard, had raised a bloody welt from cheek to chin. Not one blow, nor two, not one dozen, nor two dozen, but endlessly, infinitely, that whip-lash smote and curled about her. The sweat poured from me, and I breathed hard, clutching at the grass with my hands until I strained it out by the roots. And all the time my reason kept whispering, "Fool! Fool!" That welt on the face nearly did for me. I started to rise to my feet; but the hand of the man next to me went out to my shoulder and pressed me down.

"Easy, pardner, easy," he warned me in a low voice. I looked at him. His eyes met mine unwaveringly. He was a large man, broad-shouldered and heavy-muscled; and his face was lazy, phlegmatic, slothful, withal kindly, yet without passion, and quite soulless—a dim soul, unmalicious, unmoral, bovine, and stubborn. Just an animal he was, with no more than a faint flickering of intelligence, a good-natured brute with the strength and mental caliber of a gorilla. His hand pressed heavily upon me, and I knew the weight of the muscles behind. I looked at the other brutes, two of them unperturbed and incurious, and one of them that gloated over the spectacle; and my reason came back to me, my muscles relaxed, and I sank down in the grass.

My mind went back to the two maiden ladies with whom I had had breakfast that morning. Less than two miles, as the crow flies, separated them from this scene. Here, in the windless day, under a beneficent sun, was a sister of theirs being beaten by a brother of mine. Here was a page of life they could never see—and better so, though for lack of seeing they would never be able to understand their sisterhood, nor themselves, nor know the clay of which they were made. For it is not given to woman to live in sweet-scented, narrow rooms and at the same time be a little sister to all the world.

The whipping was finished, and the woman, no longer screaming, went back to her seat in the wagon. Nor did the other women come to her—just then. They were afraid. But they came afterward, when a decent interval had elapsed. The man put the whip away and rejoined us, flinging himself down on the other side of me. He was breathing hard from his exertions. He wiped the sweat from his eyes on his coat-sleeve, and looked challengingly at me. I returned his look carelessly; what he had done was no concern of mine. I did not go away abruptly. I lay there half an hour longer, which, under the circumstances, was tact and etiquette. I rolled cigarettes from tobacco I borrowed from them, and when I slipped down the bank to the railroad, I was equipped with the necessary information for catching the next freight bound south.

Well, and what of it? It was a page out of life, that's all; and there are many pages worse, far worse, that I have seen. I have sometimes held forth (facetiously, so my listeners believed) that the chief distinguishing trait between man and the other animals is that man is the only animal that maltreats the females of his kind. It is something of which no wolf nor cowardly coyote is ever guilty. It is something that even the dog, degenerated by domestication, will not do. The dog still retains the wild instinct in this matter, while man has lost most of his wild instincts—at least, most of the good ones.

Worse pages of life than what I have described? Read the reports on child labor in the United States,—east, west, north, and south, it doesn't matter where,—and know that all of us, profit-mongers that we are, are typesetters and printers of worse pages of life than that mere page of wife-beating on the Susquehanna.

I went down the grade a hundred yards to where the footing beside the track was good. Here I could catch my freight as it pulled slowly up the hill, and here I found half a dozen hoboes waiting for the same purpose. Several were playing seven-up with an old pack of cards. I took a hand. A coon began to shuffle the deck. He was fat, and young, and moon-faced. He beamed with good-nature. It fairly oozed from him. As he dealt the first card to me, he paused and said:—

"Say, Bo, ain't I done seen you befo'?"

"You sure have," I answered. "An' you didn't have those same duds on, either."

He was puzzled.

"D'ye remember Buffalo?" I queried.

Then he knew me, and with laughter and ejaculation hailed me as a comrade; for at Buffalo his clothes had been striped while he did his bit of time in the Erie County Penitentiary. For that matter, my clothes had been likewise striped, for I had been doing my bit of time, too.

The game proceeded, and I learned the stake for which we played. Down the bank toward the river descended a steep and narrow path that led to a spring some twenty-five feet beneath. We played on the edge of the bank. The man who was "stuck" had to take a small condensed-milk can, and with it carry water to the winners.

The first game was played and the coon was stuck. He took the small milk-tin and climbed down the bank, while we sat above and guyed him. We drank like fish. Four round trips he had to make for me alone, and the others were equally lavish with their thirst. The path was very steep, and sometimes the coon slipped when part way up, spilled the water, and had to go back for more. But he didn't get angry. He laughed as heartily as any of us; that was why he slipped so often. Also, he assured us of the prodigious quantities of water he would drink when someone else got stuck.

When our thirst was quenched, another game was started. Again the coon was stuck, and again we drank our fill. A third game and a fourth ended the same way, and each time that moon-faced darky nearly died with delight at appreciation of the fate that Chance was dealing out to him. And we nearly died with him, what of our delight. We laughed like careless children, or gods, there on the edge of the bank. I know that I laughed till it seemed the top of my head would come off, and I drank from the milk-tin till I was nigh waterlogged. Serious discussion arose as to whether we could successfully board the freight when it pulled up the grade, what of the weight of water secreted on our persons. This particular phase of the situation just about finished the coon. He had to break off from water-carrying for at least five minutes while he lay down and rolled with laughter.

The lengthening shadows stretched farther and farther across the river, and the soft, cool twilight came on, and ever we drank water, and ever our ebony cup-bearer brought more and more. Forgotten was the beaten woman of the hour before. That was a page read and turned over; I was busy now with this new page, and when the engine whistled on the grade, this page would be finished and another begun; and so the book of life goes on, page after page and pages without end—when one is young.

And then we played a game in which the coon failed to be stuck. The victim was a lean and dyspeptic-looking hobo, the one who had laughed least of all of us. We said we didn't want any water—which was the truth. Not the wealth of Ormuz and of Ind, nor the pressure of a pneumatic ram, could have forced another drop into my saturated carcass. The coon looked disappointed, then rose to the occasion and guessed he'd have some. He meant it, too. He had some, and then some, and then some. Ever the melancholy hobo climbed down and up the steep bank, and ever the coon called for more. He drank more water than all the rest of us put together. The twilight deepened into night, the stars came out, and he still drank on. I do believe that if the whistle of the freight hadn't sounded, he'd be there yet, swilling water and revenge while the melancholy hobo toiled down and up.

But the whistle sounded. The page was done. We sprang to our feet and strung out alongside the track. There she came, coughing and spluttering up the grade, the headlight turning night into day and silhouetting us in sharp relief. The engine passed us, and we were all running with the train, some boarding on the side-ladders, others "springing" the side-doors of empty box-cars and climbing in. I caught a flat-car loaded with mixed lumber and crawled away into a comfortable nook. I lay on my back with a newspaper under my head for a pillow. Above me the stars were winking and wheeling in squadrons back and forth as the train rounded the curves, and watching them I fell asleep. The day was done—one day of all my days. To-morrow would be another day, and I was young.

Chapter 4
"Pinched"

I rode into Niagara Falls in a "side-door Pullman," or, in common parlance, a box-car. A flat-car, by the way, is known amongst the fraternity as a "gondola," with the second syllable emphasized and pronounced long. But to return. I arrived in the afternoon and headed straight from the freight train to the falls. Once my eyes were filled with that wonder-vision of down-rushing water, I was lost. I could not tear myself away long enough to "batter" the "privates" (domiciles) for my supper. Even a "set-down" could not have lured me away. Night came on, a beautiful night of moonlight, and I lingered by the falls until after eleven. Then it was up to me to hunt for a place to "kip."

"Kip," "doss," "flop," "pound your ear," all mean the same thing; namely, to sleep. Somehow, I had a "hunch" that Niagara Falls was a "bad" town for hoboes, and I headed out into the country. I climbed a fence and "flopped" in a field. John Law would never find me there, I flattered myself. I lay on my back in the grass and slept like a babe. It was so balmy warm that I woke up not once all night. But with the first gray daylight my eyes opened, and I remembered the wonderful falls. I climbed the fence and started down the road to have another look at them. It was early—not more than five o'clock—and not until eight o'clock could I begin to batter for my breakfast. I could spend at least three hours by the river. Alas! I was fated never to see the river nor the falls again.

The town was asleep when I entered it. As I came along the quiet street, I saw three men coming toward me along the sidewalk. They were walking abreast. Hoboes, I decided, like myself, who had got up early. In this surmise I was not quite correct. I was only sixty-six and two-thirds per cent correct. The men on each side were hoboes all right, but the man in the middle wasn't. I directed my steps to the edge of the sidewalk in order to let the trio go by. But it didn't go by. At some word from the man in the centre, all three halted, and he of the centre addressed me.

I piped the lay on the instant. He was a "fly-cop" and the two hoboes were his prisoners. John Law was up and out after the early worm. I was a worm. Had I been richer by the experiences that were to befall me in the next several months, I should have turned and run like the very devil. He might have shot at me, but he'd have had to hit me to get me. He'd have never run after me, for two hoboes in the hand are worth more than one on the get-away. But like a dummy I stood still when he halted me. Our conversation was brief.

"What hotel are you stopping at?" he queried.

He had me. I wasn't stopping at any hotel, and, since I did not know the name of a hotel in the place, I could not claim residence in any of them. Also, I was up too early in the morning. Everything was against me.

"I just arrived," I said.

"Well, you turn around and walk in front of me, and not too far in front. There's somebody wants to see you."

I was "pinched." I knew who wanted to see me. With that "fly-cop" and the two hoboes at my heels, and under the direction of the former, I led the way to the city jail. There we were searched and our names registered. I have forgotten, now, under which name I was registered. I gave the name of Jack Drake, but when they searched me, they found letters addressed to Jack London. This caused trouble and required explanation, all of which has passed from my mind, and to this day I do not know whether I was pinched as Jack Drake or Jack London. But one or the other, it should be there to-day in the prison register of Niagara Falls. Reference can bring it to light. The time was somewhere in the latter part of June, 1894. It was only a few days after my arrest that the great railroad strike began.

From the office we were led to the "Hobo" and locked in. The "Hobo" is that part of a prison where the minor offenders are confined together in a large iron cage. Since hoboes constitute the principal division of the minor offenders, the aforesaid iron cage is called the Hobo. Here we met several hoboes who had already been pinched that morning, and every little while the door was unlocked and two or three more were thrust in on us. At last, when we totalled sixteen, we were led upstairs into the court-room. And now I shall faithfully describe what took place in that court-room, for know that my patriotic American citizenship there received a shock from which it has never fully recovered.

In the court-room were the sixteen prisoners, the judge, and two bailiffs. The judge seemed to act as his own clerk. There were no witnesses. There were no citizens of Niagara Falls present to look on and see how justice was administered in their community. The judge glanced at the list of cases before him and called out a name. A hobo stood up. The judge glanced at a bailiff. "Vagrancy, your Honor," said the bailiff. "Thirty days," said his Honor. The hobo sat down, and the judge was calling another name and another hobo was rising to his feet.

The trial of that hobo had taken just about fifteen seconds. The trial of the next hobo came off with equal celerity. The bailiff said, "Vagrancy, your Honor," and his Honor said, "Thirty days." Thus it went like clockwork, fifteen seconds to a hobo—and thirty days.

They are poor dumb cattle, I thought to myself. But wait till my turn comes; I'll give his Honor a "spiel." Part way along in the performance, his Honor, moved by some whim, gave one of us an opportunity to speak. As chance would have it, this man was not a genuine hobo. He bore none of the ear-marks of the professional "stiff." Had he approached the rest of us, while waiting at a water-tank for a freight, should have unhesitatingly classified him as a "gay-cat." Gay-cat is the synonym for tenderfoot in Hobo Land. This gay-cat was well along in years—somewhere around forty-five, I should judge. His shoulders were humped a trifle, and his face was seamed by weather-beat.

For many years, according to his story, he had driven team for some firm in (if I remember rightly) Lockport, New York. The firm had ceased to prosper, and finally, in the hard times of 1893, had gone out of business. He had been kept on to the last, though toward the last his work had been very irregular. He went on and explained at length his difficulties in getting work (when so many were out of work) during the succeeding months. In the end, deciding that he would find better opportunities for work on the Lakes, he had started for Buffalo. Of course he was "broke," and there he was. That was all.

"Thirty days," said his Honor, and called another hobo's name.

Said hobo got up. "Vagrancy, your Honor," said the bailiff, and his Honor said, "Thirty days."

And so it went, fifteen seconds and thirty days to each hobo. The machine of justice was grinding smoothly. Most likely, considering how early it was in the morning, his Honor had not yet had his breakfast and was in a hurry.

But my American blood was up. Behind me were the many generations of my American ancestry. One of the kinds of liberty those ancestors of mine had fought and died for was the right of trial by jury. This was my heritage, stained sacred by their blood, and it devolved upon me to stand up for it. All right, I threatened to myself; just wait till he gets to me.

He got to me. My name, whatever it was, was called, and I stood up. The bailiff said, "Vagrancy, your Honor," and I began to talk. But the judge began talking at the same time, and he said, "Thirty days." I started to protest, but at that moment his Honor was calling the name of the next hobo on the list. His Honor paused long enough to say to me, "Shut up!" The bailiff forced me to sit down. And the next moment that next hobo had received thirty days and the succeeding hobo was just in process of getting his.

When we had all been disposed of, thirty days to each stiff, his Honor, just as he was about to dismiss us, suddenly turned to the teamster from Lockport—the one man he had allowed to talk.

"Why did you quit your job?" his Honor asked.

Now the teamster had already explained how his job had quit him, and the question took him aback.

"Your Honor," he began confusedly, "isn't that a funny question to ask?"

"Thirty days more for quitting your job," said his Honor, and the court was closed. That was the outcome. The teamster got sixty days all together, while the rest of us got thirty days.

We were taken down below, locked up, and given breakfast. It was a pretty good breakfast, as prison breakfasts go, and it was the best I was to get for a month to come.

As for me, I was dazed. Here was I, under sentence, after a farce of a trial wherein I was denied not only my right of trial by jury, but my right to plead guilty or not guilty. Another thing my fathers had fought for flashed through my brain—habeas corpus. I'd show them. But when I asked for a lawyer, I was laughed at. Habeas corpus was all right, but of what good was it to me when I could communicate with no one outside the jail? But I'd show them. They couldn't keep me in jail forever. Just wait till I got out, that was all. I'd make them sit up. I knew something about the law and my own rights, and I'd expose their maladministration of justice. Visions of damage suits and sensational newspaper headlines were dancing before my eyes when the jailers came in and began hustling us out into the main office.

A policeman snapped a handcuff on my right wrist. (Ah, ha, thought I, a new indignity. Just wait till I get out.) On the left wrist of a negro he snapped the other handcuff of that pair. He was a very tall negro, well past six feet—so tall was he that when we stood side by side his hand lifted mine up a trifle in the manacles. Also, he was the happiest and the raggedest negro I have ever seen.

We were all handcuffed similarly, in pairs. This accomplished, a bright nickel-steel chain was brought forth, run down through the links of all the handcuffs, and locked at front and rear of the double-line. We were now a chain-gang. The command to march was given, and out we went upon the street, guarded by two officers. The tall negro and I had the place of honor. We led the procession.

After the tomb-like gloom of the jail, the outside sunshine was dazzling. I had never known it to be so sweet as now, a prisoner with clanking chains, I knew that I was soon to see the last of it for thirty days. Down through the streets of Niagara Falls we marched to the railroad station, stared at by curious passers-by, and especially by a group of tourists on the veranda of a hotel that we marched past.

There was plenty of slack in the chain, and with much rattling and clanking we sat down, two and two, in the seats of the smoking-car. Afire with indignation as I was at the outrage that had been perpetrated on me and my forefathers, I was nevertheless too prosaically practical to lose my head over it. This was all new to me. Thirty days of mystery were before me, and I looked about me to find somebody who knew the ropes. For I had already learned that I was not bound for a petty jail with a hundred or so prisoners in it, but for a full-grown penitentiary with a couple of thousand prisoners in it, doing anywhere from ten days to ten years.

In the seat behind me, attached to the chain by his wrist, was a squat, heavily-built, powerfully-muscled man. He was somewhere between thirty-five and forty years of age. I sized him up. In the corners of his eyes I saw humor and laughter and kindliness. As for the rest of him, he was a brute-beast, wholly unmoral, and with all the passion and turgid violence of the brute-beast. What saved him, what made him possible for me, were those corners of his eyes—the humor and laughter and kindliness of the beast when unaroused.

He was my "meat." I "cottoned" to him. While my cuff-mate, the tall negro, mourned with chucklings and laughter over some laundry he was sure to lose through his arrest, and while the train rolled on toward Buffalo, I talked with the man in the seat behind me. He had an empty pipe. I filled it for him with my precious tobacco—enough in a single filling to make a dozen cigarettes. Nay, the more we talked the surer I was that he was my meat, and I divided all my tobacco with him.

Now it happens that I am a fluid sort of an organism, with sufficient kinship with life to fit myself in 'most anywhere. I laid myself out to fit in with that man, though little did I dream to what extraordinary good purpose I was succeeding. He had never been in the particular penitentiary to which we were going, but he had done "one-," "two-," and "five-spots" in various other penitentiaries (a "spot" is a year), and he was filled with wisdom. We became pretty chummy, and my heart bounded when he cautioned me to follow his lead. He called me "Jack," and I called him "Jack."

The train stopped at a station about five miles from Buffalo, and we, the chain-gang, got off. I do not remember the name of this station, but I am confident that it is someone of the following: Rocklyn, Rockwood, Black Rock, Rockcastle, or Newcastle. But whatever the name of the place, we were walked a short distance and then put on a street-car. It was an old-fashioned car, with a seat, running the full length, on each side. All the passengers who sat on one side were asked to move over to the other side, and we, with a great clanking of chain, took their places. We sat facing them, I remember, and I remember, too, the awed expression on the faces of the women, who took us, undoubtedly, for convicted murderers and bank-robbers. I tried to look my fiercest, but that cuff-mate of mine, the too happy negro, insisted on rolling his eyes, laughing, and reiterating, "O Lawdy! Lawdy!"

We left the car, walked some more, and were led into the office of the Erie County Penitentiary. Here we were to register, and on that register one or the other of my names will be found. Also, we were informed that we must leave in the office all our valuables: money, tobacco, matches, pocketknives, and so forth.

My new pal shook his head at me.

"If you do not leave your things here, they will be confiscated inside," warned the official.

Still my pal shook his head. He was busy with his hands, hiding his movements behind the other fellows. (Our handcuffs had been removed.) I watched him, and followed suit, wrapping up in a bundle in my handkerchief all the things I wanted to take in. These bundles the two of us thrust into our shirts. I noticed that our fellow-prisoners, with the exception of one or two who had watches, did not turn over their belongings to the man in the office. They were determined to smuggle them in somehow, trusting to luck; but they were not so wise as my pal, for they did not wrap their things in bundles.

Our erstwhile guardians gathered up the handcuffs and chain and departed for Niagara Falls, while we, under new guardians, were led away into the prison. While we were in the office, our number had been added to by other squads of newly arrived prisoners, so that we were now a procession forty or fifty strong.

Know, ye unimprisoned, that traffic is as restricted inside a large prison as commerce was in the Middle Ages. Once inside a penitentiary, one cannot move about at will. Every few steps are encountered great steel doors or gates which are always kept locked. We were bound for the barber-shop, but we encountered delays in the unlocking of doors for us. We were thus delayed in the first "hall" we entered. A "hall" is not a corridor. Imagine an oblong cube, built out of bricks and rising six stories high, each story a row of cells, say fifty cells in a row—in short, imagine a cube of colossal honeycomb. Place this cube on the ground and enclose it in a building with a roof overhead and walls all around. Such a cube and encompassing building constitute a "hall" in the Erie County Penitentiary. Also, to complete the picture, see a narrow gallery, with steel railing, running the full length of each tier of cells and at the ends of the oblong cube see all these galleries, from both sides, connected by a fire-escape system of narrow steel stairways.

We were halted in the first hall, waiting for some guard to unlock a door. Here and there, moving about, were convicts, with close-cropped heads and shaven faces, and garbed in prison stripes. One such convict I noticed above us on the gallery of the third tier of cells. He was standing on the gallery and leaning forward, his arms resting on the railing, himself apparently oblivious of our presence. He seemed staring into vacancy. My pal made a slight hissing noise. The convict glanced down. Motioned signals passed between them. Then through the air soared the handkerchief bundle of my pal. The convict caught it, and like a flash it was out of sight in his shirt and he was staring into vacancy. My pal had told me to follow his lead. I watched my chance when the guard's back was turned, and my bundle followed the other one into the shirt of the convict.

A minute later the door was unlocked, and we filed into the barber-shop. Here were more men in convict stripes. They were the prison barbers. Also, there were bath-tubs, hot water, soap, and scrubbing-brushes. We were ordered to strip and bathe, each man to scrub his neighbor's back—a needless precaution, this compulsory bath, for the prison swarmed with vermin. After the bath, we were each given a canvas clothes-bag.

"Put all your clothes in the bags," said the guard. "It's no good trying to smuggle anything in. You've got to line up naked for inspection. Men for thirty days or less keep their shoes and suspenders. Men for more than thirty days keep nothing."

This announcement was received with consternation. How could naked men smuggle anything past an inspection? Only my pal and I were safe. But it was right here that the convict barbers got in their work. They passed among the poor newcomers, kindly volunteering to take charge of their precious little belongings, and promising to return them later in the day. Those barbers were philanthropists—to hear them talk. As in the case of Fra Lippo Lippi, never was there such prompt disemburdening. Matches, tobacco, rice-paper, pipes, knives, money, everything, flowed into the capacious shirts of the barbers. They fairly bulged with the spoil, and the guards made believe not to see. To cut the story short, nothing was ever returned. The barbers never had any intention of returning what they had taken. They considered it legitimately theirs. It was the barber-shop graft. There were many grafts in that prison, as I was to learn; and I, too, was destined to become a grafter—thanks to my new pal.

There were several chairs, and the barbers worked rapidly. The quickest shaves and hair-cuts I have ever seen were given in that shop. The men lathered themselves, and the barbers shaved them at the rate of a minute to a man. A hair-cut took a trifle longer. In three minutes the down of eighteen was scraped from my face, and my head was as smooth as a billiard-ball just sprouting a crop of bristles. Beards, mustaches, like our clothes and everything, came off. Take my word for it, we were a villainous-looking gang when they got through with us. I had not realized before how really altogether bad we were.

Then came the line-up, forty or fifty of us, naked as Kipling's heroes who stormed Lungtungpen. To search us was easy. There were only our shoes and ourselves. Two or three rash spirits, who had doubted the barbers, had the goods found on them—which goods, namely, tobacco, pipes, matches, and small change, were quickly confiscated. This over, our new clothes were brought to us—stout prison shirts, and coats and trousers conspicuously striped. I had always lingered under the impression that the convict stripes were put on a man only after he had been convicted of a felony. I lingered no longer, but put on the insignia of shame and got my first taste of marching the lock-step.

In single file, close together, each man's hands on the shoulders of the man in front, we marched on into another large hall. Here we were ranged up against the wall in a long line and ordered to strip our left arms. A youth, a medical student who was getting in his practice on cattle such as we, came down the line. He vaccinated just about four times as rapidly as the barbers shaved. With a final caution to avoid rubbing our arms against anything, and to let the blood dry so as to form the scab, we were led away to our cells. Here my pal and I parted, but not before he had time to whisper to me, "Suck it out."

As soon as I was locked in, I sucked my arm clean. And afterward I saw men who had not sucked and who had horrible holes in their arms into which I could have thrust my fist. It was their own fault. They could have sucked.

In my cell was another man. We were to be cell-mates. He was a young, manly fellow, not talkative, but very capable, indeed as splendid a fellow as one could meet with in a day's ride, and this in spite of the fact that he had just recently finished a two-year term in some Ohio penitentiary.

Hardly had we been in our cell half an hour, when a convict sauntered down the gallery and looked in. It was my pal. He had the freedom of the hall, he explained. He was unlocked at six in the morning and not locked up again till nine at night. He was in with the "push" in that hall, and had been promptly appointed a trusty of the kind technically known as "hall-man." The man who had appointed him was also a prisoner and a trusty, and was known as

"First Hall-man." There were thirteen hall-men in that hall. Ten of them had charge each of a gallery of cells, and over them were the First, Second, and Third Hall-men.

We newcomers were to stay in our cells for the rest of the day, my pal informed me, so that the vaccine would have a chance to take. Then next morning we would be put to hard labor in the prison-yard.

"But I'll get you out of the work as soon as I can," he promised. "I'll get one of the hall-men fired and have you put in his place."

He put his hand into his shirt, drew out the handkerchief containing my precious belongings, passed it in to me through the bars, and went on down the gallery.

I opened the bundle. Everything was there. Not even a match was missing. I shared the makings of a cigarette with my cell-mate. When I started to strike a match for a light, he stopped me. A flimsy, dirty comforter lay in each of our bunks for bedding. He tore off a narrow strip of the thin cloth and rolled it tightly and telescopically into a long and slender cylinder. This he lighted with a precious match. The cylinder of tight-rolled cotton cloth did not flame. On the end a coal of fire slowly smouldered. It would last for hours, and my cell-mate called it a "punk." And when it burned short, all that was necessary was to make a new punk, put the end of it against the old, blow on them, and so transfer the glowing coal. Why, we could have given Prometheus pointers on the conserving of fire.

At twelve o'clock dinner was served. At the bottom of our cage door was a small opening like the entrance of a runway in a chicken-yard. Through this were thrust two hunks of dry bread and two pannikins of "soup." A portion of soup consisted of about a quart of hot water with floating on its surface a lonely drop of grease. Also, there was some salt in that water.

We drank the soup, but we did not eat the bread. Not that we were not hungry, and not that the bread was uneatable. It was fairly good bread. But we had reasons. My cell-mate had discovered that our cell was alive with bed-bugs. In all the cracks and interstices between the bricks where the mortar had fallen out flourished great colonies. The natives even ventured out in the broad daylight and swarmed over the walls and ceiling by hundreds. My cell-mate was wise in the ways of the beasts. Like Childe Roland, dauntless the slug-horn to his lips he bore. Never was there such a battle. It lasted for hours. It was shambles. And when the last survivors fled to their brick-and-mortar fastnesses, our work was only half done. We chewed mouthfuls of our bread until it was reduced to the consistency of putty. When a fleeing belligerent escaped into a crevice between the bricks, we promptly walled him in with a daub of the chewed bread. We toiled on until the light grew dim and until every hole, nook, and cranny was closed. I shudder to think of the tragedies of starvation and cannibalism that must have ensued behind those bread-plastered ramparts.

We threw ourselves on our bunks, tired out and hungry, to wait for supper. It was a good day's work well done. In the weeks to come we at least should not suffer from the hosts of vermin. We had foregone our dinner, saved our hides at the expense of our stomachs; but we were content. Alas for the futility of human effort! Scarcely was our long task completed when a guard unlocked our door. A redistribution of prisoners was being made, and we were taken to another cell and locked in two galleries higher up.

Early next morning our cells were unlocked, and down in the hall the several hundred prisoners of us formed the lock-step and marched out into the prison-yard to go to work. The Erie Canal runs right by the back yard of the Erie County Penitentiary. Our task was to unload canal-boats, carrying huge stay-bolts on our shoulders, like railroad ties, into the prison. As I worked I sized up the situation and studied the chances for a get-away. There wasn't the ghost of a show. Along the tops of the walls marched guards armed with repeating rifles, and I was told, furthermore, that there were machine-guns in the sentry-towers.

I did not worry. Thirty days were not so long. I'd stay those thirty days, and add to the store of material I intended to use, when I got out, against the harpies of justice. I'd show what an American boy could do when his rights and privileges had been trampled on the way mine had. I had been denied my right of trial by jury; I had been denied my right to plead guilty or not guilty; I had been denied a trial even (for I couldn't consider that what I had received at Niagara Falls was a trial); I had not been allowed to communicate with a lawyer nor any one, and hence had been denied my right of suing for a writ of habeas corpus; my face had been shaved, my hair cropped close, convict stripes had been put upon my body; I was forced to toil hard on a diet of bread and water and to march the shameful lock-step with armed guards over me—and all for what? What had I done? What crime had I committed against the good citizens of Niagara Falls that all this vengeance should be wreaked upon me? I had not even violated their "sleeping-out" ordinance. I had slept outside their jurisdiction, in the country, that night. I had not even begged for a meal, or battered for a "light piece" on their streets. All that I had done was to walk along their sidewalk and gaze at their picayune waterfall. And what crime was there in that? Technically I was guilty of no misdemeanor. All right, I'd show them when I got out.

The next day I talked with a guard. I wanted to send for a lawyer. The guard laughed at me. So did the other guards. I really was *incommunicado* so far as the outside world was concerned. I tried to write a letter out, but I learned that all letters were read, and censured or confiscated, by the prison authorities, and that "short-timers" were not allowed to write letters anyway. A little later I tried smuggling letters out by men who were released, but I learned that they were searched and the letters found and destroyed. Never mind. It all helped to make it a blacker case when I did get out.

But as the prison days went by (which I shall describe in the next chapter), I "learned a few." I heard tales of the police, and police-courts, and lawyers, that were unbelievable and monstrous. Men, prisoners, told me of personal experiences with the police of great cities that were awful. And more awful were the hearsay tales they told me concerning men who had died at the hands of the police and who therefore could not testify for themselves. Years afterward, in the report of the Lexow Committee, I was to read tales true and more awful than those told to me. But in the meantime, during the first days of my imprisonment, I scoffed at what I heard.

As the days went by, however, I began to grow convinced. I saw with my own eyes, there in that prison, things unbelievable and monstrous. And the more convinced I became, the profounder grew the respect in me for the sleuth-hounds of the law and for the whole institution of criminal justice.

My indignation ebbed away, and into my being rushed the tides of fear. I saw at last, clear-eyed, what I was up against. I grew meek and lowly. Each day I resolved more emphatically to make no rumpus when I got out. All I asked, when I got out, was a chance to fade away from the landscape. And that was just what I did do when I was released. I kept my tongue between my teeth, walked softly, and sneaked for Pennsylvania, a wiser and a humbler man.

Chapter 5
The Pen

For two days I toiled in the prison-yard. It was heavy work, and, in spite of the fact that I malingered at every opportunity, I was played out. This was because of the food. No man could work hard on such food. Bread and water, that was all that was given us. Once a week we were supposed to get meat; but this meat did not always go around, and since all nutriment had first been boiled out of it in the making of soup, it didn't matter whether one got a taste of it once a week or not.

Furthermore, there was one vital defect in the bread-and-water diet. While we got plenty of water, we did not get enough of the bread. A ration of bread was about the size of one's two fists, and three rations a day were given to each prisoner. There was one good thing, I must say, about the water—it was hot. In the morning it was called "coffee," at noon it was dignified as "soup," and at night it masqueraded as "tea." But it was the same old water all the time. The prisoners called it "water bewitched." In the morning it was black water, the color being due to boiling it with burnt bread-crusts. At noon it was served minus the color, with salt and a drop of grease added. At night it was served with a purplish-auburn hue that defied all speculation; it was darn poor tea, but it was dandy hot water.

We were a hungry lot in the Erie County Pen. Only the "long-timers" knew what it was to have enough to eat. The reason for this was that they would have died after a time on the fare we "short-timers" received. I know that the long-timers got more substantial grub, because there was a whole row of them on the ground floor in our hall, and when I was a trusty, I used to steal from their grub while serving them. Man cannot live on bread alone and not enough of it.

My pal delivered the goods. After two days of work in the yard I was taken out of my cell and made a trusty, a "hall-man." At morning and night we served the bread to the prisoners in their cells; but at twelve o'clock a different method was used. The convicts marched in from work in a long line. As they entered the door of our hall, they broke the lock-step and took their hands down from the shoulders of their line-mates. Just inside the door were piled trays of bread, and here also stood the First Hall-man and two ordinary hall-men. I was one of the two. Our task was to hold the trays of bread as the line of convicts filed past. As soon as the tray, say, that I was holding was emptied, the other hall-man took my place with a full tray. And when his was emptied, I took his place with a full tray. Thus the line tramped steadily by, each man reaching with his right hand and taking one ration of bread from the extended tray.

The task of the First Hall-man was different. He used a club. He stood beside the tray and watched. The hungry wretches could never get over the delusion that sometime they could manage to get two rations of bread out of the tray. But in my experience that sometime never came. The club of the First Hall-man had a way of flashing out—quick as the stroke of a tiger's claw—to the hand that dared ambitiously. The First Hall-man was a good judge of distance, and he had smashed so many hands with that club that he had become infallible. He never missed, and he usually punished the offending convict by taking his one ration away from him and sending him to his cell to make his meal off of hot water.

And at times, while all these men lay hungry in their cells, I have seen a hundred or so extra rations of bread hidden away in the cells of the hall-men. It would seem absurd, our retaining this bread. But it was one of our grafts. We were economic masters inside our hall, turning the trick in ways quite similar to the economic masters of civilization. We controlled the food-supply of the population, and, just like our brother bandits outside, we made the people pay through the nose for it. We peddled the bread. Once a week, the men who worked in the yard received a five-cent plug of chewing tobacco. This chewing tobacco was the coin of the realm. Two or three rations of bread for a plug was the way we exchanged, and they traded, not because they loved tobacco less, but because they loved bread more. Oh, I know, it was like taking candy from a baby, but what would you? We had to live. And certainly there should be some reward for initiative and enterprise. Besides, we but patterned ourselves after our betters outside the walls, who, on a larger scale, and under the respectable disguise of merchants, bankers, and captains of industry, did precisely what we were doing. What awful things would have happened to those poor wretches if it hadn't been for us, I can't imagine. Heaven knows we put bread into circulation in the Erie County Pen. Ay, and we encouraged frugality and thrift . . . in the poor devils who forewent their tobacco. And then there was our example. In the breast of every convict there we implanted the ambition to become even as we and run a graft. Saviours of society—I guess yes.

Here was a hungry man without any tobacco. Maybe he was a profligate and had used it all up on himself. Very good; he had a pair of suspenders. I exchanged half a dozen rations of bread for it—or a dozen rations if the suspenders were very good. Now I never wore suspenders, but that didn't matter. Around the corner lodged a long-timer, doing ten years for manslaughter. He wore suspenders, and he wanted a pair. I could trade them to him for some of his meat. Meat was what I wanted. Or perhaps he had a tattered, paper-covered novel. That was treasure-trove. I could read it and then trade it off to the bakers for cake, or to the cooks for meat and vegetables, or to the firemen for decent coffee, or to someone or other for the newspaper that occasionally filtered in, heaven alone knows how. The cooks, bakers, and firemen were prisoners like myself, and they lodged in our hall in the first row of cells over us.

In short, a full-grown system of barter obtained in the Erie County Pen. There was even money in circulation. This money was sometimes smuggled in by the short-timers, more frequently came from the barber-shop graft, where the newcomers were mulcted, but most of all flowed from the cells of the long-timers—though how they got it I don't know.

What of his preeminent position, the First Hall-man was reputed to be quite wealthy. In addition to his miscellaneous grafts, he grafted on us. We farmed the general wretchedness, and the First Hall-man was Farmer-General over all of us. We held our particular grafts by his permission, and we had to pay for that permission. As I say, he was reputed to be wealthy; but we never saw his money, and he lived in a cell all to himself in solitary grandeur.

But that money was made in the Pen I had direct evidence, for I was cell-mate quite a time with the Third Hall-man. He had over sixteen dollars. He used to count his money every night after nine o'clock, when we were locked in. Also, he used to tell me each night what he would do to me if I gave away on him to the other hall-men. You see, he was afraid of being robbed, and danger threatened him from three different directions. There were the guards. A couple of them might jump upon him, give him a good beating for alleged insubordination, and throw him into the "solitaire" (the dungeon); and in the mix-up that sixteen dollars of his would take wings. Then again, the First Hall-man could have taken it all away from him by threatening to dismiss him and fire him back to hard labor in the prison-yard. And yet again, there were the ten of us who were ordinary hall-men. If we got an inkling of his wealth, there was a large liability, some quiet day, of the whole bunch of us getting him into a corner and dragging him down. Oh, we were wolves, believe me—just like the fellows who do business in Wall Street.

He had good reason to be afraid of us, and so had I to be afraid of him. He was a huge, illiterate brute, an ex-Chesapeake-Bay-oyster-pirate, an "ex-con" who had done five years in Sing Sing, and a general all-around stupidly carnivorous beast. He used to trap sparrows that flew into our hall through the open bars. When he made a capture, he hurried away with it into his cell, where I have seen him crunching bones and spitting out feathers as he bolted it raw. Oh, no, I never gave away on him to the other hall-men. This is the first time I have mentioned his sixteen dollars.

But I grafted on him just the same. He was in love with a woman prisoner who was confined in the "female department." He could neither read nor write, and I used to read her letters to him and write his replies. And I made him pay for it, too. But they were good letters. I laid myself out on them, put in my best licks, and furthermore, I won her for him; though I shrewdly guess that she was in love, not with him, but with the humble scribe. I repeat, those letters were great.

Another one of our grafts was "passing the punk." We were the celestial messengers, the fire-bringers, in that iron world of bolt and bar. When the men came in from work at night and were locked in their cells, they wanted to smoke. Then it was that we restored the divine spark, running the galleries, from cell to cell, with our smouldering punks. Those who were wise, or with whom we did business, had their punks all ready to light. Not every one got divine sparks, however. The guy who refused to dig up, went sparkless and smokeless to bed. But what did we care? We had the immortal cinch on him, and if he got fresh, two or three of us would pitch on him and give him "what-for."

You see, this was the working-theory of the hall-men. There were thirteen of us. We had something like half a thousand prisoners in our hall. We were supposed to do the work, and to keep order. The latter was the function of the guards, which they turned over to us. It was up to us to keep order; if we didn't, we'd be fired back to hard labor, most probably with a taste of the dungeon thrown in. But so long as we maintained order, that long could we work our own particular grafts.

Bear with me a moment and look at the problem. Here were thirteen beasts of us over half a thousand other beasts. It was a living hell, that prison, and it was up to us thirteen there to rule. It was impossible, considering the nature of the beasts, for us to rule by kindness. We ruled by fear. Of course, behind us, backing us up, were the guards. In extremity we called upon them for help; but it would bother them if we called upon them too often, in which event we could depend upon it that they would get more efficient trusties to take our places. But we did not call upon them often, except in a quiet sort of way, when we wanted a cell unlocked in order to get at a refractory prisoner inside. In such cases all the guard did was to unlock the door and walk away so as not to be a witness of what happened when half a dozen hall-men went inside and did a bit of man-handling.

As regards the details of this man-handling I shall say nothing. And after all, man-handling was merely one of the very minor unprintable horrors of the Erie County Pen. I say "unprintable"; and in justice I must also say "unthinkable." They were unthinkable to me until I saw them, and I was no spring chicken in the ways of the world and the awful abysses of human degradation. It would take a deep plummet to reach bottom in the Erie County Pen, and I do but skim lightly and facetiously the surface of things as I there saw them.

At times, say in the morning when the prisoners came down to wash, the thirteen of us would be practically alone in the midst of them, and every last one of them had it in for us. Thirteen against five hundred, and we ruled by fear. We could not permit the slightest infraction of rules, the slightest insolence. If we did, we were lost. Our own rule was to hit a man as soon as he opened his mouth—hit him hard, hit him with anything. A broom-handle, end-on, in the face, had a very sobering effect. But that was not all. Such a man must be made an example of; so the next rule was to wade right in and follow him up. Of course, one was sure that every hall-man in sight would come on the run to join in the chastisement; for this also was a rule. Whenever any hall-man was in trouble with a prisoner, the duty of any other hall-man who happened to be around was to lend a fist. Never mind the merits of the case—wade in and hit, and hit with anything; in short, lay the man out.

I remember a handsome young mulatto of about twenty who got the insane idea into his head that he should stand for his rights. And he did have the right of it, too; but that didn't help him any. He lived on the topmost gallery. Eight hall-men took the conceit out of him in just about a minute and a half—for that was the length of time required to travel along his gallery to the end and down five flights of steel stairs. He travelled the whole distance on every portion of his anatomy except his feet, and the eight hall-men were not idle. The mulatto struck the pavement where I was standing watching it all. He regained his feet and stood upright for a moment. In that moment he threw his arms wide apart and omitted an awful scream of terror and pain and heartbreak. At the same instant, as in a transformation scene, the shreds of his stout prison clothes fell from him, leaving him wholly naked and streaming blood from every portion of the surface of his body. Then he collapsed in a heap, unconscious. He had learned his lesson, and every convict within those walls who heard him scream had learned a lesson. So had I learned mine. It is not a nice thing to see a man's heart broken in a minute and a half.

The following will illustrate how we drummed up business in the graft of passing the punk. A row of newcomers is installed in your cells. You pass along before the bars with your punk. "Hey, Bo, give us a light," someone calls to you. Now this is an advertisement that that particular man has tobacco on him. You pass in the punk and go your way. A little later you come back and lean up casually against the bars. "Say, Bo, can you let us have a little tobacco?" is what you say. If he is not wise to the game, the chances are that he solemnly avers that he hasn't any more tobacco. All very well. You condole with him and go your way. But you know that his punk will last him only the rest of that day. Next day you come by, and he says again, "Hey, Bo, give us a light." And you say, "You haven't any tobacco and you don't need a light." And you don't give him any, either. Half an hour after, or an hour or two or three hours, you will be passing by and the man will call out to you in mild tones, "Come here, Bo." And you come. You thrust your hand between the bars and have it filled with precious tobacco. Then you give him a light.

Sometimes, however, a newcomer arrives, upon whom no grafts are to be worked. The mysterious word is passed along that he is to be treated decently. Where this word originated I could never learn. The one thing patent is that the man has a "pull." It may be with one of the superior hall-men; it may be with one of the guards in some other part of the prison; it may be that good treatment has been purchased from grafters higher up; but be it as it may, we know that it is up to us to treat him decently if we want to avoid trouble.

We hall-men were middle-men and common carriers. We arranged trades between convicts confined in different parts of the prison, and we put through the exchange. Also, we took our commissions coming and going. Sometimes the objects traded had to go through the hands of half a dozen middle-men, each of whom took his whack, or in some way or another was paid for his service.

Sometimes one was in debt for services, and sometimes one had others in his debt. Thus, I entered the prison in debt to the convict who smuggled in my things for me. A week or so afterward, one of the firemen passed a letter into my hand. It had been given to him by a barber. The barber had received it from the convict who had smuggled in my things. Because of my debt to him I was to carry the letter on. But he had not written the letter. The original sender was a long-timer in his hall. The letter was for a woman prisoner in the female department. But whether it was intended for her, or whether she, in turn, was one of the chain of go-betweens, I did not know. All that I knew was her description, and that it was up to me to get it into her hands.

Two days passed, during which time I kept the letter in my possession; then the opportunity came. The women did the mending of all the clothes worn by the convicts. A number of our hall-men had to go to the female department to bring back huge bundles of clothes. I fixed it with the First Hall-man that I was to go along. Door after door was unlocked for us as we threaded our way across the prison to the women's quarters. We entered a large room where the women sat working at their mending. My eyes were peeled for the woman who had been described to me. I located her and worked near to her. Two eagle-eyed matrons were on watch. I held the letter in my palm, and I looked my intention at the woman. She knew I had something for her; she must have been expecting it, and had set herself to divining, at the moment we entered, which of us was the messenger. But one of the matrons stood within two feet of her. Already the hall-men were picking up the bundles they were to carry away. The moment was passing. I delayed with my bundle, making believe that it was not tied securely. Would that matron ever look away? Or was I to fail? And just then another woman cut up playfully with one of the hall-men—stuck out her foot and tripped him, or pinched him, or did something or other. The matron looked that way and reprimanded the woman sharply. Now I do not know whether or not this was all planned to distract the matron's attention, but I did know that it was my opportunity. My particular woman's hand dropped from her lap down by her side. I stooped to pick up my bundle. From my stooping position I slipped the letter into her hand, and received another in exchange. The next moment the bundle was on my shoulder, the matron's gaze had returned to me because I was the last hall-man, and I was hastening to catch up with my companions. The letter I had received from the woman I turned over to the fireman, and thence it passed through the hands of the barber, of the convict who had smuggled in my things, and on to the long-timer at the other end.

Often we conveyed letters, the chain of communication of which was so complex that we knew neither sender nor sendee. We were but links in the chain. Somewhere, somehow, a convict would thrust a letter into my hand with the instruction to pass it on to the next link. All such acts were favors to be reciprocated later on, when I should be acting directly with a principal in transmitting letters, and from whom I should be receiving my pay. The whole prison was covered by a network of lines of communication. And we who were in control of the system of communication, naturally, since we were modelled after capitalistic society, exacted heavy tolls from our customers. It was service for profit with a vengeance, though we were at times not above giving service for love.

And all the time I was in the Pen I was making myself solid with my pal. He had done much for me, and in return he expected me to do as much for him. When we got out, we were to travel together, and, it goes without saying, pull off "jobs" together. For my pal was a criminal—oh, not a jewel of the first water, merely a petty criminal who would steal and rob, commit burglary, and, if cornered, not stop short of murder. Many a quiet hour we sat and talked together. He had two or three jobs in view for the immediate future, in which my work was cut out for me, and in which I joined in planning the details. I had been with and seen much of criminals, and my pal never dreamed that I was only fooling him, giving him a string thirty days long. He thought I was the real goods, liked me because I was not stupid, and liked me a bit, too, I think, for myself. Of course I had not the slightest intention of joining him in a life of sordid, petty crime; but I'd have been an idiot to throw away all the good things his friendship made possible. When one is on the hot lava of hell, he cannot pick and choose his path, and so it was with me in the Erie County Pen. I had to stay in with the "push," or do hard labor on bread and water; and to stay in with the push I had to make good with my pal.

Life was not monotonous in the Pen. Every day something was happening: men were having fits, going crazy, fighting, or the hall-men were getting drunk. Rover Jack, one of the ordinary hall-men, was our star "oryide." He was a true "profesh," a "blowed-in-the-glass" stiff, and as such received all kinds of latitude from the hall-men in authority. Pittsburg Joe, who was Second Hall-man, used to join Rover Jack in his jags; and it was a saying of the pair that the Erie County Pen was the only place where a man could get "slopped" and not be arrested. I never knew, but I was told that–bromide of potassium, gained in devious ways from the dispensary, was the dope they used. But I do know, whatever their dope was, that they got good and drunk on occasion.

Our hall was a common stews, filled with the ruck and the filth, the scum and dregs, of society—hereditary inefficients, degenerates, wrecks, lunatics, addled intelligences, epileptics, monsters, weaklings, in short, a very nightmare of humanity. Hence, fits flourished with us. These fits seemed contagious. When one man began throwing a fit, others followed his lead. I have seen seven men down with fits at the same time, making the air hideous with their cries, while as many more lunatics would be raging and gibbering up and down. Nothing was ever done for the men with fits except to throw cold water on them. It was useless to send for the medical student or the doctor. They were not to be bothered with such trivial and frequent occurrences.

There was a young Dutch boy, about eighteen years of age, who had fits most frequently of all. He usually threw one every day. It was for that reason that we kept him on the ground floor farther down in the row of cells in which we lodged. After he had had a few fits in the prison-yard, the guards refused to be bothered with him any more, and so he remained locked up in his cell all day with a Cockney cell-mate, to keep him company. Not that the Cockney was of any use. Whenever the Dutch boy had a fit, the Cockney became paralyzed with terror.

The Dutch boy could not speak a word of English. He was a farmer's boy, serving ninety days as punishment for having got into a scrap with someone. He prefaced his fits with howling. He howled like a wolf. Also, he took his fits standing up, which was very inconvenient for him, for his fits always culminated in a headlong pitch to the floor. Whenever I heard the long wolf-howl rising, I used to grab a broom and run to his cell. Now the trusties were not allowed keys to the cells, so I could not get in to him. He would stand up in the middle of his narrow cell, shivering convulsively, his eyes rolled backward till only the whites were visible, and howling like a lost soul. Try as I would, I could never get the Cockney to lend him a hand. While he stood and howled, the Cockney crouched and trembled in the upper bunk, his terror-stricken gaze fixed on that awful figure, with eyes rolled back, that howled and howled. It was hard on him, too, the poor devil of a Cockney. His own reason was not any too firmly seated, and the wonder is that he did not go mad.

All that I could do was my best with the broom. I would thrust it through the bars, train it on Dutchy's chest, and wait. As the crisis approached he would begin swaying back and forth. I followed this swaying with the broom, for there was no telling when he would take that dreadful forward pitch. But when he did, I was there with the broom, catching him and easing him down. Contrive as I would, he never came down quite gently, and his face was usually bruised by the stone floor. Once down and writhing in convulsions, I'd throw a bucket of water over him. I don't know whether cold water was the right thing or not, but it was the custom in the Erie County Pen. Nothing more than that was ever done for him. He would lie there, wet, for an hour or so, and then crawl into his bunk. I knew better than to run to a guard for assistance. What was a man with a fit, anyway?

In the adjoining cell lived a strange character—a man who was doing sixty days for eating swill out of Barnum's swill-barrel, or at least that was the way he put it. He was a badly addled creature, and, at first, very mild and gentle. The facts of his case were as he had stated them. He had strayed out to the circus ground, and, being hungry, had made his way to the barrel that contained the refuse from the table of the circus people. "And it was good bread," he often assured me; "and the meat was out of sight." A policeman had seen him and arrested him, and there he was.

Once I passed his cell with a piece of stiff thin wire in my hand. He asked me for it so earnestly that I passed it through the bars to him. Promptly, and with no tool but his fingers, he broke it into short lengths and twisted them into half a dozen very creditable safety pins. He sharpened the points on the stone floor. Thereafter I did quite a trade in safety pins. I furnished the raw material and peddled the finished product, and he did the work. As wages, I paid him extra rations of bread, and once in a while a chunk of meat or a piece of soup-bone with some marrow inside.

But his imprisonment told on him, and he grew violent day by day. The hall-men took delight in teasing him. They filled his weak brain with stories of a great fortune that had been left him. It was in order to rob him of it that he had been arrested and sent to jail. Of course, as he himself knew, there was no law against eating out of a barrel. Therefore he was wrongly imprisoned. It was a plot to deprive him of his fortune.

The first I knew of it, I heard the hall-men laughing about the string they had given him. Next he held a serious conference with me, in which he told me of his millions and the plot to deprive him of them, and in which he appointed me his detective. I did my best to let him down gently, speaking vaguely of a mistake, and that it was another man with a similar name who was the rightful heir. I left him quite cooled down; but I couldn't keep the hall-men away from him, and they continued to string him worse than ever. In the end, after a most violent scene, he threw me down, revoked my private detectiveship, and went on strike. My trade in safety pins ceased. He refused to make any more safety pins, and he peppered me with raw material through the bars of his cell when I passed by.

I could never make it up with him. The other hall-men told him that I was a detective in the employ of the conspirators. And in the meantime the hall-men drove him mad with their stringing. His fictitious wrongs preyed upon his mind, and at last he became a dangerous and homicidal lunatic. The guards refused to listen to his tale of stolen millions, and he accused them of being in the plot. One day he threw a pannikin of hot tea over one of them, and then his case was investigated. The warden talked with him a few minutes through the bars of his cell. Then he was taken away for examination before the doctors. He never came back, and I often wonder if he is dead, or if he still gibbers about his millions in some asylum for the insane.

At last came the day of days, my release. It was the day of release for the Third Hall-man as well, and the short-timer girl I had won for him was waiting for him outside the wall. They went away blissfully together. My pal and I went out together, and together we walked down into Buffalo. Were we not to be together always? We begged together on the "main-drag" that day for pennies, and what we received was spent for "shupers" of beer—I don't know how they are spelled, but they are pronounced the way I have spelled them, and they cost three cents. I was watching my chance all the time for a get-away. From some bo on the drag I managed to learn what time a certain freight pulled out. I calculated my time accordingly. When the moment came, my pal and I were in a saloon. Two foaming shupers were before us. I'd have liked to say good-by. He had been good to me. But I did not dare. I went out through the rear of the saloon and jumped the fence. It was a swift sneak, and a few minutes later I was on board a freight and heading south on the Western New York and Pennsylvania Railroad.

Chapter 6
Hoboes That Pass in the Night

In the course of my tramping I encountered hundreds of hoboes, whom I hailed or who hailed me, and with whom I waited at water-tanks, "boiled-up," cooked "mulligans," "battered" the "drag" or "privates," and beat trains, and who passed and were seen never again. On the other hand, there were hoboes who passed and repassed with amazing frequency, and others, still, who passed like ghosts, close at hand, unseen, and never seen.

It was one of the latter that I chased clear across Canada over three thousand miles of railroad, and never once did I lay eyes on him. His "monica" was Skysail Jack. I first ran into it at Montreal. Carved with a jack-knife was the skysail-yard of a ship. It was perfectly executed. Under it was "Skysail Jack." Above was "B.W. 9-15-94." This latter conveyed the information that he had passed through Montreal bound west, on October 15, 1894. He had one day the start of me. "Sailor Jack" was my monica at that particular time, and promptly I carved it alongside of his, along with the date and the information that I, too, was bound west.

I had misfortune in getting over the next hundred miles, and eight days later I picked up Skysail Jack's trail three hundred miles west of Ottawa. There it was, carved on a water-tank, and by the date I saw that he likewise had met with delay. He was only two days ahead of me. I was a "comet" and "tramp-royal," so was Skysail Jack; and it was up to my pride and reputation to catch up with him. I "rail-roaded" day and night, and I passed him; then turn about he passed me. Sometimes he was a day or so ahead, and sometimes I was. From hoboes, bound east, I got word of him occasionally, when he happened to be ahead; and from them I learned that he had become interested in Sailor Jack and was making inquiries about me.

We'd have made a precious pair, I am sure, if we'd ever got together; but get together we couldn't. I kept ahead of him clear across Manitoba, but he led the way across Alberta, and early one bitter gray morning, at the end of a division just east of Kicking Horse Pass, I learned that he had been seen the night before between Kicking Horse Pass and Rogers' Pass. It was rather curious the way the information came to me. I had been riding all night in a "side-door Pullman" (box-car), and nearly dead with cold had crawled out at the division to beg for food. A freezing fog was drifting past, and I "hit" some firemen I found in the round-house. They fixed me up with the leavings from their lunch-pails, and in addition I got out of them nearly a quart of heavenly "Java" (coffee). I heated the latter, and, as I sat down to eat, a freight pulled in from the west. I saw a side-door open and a road-kid climb out. Through the drifting fog he limped over to me. He was stiff with cold, his lips blue. I shared my Java and grub with him, learned about Skysail Jack, and then learned about him. Behold, he was from my own town, Oakland, California, and he was a member of the celebrated Boo Gang—a gang with which I had affiliated at rare intervals. We talked fast and bolted the grub in the half-hour that followed. Then my freight pulled out, and I was on it, bound west on the trail of Skysail Jack.

I was delayed between the passes, went two days without food, and walked eleven miles on the third day before I got any, and yet I succeeded in passing Skysail Jack along the Fraser River in British Columbia. I was riding "passengers" then and making time; but he must have been riding passengers, too, and with more luck or skill than I, for he got into Mission ahead of me.

Now Mission was a junction, forty miles east of Vancouver. From the junction one could proceed south through Washington and Oregon over the Northern Pacific. I wondered which way Skysail Jack would go, for I thought I was ahead of him. As for myself I was still bound west to Vancouver. I proceeded to the water-tank to leave that information, and there, freshly carved, with that day's date upon it, was Skysail Jack's monica. I hurried on into Vancouver. But he was gone. He had taken ship immediately and was still flying west on his world-adventure. Truly, Skysail Jack, you were a tramp-royal, and your mate was the "wind that tramps the world." I take off my hat to you. You were "blowed-in-the-glass" all right. A week later I, too, got my ship, and on board the steamship Umatilla, in the forecastle, was working my way down the coast to San Francisco. Skysail Jack and Sailor Jack—gee! if we'd ever got together.

Water-tanks are tramp directories. Not all in idle wantonness do tramps carve their monicas, dates, and courses. Often and often have I met hoboes earnestly inquiring if I had seen anywhere such and such a "stiff" or his monica. And more than once I have been able to give the monica of recent date, the water-tank, and the direction in which he was then bound. And promptly the hobo to whom I gave the information lit out after his pal. I have met hoboes who, in trying to catch a pal, had pursued clear across the continent and back again, and were still going.

"Monicas" are the nom-de-rails that hoboes assume or accept when thrust upon them by their fellows. Leary Joe, for instance, was timid, and was so named by his fellows. No self-respecting hobo would select Stew Bum for himself. Very few tramps care to remember their pasts during which they ignobly worked, so monicas based upon trades are very rare, though I remember having met the following: Moulder Blackey, Painter Red, Chi Plumber, Boiler-Maker, Sailor Boy, and Printer Bo. "Chi" (pronounced shy), by the way, is the argot for "Chicago."

A favorite device of hoboes is to base their monicas on the localities from which they hail, as: New York Tommy, Pacific Slim, Buffalo Smithy, Canton Tim, Pittsburg Jack, Syracuse Shine, Troy Mickey, K.L. Bill, and Connecticut Jimmy. Then there was "Slim Jim from Vinegar Hill, who never worked and never will." A "shine" is always a negro, so called, possibly, from the high lights on his countenance. Texas Shine or Toledo Shine convey both race and nativity.

Among those that incorporated their race, I recollect the following: Frisco Sheeny, New York Irish, Michigan French, English Jack, Cockney Kid, and Milwaukee Dutch. Others seem to take their monicas in part from the color-schemes stamped upon them at birth, such as: Chi Whitey, New Jersey Red, Boston Blackey, Seattle Browney, and Yellow Dick and Yellow Belly—the last a Creole from Mississippi, who, I suspect, had his monica thrust upon him.

Texas Royal, Happy Joe, Bust Connors, Burley Bo, Tornado Blackey, and Touch McCall used more imagination in rechristening themselves. Others, with less fancy, carry the names of their physical peculiarities, such as: Vancouver Slim, Detroit Shorty, Ohio Fatty, Long Jack, Big Jim, Little Joe, New York Blink, Chi Nosey, and Broken-backed Ben.

By themselves come the road-kids, sporting an infinite variety of monicas. For example, the following, whom here and there I have encountered: Buck Kid, Blind Kid, Midget Kid, Holy Kid, Bat Kid, Swift Kid, Cookey Kid, Monkey Kid, Iowa Kid, Corduroy Kid, Orator Kid (who could tell how it happened), and Lippy Kid (who was insolent, depend upon it).

On the water-tank at San Marcial, New Mexico, a dozen years ago, was the following hobo bill of fare:

1. Main-drag fair
2. Bulls not hostile.
3. Round-house good for kipping.

4. North-bound trains no good.
5. Privates no good
6. Restaurants good for cooks only
7. Railroad House good for night-work only.

Number one conveys the information that begging for money on the main street is fair; number two, that the police will not bother hoboes; number three, that one can sleep in the round-house. Number four, however, is ambiguous. The north-bound trains may be no good to beat, and they may be no good to beg. Number five means that the residences are not good to beggars, and number six means that only hoboes that have been cooks can get grub from the restaurants. Number seven bothers me. I cannot make out whether the Railroad House is a good place for any hobo to beg at night, or whether it is good only for hobo-cooks to beg at night, or whether any hobo, cook or non-cook, can lend a hand at night, helping the cooks of the Railroad House with their dirty work and getting something to eat in payment.

But to return to the hoboes that pass in the night. I remember one I met in California. He was a Swede, but he had lived so long in the United States that one couldn't guess his nationality. He had to tell it on himself. In fact, he had come to the United States when no more than a baby. I ran into him first at the mountain town of Truckee. "Which way, Bo?" was our greeting, and "Bound east" was the answer each of us gave. Quite a bunch of "stiffs" tried to ride out the overland that night, and I lost the Swede in the shuffle. Also, I lost the overland.

I arrived in Reno, Nevada, in a box-car that was promptly side-tracked. It was a Sunday morning, and after I threw my feet for breakfast, I wandered over to the Piute camp to watch the Indians gambling. And there stood the Swede, hugely interested. Of course we got together. He was the only acquaintance I had in that region, and I was his only acquaintance. We rushed together like a couple of dissatisfied hermits, and together we spent the day, threw our feet for dinner, and late in the afternoon tried to "nail" the same freight. But he was ditched, and I rode her out alone, to be ditched myself in the desert twenty miles beyond.

Of all desolate places, the one at which I was ditched was the limit. It was called a flag-station, and it consisted of a shanty dumped inconsequentially into the sand and sagebrush. A chill wind was blowing, night was coming on, and the solitary telegraph operator who lived in the shanty was afraid of me. I knew that neither grub nor bed could I get out of him. It was because of his manifest fear of me that I did not believe him when he told me that east-bound trains never stopped there. Besides, hadn't I been thrown off of an east-bound train right at that very spot not five minutes before? He assured me that it had stopped under orders, and that a year might go by before another was stopped under orders. He advised me that it was only a dozen or fifteen miles on to Wadsworth and that I'd better hike. I elected to wait, however, and I had the pleasure of seeing two west-bound freights go by without stopping, and one east-bound freight. I wondered if the Swede was on the latter. It was up to me to hit the ties to Wadsworth, and hit them I did, much to the telegraph operator's relief, for I neglected to burn his shanty and murder him. Telegraph operators have much to be thankful for. At the end of half a dozen miles, I had to get off the ties and let the east-bound overland go by. She was going fast, but I caught sight of a dim form on the first "blind" that looked like the Swede.

That was the last I saw of him for weary days. I hit the high places across those hundreds of miles of Nevada desert, riding the overlands at night, for speed, and in the day-time riding in box-cars and getting my sleep. It was early in the year, and it was cold in those upland pastures. Snow lay here and there on the level, all the mountains were shrouded in white, and at night the most miserable wind imaginable blew off from them. It was not a land in which to linger. And remember, gentle reader, the hobo goes through such a land, without shelter, without money, begging his way and sleeping at night without blankets. This last is something that can be realized only by experience.

In the early evening I came down to the depot at Ogden. The overland of the Union Pacific was pulling east, and I was bent on making connections. Out in the tangle of tracks ahead of the engine I encountered a figure slouching through the gloom. It was the

Swede. We shook hands like long-lost brothers, and discovered that our hands were gloved. "Where'd ye glahm 'em?" I asked. "Out of an engine-cab," he answered; "and where did you?" "They belonged to a fireman," said I; "he was careless."

We caught the blind as the overland pulled out, and mighty cold we found it. The way led up a narrow gorge between snow-covered mountains, and we shivered and shook and exchanged confidences about how we had covered the ground between Reno and Ogden. I had closed my eyes for only an hour or so the previous night, and the blind was not comfortable enough to suit me for a snooze. At a stop, I went forward to the engine. We had on a "double-header" (two engines) to take us over the grade.

The pilot of the head engine, because it "punched the wind," I knew would be too cold; so I selected the pilot of the second engine, which was sheltered by the first engine. I stepped on the cowcatcher and found the pilot occupied. In the darkness I felt out the form of a young boy. He was sound asleep. By squeezing, there was room for two on the pilot, and I made the boy budge over and crawled up beside him. It was a "good" night; the "shacks" (brakemen) didn't bother us, and in no time we were asleep. Once in a while hot cinders or heavy jolts aroused me, when I snuggled closer to the boy and dozed off to the coughing of the engines and the screeching of the wheels.

The overland made Evanston, Wyoming, and went no farther. A wreck ahead blocked the line. The dead engineer had been brought in, and his body attested the peril of the way. A tramp, also, had been killed, but his body had not been brought in. I talked with the boy. He was thirteen years old. He had run away from his folks in some place in Oregon, and was heading east to his grandmother. He had a tale of cruel treatment in the home he had left that rang true; besides, there was no need for him to lie to me, a nameless hobo on the track.

And that boy was going some, too. He couldn't cover the ground fast enough. When the division superintendents decided to send the overland back over the way it had come, then up on a cross "jerk" to the Oregon Short Line, and back along that road to tap the Union

Pacific the other side of the wreck, that boy climbed upon the pilot and said he was going to stay with it. This was too much for the Swede and me. It meant travelling the rest of that frigid night in order to gain no more than a dozen miles or so. We said we'd wait till the wreck was cleared away, and in the meantime get a good sleep.

Now it is no snap to strike a strange town, broke, at midnight, in cold weather, and find a place to sleep. The Swede hadn't a penny. My total assets consisted of two dimes and a nickel. From some of the town boys we learned that beer was five cents, and that the saloons kept open all night. There was our meat. Two glasses of beer would cost ten cents, there would be a stove and chairs, and we could sleep it out till morning. We headed for the lights of a saloon, walking briskly, the snow crunching under our feet, a chill little wind blowing through us.

Alas, I had misunderstood the town boys. Beer was five cents in one saloon only in the whole burg, and we didn't strike that saloon. But the one we entered was all right. A blessed stove was roaring white-hot; there were cosey, cane-bottomed arm-chairs, and a none-too-pleasant-looking barkeeper who glared suspiciously at us as we came in. A man cannot spend continuous days and nights in his clothes, beating trains, fighting soot and cinders, and sleeping anywhere, and maintain a good "front." Our fronts were decidedly against us; but what did we care? I had the price in my jeans.

"Two beers," said I nonchalantly to the barkeeper, and while he drew them, the Swede and I leaned against the bar and yearned secretly for the arm-chairs by the stove.

The barkeeper set the two foaming glasses before us, and with pride I deposited the ten cents. Now I was dead game. As soon as I learned my error in the price I'd have dug up another ten cents. Never mind if it did leave me only a nickel to my name, a stranger in a strange land. I'd have paid it all right. But that barkeeper never gave me a chance. As soon as his eyes spotted the dime I had laid down, he seized the two glasses, one in each hand, and dumped the beer into the sink behind the bar. At the same time, glaring at us malevolently, he said:—

"You've got scabs on your nose. You've got scabs on your nose. You've got scabs on your nose. See!"

I hadn't either, and neither had the Swede. Our noses were all right. The direct bearing of his words was beyond our comprehension, but the indirect bearing was clear as print: he didn't like our looks, and beer was evidently ten cents a glass.

I dug down and laid another dime on the bar, remarking carelessly, "Oh, I thought this was a five-cent joint."

"Your money's no good here," he answered, shoving the two dimes across the bar to me.

Sadly I dropped them back into my pocket, sadly we yearned toward the blessed stove and the arm-chairs, and sadly we went out the door into the frosty night.

But as we went out the door, the barkeeper, still glaring, called after us, "You've got scabs on your nose, see!"

I have seen much of the world since then, journeyed among strange lands and peoples, opened many books, sat in many lecture-halls; but to this day, though I have pondered long and deep, I have been unable to divine the meaning in the cryptic utterance of that barkeeper in Evanston, Wyoming. Our noses *were* all right.

We slept that night over the boilers in an electric-lighting plant. How we discovered that "kipping" place I can't remember. We must have just headed for it, instinctively, as horses head for water or carrier-pigeons head for the home-cote. But it was a night not pleasant to remember. A dozen hoboes were ahead of us on top the boilers, and it was too hot for all of us. To complete our misery, the engineer would not let us stand around down below. He gave us our choice of the boilers or the outside snow.

"You said you wanted to sleep, and so, damn you, sleep," said he to me, when, frantic and beaten out by the heat, I came down into the fire-room.

"Water," I gasped, wiping the sweat from my eyes, "water."

He pointed out of doors and assured me that down there somewhere in the blackness I'd find the river. I started for the river, got lost in the dark, fell into two or three drifts, gave it up, and returned half-frozen to the top of the boilers. When I had thawed out, I was thirstier than ever. Around me the hoboes were moaning, groaning, sobbing, sighing, gasping, panting, rolling and tossing and floundering heavily in their torment. We were so many lost souls toasting on a griddle in hell, and the engineer, Satan Incarnate, gave us the sole alternative of freezing in the outer cold. The Swede sat up and anathematized passionately the wanderlust in man that sent him tramping and suffering hardships such as that.

"When I get back to Chicago," he perorated, "I'm going to get a job and stick to it till hell freezes over. Then I'll go tramping again."

And, such is the irony of fate, next day, when the wreck ahead was cleared, the Swede and I pulled out of Evanston in the ice-boxes of an "orange special," a fast freight laden with fruit from sunny California. Of course, the ice-boxes were empty on account of the cold weather, but that didn't make them any warmer for us. We entered them through hatchways in the top of the car; the boxes were constructed of galvanized iron, and in that biting weather were not pleasant to the touch. We lay there, shivered and shook, and with chattering teeth held a council wherein we decided that we'd stay by the ice-boxes day and night till we got out of the inhospitable plateau region and down into the Mississippi Valley.

But we must eat, and we decided that at the next division we would throw our feet for grub and make a rush back to our ice-boxes. We arrived in the town of Green River late in the afternoon, but too early for supper. Before meal-time is the worst time for "battering" back-doors; but we put on our nerve, swung off the side-ladders as the freight pulled into the yards, and made a run for the houses. We were quickly separated; but we had agreed to meet in the ice-boxes. I had bad luck at first; but in the end, with a couple of "hand-outs" poked into my shirt, I chased for the train. It was pulling out and going fast. The particular refrigerator-car in which we were to meet had already gone by, and half a dozen cars down the train from it I swung on to the side-ladders, went up on top hurriedly, and dropped down into an ice-box.

But a shack had seen me from the caboose, and at the next stop a few miles farther on, Rock Springs, the shack stuck his head into my box and said: "Hit the grit, you son of a toad! Hit the grit!" Also he grabbed me by the heels and dragged me out. I hit the grit all right, and the orange special and the Swede rolled on without me.

Snow was beginning to fall. A cold night was coming on. After dark I hunted around in the railroad yards until I found an empty refrigerator car. In I climbed—not into the ice-boxes, but into the car itself. I swung the heavy doors shut, and their edges, covered with strips of rubber, sealed the car air-tight. The walls were thick. There was no way for the outside cold to get in. But the inside was just as cold as the outside. How to raise the temperature was the problem. But trust a "profesh" for that. Out of my pockets I dug up three or four newspapers. These I burned, one at a time, on the floor of the car. The smoke rose to the top. Not a bit of the heat could escape, and, comfortable and warm, I passed a beautiful night. I didn't wake up once.

In the morning it was still snowing. While throwing my feet for breakfast, I missed an east-bound freight. Later in the day I nailed two other freights and was ditched from both of them. All afternoon no east-bound trains went by. The snow was falling thicker than ever, but at twilight I rode out on the first blind of the overland. As I swung aboard the blind from one side, somebody swung aboard from the other. It was the boy who had run away from Oregon.

Now the first blind of a fast train in a driving snow-storm is no summer picnic. The wind goes right through one, strikes the front of the car, and comes back again. At the first stop, darkness having come on, I went forward and interviewed the fireman. I offered to "shove" coal to the end of his run, which was Rawlins, and my offer was accepted. My work was out on the tender, in the snow, breaking the lumps of coal with a sledge and shovelling it forward to him in the cab. But as I did not have to work all the time, I could come into the cab and warm up now and again.

"Say," I said to the fireman, at my first breathing spell, "there's a little kid back there on the first blind. He's pretty cold."

The cabs on the Union Pacific engines are quite spacious, and we fitted the kid into a warm nook in front of the high seat of the fireman, where the kid promptly fell asleep. We arrived at Rawlins at midnight. The snow was thicker than ever. Here the engine was to go into the round-house, being replaced by a fresh engine. As the train came to a stop, I dropped off the engine steps plump into the arms of a large man in a large overcoat. He began asking me questions, and I promptly demanded who he was. Just as promptly he informed me that he was the sheriff. I drew in my horns and listened and answered.

He began describing the kid who was still asleep in the cab. I did some quick thinking. Evidently the family was on the trail of the kid, and the sheriff had received telegraphed instructions from Oregon. Yes, I had seen the kid. I had met him first in Ogden. The date tallied with the sheriff's information. But the kid was still behind somewhere, I explained, for he had been ditched from that very overland that night when it pulled out of Rock Springs. And all the time I was praying that the kid wouldn't wake up, come down out of the cab, and put the "kibosh" on me.

The sheriff left me in order to interview the shacks, but before he left he said:—

"Bo, this town is no place for you. Understand? You ride this train out, and make no mistake about it. If I catch you after it's gone . . ."

I assured him that it was not through desire that I was in his town; that the only reason I was there was that the train had stopped there; and that he wouldn't see me for smoke the way I'd get out of his darn town.

While he went to interview the shacks, I jumped back into the cab. The kid was awake and rubbing his eyes. I told him the news and advised him to ride the engine into the round-house. To cut the story short, the kid made the same overland out, riding the pilot, with instructions to make an appeal to the fireman at the first stop for permission to ride in the engine. As for myself, I got ditched. The new fireman was young and not yet lax enough to break the rules of the Company against having tramps in the engine; so he turned down my offer to shove coal. I hope the kid succeeded with him, for all night on the pilot in that blizzard would have meant death.

Strange to say, I do not at this late day remember a detail of how I was ditched at Rawlins. I remember watching the train as it was immediately swallowed up in the snow-storm, and of heading for a saloon to warm up. Here was light and warmth. Everything was in full blast and wide open. Faro, roulette, craps, and poker tables were running, and some mad cow-punchers were making the night merry. I had just succeeded in fraternizing with them and was downing my first drink at their expense, when a heavy hand descended on my shoulder. I looked around and sighed. It was the sheriff.

Without a word he led me out into the snow.

"There's an orange special down there in the yards," said he.

"It's a damn cold night," said I.

"It pulls out in ten minutes," said he.

That was all. There was no discussion. And when that orange special pulled out, I was in the ice-boxes. I thought my feet would freeze before morning, and the last twenty miles into Laramie I stood upright in the hatchway and danced up and down. The snow was too thick for the shacks to see me, and I didn't care if they did.

My quarter of a dollar bought me a hot breakfast at Laramie, and immediately afterward I was on board the blind baggage of an overland that was climbing to the pass through the backbone of the Rockies. One does not ride blind baggages in the daytime; but in this blizzard at the top of the Rocky Mountains I doubted if the shacks would have the heart to put me off. And they didn't. They made a practice of coming forward at every stop to see if I was frozen yet.

At Ames' Monument, at the summit of the Rockies,—I forget the altitude,—the shack came forward for the last time.

"Say, Bo," he said, "you see that freight side-tracked over there to let us go by?"

I saw. It was on the next track, six feet away. A few feet more in that storm and I could not have seen it.

"Well, the 'after-push' of Kelly's Army is in one of them cars. They've got two feet of straw under them, and there's so many of them that they keep the car warm."

His advice was good, and I followed it, prepared, however, if it was a "con game" the shack had given me, to take the blind as the overland pulled out. But it was straight goods. I found the car—a big refrigerator car with the leeward door wide open for ventilation. Up I climbed and in. I stepped on a man's leg, next on some other man's arm. The light was dim, and all I could make out was arms and legs and bodies inextricably confused. Never was there such a tangle of humanity. They were all lying in the straw, and over, and under, and around one another. Eighty-four husky hoboes take up a lot of room when they are stretched out. The men I stepped on were resentful. Their bodies heaved under me like the waves of the sea, and imparted an involuntary forward movement to me. I could not find any straw to step upon, so I stepped upon more men. The resentment increased, so did my forward movement. I lost my footing and sat down with sharp abruptness. Unfortunately, it was on a man's head. The next moment he had risen on his hands and knees in wrath, and I was flying through the air. What goes up must come down, and I came down on another man's head.

What happened after that is very vague in my memory. It was like going through a threshing-machine. I was bandied about from one end of the car to the other. Those eighty-four hoboes winnowed me out till what little was left of me, by some miracle, found a bit of straw to rest upon. I was initiated, and into a jolly crowd. All the rest of that day we rode through the blizzard, and to while the time away it was decided that each man was to tell a story. It was stipulated that each story must be a good one, and, furthermore, that it must be a story no one had ever heard before. The penalty for failure was the threshing-machine. Nobody failed. And I want to say right here that never in my life have I sat at so marvellous a story-telling debauch. Here were eighty-four men from all the world—I made eighty-five; and each man told a masterpiece. It had to be, for it was either masterpiece or threshing-machine.

Late in the afternoon we arrived in Cheyenne. The blizzard was at its height, and though the last meal of all of us had been breakfast, no man cared to throw his feet for supper. All night we rolled on through the storm, and next day found us down on the sweet plains of Nebraska and still rolling. We were out of the storm and the mountains. The blessed sun was shining over a smiling land, and we had eaten nothing for twenty-four hours. We found out that the freight would arrive about noon at a town, if I remember right, that was called Grand Island.

We took up a collection and sent a telegram to the authorities of that town. The text of the message was that eighty-five healthy, hungry hoboes would arrive about noon and that it would be a good idea to have dinner ready for them. The authorities of Grand Island had two courses open to them. They could feed us, or they could throw us in jail. In the latter event they'd have to feed us anyway, and they decided wisely that one meal would be the cheaper way.

When the freight rolled into Grand Island at noon, we were sitting on the tops of the cars and dangling our legs in the sunshine. All the police in the burg were on the reception committee. They marched us in squads to the various hotels and restaurants, where dinners were spread for us. We had been thirty-six hours without food, and we didn't have to be taught what to do. After that we were marched back to the railroad station. The police had thoughtfully compelled the freight to wait for us. She pulled out slowly, and the eighty-five of us, strung out along the track, swarmed up the side-ladders. We "captured" the train.

We had no supper that evening—at least the "push" didn't, but I did. Just at supper time, as the freight was pulling out of a small town, a man climbed into the car where I was playing pedro with three other stiffs. The man's shirt was bulging suspiciously. In his hand he carried a battered quart-measure from which arose steam. I smelled "Java." I turned my cards over to one of the stiffs who was looking on, and excused myself. Then, in the other end of the car, pursued by envious glances, I sat down with the man who had climbed aboard and shared his "Java" and the hand-outs that had bulged his shirt. It was the Swede.

At about ten o'clock in the evening, we arrived at Omaha.

"Let's shake the push," said the Swede to me.

"Sure," said I.

As the freight pulled into Omaha, we made ready to do so. But the people of Omaha were also ready. The Swede and I hung upon the side-ladders, ready to drop off. But the freight did not stop. Furthermore, long rows of policemen, their brass buttons and stars glittering in the electric lights, were lined up on each side of the track. The Swede and I knew what would happen to us if we ever dropped off into their arms. We stuck by the side-ladders, and the train rolled on across the Missouri River to Council Bluffs.

"General" Kelly, with an army of two thousand hoboes, lay in camp at Chautauqua Park, several miles away. The after-push we were with was General Kelly's rear-guard, and, detraining at Council Bluffs, it started to march to camp. The night had turned cold, and heavy wind-squalls, accompanied by rain, were chilling and wetting us. Many police were guarding us and herding us to the camp. The Swede and I watched our chance and made a successful get-away.

The rain began coming down in torrents, and in the darkness, unable to see our hands in front of our faces, like a pair of blind men we fumbled about for shelter. Our instinct served us, for in no time we stumbled upon a saloon—not a saloon that was open and doing business, not merely a saloon that was closed for the night, and not even a saloon with a permanent address, but a saloon propped up on big timbers, with rollers underneath, that was being moved from somewhere to somewhere. The doors were locked. A squall of wind and rain drove down upon us. We did not hesitate. Smash went the door, and in we went.

I have made some tough camps in my time, "carried the banner" in infernal metropolises, bedded in pools of water, slept in the snow under two blankets when the spirit thermometer registered seventy-four degrees below zero (which is a mere trifle of one hundred and six degrees of frost); but I want to say right here that never did I make a tougher camp, pass a more miserable night, than that night I passed with the Swede in the itinerant saloon at Council Bluffs. In the first place, the building, perched up as it was in the air, had exposed a multitude of openings in the floor through which the wind whistled. In the second place, the bar was empty; there was no bottled fire-water with which we could warm ourselves and forget our misery. We had no blankets, and in our wet clothes, wet to the skin, we tried to sleep. I rolled under the bar, and the Swede rolled under the table. The holes and crevices in the floor made it impossible, and at the end of half an hour I crawled up on top the bar. A little later the Swede crawled up on top his table.

And there we shivered and prayed for daylight. I know, for one, that I shivered until I could shiver no more, till the shivering muscles exhausted themselves and merely ached horribly. The Swede moaned and groaned, and every little while, through chattering teeth, he muttered, "Never again; never again." He muttered this phrase repeatedly, ceaselessly, a thousand times; and when he dozed, he went on muttering it in his sleep.

At the first gray of dawn we left our house of pain, and outside, found ourselves in a mist, dense and chill. We stumbled on till we came to the railroad track. I was going back to Omaha to throw my feet for breakfast; my companion was going on to Chicago. The moment for parting had come. Our palsied hands went out to each other. We were both shivering. When we tried to speak, our teeth chattered us back into silence. We stood alone, shut off from the world; all that we could see was a short length of railroad track, both ends of which were lost in the driving mist. We stared dumbly at each other, our clasped hands shaking sympathetically. The Swede's face was blue with the cold, and I know mine must have been.

"Never again what?" I managed to articulate.

Speech strove for utterance in the Swede's throat; then faint and distant, in a thin whisper from the very bottom of his frozen soul, came the words:—

"Never again a hobo."

He paused, and, as he went on again, his voice gathered strength and huskiness as it affirmed his will.

"Never again a hobo. I'm going to get a job. You'd better do the same. Nights like this make rheumatism."

He wrung my hand.

"Good-by, Bo," said he.

"Good-by, Bo," said I.

The next we were swallowed up from each other by the mist. It was our final passing. But here's to you, Mr. Swede, wherever you are. I hope you got that job.

Chapter 7
Road-Kids and Gay-Cats

Every once in a while, in newspapers, magazines, and biographical dictionaries, I run upon sketches of my life, wherein, delicately phrased, I learn that it was in order to study sociology that I became a tramp. This is very nice and thoughtful of the biographers, but it is inaccurate. I became a tramp—well, because of the life that was in me, of the wanderlust in my blood that would not let me rest. Sociology was merely incidental; it came afterward, in the same manner that a wet skin follows a ducking. I went on "The Road" because I couldn't keep away from it; because I hadn't the price of the railroad fare in my jeans; because I was so made that I couldn't work all my life on "one same shift"; because—well, just because it was easier to than not to.

It happened in my own town, in Oakland, when I was sixteen. At that time I had attained a dizzy reputation in my chosen circle of adventurers, by whom I was known as the Prince of the Oyster Pirates. It is true, those immediately outside my circle, such as honest bay-sailors, longshoremen, yachtsmen, and the legal owners of the oysters, called me "tough," "hoodlum," "smoudge," "thief," "robber," and various other not nice things—all of which was complimentary and but served to increase the dizziness of the high place in which I sat. At that time I had not read "Paradise Lost," and later, when I read Milton's "Better to reign in hell than serve in heaven," I was fully convinced that great minds run in the same channels.

It was at this time that the fortuitous concatenation of events sent me upon my first adventure on The Road. It happened that there was nothing doing in oysters just then; that at Benicia, forty miles away, I had some blankets I wanted to get; and that at Port Costa, several miles from Benicia, a stolen boat lay at anchor in charge of the constable. Now this boat was owned by a friend of mine, by name Dinny McCrea. It had been stolen and left at Port Costa by Whiskey Bob, another friend of mine. (Poor Whiskey Bob! Only last winter his body was picked up on the beach shot full of holes by nobody knows whom.) I had come down from "up river" some time before, and reported to Dinny McCrea the whereabouts of his boat; and Dinny McCrea had promptly offered ten dollars to me if I should bring it down to Oakland to him.

Time was heavy on my hands. I sat on the dock and talked it over with Nickey the Greek, another idle oyster pirate. "Let's go," said I, and Nickey was willing. He was "broke." I possessed fifty cents and a small skiff. The former I invested and loaded into the latter in the form of crackers, canned corned beef, and a ten-cent bottle of French mustard. (We were keen on French mustard in those days.) Then, late in the afternoon, we hoisted our small spritsail and started. We sailed all night, and next morning, on the first of a glorious flood-tide, a fair wind behind us, we came booming up the Carquinez Straits to Port Costa. There lay the stolen boat, not twenty-five feet from the wharf. We ran alongside and doused our little spritsail. I sent Nickey forward to lift the anchor, while I began casting off the gaskets.

A man ran out on the wharf and hailed us. It was the constable. It suddenly came to me that I had neglected to get a written authorization from Dinny McCrea to take possession of his boat. Also, I knew that constable wanted to charge at least twenty-five dollars in fees for capturing the boat from Whiskey Bob and subsequently taking care of it. And my last fifty cents had been blown in for corned beef and French mustard, and the reward was only ten dollars anyway. I shot a glance forward to Nickey. He had the anchor up-and-down and was straining at it. "Break her out," I whispered to him, and turned and shouted back to the constable. The result was that he and I were talking at the same time, our spoken thoughts colliding in mid-air and making gibberish.

The constable grew more imperative, and perforce I had to listen. Nickey was heaving on the anchor till I thought he'd burst a blood-vessel. When the constable got done with his threats and warnings, I asked him who he was. The time he lost in telling me enabled Nickey to break out the anchor. I was doing some quick calculating. At the feet of the constable a ladder ran down the dock to the water, and to the ladder was moored a skiff. The oars were in it. But it was padlocked. I gambled everything on that padlock. I felt the breeze on my cheek, saw the surge of the tide, looked at the remaining gaskets that confined the sail, ran my eyes up the halyards to the blocks and knew that all was clear, and then threw off all dissimulation.

"In with her!" I shouted to Nickey, and sprang to the gaskets, casting them loose and thanking my stars that Whiskey Bob had tied them in square-knots instead of "grannies."

The constable had slid down the ladder and was fumbling with a key at the padlock. The anchor came aboard and the last gasket was loosed at the same instant that the constable freed the skiff and jumped to the oars.

"Peak-halyards!" I commanded my crew, at the same time swinging on to the throat-halyards. Up came the sail on the run. I belayed and ran aft to the tiller.

"Stretch her!" I shouted to Nickey at the peak. The constable was just reaching for our stern. A puff of wind caught us, and we shot away. It was great. If I'd had a black flag, I know I'd have run it up in triumph. The constable stood up in the skiff, and paled the glory of the day with the vividness of his language. Also, he wailed for a gun. You see, that was another gamble we had taken.

Anyway, we weren't stealing the boat. It wasn't the constable's. We were merely stealing his fees, which was his particular form of graft. And we weren't stealing the fees for ourselves, either; we were stealing them for my friend, Dinny McCrea.

Benicia was made in a few minutes, and a few minutes later my blankets were aboard. I shifted the boat down to the far end of Steamboat Wharf, from which point of vantage we could see anybody coming after us. There was no telling. Maybe the Port Costa constable would telephone to the Benicia constable. Nickey and I held a council of war. We lay on deck in the warm sun, the fresh breeze on our cheeks, the flood-tide rippling and swirling past. It was impossible to start back to Oakland till afternoon, when the ebb would begin to run. But we figured that the constable would have an eye out on the Carquinez Straits when the ebb started, and that nothing remained for us but to wait for the following ebb, at two o'clock next morning, when we could slip by Cerberus in the darkness.

So we lay on deck, smoked cigarettes, and were glad that we were alive. I spat over the side and gauged the speed of the current.

"With this wind, we could run this flood clear to Rio Vista," I said.

"And it's fruit-time on the river," said Nickey.

"And low water on the river," said I. "It's the best time of the year to make Sacramento."

We sat up and looked at each other. The glorious west wind was pouring over us like wine. We both spat over the side and gauged the current. Now I contend that it was all the fault of that flood-tide and fair wind. They appealed to our sailor instinct. If it had not been for them, the whole chain of events that was to put me upon The Road would have broken down.

We said no word, but cast off our moorings and hoisted sail. Our adventures up the Sacramento River are no part of this narrative. We subsequently made the city of Sacramento and tied up at a wharf. The water was fine, and we spent most of our time in swimming. On the sand-bar above the railroad bridge we fell in with a bunch of boys likewise in swimming. Between swims we lay on the bank and talked. They talked differently from the fellows I had been used to herding with. It was a new vernacular. They were road-kids, and with every word they uttered the lure of The Road laid hold of me more imperiously.

"When I was down in Alabama," one kid would begin; or, another, "Coming up on the C. & A. from K.C."; whereat, a third kid, "On the C. & A. there ain't no steps to the 'blinds.'" And I would lie silently in the sand and listen. "It was at a little town in Ohio on the Lake Shore and Michigan Southern," a kid would start; and another, "Ever ride the Cannonball on the Wabash?"; and yet another, "Nope, but I've been on the White Mail out of Chicago." "Talk about railroadin'—wait till you hit the Pennsylvania, four tracks, no water tanks, take water on the fly, that's goin' some." "The Northern Pacific's a bad road now." "Salinas is on the 'hog,' the 'bulls' is 'horstile.'" "I got 'pinched' at El Paso, along with Moke Kid." "Talkin' of 'poke-outs,' wait till you hit the French country out of Montreal—not a word of English—you say, 'Mongee, Madame, mongee, no spika da French,' an' rub your stomach an' look hungry, an' she gives you a slice of sow-belly an' a chunk of dry 'punk.'"

And I continued to lie in the sand and listen. These wanderers made my oyster-piracy look like thirty cents. A new world was calling to me in every word that was spoken—a world of rods and gunnels, blind baggages and "side-door Pullmans," "bulls" and "shacks," "floppings" and "chewin's," "pinches" and "get-aways," "strong arms" and "bindle-stiffs," "punks" and "profesh." And it all spelled Adventure. Very well; I would tackle this new world. I "lined" myself up alongside those road-kids. I was just as strong as any of them, just as quick, just as nervy, and my brain was just as good.

After the swim, as evening came on, they dressed and went up town. I went along. The kids began "battering" the "main-stem" for "light pieces," or, in other words, begging for money on the main street. I had never begged in my life, and this was the hardest thing for me to stomach when I first went on The Road. I had absurd notions about begging. My philosophy, up to that time, was that it was finer to steal than to beg; and that robbery was finer still because the risk and the penalty were proportionately greater. As an oyster pirate I had already earned convictions at the hands of justice, which, if I had tried to serve them, would have required a thousand years in state's prison. To rob was manly; to beg was sordid and despicable. But I developed in the days to come all right, all right, till I came to look upon begging as a joyous prank, a game of wits, a nerve-exerciser.

That first night, however, I couldn't rise to it; and the result was that when the kids were ready to go to a restaurant and eat, I wasn't. I was broke. Meeny Kid, I think it was, gave me the price, and we all ate together. But while I ate, I meditated. The receiver, it was said, was as bad as the thief; Meeny Kid had done the begging, and I was profiting by it. I decided that the receiver was a whole lot worse than the thief, and that it shouldn't happen again. And it didn't. I turned out next day and threw my feet as well as the next one.

Nickey the Greek's ambition didn't run to The Road. He was not a success at throwing his feet, and he stowed away one night on a barge and went down river to San Francisco. I met him, only a week ago, at a pugilistic carnival. He has progressed. He sat in a place of honor at the ring-side. He is now a manager of prize-fighters and proud of it. In fact, in a small way, in local sportdom, he is quite a shining light.

"No kid is a road-kid until he has gone over 'the hill'"—such was the law of The Road I heard expounded in Sacramento. All right, I'd go over the hill and matriculate. "The hill," by the way, was the Sierra Nevadas. The whole gang was going over the hill on a jaunt, and of course I'd go along. It was French Kid's first adventure on The Road. He had just run away from his people in San Francisco. It was up to him and me to deliver the goods. In passing, I may remark that my old title of "Prince" had vanished. I had received my "monica." I was now "Sailor Kid," later to be known as "'Frisco Kid," when I had put the Rockies between me and my native state.

At 10:20 PM the Central Pacific overland pulled out of the depot at Sacramento for the East—that particular item of time-table is indelibly engraved on my memory. There were about a dozen in our gang, and we strung out in the darkness ahead of the train ready to take her out. All the local road-kids that we knew came down to see us off—also, to "ditch" us if they could. That was their idea of a joke, and there were only about forty of them to carry it out. Their ring-leader was a crackerjack road-kid named Bob. Sacramento was his home town, but he'd hit The Road pretty well everywhere over the whole country. He took French Kid and me aside and gave us advice something like this: "We're goin' to try an' ditch your bunch, see? Youse two are weak. The rest of the push can take care of itself. So, as soon as youse two nail a blind, deck her. An' stay on the decks till youse pass Roseville Junction, at which burg the constables are horstile, sloughin' in everybody on sight."

The engine whistled and the overland pulled out. There were three blinds on her—room for all of us. The dozen of us who were trying to make her out would have preferred to slip aboard quietly; but our forty friends crowded on with the most amazing and shameless publicity and advertisement. Following Bob's advice, I immediately "decked her," that is, climbed up on top of the roof of one of the mail-cars. There I lay down, my heart jumping a few extra beats, and listened to the fun. The whole train crew was forward, and the ditching went on fast and furious. After the train had run half a mile, it stopped, and the crew came forward again and ditched the survivors. I, alone, had made the train out.

Back at the depot, about him two or three of the push that had witnessed the accident, lay French Kid with both legs off. French Kid had slipped or stumbled—that was all, and the wheels had done the rest. Such was my initiation to The Road. It was two years afterward when I next saw French Kid and examined his "stumps." This was an act of courtesy. "Cripples" always like to have their stumps examined. One of the entertaining sights on The Road is to witness the meeting of two cripples. Their common disability is a fruitful source of conversation; and they tell how it happened, describe what they know of the amputation, pass critical judgment on their own and each other's surgeons, and wind up by withdrawing to one side, taking off bandages and wrappings, and comparing stumps.

But it was not until several days later, over in Nevada, when the push caught up with me, that I learned of French Kid's accident. The push itself arrived in bad condition. It had gone through a train-wreck in the snow-sheds; Happy Joe was on crutches with two mashed legs, and the rest were nursing skins and bruises.

In the meantime, I lay on the roof of the mail-car, trying to remember whether Roseville Junction, against which burg Bob had warned me, was the first stop or the second stop. To make sure, I delayed descending to the platform of the blind until after the second stop. And then I didn't descend. I was new to the game, and I felt safer where I was. But I never told the push that I held down the decks the whole night, clear across the Sierras, through snow-sheds and tunnels, and down to Truckee on the other side, where I arrived at seven in the morning. Such a thing was disgraceful, and I'd have been a common laughing-stock. This is the first time I have confessed the truth about that first ride over the hill. As for the push, it decided that I was all right, and when I came back over the hill to Sacramento, I was a full-fledged road-kid.

Yet I had much to learn. Bob was my mentor, and he was all right. I remember one evening (it was fair-time in Sacramento, and we were knocking about and having a good time) when I lost my hat in a fight. There was I bare-headed in the street, and it was Bob to the rescue. He took me to one side from the push and told me what to do. I was a bit timid of his advice. I had just come out of jail, where I had been three days, and I knew that if the police "pinched" me again, I'd get good and "soaked." On the other hand, I couldn't show the white feather. I'd been over the hill, I was running full-fledged with the push, and it was up to me to deliver the goods. So I accepted Bob's advice, and he came along with me to see that I did it up brown.

We took our position on K Street, on the corner, I think, of Fifth. It was early in the evening and the street was crowded. Bob studied the head-gear of every Chinaman that passed. I used to wonder how the road-kids all managed to wear "five-dollar Stetson stiff-rims," and now I knew. They got them, the way I was going to get mine, from the Chinese. I was nervous—there were so many people about; but Bob was cool as an iceberg. Several times, when I started forward toward a Chinaman, all nerved and keyed up, Bob dragged me back. He wanted me to get a good hat, and one that fitted. Now a hat came by that was the right size but not new; and, after a dozen impossible hats, along would come one that was new but not the right size. And when one did come by that was new and the right size, the rim was too large or not large enough. My, Bob was finicky. I was so wrought up that I'd have snatched any kind of a head-covering.

And then, suddenly, around the corner at my back, came the bare-headed Chinaman. With him were a couple more Chinamen, and at their heels were half a dozen men and boys. I sprinted to the next corner, crossed the street, and rounded the following corner. I decided that I had surely played him out, and I dropped into a walk again. But around the corner at my heels came that persistent Mongolian. It was the old story of the hare and the tortoise. He could not run so fast as I, but he stayed with it, plodding along at a shambling and deceptive trot, and wasting much good breath in noisy imprecations. He called all Sacramento to witness the dishonor that had been done him, and a goodly portion of Sacramento heard and flocked at his heels. And I ran on like the hare, and ever that persistent Mongolian, with the increasing rabble, overhauled me. But finally, when a policeman had joined his following, I let out all my links. I twisted and turned, and I swear I ran at least twenty blocks on the straight away. And I never saw that Chinaman again. The hat was a dandy, a brand-new Stetson, just out of the shop, and it was the envy of the whole push. Furthermore, it was the symbol that I had delivered the goods. I wore it for over a year.

Road-kids are nice little chaps—when you get them alone and they are telling you "how it happened"; but take my word for it, watch out for them when they run in pack. Then they are wolves, and like wolves they are capable of dragging down the strongest man. At such times they are not cowardly. They will fling themselves upon a man and hold on with every ounce of strength in their wiry bodies, till he is thrown and helpless. More than once have I seen them do it, and I know whereof I speak. Their motive is usually robbery. And watch out for the "strong arm." Every kid in the push I travelled with was expert at it. Even French Kid mastered it before he lost his legs.

I have strong upon me now a vision of what I once saw in "The Willows." The Willows was a clump of trees in a waste piece of land near the railway depot and not more than five minutes walk from the heart of Sacramento. It is night-time and the scene is illumined by the thin light of stars. I see a husky laborer in the midst of a pack of road-kids. He is infuriated and cursing them, not a bit afraid, confident of his own strength. He weighs about one hundred and eighty pounds, and his muscles are hard; but he doesn't know what he is up against. The kids are snarling. It is not pretty. They make a rush from all sides, and he lashes out and whirls. Barber Kid is standing beside me. As the man whirls, Barber Kid leaps forward and does the trick. Into the man's back goes his knee; around the man's neck, from behind, passes his right hand, the bone of the wrist pressing against the jugular vein. Barber Kid throws his whole weight backward. It is a powerful leverage. Besides, the man's wind has been shut off. It is the strong arm.

The man resists, but he is already practically helpless. The road-kids are upon him from every side, clinging to arms and legs and body, and like a wolf at the throat of a moose Barber Kid hangs on and drags backward. Over the man goes, and down under the heap. Barber Kid changes the position of his own body, but never lets go. While some of the kids are "going through" the victim, others are holding his legs so that he cannot kick and thresh about. They improve the opportunity by taking off the man's shoes. As for him, he has given in. He is beaten. Also, what of the strong arm at his throat, he is short of wind. He is making ugly choking noises, and the kids hurry. They really don't want to kill him. All is done. At a word all holds are released at once, and the kids scatter, one of them lugging the shoes—he knows where he can get half a dollar for them. The man sits up and looks about him, dazed and helpless. Even if he wanted to, barefooted pursuit in the darkness would be hopeless. I linger a moment and watch him. He is feeling at his throat, making dry, hawking noises, and jerking his head in a quaint way as though to assure himself that the neck is not dislocated. Then I slip away to join the push, and see that man no more—though I shall always see him, sitting there in the starlight, somewhat dazed, a bit frightened, greatly dishevelled, and making quaint jerking movements of head and neck.

Drunken men are the especial prey of the road-kids. Robbing a drunken man they call "rolling a stiff"; and wherever they are, they are on the constant lookout for drunks. The drunk is their particular meat, as the fly is the particular meat of the spider. The rolling of a stiff is ofttimes an amusing sight, especially when the stiff is helpless and when interference is unlikely. At the first swoop the stiff's money and jewellery go. Then the kids sit around their victim in a sort of pow-wow. A kid generates a fancy for the stiff's necktie. Off it comes. Another kid is after underclothes. Off they come, and a knife quickly abbreviates arms and legs. Friendly hoboes may be called in to take the coat and trousers, which are too large for the kids. And in the end they depart, leaving beside the stiff the heap of their discarded rags.

Another vision comes to me. It is a dark night. My push is coming along the sidewalk in the suburbs. Ahead of us, under an electric light, a man crosses the street diagonally. There is something tentative and desultory in his walk. The kids scent the game on the instant. The man is drunk. He blunders across the opposite sidewalk and is lost in the darkness as he takes a short-cut through a vacant lot. No hunting cry is raised, but the pack flings itself forward in quick pursuit. In the middle of the vacant lot it comes upon him. But what is this?—snarling and strange forms, small and dim and menacing, are between the pack and its prey. It is another pack of road-kids, and in the hostile pause we learn that it is their meat, that they have been trailing it a dozen blocks and more and that we are butting in. But it is the world primeval. These wolves are baby wolves. (As a matter of fact, I don't think one of them was over twelve or thirteen years of age. I met some of them afterward, and learned that they had just arrived that day over the hill, and that they hailed from Denver and

Salt Lake City.) Our pack flings forward. The baby wolves squeal and screech and fight like little demons. All about the drunken man rages the struggle for the possession of him. Down he goes in the thick of it, and the combat rages over his body after the fashion of the Greeks and Trojans over the body and armor of a fallen hero. Amid cries and tears and wailings the baby wolves are dispossessed, and my pack rolls the stiff. But always I remember the poor stiff and his befuddled amazement at the abrupt eruption of battle in the vacant lot. I see him now, dim in the darkness, titubating in stupid wonder, good-naturedly essaying the role of peacemaker in that multitudinous scrap the significance of which he did not understand, and the really hurt expression on his face when he, unoffending he, was clutched at by many hands and dragged down in the thick of the press.

"Bindle-stiffs" are favorite prey of the road-kids. A bindle-stiff is a working tramp. He takes his name from the roll of blankets he carries, which is known as a "bindle." Because he does work, a bindle-stiff is expected usually to have some small change about him, and it is after that small change that the road-kids go. The best hunting-ground for bindle-stiffs is in the sheds, barns, lumber-yards, railroad-yards, etc., on the edges of a city, and the time for hunting is the night, when the bindle-stiff seeks these places to roll up in his blankets and sleep.

"Gay-cats" also come to grief at the hands of the road-kid. In more familiar parlance, gay-cats are short-horns, *chechaquos*, new chums, or tenderfeet. A gay-cat is a newcomer on The Road who is man-grown, or, at least, youth-grown. A boy on The Road, on the other hand, no matter how green he is, is never a gay-cat; he is a road-kid or a "punk," and if he travels with a "profesh," he is known possessively as a "prushun." I was never a prushun, for I did not take kindly to possession. I was first a road-kid and then a profesh. Because I started in young, I practically skipped my gay-cat apprenticeship. For a short period, during the time I was exchanging my 'Frisco Kid monica for that of Sailor Jack, I labored under the suspicion of being a gay-cat. But closer acquaintance on the part of those that suspected me quickly disabused their minds, and in a short time I acquired the unmistakable airs and ear-marks of the blowed-in-the-glass profesh. And be it known, here and now, that the profesh are the aristocracy of The Road. They are the lords and masters, the aggressive men, the primordial noblemen, the *blond beasts* so beloved of Nietzsche.

When I came back over the hill from Nevada, I found that some river pirate had stolen Dinny McCrea's boat. (A funny thing at this day is that I cannot remember what became of the skiff in which Nickey the Greek and I sailed from Oakland to Port Costa. I know that the constable didn't get it, and I know that it didn't go with us up the Sacramento River, and that is all I do know.) With the loss of Dinny McCrea's boat, I was pledged to The Road; and when I grew tired of Sacramento, I said good-by to the push (which, in its friendly way, tried to ditch me from a freight as I left town) and started on a *passear* down the valley of the San Joaquin. The Road had gripped me and would not let me go; and later, when I had voyaged to sea and done one thing and another, I returned to The Road to make longer flights, to be a "comet" and a profesh, and to plump into the bath of sociology that wet me to the skin.

Chapter 8
Two Thousand Stiffs

A "stiff" is a tramp. It was once my fortune to travel a few weeks with a "push" that numbered two thousand. This was known as "Kelly's Army." Across the wild and woolly West, clear from California, General Kelly and his heroes had captured trains; but they fell down when they crossed the Missouri and went up against the effete East. The East hadn't the slightest intention of giving free transportation to two thousand hoboes. Kelly's Army lay helplessly for some time at Council Bluffs. The day I joined it, made desperate by delay, it marched out to capture a train.

It was quite an imposing sight. General Kelly sat a magnificent black charger, and with waving banners, to the martial music of fife and drum corps, company by company, in two divisions, his two thousand stiffs countermarched before him and hit the wagon-road to the little burg of Weston, seven miles away. Being the latest recruit, I was in the last company, of the last regiment, of the Second Division, and, furthermore, in the last rank of the rear-guard. The army went into camp at Weston beside the railroad track—beside the tracks, rather, for two roads went through: the Chicago, Milwaukee, and St. Paul, and the Rock Island.

Our intention was to take the first train out, but the railroad officials "coppered" our play—and won. There was no first train. They tied up the two lines and stopped running trains. In the meantime, while we lay by the dead tracks, the good people of Omaha and Council Bluffs were bestirring themselves. Preparations were making to form a mob, capture a train in Council Bluffs, run it down to us, and make us a present of it. The railroad officials coppered that play, too. They didn't wait for the mob. Early in the morning of the second day, an engine, with a single private car attached, arrived at the station and side-tracked. At this sign that life had renewed in the dead roads, the whole army lined up beside the track.

But never did life renew so monstrously on a dead railroad as it did on those two roads. From the west came the whistle of a locomotive. It was coming in our direction, bound east. We were bound east. A stir of preparation ran down our ranks. The whistle tooted fast and furiously, and the train thundered at top speed. The hobo didn't live that could have boarded it. Another locomotive whistled, and another train came through at top speed, and another, and another, train after train, train after train, till toward the last the trains were composed of passenger coaches, box-cars, flat-cars, dead engines, cabooses, mail-cars, wrecking appliances, and all the riff-raff of worn-out and abandoned rolling-stock that collects in the yards of great railways. When the yards at Council Bluffs had been completely cleaned, the private car and engine went east, and the tracks died for keeps.

That day went by, and the next, and nothing moved, and in the meantime, pelted by sleet, and rain, and hail, the two thousand hoboes lay beside the track. But that night the good people of Council Bluffs went the railroad officials one better. A mob formed in Council Bluffs, crossed the river to Omaha, and there joined with another mob in a raid on the Union Pacific yards. First they captured an engine, next they knocked a train together, and then the united mobs piled aboard, crossed the Missouri, and ran down the Rock Island right of way to turn the train over to us. The railway officials tried to copper this play, but fell down, to the mortal terror of the section boss and one member of the section gang at Weston. This pair, under secret telegraphic orders, tried to wreck our train-load of sympathizers by tearing up the track. It happened that we were suspicious and had our patrols out. Caught red-handed at train-wrecking, and surrounded by twenty hundred infuriated hoboes, that section-gang boss and assistant prepared to meet death. I don't remember what saved them, unless it was the arrival of the train.

It was our turn to fall down, and we did, hard. In their haste, the two mobs had neglected to make up a sufficiently long train. There wasn't room for two thousand hoboes to ride. So the mobs and the hoboes had a talkfest, fraternized, sang songs, and parted, the mobs going back on their captured train to Omaha, the hoboes pulling out next morning on a hundred-and-forty-mile march to Des Moines. It was not until Kelly's Army crossed the Missouri that it began to walk, and after that it never rode again. It cost the railroads slathers of money, but they were acting on principle, and they won.

Underwood, Leola, Menden, Avoca, Walnut, Marno, Atlantic, Wyoto, Anita, Adair, Adam, Casey, Stuart, Dexter, Carlham, De Soto, Van Meter, Booneville, Commerce, Valley Junction—how the names of the towns come back to me as I con the map and trace our route through the fat Iowa country! And the hospitable Iowa farmer-folk! They turned out with their wagons and carried our baggage; gave us hot lunches at noon by the wayside; mayors of comfortable little towns made speeches of welcome and hastened us on our way; deputations of little girls and maidens came out to meet us, and the good citizens turned out by hundreds, locked arms, and marched with us down their main streets. It was circus day when we came to town, and every day was circus day, for there were many towns.

In the evenings our camps were invaded by whole populations. Every company had its campfire, and around each fire something was doing. The cooks in my company, Company L, were song-and-dance artists and contributed most of our entertainment. In another part of the encampment the glee club would be singing—one of its star voices was the "Dentist," drawn from Company L, and we were mighty proud of him. Also, he pulled teeth for the whole army, and, since the extractions usually occurred at meal-time, our digestions were stimulated by variety of incident. The Dentist had no anæsthetics, but two or three of us were always on tap to volunteer to hold down the patient. In addition to the stunts of the companies and the glee club, church services were usually held, local preachers officiating, and always there was a great making of political speeches. All these things ran neck and neck; it was a full-blown Midway. A lot of talent can be dug out of two thousand hoboes. I remember we had a picked baseball nine, and on Sundays we made a practice of putting it all over the local nines. Sometimes we did it twice on Sundays.

Last year, while on a lecturing trip, I rode into Des Moines in a Pullman—I don't mean a "side-door Pullman," but the real thing. On the outskirts of the city I saw the old stove-works, and my heart leaped. It was there, at the stove-works, a dozen years before, that the Army lay down and swore a mighty oath that its feet were sore and that it would walk no more. We took possession of the stove-works and told Des Moines that we had come to stay—that we'd walked in, but we'd be blessed if we'd walk out. Des Moines was hospitable, but this was too much of a good thing. Do a little mental arithmetic, gentle reader. Two thousand hoboes, eating three square meals, make six thousand meals per day, forty-two thousand meals per week, or one hundred and sixty-eight thousand meals per shortest month in the calendar. That's going some. We had no money. It was up to Des Moines.

Des Moines was desperate. We lay in camp, made political speeches, held sacred concerts, pulled teeth, played baseball and seven-up, and ate our six thousand meals per day, and Des Moines paid for it. Des Moines pleaded with the railroads, but they were obdurate; they had said we shouldn't ride, and that settled it. To permit us to ride would be to establish a precedent, and there weren't going to be any precedents. And still we went on eating. That was the terrifying factor in the situation. We were bound for Washington, and Des Moines would have had to float municipal bonds to pay all our railroad fares, even at special rates, and if we remained much longer, she'd have to float bonds anyway to feed us.

Then some local genius solved the problem. We wouldn't walk. Very good. We should ride. From Des Moines to Keokuk on the Mississippi flowed the Des Moines River. This particular stretch of river was three hundred miles long. We could ride on it, said the local genius; and, once equipped with floating stock, we could ride on down the Mississippi to the Ohio, and thence up the Ohio, winding up with a short portage over the mountains to Washington.

Des Moines took up a subscription. Public-spirited citizens contributed several thousand dollars. Lumber, rope, nails, and cotton for calking were bought in large quantities, and on the banks of the Des Moines was inaugurated a tremendous era of shipbuilding. Now the Des Moines is a picayune stream, unduly dignified by the appellation of "river." In our spacious western land it would be called a "creek." The oldest inhabitants shook their heads and said we couldn't make it, that there wasn't enough water to float us. Des Moines didn't care, so long as it got rid of us, and we were such well-fed optimists that we didn't care either.

On Wednesday, May 9, 1894, we got under way and started on our colossal picnic. Des Moines had got off pretty easily, and she certainly owes a statue in bronze to the local genius who got her out of her difficulty. True, Des Moines had to pay for our boats; we had eaten sixty-six thousand meals at the stove-works; and we took twelve thousand additional meals along with us in our commissary—as a precaution against famine in the wilds; but then, think what it would have meant if we had remained at Des Moines eleven months instead of eleven days. Also, when we departed, we promised Des Moines we'd come back if the river failed to float us.

It was all very well having twelve thousand meals in the commissary, and no doubt the commissary "ducks" enjoyed them; for the commissary promptly got lost, and my boat, for one, never saw it again. The company formation was hopelessly broken up during the river-trip. In any camp of men there will always be found a certain percentage of shirks, of helpless, of just ordinary, and of hustlers. There were ten men in my boat, and they were the cream of Company L. Every man was a hustler. For two reasons I was included in the ten. First, I was as good a hustler as ever "threw his feet," and next, I was "Sailor Jack." I understood boats and boating. The ten of us forgot the remaining forty men of Company L, and by the time we had missed one meal we promptly forgot the commissary. We were independent. We went down the river "on our own," hustling our "chewin's," beating every boat in the fleet, and, alas that I must say it, sometimes taking possession of the stores the farmer-folk had collected for the Army.

For a good part of the three hundred miles we were from half a day to a day or so in advance of the Army. We had managed to get hold of several American flags. When we approached a small town, or when we saw a group of farmers gathered on the bank, we ran up our flags, called ourselves the "advance boat," and demanded to know what provisions had been collected for the Army. We represented the Army, of course, and the provisions were turned over to us. But there wasn't anything small about us. We never took more than we could get away with. But we did take the cream of everything. For instance, if some philanthropic farmer had donated several dollars' worth of tobacco, we took it. So, also, we took butter and sugar, coffee and canned goods; but when the stores consisted of sacks of beans and flour, or two or three slaughtered steers, we resolutely refrained and went our way, leaving orders to turn such provisions over to the commissary boats whose business was to follow behind us.

My, but the ten of us did live on the fat of the land! For a long time General Kelly vainly tried to head us off. He sent two rowers, in a light, round-bottomed boat, to overtake us and put a stop to our piratical careers. They overtook us all right, but they were two and we were ten. They were empowered by General Kelly to make us prisoners, and they told us so. When we expressed disinclination to become prisoners, they hurried ahead to the next town to invoke the aid of the authorities. We went ashore immediately and cooked an early supper; and under the cloak of darkness we ran by the town and its authorities.

I kept a diary on part of the trip, and as I read it over now I note one persistently recurring phrase, namely, "Living fine." We did live fine. We even disdained to use coffee boiled in water. We made our coffee out of milk, calling the wonderful beverage, if I remember rightly, "pale Vienna."

While we were ahead, skimming the cream, and while the commissary was lost far behind, the main Army, coming along in the middle, starved. This was hard on the Army, I'll allow; but then, the ten of us were individualists. We had initiative and enterprise. We ardently believed that the grub was to the man who got there first, the pale Vienna to the strong. On one stretch the Army went forty-eight hours without grub; and then it arrived at a small village of some three hundred inhabitants, the name of which I do not remember, though I think it was Red Rock. This town, following the practice of all towns through which the Army passed, had appointed a committee of safety. Counting five to a family, Red Rock consisted of sixty households. Her committee of safety was scared stiff by the eruption of two thousand hungry hoboes who lined their boats two and three deep along the river bank. General Kelly was a fair man. He had no intention of working a hardship on the village. He did not expect sixty households to furnish two thousand meals. Besides, the Army had its treasure-chest.

But the committee of safety lost its head. "No encouragement to the invader" was its programme, and when General Kelly wanted to buy food, the committee turned him down. It had nothing to sell; General Kelly's money was "no good" in their burg. And then General Kelly went into action. The bugles blew. The Army left the boats and on top of the bank formed in battle array. The committee was there to see. General Kelly's speech was brief.

"Boys," he said, "when did you eat last?"

"Day before yesterday," they shouted.

"Are you hungry?"

A mighty affirmation from two thousand throats shook the atmosphere. Then General Kelly turned to the committee of safety:—

"You see, gentlemen, the situation. My men have eaten nothing in forty-eight hours. If I turn them loose upon your town, I'll not be responsible for what happens. They are desperate. I offered to buy food for them, but you refused to sell. I now withdraw my offer. Instead, I shall demand. I give you five minutes to decide. Either kill me six steers and give me four thousand rations, or I turn the men loose. Five minutes, gentlemen."

The terrified committee of safety looked at the two thousand hungry hoboes and collapsed. It didn't wait the five minutes. It wasn't going to take any chances. The killing of the steers and the collecting of the requisition began forthwith, and the Army dined.

And still the ten graceless individualists soared along ahead and gathered in everything in sight. But General Kelly fixed us. He sent horsemen down each bank, warning farmers and townspeople against us. They did their work thoroughly, all right. The erstwhile hospitable farmers met us with the icy mit. Also, they summoned the constables when we tied up to the bank, and loosed the dogs. I know. Two of the latter caught me with a barbed-wire fence between me and the river. I was carrying two buckets of milk for the pale Vienna. I didn't damage the fence any; but we drank plebian coffee boiled with vulgar water, and it was up to me to throw my feet for another pair of trousers. I wonder, gentle reader, if you ever essayed hastily to climb a barbed-wire fence with a bucket of milk in each hand. Ever since that day I have had a prejudice against barbed wire, and I have gathered statistics on the subject.

Unable to make an honest living so long as General Kelly kept his two horsemen ahead of us, we returned to the Army and raised a revolution. It was a small affair, but it devastated Company L of the Second Division. The captain of Company L refused to recognize us; said we were deserters, and traitors, and scalawags; and when he drew rations for Company L from the commissary, he wouldn't give us any. That captain didn't appreciate us, or he wouldn't have refused us grub. Promptly we intrigued with the first lieutenant. He joined us with the ten men in his boat, and in return we elected him captain of Company M. The captain of Company L raised a roar. Down upon us came General Kelly, Colonel Speed, and Colonel Baker. The twenty of us stood firm, and our revolution was ratified.

But we never bothered with the commissary. Our hustlers drew better rations from the farmers. Our new captain, however, doubted us. He never knew when he'd see the ten of us again, once we got under way in the morning, so he called in a blacksmith to clinch his captaincy. In the stern of our boat, one on each side, were driven two heavy eye-bolts of iron. Correspondingly, on the bow of his boat, were fastened two huge iron hooks. The boats were brought together, end on, the hooks dropped into the eye-bolts, and there we were, hard and fast. We couldn't lose that captain. But we were irrepressible. Out of our very manacles we wrought an invincible device that enabled us to put it all over every other boat in the fleet.

Like all great inventions, this one of ours was accidental. We discovered it the first time we ran on a snag in a bit of a rapid. The head-boat hung up and anchored, and the tail-boat swung around in the current, pivoting the head-boat on the snag. I was at the stern of the tail-boat, steering. In vain we tried to shove off. Then I ordered the men from the head-boat into the tail-boat. Immediately the head-boat floated clear, and its men returned into it. After that, snags, reefs, shoals, and bars had no terrors for us. The instant the head-boat struck, the men in it leaped into the tail-boat. Of course, the head-boat floated over the obstruction and the tail-boat then struck. Like automatons, the twenty men now in the tail-boat leaped into the head-boat, and the tail-boat floated past.

The boats used by the Army were all alike, made by the mile and sawed off. They were flat-boats, and their lines were rectangles. Each boat was six feet wide, ten feet long, and a foot and a half deep. Thus, when our two boats were hooked together, I sat at the stern steering a craft twenty feet long, containing twenty husky hoboes who "spelled" each other at the oars and paddles, and loaded with blankets, cooking outfit, and our own private commissary.

Still we caused General Kelly trouble. He had called in his horsemen, and substituted three police-boats that travelled in the van and allowed no boats to pass them. The craft containing Company M crowded the police-boats hard. We could have passed them easily, but it was against the rules. So we kept a respectful distance astern and waited. Ahead we knew was virgin farming country, unbegged and generous; but we waited. White water was all we needed, and when we rounded a bend and a rapid showed up we knew what would happen. Smash! Police-boat number one goes on a boulder and hangs up. Bang! Police-boat number two follows suit. Whop! Police-boat number three encounters the common fate of all. Of course our boat does the same things; but one, two, the men are out of the head-boat and into the tail-boat; one, two, they are out of the tail-boat and into the head-boat; and one, two, the men who belong in the tail-boat are back in it and we are dashing on. "Stop! you blankety-blank-blanks!" shriek the police-boats. "How can we?—blank the blankety-blank river, anyway!" we wail plaintively as we surge past, caught in that remorseless current that sweeps us on out of sight and into the hospitable farmer-country that replenishes our private commissary with the cream of its contributions. Again we drink pale Vienna and realize that the grub is to the man who gets there.

Poor General Kelly! He devised another scheme. The whole fleet started ahead of us. Company M of the Second Division started in its proper place in the line, which was last. And it took us only one day to put the "kibosh" on that particular scheme. Twenty-five miles of bad water lay before us—all rapids, shoals, bars, and boulders. It was over that stretch of water that the oldest inhabitants of Des Moines had shaken their heads. Nearly two hundred boats entered the bad water ahead of us, and they piled up in the most astounding manner. We went through that stranded fleet like hemlock through the fire. There was no avoiding the boulders, bars, and snags except by getting out on the bank. We didn't avoid them. We went right over them, one, two, one, two, head-boat, tail-boat, head-boat, tail-boat, all hands back and forth and back again. We camped that night alone, and loafed in camp all of next day while the Army patched and repaired its wrecked boats and straggled up to us.

There was no stopping our cussedness. We rigged up a mast, piled on the canvas (blankets), and travelled short hours while the Army worked over-time to keep us in sight. Then General Kelly had recourse to diplomacy. No boat could touch us in the straight-away. Without discussion, we were the hottest bunch that ever came down the Des Moines. The ban of the police-boats was lifted. Colonel Speed was put aboard, and with this distinguished officer we had the honor of arriving first at Keokuk on the Mississippi. And right here I want to say to General Kelly and Colonel Speed that here's my hand. You were heroes, both of you, and you were men. And I'm sorry for at least ten per cent of the trouble that was given you by the head-boat of Company M.

At Keokuk the whole fleet was lashed together in a huge raft, and, after being wind-bound a day, a steamboat took us in tow down the Mississippi to Quincy, Illinois, where we camped across the river on Goose Island. Here the raft idea was abandoned, the boats being joined together in groups of four and decked over. Somebody told me that Quincy was the richest town of its size in the United States. When I heard this, I was immediately overcome by an irresistible impulse to throw my feet. No "blowed-in-the-glass profesh" could possibly pass up such a promising burg. I crossed the river to Quincy in a small dug-out; but I came back in a large riverboat, down to the gunwales with the results of my thrown feet. Of course I kept all the money I had collected, though I paid the boat-hire; also I took my pick of the underwear, socks, cast-off clothes, shirts, "kicks," and "sky-pieces"; and when Company M had taken all it wanted there was still a respectable heap that was turned over to Company L. Alas, I was young and prodigal in those days! I told a thousand "stories" to the good people of Quincy, and every story was "good"; but since I have come to write for the magazines I have often regretted the wealth of story, the fecundity of fiction, I lavished that day in Quincy, Illinois.

It was at Hannibal, Missouri, that the ten invincibles went to pieces. It was not planned. We just naturally flew apart. The Boiler-Maker and I deserted secretly. On the same day Scotty and Davy made a swift sneak for the Illinois shore; also McAvoy and Fish achieved their get-away. This accounts for six of the ten; what became of the remaining four I do not know. As a sample of life on The Road, I make the following quotation from my diary of the several days following my desertion.

"Friday, May 25th. Boiler-Maker and I left the camp on the island. We went ashore on the Illinois side in a skiff and walked six miles on the C.B. & Q. to Fell Creek. We had gone six miles out of our way, but we got on a hand-car and rode six miles to Hull's, on the Wabash. While there, we met McAvoy, Fish, Scotty, and Davy, who had also pulled out from the Army.

> "Saturday, May 26th. At 2:11 AM. we caught the Cannonball as she slowed up at the crossing. Scotty and Davy were ditched. The four of us were ditched at the Bluffs, forty miles farther on. In the afternoon Fish and McAvoy caught a freight while Boiler-Maker and I were away getting something to eat.
>
> "Sunday, May 27th. At 3:21 AM. we caught the Cannonball and found Scotty and Davy on the blind. We were all ditched

at daylight at Jacksonville. The C. & A. runs through here, and we're going to take that. Boiler-Maker went off, but didn't return. Guess he caught a freight.

"Monday, May 28th. Boiler-Maker didn't show up. Scotty and Davy went off to sleep somewhere, and didn't get back in time to catch the K.C. passenger at 3:30 AM. I caught her and rode her till after sunrise to Masson City, 25,000 inhabitants. Caught a cattle train and rode all night.

"Tuesday, May 29th. Arrived in Chicago at 7 AM. . . ."

And years afterward, in China, I had the grief of learning that the device we employed to navigate the rapids of the Des Moines—the one-two-one-two, head-boat-tail-boat proposition—was not originated by us. I learned that the Chinese river-boatmen had for thousands of years used a similar device to negotiate "bad water." It is a good stunt all right, even if we don't get the credit. It answers Dr. Jordan's test of truth: "Will it work? Will you trust your life to it?"

Chapter 9
Bulls

If the tramp were suddenly to pass away from the United States, widespread misery for many families would follow. The tramp enables thousands of men to earn honest livings, educate their children, and bring them up God-fearing and industrious. I know. At one time my father was a constable and hunted tramps for a living. The community paid him so much per head for all the tramps he could catch, and also, I believe, he got mileage fees. Ways and means was always a pressing problem in our household, and the amount of meat on the table, the new pair of shoes, the day's outing, or the text-book for school, were dependent upon my father's luck in the chase. Well I remember the suppressed eagerness and the suspense with which I waited to learn each morning what the results of his past night's toil had been—how many tramps he had gathered in and what the chances were for convicting them. And so it was, when later, as a tramp, I succeeded in eluding some predatory constable, I could not but feel sorry for the little boys and girls at home in that constable's house; it seemed to me in a way that I was defrauding those little boys and girls of some of the good things of life.

But it's all in the game. The hobo defies society, and society's watch-dogs make a living out of him. Some hoboes like to be caught by the watch-dogs—especially in winter-time. Of course, such hoboes select communities where the jails are "good," wherein no work is performed and the food is substantial. Also, there have been, and most probably still are, constables who divide their fees with the hoboes they arrest. Such a constable does not have to hunt. He whistles, and the game comes right up to his hand. It is surprising, the money that is made out of stone-broke tramps. All through the South—at least when I was hoboing—are convict camps and plantations, where the time of convicted hoboes is bought by the farmers, and where the hoboes simply have to work. Then there are places like the quarries at Rutland, Vermont, where the hobo is exploited, the unearned energy in his body, which he has accumulated by "battering on the drag" or "slamming gates," being extracted for the benefit of that particular community.

Now I don't know anything about the quarries at Rutland, Vermont. I'm very glad that I don't, when I remember how near I was to getting into them. Tramps pass the word along, and I first heard of those quarries when I was in Indiana. But when I got into New England, I heard of them continually, and always with danger-signals flying. "They want men in the quarries," the passing hoboes said; "and they never give a 'stiff' less than ninety days." By the time I got into New Hampshire I was pretty well keyed up over those quarries, and I fought shy of railroad cops, "bulls," and constables as I never had before.

One evening I went down to the railroad yards at Concord and found a freight train made up and ready to start. I located an empty box-car, slid open the side-door, and climbed in. It was my hope to win across to White River by morning; that would bring me into Vermont and not more than a thousand miles from Rutland. But after that, as I worked north, the distance between me and the point of danger would begin to increase. In the car I found a "gay-cat," who displayed unusual trepidation at my entrance. He took me for a "shack" (brakeman), and when he learned I was only a stiff, he began talking about the quarries at Rutland as the cause of the fright I had given him. He was a young country fellow, and had beaten his way only over local stretches of road.

The freight got under way, and we lay down in one end of the box-car and went to sleep. Two or three hours afterward, at a stop, I was awakened by the noise of the right-hand door being softly slid open. The gay-cat slept on. I made no movement, though I veiled my eyes with my lashes to a little slit through which I could see out. A lantern was thrust in through the doorway, followed by the head of a shack. He discovered us, and looked at us for a moment. I was prepared for a violent expression on his part, or the customary "Hit the grit, you son of a toad!" Instead of this he cautiously withdrew the lantern and very, very softly slid the door to. This struck me as eminently unusual and suspicious. I listened, and softly I heard the hasp drop into place. The door was latched on the outside. We could not open it from the inside. One way of sudden exit from that car was blocked. It would never do. I waited a few seconds, then crept to the left-hand door and tried it. It was not yet latched. I opened it, dropped to the ground, and closed it behind me. Then I passed across the bumpers to the other side of the train. I opened the door the shack had latched, climbed in, and closed it behind me. Both exits were available again. The gay-cat was still asleep.

The train got under way. It came to the next stop. I heard footsteps in the gravel. Then the left-hand door was thrown open noisily. The gay-cat awoke, I made believe to awake; and we sat up and stared at the shack and his lantern. He didn't waste any time getting down to business.

"I want three dollars," he said.

We got on our feet and came nearer to him to confer. We expressed an absolute and devoted willingness to give him three dollars, but explained our wretched luck that compelled our desire to remain unsatisfied. The shack was incredulous. He dickered with us. He would compromise for two dollars. We regretted our condition of poverty. He said uncomplimentary things, called us sons of toads, and damned us from hell to breakfast. Then he threatened. He explained that if we didn't dig up, he'd lock us in and carry us on to White River and turn us over to the authorities. He also explained all about the quarries at Rutland.

Now that shack thought he had us dead to rights. Was not he guarding the one door, and had he not himself latched the opposite door but a few minutes before? When he began talking about quarries, the frightened gay-cat started to sidle across to the other door. The shack laughed loud and long. "Don't be in a hurry," he said; "I locked that door on the outside at the last stop." So implicitly did he believe the door to be locked that his words carried conviction. The gay-cat believed and was in despair.

The shack delivered his ultimatum. Either we should dig up two dollars, or he would lock us in and turn us over to the constable at White River—and that meant ninety days and the quarries. Now, gentle reader, just suppose that the other door had been locked. Behold the precariousness of human life. For lack of a dollar, I'd have gone to the quarries and served three months as a convict slave. So would the gay-cat. Count me out, for I was hopeless; but consider the gay-cat. He might have come out, after those ninety days, pledged to a life of crime. And later he might have broken your skull, even your skull, with a blackjack in an endeavor to take possession of the money on your person—and if not your skull, then some other poor and unoffending creature's skull.

But the door was unlocked, and I alone knew it. The gay-cat and I begged for mercy. I joined in the pleading and wailing out of sheer cussedness, I suppose. But I did my best. I told a "story" that would have melted the heart of any mug; but it didn't melt the heart of that sordid money-grasper of a shack. When he became convinced that we didn't have any money, he slid the door shut and latched it, then lingered a moment on the chance that we had fooled him and that we would now offer him the two dollars.

Then it was that I let out a few links. I called him a son of a toad. I called him all the other things he had called me. And then I called him a few additional things. I came from the West, where men knew how to swear, and I wasn't going to let any mangy shack on a measly New England "jerk" put it over me in vividness and vigor of language. At first the shack tried to laugh it down. Then he made the mistake of attempting to reply. I let out a few more links, and I cut him to the raw and therein rubbed winged and flaming epithets. Nor was my fine frenzy all whim and literary; I was indignant at this vile creature, who, in default of a dollar, would consign me to three months of slavery. Furthermore, I had a sneaking idea that he got a "drag" out of the constable fees.

But I fixed him. I lacerated his feelings and pride several dollars' worth. He tried to scare me by threatening to come in after me and kick the stuffing out of me. In return, I promised to kick him in the face while he was climbing in. The advantage of position was with me, and he saw it. So he kept the door shut and called for help from the rest of the train-crew. I could hear them answering and crunching through the gravel to him. And all the time the other door was unlatched, and they didn't know it; and in the meantime the gay-cat was ready to die with fear.

Oh, I was a hero—with my line of retreat straight behind me. I slanged the shack and his mates till they threw the door open and I could see their infuriated faces in the shine of the lanterns. It was all very simple to them. They had us cornered in the car, and they were going to come in and man-handle us. They started. I didn't kick anybody in the face. I jerked the opposite door open, and the gay-cat and I went out. The train-crew took after us.

We went over—if I remember correctly—a stone fence. But I have no doubts of recollection about where we found ourselves. In the darkness I promptly fell over a grave-stone. The gay-cat sprawled over another. And then we got the chase of our lives through that graveyard. The ghosts must have thought we were going some. So did the train-crew, for when we emerged from the graveyard and plunged across a road into a dark wood, the shacks gave up the pursuit and went back to their train. A little later that night the gay-cat and I found ourselves at the well of a farmhouse. We were after a drink of water, but we noticed a small rope that ran down one side of the well. We hauled it up and found on the end of it a gallon-can of cream. And that is as near as I got to the quarries of Rutland, Vermont.

When hoboes pass the word along, concerning a town, that "the bulls is horstile," avoid that town, or, if you must, go through softly. There are some towns that one must always go through softly. Such a town was Cheyenne, on the Union Pacific. It had a national reputation for being "horstile,"—and it was all due to the efforts of one Jeff Carr (if I remember his name aright). Jeff Carr could size up the "front" of a hobo on the instant. He never entered into discussion. In the one moment he sized up the hobo, and in the next he struck out with both fists, a club, or anything else he had handy. After he had man-handled the hobo, he started him out of town with a promise of worse if he ever saw him again. Jeff Carr knew the game. North, south, east, and west to the uttermost confines of the United States (Canada and Mexico included), the man-handled hoboes carried the word that Cheyenne was "horstile." Fortunately, I never encountered Jeff Carr. I passed through Cheyenne in a blizzard. There were eighty-four hoboes with me at the time. The strength of numbers made us pretty nonchalant on most things, but not on Jeff Carr. The connotation of "Jeff Carr" stunned our imagination, numbed our virility, and the whole gang was mortally scared of meeting him.

It rarely pays to stop and enter into explanations with bulls when they look "horstile." A swift get-away is the thing to do. It took me some time to learn this; but the finishing touch was put upon me by a bull in New York City. Ever since that time it has been an automatic process with me to make a run for it when I see a bull reaching for me. This automatic process has become a mainspring of conduct in me, wound up and ready for instant release. I shall never get over it. Should I be eighty years old, hobbling along the street on crutches, and should a policeman suddenly reach out for me, I know I'd drop the crutches and run like a deer.

The finishing touch to my education in bulls was received on a hot summer afternoon in New York City. It was during a week of scorching weather. I had got into the habit of throwing my feet in the morning, and of spending the afternoon in the little park that is hard by Newspaper Row and the City Hall. It was near there that I could buy from pushcart men current books (that had been injured in the making or binding) for a few cents each. Then, right in the park itself, were little booths where one could buy glorious, ice-cold, sterilized milk and buttermilk at a penny a glass. Every afternoon I sat on a bench and read, and went on a milk debauch. I got away with from five to ten glasses each afternoon. It was dreadfully hot weather.

So here I was, a meek and studious milk-drinking hobo, and behold what I got for it. One afternoon I arrived at the park, a fresh book-purchase under my arm and a tremendous buttermilk thirst under my shirt. In the middle of the street, in front of the City Hall, I noticed, as I came along heading for the buttermilk booth, that a crowd had formed. It was right where I was crossing the street, so I stopped to see the cause of the collection of curious men. At first I could see nothing. Then, from the sounds I heard and from a glimpse I caught, I knew that it was a bunch of gamins playing pee-wee. Now pee-wee is not permitted in the streets of New York. I didn't know that, but I learned pretty lively. I had paused possibly thirty seconds, in which time I had learned the cause of the crowd, when I heard a gamin yell "Bull!" The gamins knew their business. They ran. I didn't.

The crowd broke up immediately and started for the sidewalk on both sides of the street. I started for the sidewalk on the park-side. There must have been fifty men, who had been in the original crowd, who were heading in the same direction. We were loosely strung out. I noticed the bull, a strapping policeman in a gray suit. He was coming along the middle of the street, without haste, merely sauntering. I noticed casually that he changed his course, and was heading obliquely for the same sidewalk that I was heading for directly. He sauntered along, threading the strung-out crowd, and I noticed that his course and mine would cross each other. I was so innocent of wrong-doing that, in spite of my education in bulls and their ways, I apprehended nothing. I never dreamed that bull was after me. Out of my respect for the law I was actually all ready to pause the next moment and let him cross in front of me. The pause came all right, but it was not of my volition; also it was a backward pause. Without warning, that bull had suddenly launched out at me on the chest with both hands. At the same moment, verbally, he cast the bar sinister on my genealogy.

All my free American blood boiled. All my liberty-loving ancestors clamored in me. "What do you mean?" I demanded. You see, I wanted an explanation. And I got it. Bang! His club came down on top of my head, and I was reeling backward like a drunken man, the curious faces of the onlookers billowing up and down like the waves of the sea, my precious book falling from under my arm into the dirt, the bull advancing with the club ready for another blow. And in that dizzy moment I had a vision. I saw that club descending many times upon my head; I saw myself, bloody and battered and hard-looking, in a police-court; I heard a charge of disorderly conduct, profane language, resisting an officer, and a few other things, read by a clerk; and I saw myself across in Blackwell's Island. Oh, I knew the game. I lost all interest in explanations. I didn't stop to pick up my precious, unread book. I turned and ran. I was pretty sick, but I ran. And run I shall, to my dying day, whenever a bull begins to explain with a club.

Why, years after my tramping days, when I was a student in the University of California, one night I went to the circus. After the show and the concert I lingered on to watch the working of the transportation machinery of a great circus. The circus was leaving that night. By a bonfire I came upon a bunch of small boys. There were about twenty of them, and as they talked with one another I learned that they were going to run away with the circus. Now the circus-men didn't want to be bothered with this mess of urchins, and a telephone to police headquarters had "coppered" the play. A squad of ten policemen had been despatched to the scene to arrest the small boys for violating the nine o'clock curfew ordinance. The policemen surrounded the bonfire, and crept up close to it in the darkness. At the signal, they made a rush, each policeman grabbing at the youngsters as he would grab into a basket of squirming eels.

Now I didn't know anything about the coming of the police; and when I saw the sudden eruption of brass-buttoned, helmeted bulls, each of them reaching with both hands, all the forces and stability of my being were overthrown. Remained only the automatic process to run. And I ran. I didn't know I was running. I didn't know anything. It was, as I have said, automatic. There was no reason for me to run. I was not a hobo. I was a citizen of that community. It was my home town. I was guilty of no wrong-doing. I was a college man. I had even got my name in the papers, and I wore good clothes that had never been slept in. And yet I ran—blindly, madly, like a startled deer, for over a block. And when I came to myself, I noted that I was still running. It required a positive effort of will to stop those legs of mine.

No, I'll never get over it. I can't help it. When a bull reaches, I run. Besides, I have an unhappy faculty for getting into jail. I have been in jail more times since I was a hobo than when I was one. I start out on a Sunday morning with a young lady on a bicycle ride. Before we can get outside the city limits we are arrested for passing a pedestrian on the sidewalk. I resolve to be more careful. The next time I am on a bicycle it is night-time and my acetylene-gas-lamp is misbehaving. I cherish the sickly flame carefully, because of the ordinance. I am in a hurry, but I ride at a snail's pace so as not to jar out the flickering flame. I reach the city limits; I am beyond the jurisdiction of the ordinance; and I proceed to scorch to make up for lost time. And half a mile farther on I am "pinched" by a bull, and the next morning I forfeit my bail in the police court. The city had treacherously extended its limits into a mile of the country, and I didn't know, that was all. I remember my inalienable right of free speech and peaceable assemblage, and I get up on a soap-box to trot out the particular economic bees that buzz in my bonnet, and a bull takes me off that box and leads me to the city prison, and after that I get out on bail. It's no use. In Korea I used to be arrested about every other day. It was the same thing in Manchuria. The last time I was in Japan I broke into jail under the pretext of being a Russian spy. It wasn't my pretext, but it got me into jail just the same. There is no hope for me. I am fated to do the Prisoner-of-Chillon stunt yet. This is prophecy.

I once hypnotized a bull on Boston Common. It was past midnight and he had me dead to rights; but before I got done with him he had ponied up a silver quarter and given me the address of an all-night restaurant. Then there was a bull in Bristol, New Jersey, who caught me and let me go, and heaven knows he had provocation enough to put me in jail. I hit him the hardest I'll wager he was ever hit in his life. It happened this way. About midnight I nailed a freight out of Philadelphia. The shacks ditched me. She was pulling out slowly through the maze of tracks and switches of the freight-yards. I nailed her again, and again I was ditched. You see, I had to nail her "outside," for she was a through freight with every door locked and sealed.

The second time I was ditched the shack gave me a lecture. He told me I was risking my life, that it was a fast freight and that she went some. I told him I was used to going some myself, but it was no go. He said he wouldn't permit me to commit suicide, and I hit the grit. But I nailed her a third time, getting in between on the bumpers. They were the most meagre bumpers I had ever seen—I do not refer to the real bumpers, the iron bumpers that are connected by the coupling-link and that pound and grind on each other; what I refer to are the beams, like huge cleats, that cross the ends of freight cars just above the bumpers. When one rides the bumpers, he stands on these cleats, one foot on each, the bumpers between his feet and just beneath.

But the beams or cleats I found myself on were not the broad, generous ones that at that time were usually on box-cars. On the contrary, they were very narrow—not more than an inch and a half in breadth. I couldn't get half of the width of my sole on them. Then there was nothing to which to hold with my hands. True, there were the ends of the two box-cars; but those ends were flat, perpendicular surfaces. There were no grips. I could only press the flats of my palms against the car-ends for support. But that would have been all right if the cleats for my feet had been decently wide.

As the freight got out of Philadelphia she began to hit up speed. Then I understood what the shack had meant by suicide. The freight went faster and faster. She was a through freight, and there was nothing to stop her. On that section of the Pennsylvania four tracks run side by side, and my east-bound freight didn't need to worry about passing west-bound freights, nor about being overtaken by east-bound expresses. She had the track to herself, and she used it. I was in a precarious situation. I stood with the mere edges of my feet on the narrow projections, the palms of my hands pressing desperately against the flat, perpendicular ends of each car. And those cars moved, and moved individually, up and down and back and forth. Did you ever see a circus rider, standing on two running horses, with one foot on the back of each horse? Well, that was what I was doing, with several differences. The circus rider had the reins to hold on to, while I had nothing; he stood on the broad soles of his feet, while I stood on the edges of mine; he bent his legs and body, gaining the strength of the arch in his posture and achieving the stability of a low centre of gravity, while I was compelled to stand upright and keep my legs straight; he rode face forward, while I was riding sidewise; and also, if he fell off, he'd get only a roll in the sawdust, while I'd have been ground to pieces beneath the wheels.

And that freight was certainly going some, roaring and shrieking, swinging madly around curves, thundering over trestles, one car-end bumping up when the other was jarring down, or jerking to the right at the same moment the other was lurching to the left, and with me all the while praying and hoping for the train to stop. But she didn't stop. She didn't have to. For the first, last, and only time on The Road, I got all I wanted. I abandoned the bumpers and managed to get out on a side-ladder; it was ticklish work, for I had never encountered car-ends that were so parsimonious of hand-holds and foot-holds as those car-ends were.

I heard the engine whistling, and I felt the speed easing down. I knew the train wasn't going to stop, but my mind was made up to chance it if she slowed down sufficiently. The right of way at this point took a curve, crossed a bridge over a canal, and cut through the town of Bristol. This combination compelled slow speed. I clung on to the side-ladder and waited. I didn't know it was the town of Bristol we were approaching. I did not know what necessitated slackening in speed. All I knew was that I wanted to get off. I strained my eyes in the darkness for a street-crossing on which to land. I was pretty well down the train, and before my car was in the town the engine was past the station and I could feel her making speed again.

Then came the street. It was too dark to see how wide it was or what was on the other side. I knew I needed all of that street if I was to remain on my feet after I struck. I dropped off on the near side. It sounds easy. By "dropped off" I mean just this: I first of all, on the side-ladder, thrust my body forward as far as I could in the direction the train was going—this to give as much space as possible in which to gain backward momentum when I swung off. Then I swung, swung out and backward, backward with all my might, and let go—at the same time throwing myself backward as if I intended to strike the ground on the back of my head. The whole effort was to overcome as much as possible the primary forward momentum the train had imparted to my body. When my feet hit the grit, my body was lying backward on the air at an angle of forty-five degrees. I had reduced the forward momentum some, for when my feet struck, I did not immediately pitch forward on my face. Instead, my body rose to the perpendicular and began to incline forward. In point of fact, my body proper still retained much momentum, while my feet, through contact with the earth, had lost all their momentum. This momentum the feet had lost I had to supply anew by lifting them as rapidly as I could and running them forward in order to keep them under my forward-moving body. The result was that my feet beat a rapid and explosive tattoo clear across the street. I didn't dare stop them. If I had, I'd have pitched forward. It was up to me to keep on going.

I was an involuntary projectile, worrying about what was on the other side of the street and hoping that it wouldn't be a stone wall or a telegraph pole. And just then I hit something. Horrors! I saw it just the instant before the disaster—of all things, a bull, standing there in the darkness. We went down together, rolling over and over; and the automatic process was such in that miserable creature that in the moment of impact he reached out and clutched me and never let go. We were both knocked out, and he held on to a very lamb-like hobo while he recovered.

If that bull had any imagination, he must have thought me a traveller from other worlds, the man from Mars just arriving; for in the darkness he hadn't seen me swing from the train. In fact, his first words were: "Where did you come from?" His next words, and before I had time to answer, were: "I've a good mind to run you in." This latter, I am convinced, was likewise automatic. He was a really good bull at heart, for after I had told him a "story" and helped brush off his clothes, he gave me until the next freight to get out of town. I stipulated two things: first, that the freight be east-bound, and second, that it should not be a through freight with all doors sealed and locked. To this he agreed, and thus, by the terms of the Treaty of Bristol, I escaped being pinched.

I remember another night, in that part of the country, when I just missed another bull. If I had hit him, I'd have telescoped him, for I was coming down from above, all holds free, with several other bulls one jump behind and reaching for me. This is how it happened. I had been lodging in a livery stable in Washington. I had a box-stall and unnumbered horse-blankets all to myself. In return for such sumptuous accommodation I took care of a string of horses each morning. I might have been there yet, if it hadn't been for the bulls.

One evening, about nine o'clock, I returned to the stable to go to bed, and found a crap game in full blast. It had been a market day, and all the negroes had money. It would be well to explain the lay of the land. The livery stable faced on two streets. I entered the front, passed through the office, and came to the alley between two rows of stalls that ran the length of the building and opened out on the other street. Midway along this alley, beneath a gas-jet and between the rows of horses, were about forty negroes. I joined them as an onlooker. I was broke and couldn't play. A coon was making passes and not dragging down. He was riding his luck, and with each pass the total stake doubled. All kinds of money lay on the floor. It was fascinating. With each pass, the chances increased tremendously against the coon making another pass. The excitement was intense. And just then there came a thundering smash on the big doors that opened on the back street.

A few of the negroes bolted in the opposite direction. I paused from my flight a moment to grab at the all kinds of money on the floor. This wasn't theft: it was merely custom. Every man who hadn't run was grabbing. The doors crashed open and swung in, and through them surged a squad of bulls. We surged the other way. It was dark in the office, and the narrow door would not permit all of us to pass out to the street at the same time. Things became congested. A coon took a dive through the window, taking the sash along with him and followed by other coons. At our rear, the bulls were nailing prisoners. A big coon and myself made a dash at the door at the same time. He was bigger than I, and he pivoted me and got through first. The next instant a club swatted him on the head and he went down like a steer. Another squad of bulls was waiting outside for us. They knew they couldn't stop the rush with their hands, and so they were swinging their clubs. I stumbled over the fallen coon who had pivoted me, ducked a swat from a club, dived between a bull's legs, and was free. And then how I ran! There was a lean mulatto just in front of me, and I took his pace. He knew the town better than I did, and I knew that in the way he ran lay safety. But he, on the other hand, took me for a pursuing bull. He never looked around. He just ran. My wind was good, and I hung on to his pace and nearly killed him. In the end he stumbled weakly, went down on his knees, and surrendered to me. And when he discovered I wasn't a bull, all that saved me was that he didn't have any wind left in him.

That was why I left Washington—not on account of the mulatto, but on account of the bulls. I went down to the depot and caught the first blind out on a Pennsylvania Railroad express. After the train got good and under way and I noted the speed she was making, a misgiving smote me. This was a four-track railroad, and the engines took water on the fly. Hoboes had long since warned me never to ride the first blind on trains where the engines took water on the fly. And now let me explain. Between the tracks are shallow metal troughs. As the engine, at full speed, passes above, a sort of chute drops down into the trough. The result is that all the water in the trough rushes up the chute and fills the tender.

Somewhere along between Washington and Baltimore, as I sat on the platform of the blind, a fine spray began to fill the air. It did no harm. Ah, ha, thought I; it's all a bluff, this taking water on the fly being bad for the bo on the first blind. What does this little spray amount to? Then I began to marvel at the device. This was railroading! Talk about your primitive Western railroading—and just then the tender filled up, and it hadn't reached the end of the trough. A tidal wave of water poured over the back of the tender and down upon me. I was soaked to the skin, as wet as if I had fallen overboard.

The train pulled into Baltimore. As is the custom in the great Eastern cities, the railroad ran beneath the level of the streets on the bottom of a big "cut." As the train pulled into the lighted depot, I made myself as small as possible on the blind. But a railroad bull saw me, and gave chase. Two more joined him. I was past the depot, and I ran straight on down the track. I was in a sort of trap. On each side of me rose the steep walls of the cut, and if I ever essayed them and failed, I knew that I'd slide back into the clutches of the bulls. I ran on and on, studying the walls of the cut for a favorable place to climb up. At last I saw such a place. It came just after I had passed under a bridge that carried a level street across the cut. Up the steep slope I went, clawing hand and foot. The three railroad bulls were clawing up right after me.

At the top, I found myself in a vacant lot. On one side was a low wall that separated it from the street. There was no time for minute investigation. They were at my heels. I headed for the wall and vaulted it. And right there was where I got the surprise of my life. One is used to thinking that one side of a wall is just as high as the other side. But that wall was different. You see, the vacant lot was much higher than the level of the street. On my side the wall was low, but on the other side—well, as I came soaring over the top, all holds free, it seemed to me that I was falling feet-first, plump into an abyss. There beneath me, on the sidewalk, under the light of a street-lamp was a bull. I guess it was nine or ten feet down to the sidewalk; but in the shock of surprise in mid-air it seemed twice that distance.

I straightened out in the air and came down. At first I thought I was going to land on the bull. My clothes did brush him as my feet struck the sidewalk with explosive impact. It was a wonder he didn't drop dead, for he hadn't heard me coming. It was the man-from-Mars stunt over again. The bull did jump. He shied away from me like a horse from an auto; and then he reached for me. I didn't stop to explain. I left that to my pursuers, who were dropping over the wall rather gingerly. But I got a chase all right. I ran up one street and down another, dodged around corners, and at last got away.

After spending some of the coin I'd got from the crap game and killing off an hour of time, I came back to the railroad cut, just outside the lights of the depot, and waited for a train. My blood had cooled down, and I shivered miserably, what of my wet clothes. At last a train pulled into the station. I lay low in the darkness, and successfully boarded her when she pulled out, taking good care this time to make the second blind. No more water on the fly in mine. The train ran forty miles to the first stop. I got off in a lighted depot that was strangely familiar. I was back in Washington. In some way, during the excitement of the get-away in Baltimore, running through strange streets, dodging and turning and retracing, I had got turned around. I had taken the train out the wrong way. I had lost a night's sleep, I had been soaked to the skin, I had been chased for my life; and for all my pains I was back where I had started. Oh, no, life on The Road is not all beer and skittles. But I didn't go back to the livery stable. I had done some pretty successful grabbing, and I didn't want to reckon up with the coons. So I caught the next train out, and ate my breakfast in Baltimore.

Part Two
The Cruise of the *Snark*

Chapter 10
Forward

It began in the swimming pool at Glen Ellen. Between swims it was our wont to come out and lie in the sand and let our skins breathe the warm air and soak in the sunshine. Roscoe was a yachtsman. I had followed the sea a bit. It was inevitable that we should talk about boats. We talked about small boats, and the seaworthiness of small boats. We instanced Captain Slocum and his three years' voyage around the world in the Spray.

We asserted that we were not afraid to go around the world in a small boat, say forty feet long. We asserted furthermore that we would like to do it. We asserted finally that there was nothing in this world we'd like better than a chance to do it.

"Let us do it," we said . . . in fun.

Then I asked Charmian privily if she'd really care to do it, and she said that it was too good to be true.

The next time we breathed our skins in the sand by the swimming pool I said to Roscoe, "Let us do it."

I was in earnest, and so was he, for he said:

"When shall we start?"

I had a house to build on the ranch, also an orchard, a vineyard, and several hedges to plant, and a number of other things to do. We thought we would start in four or five years. Then the lure of the adventure began to grip us. Why not start at once? We'd never be younger, any of us. Let the orchard, vineyard, and hedges be growing up while we were away. When we came back, they would be ready for us, and we could live in the barn while we built the house.

So the trip was decided upon, and the building of the *Snark* began. We named her the *Snark* because we could not think of any other name—this information is given for the benefit of those who otherwise might think there is something occult in the name.

Our friends cannot understand why we make this voyage. They shudder, and moan, and raise their hands. No amount of explanation can make them comprehend that we are moving along the line of least resistance; that it is easier for us to go down to the sea in a small ship than to remain on dry land, just as it is easier for them to remain on dry land than to go down to the sea in the small ship. This state of mind comes of an undue prominence of the ego. They cannot get away from themselves. They cannot come out of themselves long enough to see that their line of least resistance is not necessarily everybody else's line of least resistance. They make of their own bundle of desires, likes, and dislikes a yardstick wherewith to measure the desires, likes, and dislikes of all creatures. This is unfair. I tell them so. But they cannot get away from their own miserable egos long enough to hear me. They think I am crazy. In return, I am sympathetic. It is a state of mind familiar to me. We are all prone to think there is something wrong with the mental processes of the man who disagrees with us.

The ultimate word is I LIKE. It lies beneath philosophy, and is twined about the heart of life. When philosophy has maundered ponderously for a month, telling the individual what he must do, the individual says, in an instant, "I LIKE," and does something else, and philosophy goes glimmering. It is I LIKE that makes the drunkard drink and the martyr wear a hair shirt; that makes one man a reveller and another man an anchorite; that makes one man pursue fame, another gold, another love, and another God. Philosophy is very often a man's way of explaining his own I LIKE.

But to return to the *Snark*, and why I, for one, want to journey in her around the world. The things I like constitute my set of values. The thing I like most of all is personal achievement—not achievement for the world's applause, but achievement for my own delight. It is the old "I did it! I did it! With my own hands I did it!" But personal achievement, with me, must be concrete. I'd rather win a water-fight in the swimming pool, or remain astride a horse that is trying to get out from under me, than write the great American novel. Each man to his liking. Some other fellow would prefer writing the great American novel to winning the water-fight or mastering the horse.

Possibly the proudest achievement of my life, my moment of highest living, occurred when I was seventeen. I was in a three-masted schooner off the coast of Japan. We were in a typhoon. All hands had been on deck most of the night. I was called from my bunk at seven in the morning to take the wheel. Not a stitch of canvas was set. We were running before it under bare poles, yet the schooner fairly tore along. The seas were all of an eighth of a mile apart, and the wind snatched the whitecaps from their summits, filling. The air so thick with driving spray that it was impossible to see more than two waves at a time. The schooner was almost unmanageable, rolling her rail under to starboard and to port, veering and yawing anywhere between south-east and south-west, and threatening, when the huge seas lifted under her quarter, to broach to. Had she broached to, she would ultimately have been reported lost with all hands and no tidings.

I took the wheel. The sailing-master watched me for a space. He was afraid of my youth, feared that I lacked the strength and the nerve. But when he saw me successfully wrestle the schooner through several bouts, he went below to breakfast. Fore and aft, all hands were below at breakfast. Had she broached to, not one of them would ever have reached the deck. For forty minutes I stood there alone at the wheel, in my grasp the wildly careering schooner and the lives of twenty-two men. Once we were pooped. I saw it coming, and, half-drowned, with tons of water crushing me, I checked the schooner's rush to broach to. At the end of the hour, sweating and played out, I was relieved. But I had done it! With my own hands I had done my trick at the wheel and guided a hundred tons of wood and iron through a few million tons of wind and waves.

My delight was in that I had done it—not in the fact that twenty-two men knew I had done it. Within the year over half of them were dead and gone, yet my pride in the thing performed was not diminished by half. I am willing to confess, however, that I do like a small audience. But it must be a very small audience, composed of those who love me and whom I love. When I then accomplish personal achievement, I have a feeling that I am justifying their love for me. But this is quite apart from the delight of the achievement itself. This delight is peculiarly my own and does not depend upon witnesses. When I have done some such thing, I am exalted. I glow all over. I am aware of a pride in myself that is mine, and mine alone. It is organic. Every fibre of me is thrilling with it. It is very natural. It is a mere matter of satisfaction at adjustment to environment. It is success.

Life that lives is life successful, and success is the breath of its nostrils. The achievement of a difficult feat is successful adjustment to a sternly exacting environment. The more difficult the feat, the greater the satisfaction at its accomplishment. Thus it is with the man who leaps forward from the springboard, out over the swimming pool, and with a backward half-revolution of the body, enters the water head first. Once he leaves the springboard his environment becomes immediately savage, and savage the penalty it will exact should he fail and strike the water flat. Of course, the man does not have to run the risk of the penalty. He could remain on the bank in a sweet and placid environment of summer air, sunshine, and stability. Only he is not made that way. In that swift mid-air moment he lives as he could never live on the bank.

As for myself, I'd rather be that man than the fellows who sit on the bank and watch him. That is why I am building the *Snark*. I am so made. I like, that is all. The trip around the world means big moments of living. Bear with me a moment and look at it. Here am I, a little animal called a man—a bit of vitalized matter, one hundred and sixty-five pounds of meat and blood, nerve, sinew, bones, and brain,—all of it soft and tender, susceptible to hurt, fallible, and frail. I strike a light back-handed blow on the nose of an obstreperous horse, and a bone in my hand is broken. I put my head under the water for five minutes, and I am drowned. I fall twenty feet through the air, and I am smashed. I am a creature of temperature. A few degrees one way, and my fingers and ears and toes blacken and drop off. A few degrees the other way, and my skin blisters and shrivels away from the raw, quivering flesh. A few additional degrees either way, and the life and the light in me go out. A drop of poison injected into my body from a snake, and I cease to move—for ever I cease to move. A splinter of lead from a rifle enters my head, and I am wrapped around in the eternal blackness.

Fallible and frail, a bit of pulsating, jelly-like life—it is all I am. About me are the great natural forces—colossal menaces, Titans of destruction, unsentimental monsters that have less concern for me than I have for the grain of sand I crush under my foot. They have no concern at all for me. They do not know me. They are unconscious, unmerciful, and unmoral. They are the cyclones and tornadoes, lightning flashes and cloud-bursts, tide-rips and tidal waves, undertows and waterspouts, great whirls and sucks and eddies, earthquakes and volcanoes, surfs that thunder on rock-ribbed coasts and seas that leap aboard the largest crafts that float, crushing humans to pulp or licking them off into the sea and to death—and these insensate monsters do not know that tiny sensitive creature, all nerves and weaknesses, whom men call Jack London, and who himself thinks he is all right and quite a superior being.

In the maze and chaos of the conflict of these vast and draughty Titans, it is for me to thread my precarious way. The bit of life that is I will exult over them. The bit of life that is I, in so far as it succeeds in baffling them or in bitting them to its service, will imagine that it is godlike. It is good to ride the tempest and feel godlike. I dare to assert that for a finite speck of pulsating jelly to feel godlike is a far more glorious feeling than for a god to feel godlike.

Here is the sea, the wind, and the wave. Here are the seas, the winds, and the waves of all the world. Here is ferocious environment. And here is difficult adjustment, the achievement of which is delight to the small quivering vanity that is I. I like. I am so made. It is my own particular form of vanity, that is all.

There is also another side to the voyage of the *Snark*. Being alive, I want to see, and all the world is a bigger thing to see than one small town or valley. We have done little outlining of the voyage. Only one thing is definite, and that is that our first port of call will be Honolulu. Beyond a few general ideas, we have no thought of our next port after Hawaii. We shall make up our minds as we get nearer, in a general way we know that we shall wander through the South Seas, take in Samoa, New Zealand, Tasmania, Australia, New Guinea, Borneo, and Sumatra, and go on up through the Philippines to Japan. Then will come Korea, China, India, the Red Sea, and the Mediterranean. After that the voyage becomes too vague to describe, though we know a number of things we shall surely do, and we expect to spend from one to several months in every country in Europe.

The *Snark* is to be sailed. There will be a gasolene engine on board, but it will be used only in case of emergency, such as in bad water among reefs and shoals, where a sudden calm in a swift current leaves a sailing-boat helpless. The rig of the *Snark* is to be what is called the "ketch." The ketch rig is a compromise between the yawl and the schooner. Of late years the yawl rig has proved the best for cruising. The ketch retains the cruising virtues of the yawl, and in addition manages to embrace a few of the sailing virtues of the schooner. The foregoing must be taken with a pinch of salt. It is all theory in my head. I've never sailed a ketch, nor even seen one. The theory commends itself to me. Wait till I get out on the ocean, then I'll be able to tell more about the cruising and sailing qualities of the ketch.

As originally planned, the *Snark* was to be forty feet long on the water-line. But we discovered there was no space for a bath-room, and for that reason we have increased her length to forty-five feet. Her greatest beam is fifteen feet. She has no house and no hold. There is six feet of headroom, and the deck is unbroken save for two companionways and a hatch for'ard. The fact that there is no house to break the strength of the deck will make us feel safer in case great seas thunder their tons of water down on board. A large and roomy cockpit, sunk beneath the deck, with high rail and self-bailing, will make our rough-weather days and nights more comfortable.

There will be no crew. Or, rather, Charmian, Roscoe, and I are the crew. We are going to do the thing with our own hands. With our own hands we're going to circumnavigate the globe. Sail her or sink her, with our own hands we'll do it. Of course there will be a cook and a cabin-boy. Why should we stew over a stove, wash dishes, and set the table? We could stay on land if we wanted to do those things. Besides, we've got to stand watch and work the ship. And also, I've got to work at my trade of writing in order to feed us and to get new sails and tackle and keep the *Snark* in efficient working order. And then there's the ranch; I've got to keep the vineyard, orchard, and hedges growing.

When we increased the length of the *Snark* in order to get space for a bath-room, we found that all the space was not required by the bath-room. Because of this, we increased the size of the engine. Seventy horse-power our engine is, and since we expect it to drive us along at a nine-knot clip, we do not know the name of a river with a current swift enough to defy us.

We expect to do a lot of inland work. The smallness of the *Snark* makes this possible. When we enter the land, out go the masts and on goes the engine. There are the canals of China, and the Yang-tse River. We shall spend months on them if we can get permission from the government. That will be the one obstacle to our inland voyaging—governmental permission. But if we can get that permission, there is scarcely a limit to the inland voyaging we can do.

When we come to the Nile, why we can go up the Nile. We can go up the Danube to Vienna, up the Thames to London, and we can go up the Seine to Paris and moor opposite the Latin Quarter with a bow-line out to Notre Dame and a stern-line fast to the Morgue. We can leave the Mediterranean and go up the Rhone to Lyons, there enter the Saone, cross from the Saone to the Maine through the Canal de Bourgogne, and from the Marne enter the Seine and go out the Seine at Havre. When we cross the Atlantic to the United States, we can go up the Hudson, pass through the Erie Canal, cross the Great Lakes, leave Lake Michigan at Chicago, gain the Mississippi by way of the Illinois River and the connecting canal, and go down the Mississippi to the Gulf of Mexico. And then there are the great rivers of South America. We'll know something about geography when we get back to California.

People that build houses are often sore perplexed; but if they enjoy the strain of it, I'll advise them to build a boat like the *Snark*. Just consider, for a moment, the strain of detail. Take the engine. What is the best kind of engine—the two cycle? three cycle? four cycle? My lips are mutilated with all kinds of strange jargon, my mind is mutilated with still stranger ideas and is foot-sore and weary from travelling in new and rocky realms of thought.—Ignition methods; shall it be make-and-break or jump-spark? Shall dry cells or storage batteries be used? A storage battery commends itself, but it requires a dynamo. How powerful a dynamo? And when we have installed a dynamo and a storage battery, it is simply ridiculous not to light the boat with electricity. Then comes the discussion of how many lights and how many candle-power. It is a splendid idea. But electric lights will demand a more powerful storage battery, which, in turn, demands a more powerful dynamo.

And now that we've gone in for it, why not have a searchlight? It would be tremendously useful. But the searchlight needs so much electricity that when it runs it will put all the other lights out of commission. Again we travel the weary road in the quest after more power for storage battery and dynamo. And then, when it is finally solved, someone asks, "What if the engine breaks down?" And we collapse. There are the sidelights, the binnacle light, and the anchor light. Our very lives depend upon them. So we have to fit the boat throughout with oil lamps as well.

But we are not done with that engine yet. The engine is powerful. We are two small men and a small woman. It will break our hearts and our backs to hoist anchor by hand. Let the engine do it. And then comes the problem of how to convey power for'ard from the engine to the winch. And by the time all this is settled, we redistribute the allotments of space to the engine-room, galley, bath-room, state-rooms, and cabin, and begin all over again. And when we have shifted the engine, I send off a telegram of gibberish to its makers at New York, something like this: Toggle-joint abandoned change thrust-bearing accordingly distance from forward side of flywheel to face of stern post sixteen feet six inches.

Just potter around in quest of the best steering gear, or try to decide whether you will set up your rigging with old-fashioned lanyards or with turnbuckles, if you want strain of detail. Shall the binnacle be located in front of the wheel in the centre of the beam, or shall it be located to one side in front of the wheel?—there's room right there for a library of sea-dog controversy. Then there's the problem of gasolene, fifteen hundred gallons of it—what are the safest ways to tank it and pipe it? and which is the best fire-extinguisher for a gasolene fire? Then there is the pretty problem of the life-boat and the stowage of the same. And when that is finished, come the cook and cabin-boy to confront one with nightmare possibilities. It is a small boat, and we'll be packed close together. The servant-girl problem of landsmen pales to insignificance. We did select one cabin-boy, and by that much were our troubles eased. And then the cabin-boy fell in love and resigned.

And in the meanwhile how is a fellow to find time to study navigation—when he is divided between these problems and the earning of the money wherewith to settle the problems? Neither Roscoe nor I know anything about navigation, and the summer is gone, and we are about to start, and the problems are thicker than ever, and the treasury is stuffed with emptiness. Well, anyway, it takes years to learn seamanship, and both of us are seamen. If we don't find the time, we'll lay in the books and instruments and teach ourselves navigation on the ocean between San Francisco and Hawaii.

There is one unfortunate and perplexing phase of the voyage of the *Snark*. Roscoe, who is to be my co-navigator, is a follower of one, Cyrus R. Teed. Now Cyrus R. Teed has a different cosmology from the one generally accepted, and Roscoe shares his views. Wherefore Roscoe believes that the surface of the earth is concave and that we live on the inside of a hollow sphere. Thus, though we shall sail on the one boat, the *Snark*, Roscoe will journey around the world on the inside, while I shall journey around on the outside. But of this, more anon. We threaten to be of the one mind before the voyage is completed. I am confident that I shall convert him into making the journey on the outside, while he is equally confident that before we arrive back in San Francisco I shall be on the inside of the earth. How he is going to get me through the crust I don't know, but Roscoe is ay a masterful man.

P.S.—That engine! While we've got it, and the dynamo, and the storage battery, why not have an ice-machine? Ice in the tropics! It is more necessary than bread. Here goes for the ice-machine! Now I am plunged into chemistry, and my lips hurt, and my mind hurts, and how am I ever to find the time to study navigation?

Chapter 11
The Inconceivable and Monstrous

"Spare no money," I said to Roscoe. "Let everything on the *Snark* be of the best. And never mind decoration. Plain pine boards is good enough finishing for me. But put the money into the construction. Let the *Snark* be as staunch and strong as any boat afloat. Never mind what it costs to make her staunch and strong; you see that she is made staunch and strong, and I'll go on writing and earning the money to pay for it."

And I did . . . as well as I could; for the *Snark* ate up money faster than I could earn it. In fact, every little while I had to borrow money with which to supplement my earnings. Now I borrowed one thousand dollars, now I borrowed two thousand dollars, and now I borrowed five thousand dollars. And all the time I went on working every day and sinking the earnings in the venture. I worked Sundays as well, and I took no holidays. But it was worth it. Every time I thought of the *Snark* I knew she was worth it.

For know, gentle reader, the staunchness of the *Snark*. She is forty-five feet long on the waterline. Her garboard strake is three inches thick; her planking two and one-half inches thick; her deck-planking two inches thick and in all her planking there are no butts. I know, for I ordered that planking especially from Puget Sound. Then the *Snark* has four water-tight compartments, which is to say that her length is broken by three water-tight bulkheads. Thus, no matter how large a leak the *Snark* may spring, Only one compartment can fill with water. The other three compartments will keep her afloat, anyway, and, besides, will enable us to mend the leak. There is another virtue in these bulkheads. The last compartment of all, in the very stern, contains six tanks that carry over one thousand gallons of gasoline. Now gasoline is a very dangerous article to carry in bulk on a small craft far out on the wide ocean. But when the six tanks that do not leak are themselves contained in a compartment hermetically sealed off from the rest of the boat, the danger will be seen to be very small indeed.

The *Snark* is a sail-boat. She was built primarily to sail. But incidentally, as an auxiliary, a seventy-horse-power engine was installed. This is a good, strong engine. I ought to know. I paid for it to come out all the way from New York City. Then, on deck, above the engine, is a windlass. It is a magnificent affair. It weighs several hundred pounds and takes up no end of deck-room. You see, it is ridiculous to hoist up anchor by hand-power when there is a seventy-horse-power engine on board. So we installed the windlass, transmitting power to it from the engine by means of a gear and castings specially made in a San Francisco foundry.

The *Snark* was made for comfort, and no expense was spared in this regard. There is the bath-room, for instance, small and compact, it is true, but containing all the conveniences of any bath-room upon land. The bath-room is a beautiful dream of schemes and devices, pumps, and levers, and sea-valves. Why, in the course of its building, I used to lie awake nights thinking about that bath-room. And next to the bathroom come the life-boat and the launch. They are carried on deck, and they take up what little space might have been left us for exercise. But then, they beat life insurance; and the prudent man, even if he has built as staunch and strong a craft as the *Snark,* will see to it that he has a good life-boat as well. And ours is a good one. It is a dandy. It was stipulated to cost one hundred and fifty dollars, and when I came to pay the bill, it turned out to be three hundred and ninety-five dollars. That shows how good a life-boat it is.

I could go on at great length relating the various virtues and excellences of the *Snark,* but I refrain. I have bragged enough as it is, and I have bragged to a purpose, as will be seen before my tale is ended. And please remember its title, "The Inconceivable and Monstrous." It was planned that the *Snark* should sail on October 1, 1906. That she did not so sail was inconceivable and monstrous. There was no valid reason for not sailing except that she was not ready to sail, and there was no conceivable reason why she was not ready. She was promised on November first, on November fifteenth, on December first; and yet she was never ready. On December first Charmian and I left the sweet, clean Sonoma country and came down to live in the stifling city—but not for long, oh, no, only for two weeks, for we would sail on December fifteenth. And I guess we ought to know, for Roscoe said so, and it was on his advice that we came to the city to stay two weeks. Alas, the two weeks went by, four weeks went by, six weeks went by, eight weeks went by, and we were farther away from sailing than ever. Explain it? Who?—me? I can't. It is the one thing in all my life that I have backed down on. There is no explaining it; if there were, I'd do it. I, who am an artisan of speech, confess my inability to explain why the *Snark* was not ready. As I have said, and as I must repeat, it was inconceivable and monstrous.

The eight weeks became sixteen weeks, and then, one day, Roscoe cheered us up by saying: "If we don't sail before April first, you can use my head for a football."

Two weeks later he said, "I'm getting my head in training for that match."

"Never mind," Charmian and I said to each other; "think of the wonderful boat it is going to be when it is completed."

Whereat we would rehearse for our mutual encouragement the manifold virtues and excellences of the *Snark*. Also, I would borrow more money, and I would get down closer to my desk and write harder, and I refused heroically to take a Sunday off and go out into the hills with my friends. I was building a boat, and by the eternal it was going to be a boat, and a boat spelled out all in capitals—B—O—A—T; and no matter what it cost I didn't care. So long as it was a BOAT.

And, oh, there is one other excellence of the *Snark,* upon which I must brag, namely, her bow. No sea could ever come over it. It laughs at the sea, that bow does; it challenges the sea; it snorts defiance at the sea. And withal it is a beautiful bow; the lines of it are dreamlike; I doubt if ever a boat was blessed with a more beautiful and at the same time a more capable bow. It was made to punch storms. To touch that bow is to rest one's hand on the cosmic nose of things. To look at it is to realize that expense cut no figure where it was concerned. And every time our sailing was delayed, or a new expense was tacked on, we thought of that wonderful bow and were content.

The *Snark* is a small boat. When I figured seven thousand dollars as her generous cost, I was both generous and correct. I have built barns and houses, and I know the peculiar trait such things have of running past their estimated cost. This knowledge was mine, was already mine, when I estimated the probable cost of the building of the *Snark* at seven thousand dollars. Well, she cost thirty thousand. Now don't ask me, please. It is the truth. I signed the cheques and I raised the money. Of course there is no explaining it, inconceivable and monstrous is what it is, as you will agree, I know, ere my tale is done.

Then there was the matter of delay. I dealt with forty-seven different kinds of union men and with one hundred and fifteen different firms. And not one union man and not one firm of all the union men and all the firms ever delivered anything at the time agreed upon, nor ever was on time for anything except pay-day and bill-collection. Men pledged me their immortal souls that they would deliver a certain thing on a certain date; as a rule, after such pledging, they rarely exceeded being three months late in delivery. And so it went, and Charmian and I consoled each other by saying what a splendid boat the *Snark* was, so staunch and strong; also, we would get into the small boat and row around the *Snark,* and gloat over her unbelievably wonderful bow.

"Think," I would say to Charmian, "of a gale off the China coast, and of the *Snark* hove to, that splendid bow of hers driving into the storm. Not a drop will come over that bow. She'll be as dry as a feather, and we'll be all below playing whist while the gale howls."

And Charmian would press my hand enthusiastically and exclaim: "It's worth every bit of it—the delay, and expense, and worry, and all the rest. Oh, what a truly wonderful boat!"

Whenever I looked at the bow of the *Snark* or thought of her water-tight compartments, I was encouraged. Nobody else, however, was encouraged. My friends began to make bets against the various sailing dates of the *Snark*. Mr. Wiget, who was left behind in charge of our Sonoma ranch was the first to cash his bet. He collected on New Year's Day, 1907. After that the bets came fast and furious. My friends surrounded me like a gang of harpies, making bets against every sailing date I set. I was rash, and I was stubborn. I bet, and I bet, and I continued to bet; and I paid them all. Why, the women-kind of my friends grew so brave that those among them who never bet before began to bet with me. And I paid them, too.

"Never mind," said Charmian to me; "just think of that bow and of being hove to on the China Seas."

"You see," I said to my friends, when I paid the latest bunch of wagers, "neither trouble nor cash is being spared in making the *Snark* the most seaworthy craft that ever sailed out through the Golden Gate—that is what causes all the delay."

In the meantime editors and publishers with whom I had contracts pestered me with demands for explanations. But how could I explain to them, when I was unable to explain to myself, or when there was nobody, not even Roscoe, to explain to me? The newspapers began to laugh at me, and to publish rhymes anent the *Snark's* departure with refrains like, "Not yet, but soon." And Charmian cheered me up by reminding me of the bow, and I went to a banker and borrowed five thousand more. There was one recompense for the delay, however. A friend of mine, who happens to be a critic, wrote a roast of me, of all I had done, and of all I ever was going to do; and he planned to have it published after I was out on the ocean. I was still on shore when it came out, and he has been busy explaining ever since.

And the time continued to go by. One thing was becoming apparent, namely, that it was impossible to finish the *Snark* in San Francisco. She had been so long in the building that she was beginning to break down and wear out. In fact, she had reached the stage where she was breaking down faster than she could be repaired. She had become a joke. Nobody took her seriously; least of all the men who worked on her. I said we would sail just as she was and finish building her in Honolulu. Promptly she sprang a leak that had to be attended to before we could sail. I started her for the boat-ways. Before she got to them she was caught between two huge barges and received a vigorous crushing. We got her on the ways, and, part way along, the ways spread and dropped her through, stern-first, into the mud.

It was a pretty tangle, a job for wreckers, not boat-builders. There are two high tides every twenty-four hours, and at every high tide, night and day, for a week, there were two steam tugs pulling and hauling on the *Snark*. There she was, stuck, fallen between the ways and standing on her stern. Next, and while still in that predicament, we started to use the gears and castings made in the local foundry whereby power was conveyed from the engine to the windlass. It was the first time we ever tried to use that windlass. The castings had flaws; they shattered asunder, the gears ground together, and the windlass was out of commission. Following upon that, the seventy-horse-power engine went out of commission. This engine came from New York; so did its bed-plate; there was a flaw in the bed-plate; there were a lot of flaws in the bed-plate; and the seventy-horse-power engine broke away from its shattered foundations, reared up in the air, smashed all connections and fastenings, and fell over on its side. And the *Snark* continued to stick between the spread ways, and the two tugs continued to haul vainly upon her.

"Never mind," said Charmian, "think of what a staunch, strong boat she is."

"Yes," said I, "and of that beautiful bow."

So we took heart and went at it again. The ruined engine was lashed down on its rotten foundation; the smashed castings and cogs of the power transmission were taken down and stored away—all for the purpose of taking them to Honolulu where repairs and new castings could be made. Somewhere in the dim past the *Snark* had received on the outside one coat of white paint. The intention of the colour was still evident, however, when one got it in the right light. The *Snark* had never received any paint on the inside. On the contrary, she was coated inches thick with the grease and tobacco-juice of the multitudinous mechanics who had toiled upon her. Never mind, we said; the grease and filth could be planed off, and later, when we fetched Honolulu, the *Snark* could be painted at the same time as she was being rebuilt.

By main strength and sweat we dragged the *Snark* off from the wrecked ways and laid her alongside the Oakland City Wharf. The drays brought all the outfit from home, the books and blankets and personal luggage. Along with this, everything else came on board in a torrent of confusion—wood and coal, water and water-tanks, vegetables, provisions, oil, the life-boat and the launch, all our friends, all the friends of our friends and those who claimed to be their friends, to say nothing of some of the friends of the friends of the friends of our crew. Also there were reporters, and photographers, and strangers, and cranks, and finally, and over all, clouds of coal-dust from the wharf.

We were to sail Sunday at eleven, and Saturday afternoon had arrived. The crowd on the wharf and the coal-dust were thicker than ever. In one pocket I carried a cheque-book, a fountain-pen, a dater, and a blotter; in another pocket I carried between one and two thousand dollars in paper money and gold. I was ready for the creditors, cash for the small ones and cheques for the large ones, and was waiting only for Roscoe to arrive with the balances of the accounts of the hundred and fifteen firms who had delayed me so many months. And then—

And then the inconceivable and monstrous happened once more. Before Roscoe could arrive there arrived another man. He was a United States marshal. He tacked a notice on the *Snark's* brave mast so that all on the wharf could read that the *Snark* had been libelled for debt. The marshal left a little old man in charge of the *Snark*, and himself went away. I had no longer any control of the *Snark*, nor of her wonderful bow. The little old man was now her lord and master, and I learned that I was paying him three dollars a day for being lord and master. Also, I learned the name of the man who had libelled the *Snark*. It was Sellers; the debt was two hundred and thirty-two dollars; and the deed was no more than was to be expected from the possessor of such a name. Sellers! Ye gods! Sellers!

But who under the sun was Sellers? I looked in my cheque-book and saw that two weeks before I had made him out a cheque for five hundred dollars. Other cheque-books showed me that during the many months of the building of the *Snark* I had paid him several thousand dollars. Then why in the name of common decency hadn't he tried to collect his miserable little balance instead of libelling the *Snark?* I thrust my hands into my pockets, and in one pocket encountered the cheque-book and the dater and the pen, and in the other pocket the gold money and the paper money. There was the wherewithal to settle his pitiful account a few score of times and over—why hadn't he given me a chance? There was no explanation; it was merely the inconceivable and monstrous.

To make the matter worse, the *Snark* had been libelled late Saturday afternoon; and though I sent lawyers and agents all over Oakland and San Francisco, neither United States judge, nor United States marshal, nor Mr. Sellers, nor Mr. Sellers' attorney, nor anybody could be found. They were all out of town for the weekend. And so the *Snark* did not sail Sunday morning at eleven.

The little old man was still in charge, and he said no. And Charmian and I walked out on an opposite wharf and took consolation in the *Snark's* wonderful bow and thought of all the gales and typhoons it would proudly punch.

"A bourgeois trick," I said to Charmian, speaking of Mr. Sellers and his libel; "a petty trader's panic. But never mind; our troubles will cease when once we are away from this and out on the wide ocean."

And in the end we sailed away, on Tuesday morning, April 23, 1907. We started rather lame, I confess. We had to hoist anchor by hand, because the power transmission was a wreck. Also, what remained of our seventy-horse-power engine was lashed down for ballast on the bottom of the *Snark*. But what of such things? They could be fixed in Honolulu, and in the meantime think of the magnificent rest of the boat! It is true, the engine in the launch wouldn't run, and the life-boat leaked like a sieve; but then they weren't the *Snark*; they were mere appurtenances. The things that counted were the water-tight bulkheads, the solid planking without butts, the bath-room devices—they were the *Snark*. And then there was, greatest of all, that noble, wind-punching bow.

We sailed out through the Golden Gate and set our course south toward that part of the Pacific where we could hope to pick up with the north-east trades. And right away things began to happen. I had calculated that youth was the stuff for a voyage like that of the *Snark,* and I had taken three youths—the engineer, the cook, and the cabin-boy. My calculation was only two-thirds OFF; I had forgotten to calculate on seasick youth, and I had two of them, the cook and the cabin boy. They immediately took to their bunks, and that was the end of their usefulness for a week to come. It will be understood, from the foregoing, that we did not have the hot meals we might have had, nor were things kept clean and orderly down below. But it did not matter very much anyway, for we quickly discovered that our box of oranges had at some time been frozen; that our box of apples was mushy and spoiling; that the crate of cabbages, spoiled before it was ever delivered to us, had to go overboard instanter; that kerosene had been spilled on the carrots, and that the turnips were woody and the beets rotten, while the kindling was dead wood that wouldn't burn, and the coal, delivered in rotten potato-sacks, had spilled all over the deck and was washing through the scuppers.

But what did it matter? Such things were mere accessories. There was the boat—she was all right, wasn't she? I strolled along the deck and in one minute counted fourteen butts in the beautiful planking ordered specially from Puget Sound in order that there should be no butts in it. Also, that deck leaked, and it leaked badly. It drowned Roscoe out of his bunk and ruined the tools in the engine-room, to say nothing of the provisions it ruined in the galley. Also, the sides of the *Snark* leaked, and the bottom leaked, and we had to pump her every day to keep her afloat. The floor of the galley is a couple of feet above the inside bottom of the *Snark;* and yet I have stood on the floor of the galley, trying to snatch a cold bite, and been wet to the knees by the water churning around inside four hours after the last pumping.

Then those magnificent water-tight compartments that cost so much time and money—well, they weren't water-tight after all. The water moved free as the air from one compartment to another; furthermore, a strong smell of gasolene from the after compartment leads me to suspect that someone or more of the half-dozen tanks there stored have sprung a leak. The tanks leak, and they are not hermetically sealed in their compartment. Then there was the bath-room with its pumps and levers and sea-valves—it went out of commission inside the first twenty hours. Powerful iron levers broke off short in one's hand when one tried to pump with them. The bathroom was the swiftest wreck of any portion of the *Snark*.

And the iron-work on the *Snark,* no matter what its source, proved to be mush. For instance, the bed-plate of the engine came from New York, and it was mush; so were the casting and gears for the windlass that came from San Francisco. And finally, there was the wrought iron used in the rigging, that carried away in all directions when the first strains were put upon it. Wrought iron, mind you, and it snapped like macaroni.

A gooseneck on the gaff of the mainsail broke short off. We replaced it with the gooseneck from the gaff of the storm trysail, and the second gooseneck broke short off inside fifteen minutes of use, and, mind you, it had been taken from the gaff of the storm trysail, upon which we would have depended in time of storm. At the present moment the *Snark* trails her mainsail like a broken wing, the gooseneck being replaced by a rough lashing. We'll see if we can get honest iron in Honolulu.

Man had betrayed us and sent us to sea in a sieve, but the Lord must have loved us, for we had calm weather in which to learn that we must pump every day in order to keep afloat, and that more trust could be placed in a wooden toothpick than in the most massive piece of iron to be found aboard. As the staunchness and the strength of the *Snark* went glimmering, Charmian and I pinned our faith more and more to the *Snark*'s wonderful bow. There was nothing else left to pin to. It was all inconceivable and monstrous, we knew, but that bow, at least, was rational. And then, one evening, we started to heave to.

How shall I describe it? First of all, for the benefit of the tyro, let me explain that heaving to is that sea manoeuvre which, by means of short and balanced canvas, compels a vessel to ride bow-on to wind and sea. When the wind is too strong, or the sea is too high, a vessel of the size of the *Snark* can heave to with ease, whereupon there is no more work to do on deck. Nobody needs to steer. The lookout is superfluous. All hands can go below and sleep or play whist.

Well, it was blowing half of a small summer gale, when I told Roscoe we'd heave to. Night was coming on. I had been steering nearly all day, and all hands on deck (Roscoe and Bert and Charmian) were tired, while all hands below were seasick. It happened that we had already put two reefs in the big mainsail. The flying-jib and the jib were taken in, and a reef put in the fore-staysail. The mizzen was also taken in. About this time the flying jib-boom buried itself in a sea and broke short off. I started to put the wheel down in order to heave to. The *Snark* at the moment was rolling in the trough. She continued rolling in the trough. I put the spokes down harder and harder. She never budged from the trough. (The trough, gentle reader, is the most dangerous position all in which to lay a vessel.) I put the wheel hard down, and still the *Snark* rolled in the trough. Eight points was the nearest I could get her to the wind. I had Roscoe and Bert come in on the main-sheet. The *Snark* rolled on in the trough, now putting her rail under on one side and now under on the other side.

Again the inconceivable and monstrous was showing its grizzly head. It was grotesque, impossible. I refused to believe it. Under double-reefed mainsail and single-reefed staysail the *Snark* refused to heave to. We flattened the mainsail down. It did not alter the *Snark's* course a tenth of a degree. We slacked the mainsail off with no more result. We set a storm trysail on the mizzen, and took in the mainsail. No change. The *Snark* roiled on in the trough. That beautiful bow of hers refused to come up and face the wind.

Next we took in the reefed staysail. Thus, the only bit of canvas left on her was the storm trysail on the mizzen. If anything would bring her bow up to the wind, that would. Maybe you won't believe me when I say it failed, but I do say it failed. And I say it failed because I saw it fail, and not because I believe it failed. I don't believe it did fail. It is unbelievable, and I am not telling you what I believe; I am telling you what I saw.

Now, gentle reader, what would you do if you were on a small boat, rolling in the trough of the sea, a trysail on that small boat's stern that was unable to swing the bow up into the wind? Get out the sea-anchor. It's just what we did. We had a patent one, made to order and warranted not to dive. Imagine a hoop of steel that serves to keep open the mouth of a large, conical, canvas bag, and you have a sea-anchor. Well, we made a line fast to the sea-anchor and to the bow of the *Snark,* and then dropped the sea-anchor overboard. It promptly dived. We had a tripping line on it, so we tripped the sea-anchor and hauled it in. We attached a big timber as a float, and dropped the sea-anchor over again. This time it floated. The line to the bow grew taut. The trysail on the mizzen tended to swing the bow into the wind, but, in spite of this tendency, the *Snark* calmly took that sea-anchor in her teeth, and went on ahead, dragging it after her, still in the trough of the sea. And there you are. We even took in the trysail, hoisted the full mizzen in its place, and hauled the full mizzen down flat, and the *Snark* wallowed in the trough and dragged the sea-anchor behind her. Don't believe me. I don't believe it myself. I am merely telling you what I saw.

Now I leave it to you. Who ever heard of a sailing-boat that wouldn't heave to?—that wouldn't heave to with a sea-anchor to help it? Out of my brief experience with boats I know I never did. And I stood on deck and looked on the naked face of the inconceivable and monstrous—the *Snark* that wouldn't heave to. A stormy night with broken moonlight had come on. There was a splash of wet in the air, and up to windward there was a promise of rain-squalls; and then there was the trough of the sea, cold and cruel in the moonlight, in which the *Snark* complacently rolled. And then we took in the sea-anchor and the mizzen, hoisted the reefed staysail, ran the *Snark* off before it, and went below—not to the hot meal that should have awaited us, but to skate across the slush and slime on the cabin floor, where cook and cabin-boy lay like dead men in their bunks, and to lie down in our own bunks, with our clothes on ready for a call, and to listen to the bilge-water spouting knee-high on the galley floor.

In the Bohemian Club of San Francisco there are some crack sailors. I know, because I heard them pass judgment on the *Snark* during the process of her building. They found only one vital thing the matter with her, and on this they were all agreed, namely, that she could not run. She was all right in every particular, they said, except that I'd never be able to run her before it in a stiff wind and sea. "Her lines," they explained enigmatically, "it is the fault of her lines. She simply cannot be made to run, that is all." Well, I wish I'd only had those crack sailors of the Bohemian Club on board the *Snark* the other night for them to see for themselves their one, vital, unanimous judgment absolutely reversed. Run? It is the one thing the *Snark* does to perfection. Run? She ran with a sea-anchor fast for'ard and a full mizzen flattened down aft. Run? At the present moment, as I write this, we are bowling along before it, at a six-knot clip, in the north-east trades. Quite a tidy bit of sea is running. There is nobody at the wheel, the wheel is not even lashed and is set over a half-spoke weather helm. To be precise, the wind is north-east; the *Snark*'s mizzen is furled, her mainsail is over to starboard, her head-sheets are hauled flat: and the *Snark*'s course is south-south-west. And yet there are men who have sailed the seas for forty years and who hold that no boat can run before it without being steered. They'll call me a liar when they read this; it's what they called Captain Slocum when he said the same of his Spray.

As regards the future of the *Snark* I'm all at sea. I don't know. If I had the money or the credit, I'd build another *Snark* that WOULD heave to. But I am at the end of my resources. I've got to put up with the present *Snark* or quit—and I can't quit. So I guess I'll have to try to get along with heaving the *Snark* to stern first. I am waiting for the next gale to see how it will work. I think it can be done. It all depends on how her stern takes the seas. And who knows but that some wild morning on the China Sea, some gray-beard skipper will stare, rub his incredulous eyes and stare again, at the spectacle of a weird, small craft very much like the *Snark*, hove to stern-first and riding out the gale?

P.S. On my return to California after the voyage, I learned that the *Snark* was forty-three feet on the water-line instead of forty-five. This was due to the fact that the builder was not on speaking terms with the tape-line or two-foot rule.

Chapter 12
Adventure

No, adventure is not dead, and in spite of the steam engine and of Thomas Cook & Son. When the announcement of the contemplated voyage of the *Snark* was made, young men of "roving disposition" proved to be legion, and young women as well—to say nothing of the elderly men and women who volunteered for the voyage. Why, among my personal friends there were at least half a dozen who regretted their recent or imminent marriages; and there was one marriage I know of that almost failed to come off because of the *Snark*.

Every mail to me was burdened with the letters of applicants who were suffocating in the "man-stifled towns," and it soon dawned upon me that a twentieth century Ulysses required a corps of stenographers to clear his correspondence before setting sail. No, adventure is certainly not dead—not while one receives letters that begin:

> "There is no doubt that when you read this soul-plea from a female stranger in New York City," etc.; and wherein one learns, a little farther on, that this female stranger weighs only ninety pounds, wants to be cabin-boy, and "yearns to see the countries of the world."

The possession of a "passionate fondness for geography," was the way one applicant expressed the wander-lust that was in him; while another wrote, "I am cursed with an eternal yearning to be always on the move, consequently this letter to you." But best of all was the fellow who said he wanted to come because his feet itched.

There were a few who wrote anonymously, suggesting names of friends and giving said friends' qualifications; but to me there was a hint of something sinister in such proceedings, and I went no further in the matter.

With two or three exceptions, all the hundreds that volunteered for my crew were very much in earnest. Many of them sent their photographs. Ninety percent offered to work in any capacity, and ninety-nine percent offered to work without salary. "Contemplating your voyage on the *Snark*," said one, "and notwithstanding its attendant dangers, to accompany you (in any capacity whatever) would be the climax of my ambitions." Which reminds me of the young fellow who was "seventeen years old and ambicious," and who, at the end of his letter, earnestly requested "but please do not let this git into the papers or magazines." Quite different was the one who said, "I would be willing to work like hell and not demand pay." Almost all of them wanted me to telegraph, at their expense, my acceptance of their services; and quite a number offered to put up a bond to guarantee their appearance on sailing date.

Some were rather vague in their own minds concerning the work to be done on the *Snark*; as, for instance, the one who wrote: "I am taking the liberty of writing you this note to find out if there would be any possibility of my going with you as one of the crew of your boat to make sketches and illustrations." Several, unaware of the needful work on a small craft like the *Snark*, offered to serve, as one of them phrased it, "as assistant in filing materials collected for books and novels." That's what one gets for being prolific.

"Let me give my qualifications for the job," wrote one. "I am an orphan living with my uncle, who is a hot revolutionary socialist and who says a man without the red blood of adventure is an animated dish-rag." Said another: "I can swim some, though I don't know any of the new strokes. But what is more important than strokes, the water is a friend of mine." "If I was put alone in a sail-boat, I could get her anywhere I wanted to go," was the qualification of a third—and a better qualification than the one that follows, "I have also watched the fish-boats unload." But possibly the prize should go to this one, who very subtly conveys his deep knowledge of the world and life by saying: "My age, in years, is twenty-two."

Then there were the simple straight-out, homely, and unadorned letters of young boys, lacking in the felicities of expression, it is true, but desiring greatly to make the voyage. These were the hardest of all to decline, and each time I declined one it seemed as if I had struck Youth a slap in the face. They were so earnest, these boys, they wanted so much to go. "I am sixteen but large for my age," said one; and another, "Seventeen but large and healthy." "I am as strong at least as the average boy of my size," said an evident weakling. "Not afraid of any kind of work," was what many said, while one in particular, to lure me no doubt by inexpensiveness, wrote: "I can pay my way to the Pacific coast, so that part would probably be acceptable to you." "Going around the world is THE ONE THING I want to do," said one, and it seemed to be the one thing that a few hundred wanted to do. "I have no one who cares whether I go or not," was the pathetic note sounded by another. One had sent his photograph, and speaking of it, said, "I'm a homely-looking sort of a chap, but looks don't always count." And I am confident that the lad who wrote the following would have turned out all right: "My age is 19 years, but I am rather small and consequently won't take up much room, but I'm tough as the devil." And there was one thirteen-year-old applicant that Charmian and I fell in love with, and it nearly broke our hearts to refuse him.

But it must not be imagined that most of my volunteers were boys; on the contrary, boys constituted a very small proportion. There were men and women from every walk in life. Physicians, surgeons, and dentists offered in large numbers to come along, and, like all the professional men, offered to come without pay, to serve in any capacity, and to pay, even, for the privilege of so serving.

There was no end of compositors and reporters who wanted to come, to say nothing of experienced valets, chefs, and stewards. Civil engineers were keen on the voyage; "lady" companions galore cropped up for Charmian; while I was deluged with the applications of would-be private secretaries. Many high school and university students yearned for the voyage, and every trade in the working class developed a few applicants, the machinists, electricians, and engineers being especially strong on the trip. I was surprised at the number, who, in musty law offices, heard the call of adventure; and I was more than surprised by the number of elderly and retired sea captains who were still thralls to the sea. Several young fellows, with millions coming to them later on, were wild for the adventure, as were also several county superintendents of schools.

Fathers and sons wanted to come, and many men with their wives, to say nothing of the young woman stenographer who wrote: "Write immediately if you need me. I shall bring my typewriter on the first train." But the best of all is the following—observe the delicate way in which he worked in his wife: "I thought I would drop you a line of inquiry as to the possibility of making the trip with you, am 24 years of age, married and broke, and a trip of that kind would be just what we are looking for."

Come to think of it, for the average man it must be fairly difficult to write an honest letter of self-recommendation. One of my correspondents was so stumped that he began his letter with the words, "This is a hard task"; and, after vainly trying to describe his good points, he wound up with, "It is a hard job writing about one's self." Nevertheless, there was one who gave himself a most glowing and lengthy character, and in conclusion stated that he had greatly enjoyed writing it.

"But suppose this: your cabin-boy could run your engine, could repair it when out of order. Suppose he could take his turn at the wheel, could do any carpenter or machinist work. Suppose he is strong, healthy, and willing to work. Would you not rather have him than a kid that gets seasick and can't do anything but wash dishes?" It was letters of this sort that I hated to decline. The writer of it, self-taught in English, had been only two years in the United States, and, as he said, "I am not wishing to go with you to earn my living, but I wish to learn and see." At the time of writing to me he was a designer for one of the big motor manufacturing companies; he had been to sea quite a bit, and had been used all his life to the handling of small boats.

"I have a good position, but it matters not so with me as I prefer travelling," wrote another. "As to salary, look at me, and if I am worth a dollar or two, all right, and if I am not, nothing said. As to my honesty and character, I shall be pleased to show you my employers. Never drink, no tobacco, but to be honest, I myself, after a little more experience, want to do a little writing."

"I can assure you that I am eminently respectable, but find other respectable people tiresome." The man who wrote the foregoing certainly had me guessing, and I am still wondering whether or not he'd have found me tiresome, or what the deuce he did mean.

"I have seen better days than what I am passing through to-day," wrote an old salt, "but I have seen them a great deal worse also."

But the willingness to sacrifice on the part of the man who wrote the following was so touching that I could not accept: "I have a father, a mother, brothers and sisters, dear friends and a lucrative position, and yet I will sacrifice all to become one of your crew."

Another volunteer I could never have accepted was the finicky young fellow who, to show me how necessary it was that I should give him a chance, pointed out that "to go in the ordinary boat, be it schooner or steamer, would be impracticable, for I would have to mix among and live with the ordinary type of seamen, which as a rule is not a clean sort of life."

Then there was the young fellow of twenty-six, who had "run through the gamut of human emotions," and had "done everything from cooking to attending Stanford University," and who, at the present writing, was "A vaquero on a fifty-five-thousand-acre range." Quite in contrast was the modesty of the one who said, "I am not aware of possessing any particular qualities that would be likely to recommend me to your consideration. But should you be impressed, you might consider it worth a few minutes' time to answer. Otherwise, there's always work at the trade. Not expecting, but hoping, I remain, etc."

But I have held my head in both my hands ever since, trying to figure out the intellectual kinship between myself and the one who wrote: "Long before I knew of you, I had mixed political economy and history and deducted therefrom many of your conclusions in concrete."

Here, in its way, is one of the best, as it is the briefest, that I received: "If any of the present company signed on for cruise happens to get cold feet and you need one more who understands boating, engines, etc., would like to hear from you, etc." Here is another brief one: "Point blank, would like to have the job of cabin-boy on your trip around the world, or any other job on board. Am nineteen years old, weigh one hundred and forty pounds, and am an American."

And here is a good one from a man a "little over five feet long": "When I read about your manly plan of sailing around the world in a small boat with Mrs. London, I was so much rejoiced that I felt I was planning it myself, and I thought to write you about filling either position of cook or cabin-boy myself, but for some reason I did not do it, and I came to Denver from Oakland to join my friend's business last month, but everything is worse and unfavourable. But fortunately you have postponed your departure on account of the great earthquake, so I finally decided to propose you to let me fill either of the positions. I am not very strong, being a man of a little over five feet long, although I am of sound health and capability."

"I think I can add to your outfit an additional method of utilizing the power of the wind," wrote a well-wisher, "which, while not interfering with ordinary sails in light breezes, will enable you to use the whole force of the wind in its mightiest blows, so that even when its force is so great that you may have to take in every inch of canvas used in the ordinary way, you may carry the fullest spread with my method. With my attachment your craft could not be UPSET."

The foregoing letter was written in San Francisco under the date of April 16, 1906. And two days later, on April 18, came the Great Earthquake. And that's why I've got it in for that earthquake, for it made a refugee out of the man who wrote the letter, and prevented us from ever getting together.

Many of my brother socialists objected to my making the cruise, of which the following is typical: "The Socialist Cause and the millions of oppressed victims of Capitalism has a right and claim upon your life and services. If, however, you persist, then, when you swallow the last mouthful of salt chuck you can hold before sinking, remember that we at least protested."

One wanderer over the world who "could, if opportunity afforded, recount many unusual scenes and events," spent several pages ardently trying to get to the point of his letter, and at last achieved the following: "Still I am neglecting the point I set out to write you about. So will say at once that it has been stated in print that you and one or two others are going to take a cruise around the world a little fifty-or sixty-foot boat. I therefore cannot get myself to think that a man of your attainments and experience would attempt such a proceeding, which is nothing less than courting death in that way. And even if you were to escape for some time, your whole Person, and those with you would be bruised from the ceaseless motion of a craft of the above size, even if she were padded, a thing not usual at sea." Thank you, kind friend, thank you for that qualification, "a thing not usual at sea." Nor is this friend ignorant of the sea. As he says of himself, "I am not a land-lubber, and I have sailed every sea and ocean." And he winds up his letter with: "Although not wishing to offend, it would be madness to take any woman outside the bay even, in such a craft."

And yet, at the moment of writing this, Charmian is in her stateroom at the typewriter, Martin is cooking dinner, Tochigi is setting the table, Roscoe and Bert are caulking the deck, and the *Snark* is steering herself some five knots an hour in a rattling good sea—and the *Snark* is not padded, either.

"Seeing a piece in the paper about your intended trip, would like to know if you would like a good crew, as there is six of us boys all good sailor men, with good discharges from the Navy and Merchant Service, all true Americans, all between the ages of 20 and 22, and at present are employed as riggers at the Union Iron Works, and would like very much to sail with you."—It was letters like this that made me regret the boat was not larger.

And here writes the one woman in all the world—outside of Charmian—for the cruise: "If you have not succeeded in getting a cook I would like very much to take the trip in that capacity. I am a woman of fifty, healthy and capable, and can do the work for the small company that compose the crew of the *Snark*. I am a very good cook and a very good sailor and something of a traveller, and the length of the voyage, if of ten years' duration, would suit me better than one. References, etc."

Some day, when I have made a lot of money, I'm going to build a big ship, with room in it for a thousand volunteers. They will have to do all the work of navigating that boat around the world, or they'll stay at home. I believe that they'll work the boat around the world, for I know that Adventure is not dead. I know Adventure is not dead because I have had a long and intimate correspondence with Adventure.

Chapter 13
Finding One's Way About

"But," our friends objected, "how dare you go to sea without a navigator on board? You're not a navigator, are you?"

I had to confess that I was not a navigator, that I had never looked through a sextant in my life, and that I doubted if I could tell a sextant from a nautical almanac. And when they asked if Roscoe was a navigator, I shook my head. Roscoe resented this. He had glanced at the "Epitome," bought for our voyage, knew how to use logarithm tables, had seen a sextant at some time, and, what of this and of his seafaring ancestry, he concluded that he did know navigation. But Roscoe was wrong, I still insist. When a young boy he came from Maine to California by way of the Isthmus of Panama, and that was the only time in his life that he was out of sight of land. He had never gone to a school of navigation, nor passed an examination in the same; nor had he sailed the deep sea and learned the art from some other navigator. He was a San Francisco Bay yachtsman, where land is always only several miles away and the art of navigation is never employed.

So the *Snark* started on her long voyage without a navigator. We beat through the Golden Gate on April 23, and headed for the Hawaiian Islands, twenty-one hundred sea-miles away as the gull flies. And the outcome was our justification. We arrived. And we arrived, furthermore, without any trouble, as you shall see; that is, without any trouble to amount to anything. To begin with, Roscoe tackled the navigating. He had the theory all right, but it was the first time he had ever applied it, as was evidenced by the erratic behaviour of the *Snark*. Not but what the *Snark* was perfectly steady on the sea; the pranks she cut were on the chart. On a day with a light breeze she would make a jump on the chart that advertised "a wet sail and a flowing sheet," and on a day when she just raced over the ocean, she scarcely changed her position on the chart. Now when one's boat has logged six knots for twenty-four consecutive hours, it is incontestable that she has covered one hundred and forty-four miles of ocean. The ocean was all right, and so was the patent log; as for speed, one saw it with his own eyes. Therefore the thing that was not all right was the figuring that refused to boost the *Snark* along over the chart. Not that this happened every day, but that it did happen. And it was perfectly proper and no more than was to be expected from a first attempt at applying a theory.

The acquisition of the knowledge of navigation has a strange effect on the minds of men. The average navigator speaks of navigation with deep respect. To the layman navigation is a deed and awful mystery, which feeling has been generated in him by the deep and awful respect for navigation that the layman has seen displayed by navigators. I have known frank, ingenuous, and modest young men, open as the day, to learn navigation and at once betray secretiveness, reserve, and self-importance as if they had achieved some tremendous intellectual attainment. The average navigator impresses the layman as a priest of some holy rite. With bated breath, the amateur yachtsman navigator invites one in to look at his chronometer. And so it was that our friends suffered such apprehension at our sailing without a navigator.

During the building of the *Snark*, Roscoe and I had an agreement, something like this: "I'll furnish the books and instruments," I said, "and do you study up navigation now. I'll be too busy to do any studying. Then, when we get to sea, you can teach me what you have learned." Roscoe was delighted. Furthermore, Roscoe was as frank and ingenuous and modest as the young men I have described. But when we got out to sea and he began to practise the holy rite, while I looked on admiringly, a change, subtle and distinctive, marked his bearing. When he shot the sun at noon, the glow of achievement wrapped him in lambent flame. When he went below, figured out his observation, and then returned on deck and announced our latitude and longitude, there was an authoritative ring in his voice that was new to all of us. But that was not the worst of it. He became filled with incommunicable information. And the more he discovered the reasons for the erratic jumps of the *Snark* over the chart, and the less the *Snark* jumped, the more incommunicable and holy and awful became his information. My mild suggestions that it was about time that I began to learn, met with no hearty response, with no offers on his part to help me. He displayed not the slightest intention of living up to our agreement.

Now this was not Roscoe's fault; he could not help it. He had merely gone the way of all the men who learned navigation before him. By an understandable and forgivable confusion of values, plus a loss of orientation, he felt weighted by responsibility, and experienced the possession of power that was like unto that of a god. All his life Roscoe had lived on land, and therefore in sight of land. Being constantly in sight of land, with landmarks to guide him, he had managed, with occasional difficulties, to steer his body around and about the earth. Now he found himself on the sea, wide-stretching, bounded only by the eternal circle of the sky. This circle looked always the same. There were no landmarks. The sun rose to the east and set to the west and the stars wheeled through the night. But who may look at the sun or the stars and say, "My place on the face of the earth at the present moment is four and three-quarter miles to the west of Jones's Cash Store of Smithersville"? or "I know where I am now, for the Little Dipper informs me that Boston is three miles away on the second turning to the right"? And yet that was precisely what Roscoe did. That he was astounded by the achievement, is putting it mildly. He stood in reverential awe of himself; he had performed a miraculous feat. The act of finding himself on the face of the waters became a rite, and he felt himself a superior being to the rest of us who knew not this rite and were dependent on him for being shepherded across the heaving and limitless waste, the briny highroad that connects the continents and whereon there are no mile-stones. So, with the sextant he made obeisance to the sun-god, he consulted ancient tomes and tables of magic characters, muttered prayers in a strange tongue that sounded like INDEXERRORPARALLAXREFRACTION, made cabalistic signs on paper, added and carried one, and then, on a piece of holy script called the Grail—I mean the Chart—he placed his finger on a certain space conspicuous for its blankness and said, "Here we are." When we looked at the blank space and asked, "And where is that?" he answered in the cipher-code of the higher priesthood, "31-15-47 north, 133-5-30 west." And we said "Oh," and felt mighty small.

So I aver, it was not Roscoe's fault. He was like unto a god, and he carried us in the hollow of his hand across the blank spaces on the chart. I experienced a great respect for Roscoe; this respect grew so profound that had he commanded, "Kneel down and worship me," I know that I should have flopped down on the deck and yammered. But, one day, there came a still small thought to me that said: "This is not a god; this is Roscoe, a mere man like myself. What he has done, I can do. Who taught him? Himself. Go you and do likewise—be your own teacher." And right there Roscoe crashed, and he was high priest of the *Snark* no longer. I invaded the sanctuary and demanded the ancient tomes and magic tables, also the prayer-wheel—the sextant, I mean.

And now, in simple language. I shall describe how I taught myself navigation. One whole afternoon I sat in the cockpit, steering with one hand and studying logarithms with the other. Two afternoons, two hours each, I studied the general theory of navigation and the particular process of taking a meridian altitude. Then I took the sextant, worked out the index error, and shot the sun. The figuring from the data of this observation was child's play. In the "Epitome" and the "Nautical Almanac" were scores of cunning tables, all worked out by mathematicians and astronomers. It was like using interest tables and lightning-calculator tables such as you all know. The mystery was mystery no longer. I put my finger on the chart and announced that that was where we were. I was right too, or at least I was as right as Roscoe, who selected a spot a quarter of a mile away from mine. Even he was willing to split the distance with me. I had exploded the mystery, and yet, such was the miracle of it, I was conscious of new power in me, and I felt the thrill and tickle of pride. And when Martin asked me, in the same humble and respectful way I had previously asked Roscoe, as to where we were, it was with exaltation and spiritual chest-throwing that I answered in the cipher-code of the higher priesthood and heard Martin's self-abasing and worshipful "Oh." As for Charmian, I felt that in a new way I had proved my right to her; and I was aware of another feeling, namely, that she was a most fortunate woman to have a man like me.

I couldn't help it. I tell it as a vindication of Roscoe and all the other navigators. The poison of power was working in me. I was not as other men—most other men; I knew what they did not know,— the mystery of the heavens, that pointed out the way across the deep. And the taste of power I had received drove me on. I steered at the wheel long hours with one hand, and studied mystery with the other. By the end of the week, teaching myself, I was able to do diverse things. For instance, I shot the North Star, at night, of course; got its altitude, corrected for index error, dip, etc., and found our latitude. And this latitude agreed with the latitude of the previous noon corrected by dead reckoning up to that moment. Proud? Well, I was even prouder with my next miracle. I was going to turn in at nine o'clock. I worked out the problem, self-instructed, and learned what star of the first magnitude would be passing the meridian around half-past eight. This star proved to be Alpha Crucis. I had never heard of the star before. I looked it up on the star map. It was one of the stars of the Southern Cross. What! thought I; have we been sailing with the Southern Cross in the sky of nights and never known it? Dolts that we are! Gudgeons and moles! I couldn't believe it. I went over the problem again, and verified it. Charmian had the wheel from eight till ten that evening. I told her to keep her eyes open and look due south for the Southern Cross. And when the stars came out, there shone the Southern Cross low on the horizon. Proud? No medicine man nor high priest was ever prouder. Furthermore, with the prayer-wheel I shot Alpha Crucis and from its altitude worked out our latitude. And still furthermore, I shot the North Star, too, and it agreed with what had been told me by the Southern Cross. Proud? Why, the language of the stars was mine, and I listened and heard them telling me my way over the deep.

Proud? I was a worker of miracles. I forgot how easily I had taught myself from the printed page. I forgot that all the work (and a tremendous work, too) had been done by the masterminds before me, the astronomers and mathematicians, who had discovered and elaborated the whole science of navigation and made the tables in the "Epitome." I remembered only the everlasting miracle of it—that I had listened to the voices of the stars and been told my place upon the highway of the sea. Charmian did not know, Martin did not know, Tochigi, the cabin-boy, did not know. But I told them. I was God's messenger. I stood between them and infinity. I translated the high celestial speech into terms of their ordinary understanding. We were heaven-directed, and it was I who could read the sign-post of the sky!—I! I!

And now, in a cooler moment, I hasten to blab the whole simplicity of it, to blab on Roscoe and the other navigators and the rest of the priesthood, all for fear that I may become even as they, secretive, immodest, and inflated with self-esteem. And I want to say this now: any young fellow with ordinary gray matter, ordinary education, and with the slightest trace of the student-mind, can get the books, and charts, and instruments and teach himself navigation. Now I must not be misunderstood. Seamanship is an entirely different matter. It is not learned in a day, nor in many days; it requires years. Also, navigating by dead reckoning requires long study and practice. But navigating by observations of the sun, moon, and stars, thanks to the astronomers and mathematicians, is child's play. Any average young fellow can teach himself in a week. And yet again I must not be misunderstood. I do not mean to say that at the end of a week a young fellow could take charge of a fifteen-thousand-ton steamer, driving twenty knots an hour through the brine, racing from land to land, fair weather and foul, clear sky or cloudy, steering by degrees on the compass card and making landfalls with most amazing precision. But what I do mean is just this: the average young fellow I have described can get into a staunch sail-boat and put out across the ocean, without knowing anything about navigation, and at the end of the week he will know enough to know where he is on the chart. He will be able to take a meridian observation with fair accuracy, and from that observation, with ten minutes of figuring, work out his latitude and longitude. And, carrying neither freight nor passengers, being under no press to reach his destination, he can jog comfortably along, and if at any time he doubts his own navigation and fears an imminent landfall, he can heave to all night and proceed in the morning.

Joshua Slocum sailed around the world a few years ago in a thirty-seven-foot boat all by himself. I shall never forget, in his narrative of the voyage, where he heartily endorsed the idea of young men, in similar small boats, making similar voyage. I promptly endorsed his idea, and so heartily that I took my wife along. While it certainly makes a Cook's tour look like thirty cents, on top of that, amid on top of the fun and pleasure, it is a splendid education for a young man—oh, not a mere education in the things of the world outside, of lands, and peoples, and climates, but an education in the world inside, an education in one's self, a chance to learn one's own self, to get on speaking terms with one's soul. Then there is the training and the disciplining of it. First, naturally, the young fellow will learn his limitations; and next, inevitably, he will proceed to press back those limitations. And he cannot escape returning from such a voyage a bigger and better man. And as for sport, it is a king's sport, taking one's self around the world, doing it with one's own hands, depending on no one but one's self, and at the end, back at the starting-point, contemplating with inner vision the planet rushing through space, and saying, "I did it; with my own hands I did it. I went clear around that whirling sphere, and I can travel alone, without any nurse of a sea-captain to guide my steps across the seas. I may not fly to other stars, but of this star I myself am master."

As I write these lines I lift my eyes and look seaward. I am on the beach of Waikiki on the island of Oahu. Far, in the azure sky, the trade-wind clouds drift low over the blue-green turquoise of the deep sea. Nearer, the sea is emerald and light olive-green.

Then comes the reef, where the water is all slaty purple flecked with red. Still nearer are brighter greens and tans, lying in alternate stripes and showing where sandbeds lie between the living coral banks. Through and over and out of these wonderful colours tumbles and thunders a magnificent surf. As I say, I lift my eyes to all this, and through the white crest of a breaker suddenly appears a dark figure, erect, a man-fish or a sea-god, on the very forward face of the crest where the top falls over and down, driving in toward shore, buried to his loins in smoking spray, caught up by the sea and flung landward, bodily, a quarter of a mile. It is a Kanaka on a surf-board. And I know that when I have finished these lines I shall be out in that riot of colour and pounding surf, trying to bit those breakers even as he, and failing as he never failed, but living life as the best of us may live it. And the picture of that coloured sea and that flying sea-god Kanaka becomes another reason for the young man to go west, and farther west, beyond the Baths of Sunset, and still west till he arrives home again.

But to return. Please do not think that I already know it all. I know only the rudiments of navigation. There is a vast deal yet for me to learn. On the *Snark* there is a score of fascinating books on navigation waiting for me. There is the danger-angle of Lecky, there is the line of Sumner, which, when you know least of all where you are, shows most conclusively where you are, and where you are not. There are dozens and dozens of methods of finding one's location on the deep, and one can work years before he masters it all in all its fineness.

Even in the little we did learn there were slips that accounted for the apparently antic behaviour of the *Snark*. On Thursday, May 16, for instance, the trade wind failed us. During the twenty-four hours that ended Friday at noon, by dead reckoning we had not sailed twenty miles. Yet here are our positions, at noon, for the two days, worked out from our observations:

Thursday: 20 degrees 57 minutes 9 seconds N
152 degrees 40 minutes 30 seconds W

Friday: 21 degrees 15 minutes 33 seconds N
154 degrees 12 minutes W

The difference between the two positions was something like eighty miles. Yet we knew we had not travelled twenty miles. Now our figuring was all right. We went over it several times. What was wrong was the observations we had taken. To take a correct observation requires practice and skill, and especially so on a small craft like the *Snark*. The violently moving boat and the closeness of the observer's eye to the surface of the water are to blame. A big wave that lifts up a mile off is liable to steal the horizon away.

But in our particular case there was another perturbing factor. The sun, in its annual march north through the heavens, was increasing its declination. On the 19th parallel of north latitude in the middle of May the sun is nearly overhead. The angle of arc was between eighty-eight and eighty-nine degrees. Had it been ninety degrees it would have been straight overhead. It was on another day that we learned a few things about taking the altitude of the almost perpendicular sun. Roscoe started in drawing the sun down to the eastern horizon, and he stayed by that point of the compass despite the fact that the sun would pass the meridian to the south. I, on the other hand, started in to draw the sun down to south-east and strayed away to the south-west. You see, we were teaching ourselves. As a result, at twenty-five minutes past twelve by the ship's time, I called twelve o'clock by the sun. Now this signified that we had changed our location on the face of the world by twenty-five minutes, which was equal to something like six degrees of longitude, or three hundred and fifty miles. This showed the *Snark* had travelled fifteen knots per hour for twenty-four consecutive hours—and we had never noticed it! It was absurd and grotesque. But Roscoe, still looking east, averred that it was not yet twelve o'clock. He was bent on giving us a twenty-knot clip. Then we began to train our sextants rather wildly all around the horizon, and wherever we looked, there was the sun, puzzlingly close to the sky-line, sometimes above it and sometimes below it. In one direction the sun was proclaiming morning, in another direction it was proclaiming afternoon. The sun was all right—we knew that; therefore we were all wrong. And the rest of the afternoon we spent in the cockpit reading up the matter in the books and finding out what was wrong. We missed the observation that day, but we didn't the next. We had learned.

And we learned well, better than for a while we thought we had. At the beginning of the second dog-watch one evening, Charmian and I sat down on the forecastle-head for a rubber of cribbage. Chancing to glance ahead, I saw cloud-capped mountains rising from the sea. We were rejoiced at the sight of land, but I was in despair over our navigation. I thought we had learned something, yet our position at noon, plus what we had run since, did not put us within a hundred miles of land. But there was the land, fading away before our eyes in the fires of sunset. The land was all right. There was no disputing it. Therefore our navigation was all wrong. But it wasn't. That land we saw was the summit of Haleakala, the House of the Sun, the greatest extinct volcano in the world. It towered ten thousand feet above the sea, and it was all of a hundred miles away. We sailed all night at a seven-knot clip, and in the morning the House of the Sun was still before us, and it took a few more hours of sailing to bring it abreast of us. "That island is Maui," we said, verifying by the chart. "That next island sticking out is Molokai, where the lepers are. And the island next to that is Oahu. There is Makapuu Head now. We'll be in Honolulu to-morrow. Our navigation is all right."

Chapter 14
First Landfall

"It will not be so monotonous at sea," I promised my fellow-voyagers on the *Snark*. "The sea is filled with life. It is so populous that every day something new is happening. Almost as soon as we pass through the Golden Gate and head south we'll pick up with the flying fish. We'll be having them fried for breakfast. We'll be catching bonita and dolphin, and spearing porpoises from the bowsprit. And then there are the sharks—sharks without end."

We passed through the Golden Gate and headed south. We dropped the mountains of California beneath the horizon, and daily the surf grew warmer. But there were no flying fish, no bonita and dolphin. The ocean was bereft of life. Never had I sailed on so forsaken a sea. Always, before, in the same latitudes, had I encountered flying fish.

"Never mind," I said. "Wait till we get off the coast of Southern California. Then we'll pick up the flying fish."

We came abreast of Southern California, abreast of the Peninsula of Lower California, abreast of the coast of Mexico; and there were no flying fish. Nor was there anything else. No life moved. As the days went by the absence of life became almost uncanny.

"Never mind," I said. "When we do pick up with the flying fish we'll pick up with everything else. The flying fish is the staff of life for all the other breeds. Everything will come in a bunch when we find the flying fish."

When I should have headed the *Snark* south-west for Hawaii, I still held her south. I was going to find those flying fish. Finally the time came when, if I wanted to go to Honolulu, I should have headed the *Snark* due west, instead of which I kept her south. Not until latitude 19 degrees did we encounter the first flying fish. He was very much alone. I saw him. Five other pairs of eager eyes scanned the sea all day, but never saw another. So sparse were the flying fish that nearly a week more elapsed before the last one on board saw his first flying fish. As for the dolphin, bonita, porpoise, and all the other hordes of life—there weren't any.

Not even a shark broke surface with his ominous dorsal fin. Bert took a dip daily under the bowsprit, hanging on to the stays and dragging his body through the water. And daily he canvassed the project of letting go and having a decent swim. I did my best to dissuade him. But with him I had lost all standing as an authority on sea life.

"If there are sharks," he demanded, "why don't they show up?"

I assured him that if he really did let go and have a swim the sharks would promptly appear. This was a bluff on my part. I didn't believe it. It lasted as a deterrent for two days. The third day the wind fell calm, and it was pretty hot. The *Snark* was moving a knot an hour. Bert dropped down under the bowsprit and let go. And now behold the perversity of things. We had sailed across two thousand miles and more of ocean and had met with no sharks. Within five minutes after Bert finished his swim, the fin of a shark was cutting the surface in circles around the *Snark*.

There was something wrong about that shark. It bothered me. It had no right to be there in that deserted ocean. The more I thought about it, the more incomprehensible it became. But two hours later we sighted land and the mystery was cleared up. He had come to us from the land, and not from the uninhabited deep. He had presaged the landfall. He was the messenger of the land.

Twenty-seven days out from San Francisco we arrived at the island of Oahu, Territory of Hawaii. In the early morning we drifted around Diamond Head into full view of Honolulu; and then the ocean burst suddenly into life. Flying fish cleaved the air in glittering squadrons. In five minutes we saw more of them than during the whole voyage. Other fish, large ones, of various sorts, leaped into the air. There was life everywhere, on sea and shore. We could see the masts and funnels of the shipping in the harbour, the hotels and bathers along the beach at Waikiki, the smoke rising from the dwelling-houses high up on the volcanic slopes of the Punch Bowl and Tantalus. The custom-house tug was racing toward us and a big school of porpoises got under our bow and began cutting the most ridiculous capers. The port doctor's launch came charging out at us, and a big sea turtle broke the surface with his back and took a look at us. Never was there such a burgeoning of life. Strange faces were on our decks, strange voices were speaking, and copies of that very morning's newspaper, with cable reports from all the world, were thrust before our eyes. Incidentally, we read that the *Snark* and all hands had been lost at sea, and that she had been a very unseaworthy craft anyway. And while we read this information a wireless message was being received by the congressional party on the summit of Haleakala announcing the safe arrival of the *Snark*.

It was the *Snark's* first landfall—and such a landfall! For twenty-seven days we had been on the deserted deep, and it was pretty hard to realize that there was so much life in the world. We were made dizzy by it. We could not take it all in at once. We were like awakened Rip Van Winkles, and it seemed to us that we were dreaming. On one side the azure sea lapped across the horizon into the azure sky; on the other side the sea lifted itself into great breakers of emerald that fell in a snowy smother upon a white coral beach. Beyond the beach, green plantations of sugar-cane undulated gently upward to steeper slopes, which, in turn, became jagged volcanic crests, drenched with tropic showers and capped by stupendous masses of trade-wind clouds. At any rate, it was a most beautiful dream. The *Snark* turned and headed directly in toward the emerald surf, till it lifted and thundered on either hand; and on either hand, scarce a biscuit-toss away, the reef showed its long teeth, pale green and menacing.

Abruptly the land itself, in a riot of olive-greens of a thousand hues, reached out its arms and folded the *Snark* in. There was no perilous passage through the reef, no emerald surf and azure sea—nothing but a warm soft land, a motionless lagoon, and tiny beaches on which swam dark-skinned tropic children. The sea had disappeared. The *Snark's* anchor rumbled the chain through the hawse-pipe, and we lay without movement on a "lineless, level floor." It was all so beautiful and strange that we could not accept it as real. On the chart this place was called Pearl Harbour, but we called it Dream Harbour.

A launch came off to us; in it were members of the Hawaiian Yacht Club, come to greet us and make us welcome, with true Hawaiian hospitality, to all they had. They were ordinary men, flesh and blood and all the rest; but they did not tend to break our dreaming. Our last memories of men were of United States marshals and of panicky little merchants with rusty dollars for souls, who, in a reeking atmosphere of soot and coal-dust, laid grimy hands upon the *Snark* and held her back from her world adventure. But these men who came to meet us were clean men. A healthy tan was on their cheeks, and their eyes were not dazzled and bespectacled from gazing overmuch at glittering dollar-heaps. No, they merely verified the dream. They clinched it with their unsmirched souls.

So we went ashore with them across a level flashing sea to the wonderful green land. We landed on a tiny wharf, and the dream became more insistent; for know that for twenty-seven days we had been rocking across the ocean on the tiny *Snark*. Not once in all those twenty-seven days had we known a moment's rest, a moment's cessation from movement. This ceaseless movement had become ingrained. Body and brain we had rocked and rolled so long that when we climbed out on the tiny wharf kept on rocking and rolling. This, naturally, we attributed to the wharf. It was projected psychology. I spraddled along the wharf and nearly fell into the water. I glanced at Charmian, and the way she walked made me sad. The wharf had all the seeming of a ship's deck. It lifted, tilted, heaved and sank; and since there were no handrails on it, it kept Charmian and me busy avoiding falling in. I never saw such a preposterous little wharf. Whenever I watched it closely, it refused to roll; but as soon as I took my attention off from it, away it went, just like the *Snark*. Once, I caught it in the act, just as it upended, and I looked down the length of it for two hundred feet, and for all the world it was like the deck of a ship ducking into a huge head-sea.

At last, however, supported by our hosts, we negotiated the wharf and gained the land. But the land was no better. The very first thing it did was to tilt up on one side, and far as the eye could see I watched it tilt, clear to its jagged, volcanic backbone, and I saw the clouds above tilt, too. This was no stable, firm-founded land, else it would not cut such capers. It was like all the rest of our landfall, unreal. It was a dream. At any moment, like shifting vapour, it might dissolve away. The thought entered my head that perhaps it was my fault, that my head was swimming or that something I had eaten had disagreed with me. But I glanced at Charmian and her sad walk, and even as I glanced I saw her stagger and bump into the yachtsman by whose side she walked. I spoke to her, and she complained about the antic behaviour of the land.

We walked across a spacious, wonderful lawn and down an avenue of royal palms, and across more wonderful lawn in the gracious shade of stately trees. The air was filled with the songs of birds and was heavy with rich warm fragrances—wafture from great lilies, and blazing blossoms of hibiscus, and other strange gorgeous tropic flowers. The dream was becoming almost impossibly beautiful to us who for so long had seen naught but the restless, salty sea. Charmian reached out her hand and clung to me—for support against the ineffable beauty of it, thought I. But no. As I supported her I braced my legs, while the flowers and lawns reeled and swung around me. It was like an earthquake, only it quickly passed without doing any harm. It was fairly difficult to catch the land playing these tricks. As long as I kept my mind on it, nothing happened. But as soon as my attention was distracted, away it went, the whole panorama, swinging and heaving and tilting at all sorts of angles. Once, however, I turned my head suddenly and caught that stately line of royal palms swinging in a great arc across the sky. But it stopped, just as soon as I caught it, and became a placid dream again.

Next we came to a house of coolness, with great sweeping veranda, where lotus-eaters might dwell. Windows and doors were wide open to the breeze, and the songs and fragrances blew lazily in and out. The walls were hung with tapa-cloths. Couches with grass-woven covers invited everywhere, and there was a grand piano, that played, I was sure, nothing more exciting than lullabies. Servants—Japanese maids in native costume—drifted around and about, noiselessly, like butterflies. Everything was preternaturally cool. Here was no blazing down of a tropic sun upon an unshrinking sea. It was too good to be true. But it was not real. It was a dream-dwelling. I knew, for I turned suddenly and caught the grand piano cavorting in a spacious corner of the room. I did not say anything, for just then we were being received by a gracious woman, a beautiful Madonna, clad in flowing white and shod with sandals, who greeted us as though she had known us always.

We sat at table on the lotus-eating veranda, served by the butterfly maids, and ate strange foods and partook of a nectar called poi. But the dream threatened to dissolve. It shimmered and trembled like an iridescent bubble about to break. I was just glancing out at the green grass and stately trees and blossoms of hibiscus, when suddenly I felt the table move. The table, and the Madonna across from me, and the veranda of the lotus-eaters, the scarlet hibiscus, the greensward and the trees—all lifted and tilted before my eyes, and heaved and sank down into the trough of a monstrous sea. I gripped my chair convulsively and held on. I had a feeling that I was holding on to the dream as well as the chair. I should not have been surprised had the sea rushed in and drowned all that fairyland and had I found myself at the wheel of the *Snark* just looking up casually from the study of logarithms. But the dream persisted. I looked covertly at the Madonna and her husband. They evidenced no perturbation. The dishes had not moved upon the table. The hibiscus and trees and grass were still there. Nothing had changed. I partook of more nectar, and the dream was more real than ever.

"Will you have some iced tea?" asked the Madonna; and then her side of the table sank down gently and I said yes to her at an angle of forty-five degrees.

"Speaking of sharks," said her husband, "up at Niihau there was a man—" And at that moment the table lifted and heaved, and I gazed upward at him at an angle of forty-five degrees.

So the luncheon went on, and I was glad that I did not have to bear the affliction of watching Charmian walk. Suddenly, however, a mysterious word of fear broke from the lips of the lotus-eaters. "Ah, ah," thought I, "now the dream goes glimmering." I clutched the chair desperately, resolved to drag back to the reality of the *Snark* some tangible vestige of this lotus land. I felt the whole dream lurching and pulling to be gone. Just then the mysterious word of fear was repeated. It sounded like REPORTERS. I looked and saw three of them coming across the lawn. Oh, blessed reporters! Then the dream was indisputably real after all. I glanced out across the shining water and saw the *Snark* at anchor, and I remembered that I had sailed in her from San Francisco to Hawaii, and that this was Pearl Harbour, and that even then I was acknowledging introductions and saying, in reply to the first question, "Yes, we had delightful weather all the way down."

Chapter 15
Royal Sport

That is what it is, a royal sport for the natural kings of earth. The grass grows right down to the water at Waikiki Beach, and within fifty feet of the everlasting sea. The trees also grow down to the salty edge of things, and one sits in their shade and looks seaward at a majestic surf thundering in on the beach to one's very feet. Half a mile out, where is the reef, the white-headed combers thrust suddenly skyward out of the placid turquoise-blue and come rolling in to shore. One after another they come, a mile long, with smoking crests, the white battalions of the infinite army of the sea. And one sits and listens to the perpetual roar, and watches the unending procession, and feels tiny and fragile before this tremendous force expressing itself in fury and foam and sound. Indeed, one feels microscopically small, and the thought that one may wrestle with this sea raises in one's imagination a thrill of apprehension, almost of fear. Why, they are a mile long, these bull-mouthed monsters, and they weigh a thousand tons, and they charge in to shore faster than a man can run. What chance? No chance at all, is the verdict of the shrinking ego; and one sits, and looks, and listens, and thinks the grass and the shade are a pretty good place in which to be.

And suddenly, out there where a big smoker lifts skyward, rising like a sea-god from out of the welter of spume and churning white, on the giddy, toppling, overhanging and downfalling, precarious crest appears the dark head of a man. Swiftly he rises through the rushing white. His black shoulders, his chest, his loins, his limbs—all is abruptly projected on one's vision. Where but the moment before was only the wide desolation and invincible roar, is now a man, erect, full-statured, not struggling frantically in that wild movement, not buried and crushed and buffeted by those mighty monsters, but standing above them all, calm and superb, poised on the giddy summit, his feet buried in the churning foam, the salt smoke rising to his knees, and all the rest of him in the free air and flashing sunlight, and he is flying through the air, flying forward, flying fast as the surge on which he stands. He is a Mercury—a brown Mercury. His heels are winged, and in them is the swiftness of the sea. In truth, from out of the sea he has leaped upon the back of the sea, and he is riding the sea that roars and bellows and cannot shake him from its back. But no frantic outreaching and balancing is his. He is impassive, motionless as a statue carved suddenly by some miracle out of the sea's depth from which he rose. And straight on toward shore he flies on his winged heels and the white crest of the breaker. There is a wild burst of foam, a long tumultuous rushing sound as the breaker falls futile and spent on the beach at your feet; and there, at your feet steps calmly ashore a Kanaka, burnt, golden and brown by the tropic sun. Several minutes ago he was a speck a quarter of a mile away. He has "bitted the bull-mouthed breaker" and ridden it in, and the pride in the feat shows in the carriage of his magnificent body as he glances for a moment carelessly at you who sit in the shade of the shore. He is a Kanaka—and more, he is a man, a member of the kingly species that has mastered matter and the brutes and lorded it over creation.

And one sits and thinks of Tristram's last wrestle with the sea on that fatal morning; and one thinks further, to the fact that that Kanaka has done what Tristram never did, and that he knows a joy of the sea that Tristram never knew. And still further one thinks. It is all very well, sitting here in cool shade of the beach, but you are a man, one of the kingly species, and what that Kanaka can do, you can do yourself. Go to. Strip off your clothes that are a nuisance in this mellow clime. Get in and wrestle with the sea; wing your heels with the skill and power that reside in you; bit the sea's breakers, master them, and ride upon their backs as a king should.

And that is how it came about that I tackled surf-riding. And now that I have tackled it, more than ever do I hold it to be a royal sport. But first let me explain the physics of it. A wave is a communicated agitation. The water that composes the body of a wave does not move. If it did, when a stone is thrown into a pond and the ripples spread away in an ever widening circle, there would appear at the centre an ever increasing hole. No, the water that composes the body of a wave is stationary. Thus, you may watch a particular portion of the ocean's surface and you will see the sane water rise and fall a thousand times to the agitation communicated by a thousand successive waves. Now imagine this communicated agitation moving shoreward. As the bottom shoals, the lower portion of the wave strikes land first and is stopped. But water is fluid, and the upper portion has not struck anything, wherefore it keeps on communicating its agitation, keeps on going. And when the top of the wave keeps on going, while the bottom of it lags behind, something is bound to happen. The bottom of the wave drops out from under and the top of the wave falls over, forward, and down, curling and cresting and roaring as it does so. It is the bottom of a wave striking against the top of the land that is the cause of all surfs.

But the transformation from a smooth undulation to a breaker is not abrupt except where the bottom shoals abruptly. Say the bottom shoals gradually for from quarter of a mile to a mile, then an equal distance will be occupied by the transformation. Such a bottom is that off the beach of Waikiki, and it produces a splendid surf-riding surf. One leaps upon the back of a breaker just as it begins to break, and stays on it as it continues to break all the way in to shore.

And now to the particular physics of surf-riding. Get out on a flat board, six feet long, two feet wide, and roughly oval in shape. Lie down upon it like a small boy on a coaster and paddle with your hands out to deep water, where the waves begin to crest. Lie out there quietly on the board. Sea after sea breaks before, behind, and under and over you, and rushes in to shore, leaving you behind. When a wave crests, it gets steeper. Imagine yourself, on your hoard, on the face of that steep slope. If it stood still, you would slide down just as a boy slides down a hill on his coaster. "But," you object, "the wave doesn't stand still." Very true, but the water composing the wave stands still, and there you have the secret. If ever you start sliding down the face of that wave, you'll keep on sliding and you'll never reach the bottom. Please don't laugh. The face of that wave may be only six feet, yet you can slide down it a quarter of a mile, or half a mile, and not reach the bottom. For, see, since a wave is only a communicated agitation or impetus, and since the water that composes a wave is changing every instant, new water is rising into the wave as fast as the wave travels. You slide down this new water, and yet remain in your old position on the wave, sliding down the still newer water that is rising and forming the wave. You slide precisely as fast as the wave travels. If it travels fifteen miles an hour, you slide fifteen miles an hour. Between you and shore stretches a quarter of mile of water. As the wave travels, this water obligingly heaps itself into the wave, gravity does the rest, and down you go, sliding the whole length of it. If you still cherish the notion, while sliding, that the water is moving with you, thrust your arms into it and attempt to paddle; you will find that you have to be remarkably quick to get a stroke, for that water is dropping astern just as fast as you are rushing ahead.

And now for another phase of the physics of surf-riding. All rules have their exceptions. It is true that the water in a wave does not travel forward. But there is what may be called the send of the sea. The water in the overtoppling crest does move forward, as you will speedily realize if you are slapped in the face by it, or if you are caught under it and are pounded by one mighty blow down under the surface panting and gasping for half a minute. The water in the top of a wave rests upon the water in the bottom of the wave. But when the bottom of the wave strikes the land, it stops, while the top goes on. It no longer has the bottom of the wave to hold it up. Where was solid water beneath it, is now air, and for the first time it feels the grip of gravity, and down it falls, at the same time being torn asunder from the lagging bottom of the wave and flung forward. And it is because of this that riding a surf-board is something more than a mere placid sliding down a hill. In truth, one is caught up and hurled shoreward as by some Titan's hand.

I deserted the cool shade, put on a swimming suit, and got hold of a surf-board. It was too small a board. But I didn't know, and nobody told me. I joined some little Kanaka boys in shallow water, where the breakers were well spent and small—a regular kindergarten school. I watched the little Kanaka boys. When a likely-looking breaker came along, they flopped upon their stomachs on their boards, kicked like mad with their feet, and rode the breaker in to the beach. I tried to emulate them. I watched them, tried to do everything that they did, and failed utterly. The breaker swept past, and I was not on it. I tried again and again. I kicked twice as madly as they did, and failed. Half a dozen would be around. We would all leap on our boards in front of a good breaker. Away our feet would churn like the stern-wheels of river steamboats, and away the little rascals would scoot while I remained in disgrace behind.

I tried for a solid hour, and not one wave could I persuade to boost me shoreward. And then arrived a friend, Alexander Hume

Ford, a globe trotter by profession, bent ever on the pursuit of sensation. And he had found it at Waikiki. Heading for Australia, he had stopped off for a week to find out if there were any thrills in surf-riding, and he had become wedded to it. He had been at it every day for a month and could not yet see any symptoms of the fascination lessening on him. He spoke with authority.

"Get off that board," he said. "Chuck it away at once. Look at the way you're trying to ride it. If ever the nose of that board hits bottom, you'll be disembowelled. Here, take my board. It's a man's size."

I am always humble when confronted by knowledge. Ford knew. He showed me how properly to mount his board. Then he waited for a good breaker, gave me a shove at the right moment, and started me in. Ah, delicious moment when I felt that breaker grip and fling me.

On I dashed, a hundred and fifty feet, and subsided with the breaker on the sand. From that moment I was lost. I waded back to Ford with his board. It was a large one, several inches thick, and weighed all of seventy-five pounds. He gave me advice, much of it. He had had no one to teach him, and all that he had laboriously learned in several weeks he communicated to me in half an hour. I really learned by proxy. And inside of half an hour I was able to start myself and ride in. I did it time after time, and Ford applauded and advised. For instance, he told me to get just so far forward on the board and no farther. But I must have got some farther, for as I came charging in to land, that miserable board poked its nose down to bottom, stopped abruptly, and turned a somersault, at the same time violently severing our relations. I was tossed through the air like a chip and buried ignominiously under the downfalling breaker. And I realized that if it hadn't been for Ford, I'd have been disembowelled. That particular risk is part of the sport, Ford says. Maybe he'll have it happen to him before he leaves Waikiki, and then, I feel confident, his yearning for sensation will be satisfied for a time.

When all is said and done, it is my steadfast belief that homicide is worse than suicide, especially if, in the former case, it is a woman. Ford saved me from being a homicide. "Imagine your legs are a rudder," he said. "Hold them close together, and steer with them." A few minutes later I came charging in on a comber. As I neared the beach, there, in the water, up to her waist, dead in front of me, appeared a woman. How was I to stop that comber on whose back I was? It looked like a dead woman. The board weighed seventy-five pounds, I weighed a hundred and sixty-five. The added weight had a velocity of fifteen miles per hour. The board and I constituted a projectile. I leave it to the physicists to figure out the force of the impact upon that poor, tender woman. And then I remembered my guardian angel, Ford. "Steer with your legs!" rang through my brain. I steered with my legs, I steered sharply, abruptly, with all my legs and with all my might. The board sheered around broadside on the crest. Many things happened simultaneously. The wave gave me a passing buffet, a light tap as the taps of waves go, but a tap sufficient to knock me off the board and smash me down through the rushing water to bottom, with which I came in violent collision and upon which I was rolled over and over. I got my head out for a breath of air and then gained my feet. There stood the woman before me. I felt like a hero. I had saved her life. And she laughed at me. It was not hysteria. She had never dreamed of her danger. Anyway, I solaced myself, it was not I but Ford that saved her, and I didn't have to feel like a hero. And besides, that leg-steering was great. In a few minutes more of practice I was able to thread my way in and out past several bathers and to remain on top my breaker instead of going under it.

"To-morrow," Ford said, "I am going to take you out into the blue water."

I looked seaward where he pointed, and saw the great smoking combers that made the breakers I had been riding look like ripples. I don't know what I might have said had I not recollected just then that I was one of a kingly species. So all that I did say was, "All right, I'll tackle them to-morrow."

The water that rolls in on Waikiki Beach is just the same as the water that laves the shores of all the Hawaiian Islands; and in ways, especially from the swimmer's standpoint, it is wonderful water. It is cool enough to be comfortable, while it is warm enough to permit a swimmer to stay in all day without experiencing a chill. Under the sun or the stars, at high noon or at midnight, in midwinter or in midsummer, it does not matter when, it is always the same temperature—not too warm, not too cold, just right. It is wonderful water, salt as old ocean itself, pure and crystal-clear. When the nature of the water is considered, it is not so remarkable after all that the Kanakas are one of the most expert of swimming races.

So it was, next morning, when Ford came along, that I plunged into the wonderful water for a swim of indeterminate length. Astride of our surf-boards, or, rather, flat down upon them on our stomachs, we paddled out through the kindergarten where the little Kanaka boys were at play. Soon we were out in deep water where the big smokers came roaring in. The mere struggle with them, facing them and paddling seaward over them and through them, was sport enough in itself. One had to have his wits about him, for it was a battle in which mighty blows were struck, on one side, and in which cunning was used on the other side—a struggle between insensate force and intelligence. I soon learned a bit. When a breaker curled over my head, for a swift instant I could see the light of day through its emerald body; then down would go my head, and I would clutch the board with all my strength. Then would come the blow, and to the onlooker on shore I would be blotted out. In reality the board and I have passed through the crest and emerged in the respite of the other side. I should not recommend those smashing blows to an invalid or delicate person. There is weight behind them, and the impact of the driven water is like a sandblast. Sometimes one passes through half a dozen combers in quick succession, and it is just about that time that he is liable to discover new merits in the stable land and new reasons for being on shore.

Out there in the midst of such a succession of big smoky ones, a third man was added to our party, one Freeth. Shaking the water from my eyes as I emerged from one wave and peered ahead to see what the next one looked like, I saw him tearing in on the back of it, standing upright on his board, carelessly poised, a young god bronzed with sunburn. We went through the wave on the back of which he rode. Ford called to him. He turned an airspring from his wave, rescued his board from its maw, paddled over to us and joined Ford in showing me things. One thing in particular I learned from Freeth, namely, how to encounter the occasional breaker of exceptional size that rolled in. Such breakers were really ferocious, and it was unsafe to meet them on top of the board. But Freeth showed me, so that whenever I saw one of that calibre rolling down on me, I slid off the rear end of the board and dropped down beneath the surface, my arms over my head and holding the board. Thus, if the wave ripped the board out of my hands and tried to strike me with it (a common trick of such waves), there would be a cushion of water a foot or more in depth, between my head and the blow. When the wave passed, I climbed upon the board and paddled on. Many men have been terribly injured, I learn, by being struck by their boards.

The whole method of surf-riding and surf-fighting, learned, is one of non-resistance. Dodge the blow that is struck at you. Dive through the wave that is trying to slap you in the face. Sink down, feet first, deep under the surface, and let the big smoker that is trying to smash you go by far overhead. Never be rigid. Relax. Yield yourself to the waters that are ripping and tearing at you. When the undertow catches you and drags you seaward along the bottom, don't struggle against it. If you do, you are liable to be drowned, for it is stronger than you. Yield yourself to that undertow. Swim with it, not against it, and you will find the pressure removed. And, swimming with it, fooling it so that it does not hold you, swim upward at the same time. It will be no trouble at all to reach the surface.

The man who wants to learn surf-riding must be a strong swimmer, and he must be used to going under the water. After that, fair strength and common-sense are all that is required. The force of the big comber is rather unexpected. There are mix-ups in which board and rider are torn apart and separated by several hundred feet. The surf-rider must take care of himself. No matter how many riders swim out with him, he cannot depend upon any of them for aid. The fancied security I had in the presence of Ford and Freeth made me forget that it was my first swim out in deep water among the big ones. I recollected, however, and rather suddenly, for a big wave came in, and away went the two men on its back all the way to shore. I could have been drowned a dozen different ways before they got back to me.

One slides down the face of a breaker on his surf-board, but he has to get started to sliding. Board and rider must be moving shoreward at a good rate before the wave overtakes them. When you see the wave coming that you want to ride in, you turn tail to it and paddle shoreward with all your strength, using what is called the windmill stroke. This is a sort of spurt performed immediately in front of the wave. If the board is going fast enough, the wave accelerates it, and the board begins its quarter-of-a-mile slide.

I shall never forget the first big wave I caught out there in the deep water. I saw it coming, turned my back on it and paddled for dear life. Faster and faster my board went, till it seemed my arms would drop off. What was happening behind me I could not tell. One cannot look behind and paddle the windmill stroke. I heard the crest of the wave hissing and churning, and then my board was lifted and flung forward. I scarcely knew what happened the first half-minute. Though I kept my eyes open, I could not see anything, for I was buried in the rushing white of the crest. But I did not mind. I was chiefly conscious of ecstatic bliss at having caught the wave. At the end, of the half-minute, however, I began to see things, and to breathe. I saw that three feet of the nose of my board was clear out of water and riding on the air. I shifted my weight forward, and made the nose come down. Then I lay, quite at rest in the midst of the wild movement, and watched the shore and the bathers on the beach grow distinct. I didn't cover quite a quarter of a mile on that wave, because, to prevent the board from diving, I shifted my weight back, but shifted it too far and fell down the rear slope of the wave.

It was my second day at surf-riding, and I was quite proud of myself. I stayed out there four hours, and when it was over, I was resolved that on the morrow I'd come in standing up. But that resolution paved a distant place. On the morrow I was in bed. I was not sick, but I was very unhappy, and I was in bed. When describing the wonderful water of Hawaii I forgot to describe the wonderful sun of Hawaii. It is a tropic sun, and, furthermore, in the first part of June, it is an overhead sun. It is also an insidious, deceitful sun. For the first time in my life I was sunburned unawares. My arms, shoulders, and back had been burned many times in the past and were tough; but not so my legs. And for four hours I had exposed the tender backs of my legs, at right-angles, to that perpendicular Hawaiian sun. It was not until after I got ashore that I discovered the sun had touched me. Sunburn at first is merely warm; after that it grows intense and the blisters come out. Also, the joints, where the skin wrinkles, refuse to bend. That is why I spent the next day in bed. I couldn't walk. And that is why, to-day, I am writing this in bed. It is easier to than not to. But to-morrow, ah, to-morrow, I shall be out in that wonderful water, and I shall come in standing up, even as Ford and Freeth. And if I fail to-morrow, I shall do it the next day, or the next. Upon one thing I am resolved: the *Snark* shall not sail from Honolulu until I, too, wing my heels with the swiftness of the sea, and become a sun-burned, skin-peeling Mercury.

Chapter 16
Lepers of Molokai

When the *Snark* sailed along the windward coast of Molokai, on her way to Honolulu, I looked at the chart, then pointed to a low-lying peninsula backed by a tremendous cliff varying from two to four thousand feet in height, and said: "The pit of hell, the most cursed place on Earth." I should have been shocked, if, at that moment, I could have caught a vision of myself a month later, ashore in the most cursed place on Earth and having a disgracefully good time along with eight hundred of the lepers who were likewise having a good time. Their good time was not disgraceful; but mine was, for in the midst of so much misery it was not meet for me to have a good time. That is the way I felt about it, and my only excuse is that I couldn't help having a good time.

For instance, in the afternoon of the Fourth of July all the lepers gathered at the race-track for the sports. I had wandered away from the Superintendent and the physicians in order to get a snapshot of the finish of one of the races. It was an interesting race, and partisanship ran high. Three horses were entered, one ridden by a Chinese, one by an Hawaiian, and one by a Portuguese boy. All three riders were lepers; so were the judges and the crowd. The race was twice around the track. The Chinese and the Hawaiian got away together and rode neck and neck, the Portuguese boy toiling along two hundred feet behind. Around they went in the same positions. Halfway around on the second and final lap the Chinese pulled away and got one length ahead of the Hawaiian. At the same time the Portuguese boy was beginning to crawl up. But it looked hopeless. The crowd went wild. All the lepers were passionate lovers of horseflesh. The Portuguese boy crawled nearer and nearer. I went wild, too. They were on the home stretch. The Portuguese boy passed the Hawaiian. There was a thunder of hoofs, a rush of the three horses bunched together, the jockeys plying their whips, and every last onlooker bursting his throat, or hers, with shouts and yells. Nearer, nearer, inch by inch, the Portuguese boy crept up, and passed, yes, passed, winning by a head from the Chinese. I came to myself in a group of lepers. They were yelling, tossing their hats, and dancing around like fiends. So was I. When I came to I was waving my hat and murmuring ecstatically: "By golly, the boy wins! The boy wins!"

I tried to check myself. I assured myself that I was witnessing one of the horrors of Molokai, and that it was shameful for me, under such circumstances, to be so light-hearted and light-headed.

But it was no use. The next event was a donkey-race, and it was just starting; so was the fun. The last donkey in was to win the race, and what complicated the affair was that no rider rode his own donkey. They rode one another's donkeys, the result of which was that each man strove to make the donkey he rode beat his own donkey ridden by someone else, Naturally, only men possessing very slow or extremely obstreperous donkeys had entered them for the race. One donkey had been trained to tuck in its legs and lie down whenever its rider touched its sides with his heels. Some donkeys strove to turn around and come back; others developed a penchant for the side of the track, where they stuck their heads over the railing and stopped; while all of them dawdled. Halfway around the track one donkey got into an argument with its rider. When all the rest of the donkeys had crossed the wire, that particular donkey was still arguing. He won the race, though his rider lost it and came in on foot. And all the while nearly a thousand lepers were laughing uproariously at the fun. Anybody in my place would have joined with them in having a good time.

All the foregoing is by way of preamble to the statement that the horrors of Molokai, as they have been painted in the past, do not exist. The Settlement has been written up repeatedly by sensationalists, and usually by sensationalists who have never laid eyes on it. Of course, leprosy is leprosy, and it is a terrible thing; but so much that is lurid has been written about Molokai that neither the lepers, nor those who devote their lives to them, have received a fair deal. Here is a case in point. A newspaper writer, who, of course, had never been near the Settlement, vividly described Superintendent McVeigh, crouching in a grass hut and being besieged nightly by starving lepers on their knees, wailing for food. This hair-raising account was copied by the press all over the United States and was the cause of many indignant and protesting editorials. Well, I lived and slept for five days in Mr. McVeigh's "grass hut" (which was a comfortable wooden cottage, by the way; and there isn't a grass house in the whole Settlement), and I heard the lepers wailing for food—only the wailing was peculiarly harmonious and rhythmic, and it was accompanied by the music of stringed instruments, violins, guitars, ukuleles, and banjos. Also, the wailing was of various sorts. The leper brass band wailed, and two singing societies wailed, and lastly a quintet of excellent voices wailed. So much for a lie that should never have been printed. The wailing was the serenade which the glee clubs always give Mr. McVeigh when he returns from a trip to Honolulu.

Leprosy is not so contagious as is imagined. I went for a week's visit to the Settlement, and I took my wife along—all of which would not have happened had we had any apprehension of contracting the disease. Nor did we wear long, gauntleted gloves and keep apart from the lepers. On the contrary, we mingled freely with them, and before we left, knew scores of them by sight and name. The precautions of simple cleanliness seem to be all that is necessary. On returning to their own houses, after having been among and handling lepers, the non-lepers, such as the physicians and the superintendent, merely wash their faces and hands with mildly antiseptic soap and change their coats.

That a leper is unclean, however, should be insisted upon; and the segregation of lepers, from what little is known of the disease, should be rigidly maintained. On the other hand, the awful horror with which the leper has been regarded in the past, and the frightful treatment he has received, have been unnecessary and cruel. In order to dispel some of the popular misapprehensions of leprosy, I want to tell something of the relations between the lepers and non-lepers as I observed them at Molokai. On the morning after our arrival Charmian and I attended a shoot of the Kalaupapa Rifle Club, and caught our first glimpse of the democracy of affliction and alleviation that obtains. The club was just beginning a prize shoot for a cup put up by Mr. McVeigh, who is also a member of the club, as also are Dr. Goodhue and Dr. Hollmann, the resident physicians (who, by the way, live in the Settlement with their wives). All about us, in the shooting booth, were the lepers. Lepers and non-lepers were using the same guns, and all were rubbing shoulders in the confined space. The majority of the lepers were Hawaiians. Sitting beside me on a bench was a Norwegian. Directly in front of me, in the stand, was an American, a veteran of the Civil War, who had fought on the Confederate side. He was sixty-five years of age, but that did not prevent him from running up a good score. Strapping Hawaiian policemen, lepers, khaki-clad, were also shooting, as were Portuguese, Chinese, and kokuas—the latter are native helpers in the Settlement who are non-lepers. And on the afternoon that Charmian and I climbed the two-thousand-foot pali and looked our last upon the Settlement, the superintendent, the doctors, and the mixture of nationalities and of diseased and non-diseased were all engaged in an exciting baseball game.

Not so was the leper and his greatly misunderstood and feared disease treated during the middle ages in Europe. At that time the leper was considered legally and politically dead. He was placed in a funeral procession and led to the church, where the burial service was read over him by the officiating clergyman. Then a spadeful of earth was dropped upon his chest and he was dead-living dead. While this rigorous treatment was largely unnecessary, nevertheless, one thing was learned by it. Leprosy was unknown in Europe until it was introduced by the returning Crusaders, whereupon it spread slowly until it had seized upon large numbers of the people. Obviously, it was a disease that could be contracted by contact. It was a contagion, and it was equally obvious that it could be eradicated by segregation. Terrible and monstrous as was the treatment of the leper in those days, the great lesson of segregation was learned. By its means leprosy was stamped out.

And by the same means leprosy is even now decreasing in the Hawaiian Islands. But the segregation of the lepers on Molokai is not the horrible nightmare that has been so often exploited by YELLOW writers. In the first place, the leper is not torn ruthlessly from his family. When a suspect is discovered, he is invited by the Board of Health to come to the Kalihi receiving station at Honolulu. His fare and all expenses are paid for him. He is first passed upon by microscopical examination by the bacteriologist of the Board of Health. If the bacillus leprae is found, the patient is examined by the Board of Examining Physicians, five in number. If found by them to be a leper, he is so declared, which finding is later officially confirmed by the Board of Health, and the leper is ordered straight to Molokai. Furthermore, during the thorough trial that is given his case, the patient has the right to be represented by a physician whom he can select and employ for himself. Nor, after having been declared a leper, is the patient immediately rushed off to Molokai. He is given ample time, weeks, and even months, sometimes, during which he stays at Kalihi and winds up or arranges all his business affairs. At Molokai, in turn, he may be visited by his relatives, business agents, etc., though they are not permitted to eat and sleep in his house. Visitors' houses, kept "clean," are maintained for this purpose.

I saw an illustration of the thorough trial given the suspect, when I visited Kalihi with Mr. Pinkham, president of the Board of Health. The suspect was an Hawaiian, seventy years of age, who for thirty-four years had worked in Honolulu as a pressman in a printing office. The bacteriologist had decided that he was a leper, the Examining Board had been unable to make up its mind, and that day all had come out to Kalihi to make another examination.

When at Molokai, the declared leper has the privilege of re-examination, and patients are continually coming back to Honolulu for that purpose. The steamer that took me to Molokai had on board two returning lepers, both young women, one of whom had come to Honolulu to settle up some property she owned, and the other had come to Honolulu to see her sick mother. Both had remained at Kalihi for a month.

The Settlement of Molokai enjoys a far more delightful climate than even Honolulu, being situated on the windward side of the island in the path of the fresh north-east trades. The scenery is magnificent; on one side is the blue sea, on the other the wonderful wall of the pali, receding here and there into beautiful mountain valleys. Everywhere are grassy pastures over which roam the hundreds of horses which are owned by the lepers. Some of them have their own carts, rigs, and traps. In the little harbour of Kalaupapa lie fishing boats and a steam launch, all of which are privately owned and operated by lepers. Their bounds upon the sea are, of course, determined: otherwise no restriction is put upon their sea-faring. Their fish they sell to the Board of Health, and the money they receive is their own. While I was there, one night's catch was four thousand pounds.

And as these men fish, others farm. All trades are followed. One leper, a pure Hawaiian, is the boss painter. He employs eight men, and takes contracts for painting buildings from the Board of Health. He is a member of the Kalaupapa Rifle Club, where I met him, and I must confess that he was far better dressed than I. Another man, similarly situated, is the boss carpenter. Then, in addition to the Board of Health store, there are little privately owned stores, where those with shopkeeper's souls may exercise their peculiar instincts. The Assistant Superintendent, Mr. Waiamau, a finely educated and able man, is a pure Hawaiian and a leper. Mr. Bartlett, who is the present storekeeper, is an American who was in business in Honolulu before he was struck down by the disease. All that these men earn is that much in their own pockets. If they do not work, they are taken care of anyway by the territory, given food, shelter, clothes, and medical attendance. The Board of Health carries on agriculture, stock-raising, and dairying, for local use, and employment at fair wages is furnished to all that wish to work. They are not compelled to work, however, for they are the wards of the territory. For the young, and the very old, and the helpless there are homes and hospitals.

Major Lee, an American and long a marine engineer for the Inter Island Steamship Company, I met actively at work in the new steam laundry, where he was busy installing the machinery. I met him often, afterwards, and one day he said to me:

"Give us a good breeze about how we live here. For heaven's sake write us up straight. Put your foot down on this chamber-of-horrors rot and all the rest of it. We don't like being misrepresented. We've got some feelings. Just tell the world how we really are in here."

Man after man that I met in the Settlement, and woman after woman, in one way or another expressed the same sentiment. It was patent that they resented bitterly the sensational and untruthful way in which they have been exploited in the past.

In spite of the fact that they are afflicted by disease, the lepers form a happy colony, divided into two villages and numerous country and seaside homes, of nearly a thousand souls. They have six churches, a Young Men's Christian Association building, several assembly halls, a band stand, a race-track, baseball grounds, shooting ranges, an athletic club, numerous glee clubs, and two brass bands.

"They are so contented down there," Mr. Pinkham told me, "that you can't drive them away with a shot-gun."

This I later verified for myself. In January of this year, eleven of the lepers, on whom the disease, after having committed certain ravages, showed no further signs of activity, were brought back to Honolulu for re-examination. They were loath to come; and, on being asked whether or not they wanted to go free if found clean of leprosy, one and all answered, "Back to Molokai."

In the old days, before the discovery of the leprosy bacillus, a small number of men and women, suffering from various and wholly different diseases, were adjudged lepers and sent to Molokai. Years afterward they suffered great consternation when the bacteriologists declared that they were not afflicted with leprosy and never had been. They fought against being sent away from Molokai, and in one way or another, as helpers and nurses, they got jobs from the Board of Health and remained. The present jailer is one of these men. Declared to be a non-leper, he accepted, on salary, the charge of the jail, in order to escape being sent away.

At the present moment, in Honolulu, there is a bootblack. He is an American negro. Mr. McVeigh told me about him. Long ago, before the bacteriological tests, he was sent to Molokai as a leper. As a ward of the state he developed a superlative degree of independence and fomented much petty mischief. And then, one day, after having been for years a perennial source of minor annoyances, the bacteriological test was applied, and he was declared a non-leper.

"Ah, ha!" chortled Mr. McVeigh. "Now I've got you! Out you go on the next steamer and good riddance!"

But the negro didn't want to go. Immediately he married an old woman, in the last stages of leprosy, and began petitioning the

Board of Health for permission to remain and nurse his sick wife. There was no one, he said pathetically, who could take care of his poor wife as well as he could. But they saw through his game, and he was deported on the steamer and given the freedom of the world. But he preferred Molokai. Landing on the leeward side of Molokai, he sneaked down the pali one night and took up his abode in the Settlement. He was apprehended, tried and convicted of trespass, sentenced to pay a small fine, and again deported on the steamer with the warning that if he trespassed again, he would be fined one hundred dollars and be sent to prison in Honolulu. And now, when Mr. McVeigh comes up to Honolulu, the bootblack shines his shoes for him and says:

"Say, Boss, I lost a good home down there. Yes, sir, I lost a good home." Then his voice sinks to a confidential whisper as he says, "Say, Boss, can't I go back? Can't you fix it for me so as I can go back?"

He had lived nine years on Molokai, and he had had a better time there than he has ever had, before and after, on the outside.

As regards the fear of leprosy itself, nowhere in the Settlement among lepers, or non-lepers, did I see any sign of it. The chief horror of leprosy obtains in the minds of those who have never seen a leper and who do not know anything about the disease. At the hotel at Waikiki a lady expressed shuddering amazement at my having the hardihood to pay a visit to the Settlement. On talking with her I learned that she had been born in Honolulu, had lived there all her life, and had never laid eyes on a leper. That was more than I could say of myself in the United States, where the segregation of lepers is loosely enforced and where I have repeatedly seen lepers on the streets of large cities.

Leprosy is terrible, there is no getting away from that; but from what little I know of the disease and its degree of contagiousness, I would by far prefer to spend the rest of my days in Molokai than in any tuberculosis sanatorium. In every city and county hospital for poor people in the United States, or in similar institutions in other countries, sights as terrible as those in Molokai can be witnessed, and the sum total of these sights is vastly more terrible. For that matter, if it were given me to choose between being compelled to live in Molokai for the rest of my life, or in the East End of London, the East Side of New York, or the Stockyards of Chicago, I would select Molokai without debate. I would prefer one year of life in Molokai to five years of life in the above-mentioned cesspools of human degradation and misery.

In Molokai the people are happy. I shall never forget the celebration of the Fourth of July I witnessed there. At six o'clock in the morning the "horribles" were out, dressed fantastically, astride horses, mules, and donkeys (their own property), and cutting capers all over the Settlement. Two brass bands were out as well. Then there were the pa-u riders, thirty or forty of them, Hawaiian women all, superb horsewomen dressed gorgeously in the old, native riding costume, and dashing about in twos and threes and groups. In the afternoon Charmian and I stood in the judge's stand and awarded the prizes for horsemanship and costume to the pa-u riders. All about were the hundreds of lepers, with wreaths of flowers on heads and necks and shoulders, looking on and making merry. And always, over the brows of hills and across the grassy level stretches, appearing and disappearing, were the groups of men and women, gaily dressed, on galloping horses, horses and riders flower-bedecked and flower-garlanded, singing, and laughing, and riding like the wind. And as I stood in the judge's stand and looked at all this, there came to my recollection the lazar house of Havana, where I had once beheld some two hundred lepers, prisoners inside four restricted walls until they died. No, there are a few thousand places I wot of in this world over which I would select Molokai as a place of permanent residence. In the evening we went to one of the leper assembly halls, where, before a crowded audience, the singing societies contested for prizes, and where the night wound up with a dance. I have seen the Hawaiians living in the slums of Honolulu, and, having seen them, I can readily understand why the lepers, brought up from the Settlement for re-examination, shouted one and all, "Back to Molokai!"

One thing is certain. The leper in the Settlement is far better off than the leper who lies in hiding outside. Such a leper is a lonely outcast, living in constant fear of discovery and slowly and surely rotting away. The action of leprosy is not steady. It lays hold of its victim, commits a ravage, and then lies dormant for an indeterminate period. It may not commit another ravage for five years, or ten years, or forty years, and the patient may enjoy uninterrupted good health. Rarely, however, do these first ravages cease of themselves. The skilled surgeon is required, and the skilled surgeon cannot be called in for the leper who is in hiding. For instance, the first ravage may take the form of a perforating ulcer in the sole of the foot. When the bone is reached, necrosis sets in. If the leper is in hiding, he cannot be operated upon, the necrosis will continue to eat its way up the bone of the leg, and in a brief and horrible time that leper will die of gangrene or some other terrible complication. On the other hand, if that same leper is in Molokai, the surgeon will operate upon the foot, remove the ulcer, cleanse the bone, and put a complete stop to that particular ravage of the disease. A month after the operation the leper will be out riding horseback, running foot races, swimming in the breakers, or climbing the giddy sides of the valleys for mountain apples. And as has been stated before, the disease, lying dormant, may not again attack him for five, ten, or forty years.

The old horrors of leprosy go back to the conditions that obtained before the days of antiseptic surgery, and before the time when physicians like Dr. Goodhue and Dr. Hollmann went to live at the Settlement. Dr. Goodhue is the pioneer surgeon there, and too much praise cannot be given him for the noble work he has done. I spent one morning in the operating room with him and of the three operations he performed, two were on men, newcomers, who had arrived on the same steamer with me. In each case, the disease had attacked in one spot only. One had a perforating ulcer in the ankle, well advanced, and the other man was suffering from a similar affliction, well advanced, under his arm. Both cases were well advanced because the man had been on the outside and had not been treated. In each case, Dr. Goodhue put an immediate and complete stop to the ravage, and in four weeks those two men will be as well and able-bodied as they ever were in their lives. The only difference between them and you or me is that the disease is lying dormant in their bodies and may at any future time commit another ravage.

Leprosy is as old as history. References to it are found in the earliest written records. And yet to-day practically nothing more is known about it than was known then. This much was known then, namely, that it was contagious and that those afflicted by it should be segregated. The difference between then and now is that to-day the leper is more rigidly segregated and more humanely treated. But leprosy itself still remains the same awful and profound mystery. A reading of the reports of the physicians and specialists of all countries reveals the baffling nature of the disease. These leprosy specialists are unanimous on no one phase of the disease. They do not know. In the past they rashly and dogmatically generalized. They generalize no longer. The one possible generalization that can be drawn from all the investigation that has been made is that leprosy is FEEBLY CONTAGIOUS. But in what manner it is feebly contagious is not known. They have isolated the bacillus of leprosy. They can determine by bacteriological examination whether or not a person is a leper; but they are as far away as ever from knowing how that bacillus finds its entrance into the body of a non-leper. They do not know the length of time of incubation. They have tried to inoculate all sorts of animals with leprosy, and have failed.

They are baffled in the discovery of a serum wherewith to fight the disease. And in all their work, as yet, they have found no clue, no cure. Sometimes there have been blazes of hope, theories of causation and much heralded cures, but every time the darkness of failure quenched the flame. A doctor insists that the cause of leprosy is a long-continued fish diet, and he proves his theory voluminously till a physician from the highlands of India demands why the natives of that district should therefore be afflicted by leprosy when they have never eaten fish, nor all the generations of their fathers before them. A man treats a leper with a certain kind of oil or drug, announces a cure, and five, ten, or forty years afterwards the disease breaks out again. It is this trick of leprosy lying dormant in the body for indeterminate periods that is responsible for many alleged cures. But this much is certain: AS YET THERE HAS BEEN NO AUTHENTIC CASE OF A CURE.

Leprosy is FEEBLY CONTAGIOUS, but how is it contagious? An Austrian physician has inoculated himself and his assistants with leprosy and failed to catch it. But this is not conclusive, for there is the famous case of the Hawaiian murderer who had his sentence of death commuted to life imprisonment on his agreeing to be inoculated with the bacillus leprae. Some time after inoculation, leprosy made its appearance, and the man died a leper on Molokai. Nor was this conclusive, for it was discovered that at the time he was inoculated several members of his family were already suffering from the disease on Molokai. He may have contracted the disease from them, and it may have been well along in its mysterious period of incubation at the time he was officially inoculated. Then there is the case of that hero of the Church, Father Damien, who went to Molokai a clean man and died a leper. There have been many theories as to how he contracted leprosy, but nobody knows. He never knew himself. But every chance that he ran has certainly been run by a woman at present living in the Settlement; who has lived there many years; who has had five leper husbands, and had children by them; and who is to-day, as she always has been, free of the disease.

As yet no light has been shed upon the mystery of leprosy. When more is learned about the disease, a cure for it may be expected. Once an efficacious serum is discovered, and leprosy, because it is so feebly contagious, will pass away swiftly from the earth. The battle waged with it will be short and sharp. In the meantime, how to discover that serum, or some other unguessed weapon? In the present it is a serious matter. It is estimated that there are half a million lepers, not segregated, in India alone. Carnegie libraries, Rockefeller universities, and many similar benefactions are all very well; but one cannot help thinking how far a few thousands of dollars would go, say in the leper Settlement of Molokai. The residents there are accidents of fate, scapegoats to some mysterious natural law of which man knows nothing, isolated for the welfare of their fellows who else might catch the dread disease, even as they have caught it, nobody knows how. Not for their sakes merely, but for the sake of future generations, a few thousands of dollars would go far in a legitimate and scientific search after a cure for leprosy, for a serum, or for some undreamed discovery that will enable the medical world to exterminate the bacillus leprae. There's the place for your money, you philanthropists.

Chapter 17
The House of the Sun

There are hosts of people who journey like restless spirits round and about this earth in search of seascapes and landscapes and the wonders and beauties of nature. They overrun Europe in armies; they can be met in droves and herds in Florida and the West Indies, at the Pyramids, and on the slopes and summits of the Canadian and American Rockies; but in the House of the Sun they are as rare as live and wriggling dinosaurs. Haleakala is the Hawaiian name for "the House of the Sun." It is a noble dwelling, situated on the Island of Maui; but so few tourists have ever peeped into it, much less entered it, that their number may be practically reckoned as zero. Yet I venture to state that for natural beauty and wonder the nature-lover may see dissimilar things as great as Haleakala, but no greater, while he will never see elsewhere anything more beautiful or wonderful. Honolulu is six days' steaming from San Francisco; Maui is a night's run on the steamer from Honolulu; and six hours more if he is in a hurry, can bring the arvelou to Kolikoli, which is ten thousand and thirty-two feet above the sea and which stands hard by the entrance portal to the House of the Sun. Yet the tourist comes not, and Haleakala sleeps on in lonely and unseen grandeur.

Not being tourists, we of the *Snark* went to Haleakala. On the slopes of that monster mountain there is a cattle ranch of some fifty thousand acres, where we spent the night at an altitude of two thousand feet. The next morning it was boots and saddles, and with cow-boys and pack-horses we climbed to Ukulele, a mountain ranch-house, the altitude of which, fifty-five hundred feet, gives a severely temperate climate, compelling blankets at night and a roaring fireplace in the living-room. Ukulele, by the way, is the Hawaiian for "jumping flea" as it is also the Hawaiian for a certain musical instrument that may be likened to a young guitar. It is my opinion that the mountain ranch-house was named after the young guitar. We were not in a hurry, and we spent the day at Ukulele, learnedly discussing altitudes and barometers and shaking our particular barometer whenever any one's argument stood in need of demonstration. Our barometer was the most graciously acquiescent instrument I have ever seen. Also, we gathered mountain raspberries, large as hen's eggs and larger, gazed up the pasture-covered lava slopes to the summit of Haleakala, forty-five hundred feet above us, and looked down upon a mighty battle of the clouds that was being fought beneath us, ourselves in the bright sunshine.

Every day and every day this unending battle goes on. Ukiukiu is the name of the trade-wind that comes raging down out of the north-east and hurls itself upon Haleakala. Now Haleakala is so bulky and tall that it turns the north-east trade-wind aside on either hand, so that in the lee of Haleakala no trade-wind blows at all. On the contrary, the wind blows in the counter direction, in the teeth of the north-east trade. This wind is called Naulu. And day and night and always Ukiukiu and Naulu strive with each other, advancing, retreating, flanking, curving, curling, and turning and twisting, the conflict made visible by the cloud-masses plucked from the heavens and hurled back and forth in squadrons, battalions, armies, and great mountain ranges. Once in a while, Ukiukiu, in mighty gusts, flings immense cloud-masses clear over the summit of Haleakala; whereupon Naulu craftily captures them, lines them up in new battle-formation, and with them smites back at his ancient and eternal antagonist. Then Ukiukiu sends a great cloud-army around the eastern-side of the mountain. It is a flanking movement, well executed. But Naulu, from his lair on the leeward side, gathers the flanking army in, pulling and twisting and dragging it, hammering it into shape, and sends it charging back against Ukiukiu around the western side of the mountain. And all the while, above and below the main battle-field, high up the slopes toward the sea, Ukiukiu and Naulu are continually sending out little wisps of cloud, in ragged skirmish line, that creep and crawl over the ground, among the trees and through the canyons, and that spring upon and capture one another in sudden ambuscades and sorties. And sometimes Ukiukiu or Naulu, abruptly sending out a heavy charging column, captures the ragged little skirmishers or drives them skyward, turning over and over, in vertical whirls, thousands of feet in the air.

But it is on the western slopes of Haleakala that the main battle goes on. Here Naulu masses his heaviest formations and wins his greatest victories. Ukiukiu grows weak toward late afternoon, which is the way of all trade-winds, and is driven backward by Naulu. Naulu's generalship is excellent. All day he has been gathering and packing away immense reserves. As the afternoon draws on, he welds them into a solid column, sharp-pointed, miles in length, a mile in width, and hundreds of feet thick. This column he slowly thrusts forward into the broad battle-front of Ukiukiu, and slowly and surely Ukiukiu, weakening fast, is split asunder. But it is not all bloodless. At times Ukiukiu struggles wildly, and with fresh accessions of strength from the limitless north-east, smashes away half a mile at a time of Naulu's column and sweeps it off and away toward West Maui. Sometimes, when the two charging armies meet end-on, a tremendous perpendicular whirl results, the cloud-masses, locked together, mounting thousands of feet into the air and turning over and over. A favourite device of Ukiukiu is to send a low, squat formation, densely packed, forward along the ground and under Naulu. When Ukiukiu is under, he proceeds to buck. Naulu's mighty middle gives to the blow and bends upward, but usually he turns the attacking column back upon itself and sets it milling. And all the while the ragged little skirmishers, stray and detached, sneak through the trees and canyons, crawl along and through the grass, and surprise one another with unexpected leaps and rushes; while above, far above, serene and lonely in the rays of the setting sun, Haleakala looks down upon the conflict. And so, the night. But in the morning, after the fashion of trade-winds, Ukiukiu gathers strength and sends the hosts of Naulu rolling back in confusion and rout. And one day is like another day in the battle of the clouds, where Ukiukiu and Naulu strive eternally on the slopes of Haleakala.

Again in the morning, it was boots and saddles, cow-boys, and packhorses, and the climb to the top began. One packhorse carried twenty gallons of water, slung in five-gallon bags on either side; for water is precious and rare in the crater itself, in spite of the fact that several miles to the north and east of the crater-rim more rain comes down than in any other place in the world. The way led upward across countless lava flows, without regard for trails, and never have I seen horses with such perfect footing as that of the thirteen that composed our outfit. They climbed or dropped down perpendicular places with the sureness and coolness of mountain goats, and never a horse fell or baulked.

There is a familiar and strange illusion experienced by all who climb isolated mountains. The higher one climbs, the more of the earth's surface becomes visible, and the effect of this is that the horizon seems up-hill from the observer. This illusion is especially notable on Haleakala, for the old volcano rises directly from the sea without buttresses or connecting ranges. In consequence, as fast as we climbed up the grim slope of Haleakala, still faster did Haleakala, ourselves, and all about us, sink down into the centre of what appeared a profound abyss. Everywhere, far above us, towered the horizon. The ocean sloped down from the horizon to us. The higher we climbed, the deeper did we seem to sink down, the farther above us shone the horizon, and the steeper pitched the grade up to that horizontal line where sky and ocean met. It was weird and unreal, and vagrant thoughts of Simm's Hole and of the volcano through which Jules Verne journeyed to the centre of the earth flitted through one's mind.

And then, when at last we reached the summit of that monster mountain, which summit was like the bottom of an inverted cone situated in the centre of an awful cosmic pit, we found that we were at neither top nor bottom. Far above us was the heaven-towering horizon, and far beneath us, where the top of the mountain should have been, was a deeper deep, the great crater, the House of the Sun. Twenty-three miles around stretched the dizzy wells of the crater. We stood on the edge of the nearly vertical western wall, and the floor of the crater lay nearly half a mile beneath. This floor, broken by lava-flows and cinder-cones, was as red and fresh and uneroded as if it were but yesterday that the fires went out. The cinder-cones, the smallest over four hundred feet in height and the largest over nine hundred, seemed no more than puny little sand-hills, so mighty was the magnitude of the setting. Two gaps, thousands of feet deep, broke the rim of the crater, and through these Ukiukiu vainly strove to drive his fleecy herds of trade-wind clouds. As fast as they advanced through the gaps, the heat of the crater dissipated them into thin air, and though they advanced always, they got nowhere.

It was a scene of vast bleakness and desolation, stern, forbidding, fascinating. We gazed down upon a place of fire and earthquake. The tie-ribs of Earth lay bare before us. It was a workshop of nature still cluttered with the raw beginnings of world-making. Here and there great dikes of primordial rock had thrust themselves up from the bowels of earth, straight through the molten surface-ferment that had evidently cooled only the other day. It was all unreal and unbelievable. Looking upward, far above us (in reality beneath us) floated the cloud-battle of Ukiukiu and Naulu. And higher up the slope of the seeming abyss, above the cloud-battle, in the air and sky, hung the islands of Lanai and Molokai. Across the crater, to the south-east, still apparently looking upward, we saw ascending, first, the turquoise sea, then the white surf-line of the shore of Hawaii; above that the belt of trade-clouds, and next, eighty miles away, rearing their stupendous hulks out of the azure sky, tipped with snow, wreathed with cloud, trembling like a mirage, the peaks of Mauna Kea and Mauna Loa hung poised on the wall of heaven.

It is told that long ago, one Maui, the son of Hina, lived on what is now known as West Maui. His mother, Hina, employed her time in the making of kapas. She must have made them at night, for her days were occupied in trying to dry the kapas. Each morning, and all morning, she toiled at spreading them out in the sun. But no sooner were they out, than she began taking them in, in order to have them all under shelter for the night. For know that the days were shorter then than now. Maui watched his mother's futile toil and felt sorry for her. He decided to do something—oh, no, not to help her hang out and take in the kapas. He was too clever for that. His idea was to make the sun go slower. Perhaps he was the first Hawaiian astronomer. At any rate, he took a series of observations of the sun from various parts of the island. His conclusion was that the sun's path was directly across Haleakala. Unlike Joshua, he stood in no need of divine assistance. He gathered a huge quantity of coconuts, from the fibre of which he braided a stout cord, and in one end of which he made a noose, even as the cow-boys of Haleakala do to this day. Next he climbed into the House of the Sun and laid in wait. When the sun came tearing along the path, bent on completing its journey in the shortest time possible, the valiant youth threw his lariat around one of the sun's largest and strongest beams. He made the sun slow down some; also, he broke the beam short off. And he kept on roping and breaking off beams till the sun said it was willing to listen to reason. Maui set forth his terms of peace, which the sun accepted, agreeing to go more slowly thereafter. Wherefore Hina had ample time in which to dry her kapas, and the days are longer than they used to be, which last is quite in accord with the teachings of modern astronomy.

We had a lunch of jerked beef and hard poi in a stone corral, used of old time for the night-impounding of cattle being driven across the island. Then we skirted the rim for half a mile and began the descent into the crater. Twenty-five hundred feet beneath lay the floor, and down a steep slope of loose volcanic cinders we dropped, the sure-footed horses slipping and sliding, but always keeping their feet. The black surface of the cinders, when broken by the horses' hoofs, turned to a yellow ochre dust, virulent in appearance and acid of taste, that arose in clouds. There was a gallop across a level stretch to the mouth of a convenient blow-hole, and then the descent continued in clouds of volcanic dust, winding in and out among cinder-cones, brick-red, old rose, and purplish black of colour. Above us, higher and higher, towered the crater-walls, while we journeyed on across innumerable lava-flows, turning and twisting a devious way among the adamantine billows of a petrified sea. Saw-toothed waves of lava vexed the surface of this weird ocean, while on either hand arose jagged crests and spiracles of fantastic shape. Our way led on past a bottomless pit and along and over the main stream of the latest lava-flow for seven miles.

At the lower end of the crater was our camping spot, in a small grove of olapa and kolea trees, tucked away in a corner of the crater at the base of walls that rose perpendicularly fifteen hundred feet. Here was pasturage for the horses, but no water, and first we turned aside and picked our way across a mile of lava to a known water-hole in a crevice in the crater-wall. The water-hole was empty. But on climbing fifty feet up the crevice, a pool was found containing half a dozen barrels of water. A pail was carried up, and soon a steady stream of the precious liquid was running down the rock and filling the lower pool, while the cow-boys below were busy fighting the horses back, for there was room for one only to drink at a time. Then it was on to camp at the foot of the wall, up which herds of wild goats scrambled and blatted, while the tent arose to the sound of rifle-firing. Jerked beef, hard poi, and broiled kid were the menu. Over the crest of the crater, just above our heads, rolled a sea of clouds, driven on by Ukiukiu. Though this sea rolled over the crest unceasingly, it never blotted out nor dimmed the moon, for the heat of the crater dissolved the clouds as fast as they rolled in. Through the moonlight, attracted by the camp-fire, came the crater cattle to peer and challenge. They were rolling fat, though they rarely drank water, the morning dew on the grass taking its place. It was because of this dew that the tent made a welcome bedchamber, and we fell asleep to the chanting of hulas by the unwearied Hawaiian cowboys, in whose veins, no doubt, ran the blood of Maui, their valiant forebear.

The camera cannot do justice to the House of the Sun. The sublimated chemistry of photography may not lie, but it certainly does not tell all the truth. The Koolau Gap may be faithfully reproduced, just as it impinged on the retina of the camera, yet in the resulting picture the gigantic scale of things would be missing. Those walls that seem several hundred feet in height are almost as many thousand; that entering wedge of cloud is a mile and a half wide in the gap itself, while beyond the gap it is a veritable ocean; and that foreground of cinder-cone and volcanic ash, mushy and colourless in appearance, is in truth gorgeous-hued in brick-red, terra-cotta rose, yellow ochre, and purplish black. Also, words are a vain thing and drive to despair. To say that a crater-wall is two thousand feet high is to say just precisely that it is two thousand feet high; but there is a vast deal more to that crater-wall than a mere statistic. The sun is ninety-three millions of miles distant, but to mortal conception the adjoining county is farther away. This frailty of the human brain is hard on the sun. It is likewise hard on the House of the Sun. Haleakala has a message of beauty and wonder for the human soul that cannot be delivered by proxy. Kolikoli is six hours from Kahului; Kahului is a night's run from Honolulu; Honolulu is six days from San Francisco; and there you are.

We climbed the crater-walls, put the horses over impossible places, rolled stones, and shot wild goats. I did not get any goats. I was too busy rolling stones. One spot in particular I remember, where we started a stone the size of a horse. It began the descent easy enough, rolling over, wobbling, and threatening to stop; but in a few minutes it was soaring through the air two hundred feet at a jump. It grew rapidly smaller until it struck a slight slope of volcanic sand, over which it darted like a startled jackrabbit, kicking up behind it a tiny trail of yellow dust. Stone and dust diminished in size, until some of the party said the stone had stopped. That was because they could not see it any longer. It had vanished into the distance beyond their ken. Others saw it rolling farther on—I know I did; and it is my firm conviction that that stone is still rolling.

Our last day in the crater, Ukiukiu gave us a taste of his strength. He smashed Naulu back all along the line, filled the House of the Sun to overflowing with clouds, and drowned us out. Our rain-gauge was a pint cup under a tiny hole in the tent. That last night of storm and rain filled the cup, and there was no way of measuring the water that spilled over into the blankets. With the rain-gauge out of business there was no longer any reason for remaining; so we broke camp in the wet-gray of dawn, and plunged eastward across the lava to the Kaupo Gap. East Maui is nothing more or less than the vast lava stream that flowed long ago through the Kaupo Gap; and down this stream we picked our way from an altitude of six thousand five hundred feet to the sea. This was a day's work in itself for the horses; but never were there such horses. Safe in the bad places, never rushing, never losing their heads, as soon as they found a trail wide and smooth enough to run on, they ran. There was no stopping them until the trail became bad again, and then they stopped of themselves. Continuously, for days, they had performed the hardest kind of work, and fed most of the time on grass foraged by themselves at night while we slept, and yet that day they covered twenty-eight leg-breaking miles and galloped into Hana like a bunch of colts. Also, there were several of them, reared in the dry region on the leeward side of Haleakala, that had never worn shoes in all their lives. Day after day, and all day long, unshod, they had travelled over the sharp lava, with the extra weight of a man on their backs, and their hoofs were in better condition than those of the shod horses.

The scenery between Vieiras's (where the Kaupo Gap empties into the sea) and Lana, which we covered in half a day, is well worth a week or month; but, wildly beautiful as it is, it becomes pale and small in comparison with the wonderland that lies beyond the rubber plantations between Hana and the Honomanu Gulch. Two days were required to cover this marvelous stretch, which lies on the windward side of Haleakala. The people who dwell there call it the "ditch country," an unprepossessing name, but it has no other. Nobody else ever comes there. Nobody else knows anything about it. With the exception of a handful of men, whom business has brought there, nobody has heard of the ditch country of Maui. Now a ditch is a ditch, assumably muddy, and usually traversing uninteresting and monotonous landscapes. But the Nahiku Ditch is not an ordinary ditch. The windward side of Haleakala is serried by a thousand precipitous gorges, down which rush as many torrents, each torrent of which achieves a score of cascades and waterfalls before it reaches the sea. More rain comes down here than in any other region in the world. In 1904 the year's downpour was four hundred and twenty inches. Water means sugar, and sugar is the backbone of the territory of Hawaii, wherefore the Nahiku Ditch, which is not a ditch, but a chain of tunnels. The water travels underground, appearing only at intervals to leap a gorge, travelling high in the air on a giddy flume and plunging into and through the opposing mountain. This magnificent waterway is called a "ditch," and with equal appropriateness can Cleopatra's barge be called a box-car.

There are no carriage roads through the ditch country, and before the ditch was built, or bored, rather, there was no horse-trail. Hundreds of inches of rain annually, on fertile soil, under a tropic sun, means a steaming jungle of vegetation. A man, on foot, cutting his way through, might advance a mile a day, but at the end of a week he would be a wreck, and he would have to crawl hastily back if he wanted to get out before the vegetation overran the passage way he had cut. O'Shaughnessy was the daring engineer who conquered the jungle and the gorges, ran the ditch and made the horse-trail. He built enduringly, in concrete and masonry, and made one of the most remarkable water-farms in the world. Every little runlet and dribble is harvested and conveyed by subterranean channels to the main ditch. But so heavily does it rain at times that countless spillways let the surplus escape to the sea.

The horse-trail is not very wide. Like the engineer who built it, it dares anything. Where the ditch plunges through the mountain, it climbs over; and where the ditch leaps a gorge on a flume, the horse-trail takes advantage of the ditch and crosses on top of the flume. That careless trail thinks nothing of travelling up or down the faces of precipices. It gouges its narrow way out of the wall, dodging around waterfalls or passing under them where they thunder down in white fury; while straight overhead the wall rises hundreds of feet, and straight beneath it sinks a thousand. And those arvelous mountain horses are as unconcerned as the trail. They fox-trot along it as a matter of course, though the footing is slippery with rain, and they will gallop with their hind feet slipping over the edge if you let them. I advise only those with steady nerves and cool heads to tackle the Nahiku Ditch trail. One of our cow-boys was noted as the strongest and bravest on the big ranch. He had ridden mountain horses all his life on the rugged western slopes of Haleakala. He was first in the horse-breaking; and when the others hung back, as a matter of course, he would go in to meet a wild bull in the cattle-pen. He had a reputation. But he had never ridden over the Nahiku Ditch. It was there he lost his reputation. When he faced the first flume, spanning a hair-raising gorge, narrow, without railings, with a bellowing waterfall above, another below, and directly beneath a wild cascade, the air filled with driving spray and rocking to the clamour and rush of sound and motion—well, that cow-boy dismounted from his horse, explained briefly that he had a wife and two children, and crossed over on foot, leading the horse behind him.

The only relief from the flumes was the precipices; and the only relief from the precipices was the flumes, except where the ditch was far under ground, in which case we crossed one horse and rider at a time, on primitive log-bridges that swayed and teetered and threatened to carry away. I confess that at first I rode such places with my feet loose in the stirrups, and that on the sheer walls I saw to it, by a definite, conscious act of will, that the foot in the outside stirrup, overhanging the thousand feet of fall, was exceedingly loose. I say "at first"; for, as in the crater itself we quickly lost our conception of magnitude, so, on the Nahiku Ditch, we quickly lost our apprehension of depth. The ceaseless iteration of height and depth produced a state of consciousness in which height and depth were accepted as the ordinary conditions of existence; and from the horse's back to look sheer down four hundred or five hundred feet became quite commonplace and non-productive of thrills. And as carelessly as the trail and the horses, we swung along the dizzy heights and ducked around or through the waterfalls.

And such a ride! Falling water was everywhere. We rode above the clouds, under the clouds, and through the clouds! And every now and then a shaft of sunshine penetrated like a search-light to the depths yawning beneath us, or flashed upon some pinnacle of the crater-rim thousands of feet above. At every turn of the trail a waterfall or a dozen waterfalls, leaping hundreds of feet through the air, burst upon our vision. At our first night's camp, in the Keanae Gulch, we counted thirty-two waterfalls from a single viewpoint. The vegetation ran riot over that wild land. There were forests of koa and kolea trees, and candlenut trees; and then there were the trees called ohia-ai, which bore red mountain apples, mellow and juicy and most excellent to eat. Wild bananas grew everywhere, clinging to the sides of the gorges, and, overborne by their great bunches of ripe fruit, falling across the trail and blocking the way. And over the forest surged a sea of green life, the climbers of a thousand varieties, some that floated airily, in lacelike filaments, from the tallest branches others that coiled and wound about the trees like huge serpents; and one, the ei-ei, that was for all the world like a climbing palm, swinging on a thick stem from branch to branch and tree to tree and throttling the supports whereby it climbed. Through the sea of green, lofty tree-ferns thrust their great delicate fronds, and the lehua flaunted its scarlet blossoms. Underneath the climbers, in no less profusion, grew the warm-coloured, strangely-marked plants that in the United States one is accustomed to seeing preciously conserved in hot-houses. In fact, the ditch country of Maui is nothing more nor less than a huge conservatory. Every familiar variety of fern flourishes, and more varieties that are unfamiliar, from the tiniest maidenhair to the gross and voracious staghorn, the latter the terror of the woodsmen, interlacing with itself in tangled masses five or six feet deep and covering acres.

Never was there such a ride. For two days it lasted, when we emerged into rolling country, and, along an actual wagon-road, came home to the ranch at a gallop. I know it was cruel to gallop the horses after such a long, hard journey; but we blistered our hands in vain effort to hold them in. That's the sort of horses they grow on Haleakala. At the ranch there was great festival of cattle-driving, branding, and horse-breaking. Overhead Ukiukiu and Naulu battled valiantly, and far above, in the sunshine, towered the mighty summit of Haleakala.

Chapter 18
A Pacific Traverse

Sandwich Islands to Tahiti.—There is great difficulty in making this passage across the trades. The whalers and all others speak with great doubt of fetching Tahiti from the Sandwich islands. Capt. Bruce says that a vessel should keep to the northward until she gets a start of wind before bearing for her destination. In his passage between them in November, 1837, he had no variables near the line in coming south, and never could make easting on either tack, though he endeavoured by every means to do so.

So say the sailing directions for the South Pacific Ocean; and that is all they say. There is not a word more to help the weary voyager in making this long traverse—nor is there any word at all concerning the passage from Hawaii to the Marquesas, which lie some eight hundred miles to the northeast of Tahiti and which are the more difficult to reach by just that much. The reason for the lack of directions is, I imagine, that no voyager is supposed to make himself weary by attempting so impossible a traverse. But the impossible did not deter the *Snark,*—principally because of the fact that we did not read that particular little paragraph in the sailing directions until after we had started. We sailed from Hilo, Hawaii, on October 7, and arrived at Nuka-hiva, in the Marquesas, on December 6. The distance was two thousand miles as the crow flies, while we actually travelled at least four thousand miles to accomplish it, thus proving for once and for ever that the shortest distance between two points is not always a straight line. Had we headed directly for the Marquesas, we might have travelled five or six thousand miles.

Upon one thing we were resolved: we would not cross the Line west of 130 degrees west longitude. For here was the problem. To cross the Line to the west of that point, if the southeast trades were well around to the southeast, would throw us so far to leeward of the Marquesas that a head-beat would be maddeningly impossible. Also, we had to remember the equatorial current, which moves west at a rate of anywhere from twelve to seventy-five miles a day. A pretty pickle, indeed, to be to leeward of our destination with such a current in our teeth. No; not a minute, nor a second, west of 130 degrees west longitude would we cross the Line. But since the southeast trades were to be expected five or six degrees north of the Line (which, if they were well around to the southeast or south-southeast, would necessitate our sliding off toward south-southwest), we should have to hold to the eastward, north of the Line, and north of the southeast trades, until we gained at least 128 degrees west longitude.

I have forgotten to mention that the seventy-horse-power gasolene engine, as usual, was not working, and that we could depend upon wind alone. Neither was the launch engine working. And while I am about it, I may as well confess that the five-horse-power, which ran the lights, fans, and pumps, was also on the sick-list. A striking title for a book haunts me, waking and sleeping. I should like to write that book some day and to call it "Around the World with Three Gasolene Engines and a Wife." But I am afraid I shall not write it, for fear of hurting the feelings of some of the young gentlemen of San Francisco, Honolulu, and Hilo, who learned their trades at the expense of the *Snark*'s engines.

It looked easy on paper. Here was Hilo and there was our objective, 128 degrees west longitude. With the northeast trade blowing we could travel a straight line between the two points, and even slack our sheets off a goodly bit. But one of the chief troubles with the trades is that one never knows just where he will pick them up and just in what direction they will be blowing. We picked up the northeast trade right outside of Hilo harbour, but the miserable breeze was away around into the east. Then there was the north equatorial current setting westward like a mighty river. Furthermore, a small boat, by the wind and bucking into a big headsea, does not work to advantage. She jogs up and down and gets nowhere. Her sails are full and straining, every little while she presses her lee-rail under, she flounders, and bumps, and splashes, and that is all. Whenever she begins to gather way, she runs ker-chug into a big mountain of water and is brought to a standstill. So, with the *Snark*, the resultant of her smallness, of the trade around into the east, and of the strong equatorial current, was a long sag south. Oh, she did not go quite south. But the easting she made was distressing. On October 11, she made forty miles easting; October 12, fifteen miles; October 13, no easting; October 14, thirty miles; October 15, twenty-three miles; October 16, eleven miles; and on October 17, she actually went to the westward four miles. Thus, in a week she made one hundred and fifteen miles easting, which was equivalent to sixteen miles a day. But, between the longitude of Hilo and 128 degrees west longitude is a difference of twenty-seven degrees, or, roughly, sixteen hundred miles. At sixteen miles a day, one hundred days would be required to accomplish this distance. And even then, our objective, 128 degrees west longitude, was five degrees north of the Line, while Nuka-hiva, in the Marquesas, lay nine degrees south of the Line and twelve degrees to the west!

There remained only one thing to do—to work south out of the trade and into the variables. It is true that Captain Bruce found no variables on his traverse, and that he "never could make easting on either tack." It was the variables or nothing with us, and we prayed for better luck than he had had. The variables constitute the belt of ocean lying between the trades and the doldrums, and are conjectured to be the draughts of heated air which rise in the doldrums, flow high in the air counter to the trades, and gradually sink down till they fan the surface of the ocean where they are found. And they are found where they are found; for they are wedged between the trades and the doldrums, which same shift their territory from day to day and month to month.

We found the variables in 11 degrees north latitude, and 11 degrees north latitude we hugged jealously. To the south lay the doldrums. To the north lay the northeast trade that refused to blow from the northeast. The days came and went, and always they found the *Snark* somewhere near the eleventh parallel. The variables were truly variable. A light head-wind would die away and leave us rolling in a calm for forty-eight hours. Then a light head-wind would spring up, blow for three hours, and leave us rolling in another calm for forty-eight hours. Then—hurrah!—the wind would come out of the west, fresh, beautifully fresh, and send the *Snark* along, wing and wing, her wake bubbling, the log-line straight astern. At the end of half an hour, while we were preparing to set the spinnaker, with a few sickly gasps the wind would die away. And so it went. We wagered optimistically on every favourable fan of air that lasted over five minutes; but it never did any good. The fans faded out just the same.

But there were exceptions. In the variables, if you wait long enough, something is bound to happen, and we were so plentifully stocked with food and water that we could afford to wait. On October 26, we actually made one hundred and three miles of easting, and we talked about it for days afterwards. Once we caught a moderate gale from the south, which blew itself out in eight hours, but it helped us to seventy-one miles of easting in that particular twenty-four hours. And then, just as it was expiring, the wind came straight out from the north (the directly opposite quarter), and fanned us along over another degree of easting.

In years and years no sailing vessel has attempted this traverse, and we found ourselves in the midst of one of the loneliest of the Pacific solitudes. In the sixty days we were crossing it we sighted no sail, lifted no steamer's smoke above the horizon. A disabled vessel could drift in this deserted expanse for a dozen generations, and there would be no rescue. The only chance of rescue would be from a vessel like the *Snark*, and the *Snark* happened to be there principally because of the fact that the traverse had been begun before the particular paragraph in the sailing directions had been read. Standing upright on deck, a straight line drawn from the eye to the horizon would measure three miles and a half. Thus, seven miles was the diameter of the circle of the sea in which we had our centre. Since we remained always in the centre, and since we constantly were moving in some direction, we looked upon many circles. But all circles looked alike. No tufted islets, gray headlands, nor glistening patches of white canvas ever marred the symmetry of that unbroken curve. Clouds came and went, rising up over the rim of the circle, flowing across the space of it, and spilling away and down across the opposite rim.

The world faded as the procession of the weeks marched by. The world faded until at last there ceased to be any world except the little world of the *Snark*, freighted with her seven souls and floating on the expanse of the waters. Our memories of the world, the great world, became like dreams of former lives we had lived somewhere before we came to be born on the *Snark*. After we had been out of fresh vegetables for some time, we mentioned such things in much the same way I have heard my father mention the vanished apples of his boyhood. Man is a creature of habit, and we on the *Snark* had got the habit of the *Snark*. Everything about her and aboard her was as a matter of course, and anything different would have been an irritation and an offence.

There was no way by which the great world could intrude. Our bell rang the hours, but no caller ever rang it. There were no guests to dinner, no telegrams, no insistent telephone jangles invading our privacy. We had no engagements to keep, no trains to catch, and there were no morning newspapers over which to waste time in learning what was happening to our fifteen hundred million other fellow-creatures.

But it was not dull. The affairs of our little world had to be regulated, and, unlike the great world, our world had to be steered in its journey through space. Also, there were cosmic disturbances to be encountered and baffled, such as do not afflict the big earth in its frictionless orbit through the windless void. And we never knew, from moment to moment, what was going to happen next. There were spice and variety enough and to spare. Thus, at four in the morning, I relieve Hermann at the wheel.

"East-northeast," he gives me the course. "She's eight points off, but she ain't steering."

Small wonder. The vessel does not exist that can be steered in so absolute a calm.

"I had a breeze a little while ago—maybe it will come back again," Hermann says hopefully, ere he starts forward to the cabin and his bunk.

The mizzen is in and fast furled. In the night, what of the roll and the absence of wind, it had made life too hideous to be permitted to go on rasping at the mast, smashing at the tackles, and buffeting the empty air into hollow outbursts of sound. But the big mainsail is still on, and the staysail, jib, and flying-jib are snapping and slashing at their sheets with every roll. Every star is out. Just for luck I put the wheel hard over in the opposite direction to which it had been left by Hermann, and I lean back and gaze up at the stars. There is nothing else for me to do. There is nothing to be done with a sailing vessel rolling in a stark calm.

Then I feel a fan on my cheek, faint, so faint, that I can just sense it ere it is gone. But another comes, and another, until a real and just perceptible breeze is blowing. How the *Snark*'s sails manage to feel it is beyond me, but feel it they do, as she does as well, for the compass card begins slowly to revolve in the binnacle. In reality, it is not revolving at all. It is held by terrestrial magnetism in one place, and it is the *Snark* that is revolving, pivoted upon that delicate cardboard device that floats in a closed vessel of alcohol.

So the *Snark* comes back on her course. The breath increases to a tiny puff. The *Snark* feels the weight of it and actually heels over a trifle. There is flying scud overhead, and I notice the stars being blotted out. Walls of darkness close in upon me, so that, when the last star is gone, the darkness is so near that it seems I can reach out and touch it on every side. When I lean toward it, I can feel it loom against my face. Puff follows puff, and I am glad the mizzen is furled. Phew! that was a stiff one! The *Snark* goes over and down until her lee-rail is buried and the whole Pacific Ocean is pouring in. Four or five of these gusts make me wish that the jib and flying-jib were in. The sea is picking up, the gusts are growing stronger and more frequent, and there is a splatter of wet in the air. There is no use in attempting to gaze to windward. The wall of blackness is within arm's length. Yet I cannot help attempting to see and gauge the blows that are being struck at the *Snark*. There is something ominous and menacing up there to windward, and I have a feeling that if I look long enough and strong enough, I shall divine it. Futile feeling. Between two gusts I leave the wheel and run forward to the cabin companionway, where I light matches and consult the barometer. "29-90" it reads. That sensitive instrument refuses to take notice of the disturbance which is humming with a deep, throaty voice in the rigging. I get back to the wheel just in time to meet another gust, the strongest yet. Well, anyway, the wind is abeam and the *Snark* is on her course, eating up easting. That at least is well.

The jib and flying-jib bother me, and I wish they were in. She would make easier weather of it, and less risky weather likewise. The wind snorts, and stray raindrops pelt like birdshot. I shall certainly have to call all hands, I conclude; then conclude the next instant to hang on a little longer. Maybe this is the end of it, and I shall have called them for nothing. It is better to let them sleep.

I hold the *Snark* down to her task, and from out of the darkness, at right angles, comes a deluge of rain accompanied by shrieking wind. Then everything eases except the blackness, and I rejoice in that I have not called the men.

No sooner does the wind ease than the sea picks up. The combers are breaking now, and the boat is tossing like a cork. Then out of the blackness the gusts come harder and faster than before. If only I knew what was up there to windward in the blackness! The *Snark* is making heavy weather of it, and her lee-rail is buried oftener than not. More shrieks and snorts of wind. Now, if ever, is the time to call the men. I WILL call them, I resolve. Then there is a burst of rain, a slackening of the wind, and I do not call. But it is rather lonely, there at the wheel, steering a little world through howling blackness. It is quite a responsibility to be all alone on the surface of a little world in time of stress, doing the thinking for its sleeping inhabitants. I recoil from the responsibility as more gusts begin to strike and as a sea licks along the weather rail and splashes over into the cockpit. The salt water seems strangely warm to my body and is shot through with ghostly nodules of phosphorescent light. I shall surely call all hands to shorten sail. Why should they sleep? I am a fool to have any compunctions in the matter. My intellect is arrayed against my heart. It was my heart that said, "Let them sleep." Yes, but it was my intellect that backed up my heart in that judgment. Let my intellect then reverse the judgment; and, while I am speculating as to what particular entity issued that command to my intellect, the gusts die away. Solicitude for mere bodily comfort has no place in practical seamanship, I conclude sagely; but study the feel of the next series of gusts and do not call the men. After all, it IS my intellect, behind everything, procrastinating, measuring its knowledge of what the *Snark* can endure against the blows being struck at her, and waiting the call of all hands against the striking of still severer blows.

Daylight, gray and violent, steals through the cloud-pall and shows a foaming sea that flattens under the weight of recurrent and increasing squalls. Then comes the rain, filling the windy valleys of the sea with milky smoke and further flattening the waves, which but wait for the easement of wind and rain to leap more wildly than before. Come the men on deck, their sleep out, and among them Hermann, his face on the broad grin in appreciation of the breeze of wind I have picked up. I turn the wheel over to Warren and start to go below, pausing on the way to rescue the galley stovepipe which has gone adrift. I am barefooted, and my toes have had an excellent education in the art of clinging; but, as the rail buries itself in a green sea, I suddenly sit down on the streaming deck. Hermann good-naturedly elects to question my selection of such a spot. Then comes the next roll, and he sits down, suddenly, and without premeditation. The *Snark* heels over and down, the rail takes it green, and Hermann and I, clutching the precious stove-pipe, are swept down into the lee-scuppers. After that I finish my journey below, and while changing my clothes grin with satisfaction—the *Snark* is making easting.

No, it is not all monotony. When we had worried along our easting to 126 degrees west longitude, we left the variables and headed south through the doldrums, where was much calm weather and where, taking advantage of every fan of air, we were often glad to make a score of miles in as many hours. And yet, on such a day, we might pass through a dozen squalls and be surrounded by dozens more. And every squall was to be regarded as a bludgeon capable of crushing the *Snark*. We were struck sometimes by the centres and sometimes by the sides of these squalls, and we never knew just where or how we were to be hit. The squall that rose up, covering half the heavens, and swept down upon us, as likely as not split into two squalls which passed us harmlessly on either side while the tiny, innocent looking squall that appeared to carry no more than a hogshead of water and a pound of wind, would abruptly assume cyclopean proportions, deluging us with rain and overwhelming us with wind. Then there were treacherous squalls that went boldly astern and sneaked back upon us from a mile to leeward. Again, two squalls would tear along, one on each side of us, and we would get a fillip from each of them. Now a gale certainly grows tiresome after a few hours, but squalls never. The thousandth squall in one's experience is as interesting as the first one, and perhaps a bit more so. It is the tyro who has no apprehension of them. The man of a thousand squalls respects a squall. He knows what they are.

It was in the doldrums that our most exciting event occurred. On November 20, we discovered that through an accident we had lost over one-half of the supply of fresh water that remained to us. Since we were at that time forty-three days out from Hilo, our supply of fresh water was not large. To lose over half of it was a catastrophe. On close allowance, the remnant of water we possessed would last twenty days. But we were in the doldrums; there was no telling where the southeast trades were, nor where we would pick them up.

The handcuffs were promptly put upon the pump, and once a day the water was portioned out. Each of us received a quart for personal use, and eight quarts were given to the cook. Enters now the psychology of the situation. No sooner had the discovery of the water shortage been made than I, for one, was afflicted with a burning thirst. It seemed to me that I had never been so thirsty in my life. My little quart of water I could easily have drunk in one draught, and to refrain from doing so required a severe exertion of will. Nor was I alone in this. All of us talked water, thought water, and dreamed water when we slept. We examined the charts for possible islands to which to run in extremity, but there were no such islands. The Marquesas were the nearest, and they were the other side of the Line, and of the doldrums, too, which made it even worse. We were in 3 degrees north latitude, while the Marquesas were 9 degrees south latitude—a difference of over a thousand miles. Furthermore, the Marquesas lay some fourteen degrees to the west of our longitude. A pretty pickle for a handful of creatures sweltering on the ocean in the heat of tropic calms.

We rigged lines on either side between the main and mizzen riggings. To these we laced the big deck awning, hoisting it up aft with a sailing pennant so that any rain it might collect would run forward where it could be caught. Here and there squalls passed across the circle of the sea. All day we watched them, now to port or starboard, and again ahead or astern. But never one came near enough to wet us. In the afternoon a big one bore down upon us. It spread out across the ocean as it approached, and we could see it emptying countless thousands of gallons into the salt sea. Extra attention was paid to the awning and then we waited. Warren, Martin, and Hermann made a vivid picture. Grouped together, holding on to the rigging, swaying to the roll, they were gazing intently at the squall. Strain, anxiety, and yearning were in every posture of their bodies. Beside them was the dry and empty awning. But they seemed to grow limp and to droop as the squall broke in half, one part passing on ahead, the other drawing astern and going to leeward.

But that night came rain. Martin, whose psychological thirst had compelled him to drink his quart of water early, got his mouth down to the lip of the awning and drank the deepest draught I ever have seen drunk. The precious water came down in bucketfuls and tubfuls, and in two hours we caught and stored away in the tanks one hundred and twenty gallons. Strange to say, in all the rest of our voyage to the Marquesas not another drop of rain fell on board. If that squall had missed us, the handcuffs would have remained on the pump, and we would have busied ourselves with utilizing our surplus gasolene for distillation purposes.

Then there was the fishing. One did not have to go in search of it, for it was there at the rail. A three-inch steel hook, on the end of a stout line, with a piece of white rag for bait, was all that was necessary to catch bonitas weighing from ten to twenty-five pounds. Bonitas feed on flying-fish, wherefore they are unaccustomed to nibbling at the hook. They strike as gamely as the gamest fish in the sea, and their first run is something that no man who has ever caught them will forget. Also, bonitas are the veriest cannibals. The instant one is hooked he is attacked by his fellows. Often and often we hauled them on board with fresh, clean-bitten holes in them the size of teacups.

One school of bonitas, numbering many thousands, stayed with us day and night for more than three weeks. Aided by the *Snark*, it was great hunting; for they cut a swath of destruction through the ocean half a mile wide and fifteen hundred miles in length. They ranged along abreast of the *Snark* on either side, pouncing upon the flying-fish her forefoot scared up. Since they were continually pursuing astern the flying-fish that survived for several flights, they were always overtaking the *Snark*, and at any time one could glance astern and on the front of a breaking wave see scores of their silvery forms coasting down just under the surface. When they had eaten their fill, it was their delight to get in the shadow of the boat, or of her sails, and a hundred or so were always to be seen lazily sliding along and keeping cool.

But the poor flying-fish! Pursued and eaten alive by the bonitas and dolphins, they sought flight in the air, where the swooping seabirds drove them back into the water. Under heaven there was no refuge for them. Flying-fish do not play when they essay the air. It is a life-and-death affair with them. A thousand times a day we could lift our eyes and see the tragedy played out. The swift, broken circling of a guny might attract one's attention. A glance beneath shows the back of a dolphin breaking the surface in a wild rush. Just in front of its nose a shimmering palpitant streak of silver shoots from the water into the air—a delicate, organic mechanism of flight, endowed with sensation, power of direction, and love of life. The guny swoops for it and misses, and the flying-fish, gaining its altitude by rising, kite-like, against the wind, turns in a half-circle and skims off to leeward, gliding on the bosom of the wind. Beneath it, the wake of the dolphin shows in churning foam. So he follows, gazing upward with large eyes at the flashing breakfast that navigates an element other than his own. He cannot rise to so lofty occasion, but he is a thorough-going empiricist, and he knows, sooner or later, if not gobbled up by the guny, that the flying-fish must return to the water. And then—breakfast. We used to pity the poor winged fish. It was sad to see such sordid and bloody slaughter. And then, in the night watches, when a forlorn little flying-fish struck the mainsail and fell gasping and splattering on the deck, we would rush for it just as eagerly, just as greedily, just as voraciously, as the dolphins and bonitas. For know that flying-fish are most toothsome for breakfast. It is always a wonder to me that such dainty meat does not build dainty tissue in the bodies of the devourers. Perhaps the dolphins and bonitas are coarser-fibred because of the high speed at which they drive their bodies in order to catch their prey. But then again, the flying-fish drive their bodies at high speed, too.

Sharks we caught occasionally, on large hooks, with chain-swivels, bent on a length of small rope. And sharks meant pilot-fish, and remoras, and various sorts of parasitic creatures. Regular man-eaters some of the sharks proved, tiger-eyed and with twelve rows of teeth, razor-sharp. By the way, we of the *Snark* are agreed that we have eaten many fish that will not compare with baked shark smothered in tomato dressing. In the calms we occasionally caught a fish called "hake" by the Japanese cook. And once, on a spoon-hook trolling a hundred yards astern, we caught a snake-like fish, over three feet in length and not more than three inches in diameter, with four fangs in his jaw. He proved the most delicious fish—delicious in meat and flavour—that we have ever eaten on board.

The most welcome addition to our larder was a green sea-turtle, weighing a full hundred pounds and appearing on the table most appetizingly in steaks, soups, and stews, and finally in a wonderful curry which tempted all hands into eating more rice than was good for them. The turtle was sighted to windward, calmly sleeping on the surface in the midst of a huge school of curious dolphins. It was a deep-sea turtle of a surety, for the nearest land was a thousand miles away. We put the *Snark* about and went back for him, Hermann driving the granes into his head and neck. When hauled aboard, numerous remora were clinging to his shell, and out of the hollows at the roots of his flippers crawled several large crabs. It did not take the crew of the *Snark* longer than the next meal to reach the unanimous conclusion that it would willingly put the *Snark* about any time for a turtle.

But it is the dolphin that is the king of deep-sea fishes. Never is his colour twice quite the same. Swimming in the sea, an ethereal creature of palest azure, he displays in that one guise a miracle of colour. But it is nothing compared with the displays of which he is capable. At one time he will appear green—pale green, deep green, phosphorescent green; at another time blue—deep blue, electric blue, all the spectrum of blue. Catch him on a hook, and he turns to gold, yellow gold, all gold. Haul him on deck, and he excels the spectrum, passing through inconceivable shades of blues, greens, and yellows, and then, suddenly, turning a ghostly white, in the midst of which are bright blue spots, and you suddenly discover that he is speckled like a trout. Then back from white he goes, through all the range of colours, finally turning to a mother-of-pearl.

For those who are devoted to fishing, I can recommend no finer sport than catching dolphin. Of course, it must be done on a thin line with reel and pole. A No. 7, O'Shaughnessy tarpon hook is just the thing, baited with an entire flying-fish. Like the bonita, the dolphin's fare consists of flying-fish, and he strikes like lightning at the bait. The first warning is when the reel screeches and you see the line smoking out at right angles to the boat. Before you have time to entertain anxiety concerning the length of your line, the fish rises into the air in a succession of leaps. Since he is quite certain to be four feet long or over, the sport of landing so gamey a fish can be realized. When hooked, he invariably turns golden. The idea of the series of leaps is to rid himself of the hook, and the man who has made the strike must be of iron or decadent if his heart does not beat with an extra flutter when he beholds such gorgeous fish, glittering in golden mail and shaking itself like a stallion in each mid-air leap. 'Ware slack! If you don't, on one of those leaps the hook will be flung out and twenty feet away. No slack, and away he will go on another run, culminating in another series of leaps. About this time one begins to worry over the line, and to wish that he had had nine hundred feet on the reel originally instead of six hundred. With careful playing the line can be saved, and after an hour of keen excitement the fish can be brought to gaff. One such dolphin I landed on the *Snark* measured four feet and seven inches.

Hermann caught dolphins more prosaically. A hand-line and a chunk of shark-meat were all he needed. His hand-line was very thick, but on more than one occasion it parted and lost the fish. One day a dolphin got away with a lure of Hermann's manufacture, to which were lashed four O'Shaughnessy hooks. Within an hour the same dolphin was landed with the rod, and on dissecting him the four hooks were recovered. The dolphins, which remained with us over a month, deserted us north of the line, and not one was seen during the remainder of the traverse.

So the days passed. There was so much to be done that time never dragged. Had there been little to do, time could not have dragged with such wonderful seascapes and cloudscapes—dawns that were like burning imperial cities under rainbows that arched nearly to the zenith; sunsets that bathed the purple sea in rivers of rose-coloured light, flowing from a sun whose diverging, heaven-climbing rays were of the purest blue. Overside, in the heat of the day, the sea was an azure satiny fabric, in the depths of which the sunshine focussed in funnels of light. Astern, deep down, when there was a breeze, bubbled a procession of milky-turquoise ghosts—the foam flung down by the hull of the *Snark* each time she floundered against a sea. At night the wake was phosphorescent fire, where the medusa slime resented our passing bulk, while far down could be observed the unceasing flight of comets, with long, undulating, nebulous tails—caused by the passage of the bonitas through the resentful medusa slime. And now and again, from out of the darkness on either hand, just under the surface, larger phosphorescent organisms flashed up like electric lights, marking collisions with the careless bonitas skurrying ahead to the good hunting just beyond our bowsprit.

We made our easting, worked down through the doldrums, and caught a fresh breeze out of south-by-west. Hauled up by the wind, on such a slant, we would fetch past the Marquesas far away to the westward. But the next day, on Tuesday, November 26, in the thick of a heavy squall, the wind shifted suddenly to the southeast. It was the trade at last. There were no more squalls, naught but fine weather, a fair wind, and a whirling log, with sheets slacked off and with spinnaker and mainsail swaying and bellying on either side. The trade backed more and more, until it blew out of the northeast, while we steered a steady course to the southwest. Ten days of this, and on the morning of December 6, at five o'clock, we sighted land "just where it ought to have been," dead ahead. We passed to leeward of Ua-huka, skirted the southern edge of Nuka-hiva, and that night, in driving squalls and inky darkness, fought our way in to an anchorage in the narrow bay of Taiohae. The anchor rumbled down to the blatting of wild goats on the cliffs, and the air we breathed was heavy with the perfume of flowers. The traverse was accomplished. Sixty days from land to land, across a lonely sea above whose horizons never rise the straining sails of ships.

Chapter 19
Typee

To the eastward Ua-huka was being blotted out by an evening rain-squall that was fast overtaking the *Snark*. But that little craft, her big spinnaker filled by the southeast trade, was making a good race of it. Cape Martin, the southeasternmost point of Nuku-hiva, was abeam, and Comptroller Bay was opening up as we fled past its wide entrance, where Sail Rock, for all the world like the spritsail of a Columbia River salmon-boat, was making brave weather of it in the smashing southeast swell.

"What do you make that out to be?" I asked Hermann, at the wheel.

"A fishing-boat, sir," he answered after careful scrutiny.

Yet on the chart it was plainly marked, "Sail Rock."

But we were more interested in the recesses of Comptroller Bay, where our eyes eagerly sought out the three bights of land and centred on the midmost one, where the gathering twilight showed the dim walls of a valley extending inland. How often we had pored over the chart and centred always on that midmost bight and on the valley it opened—the Valley of Typee. "Taipi" the chart spelled it, and spelled it correctly, but I prefer "Typee," and I shall always spell it "Typee." When I was a little boy, I read a book spelled in that manner—Herman Melville's "Typee"; and many long hours I dreamed over its pages. Nor was it all dreaming. I resolved there and then, mightily, come what would, that when I had gained strength and years, I, too, would voyage to Typee. For the wonder of the world was penetrating to my tiny consciousness—the wonder that was to lead me to many lands, and that leads and never pails. The years passed, but Typee was not forgotten. Returned to San Francisco from a seven months' cruise in the North Pacific, I decided the time had come. The brig Galilee was sailing for the Marquesas, but her crew was complete and I, who was an able-seaman before the mast and young enough to be overweeningly proud of it, was willing to condescend to ship as cabin-boy in order to make the pilgrimage to Typee. Of course, the Galilee would have sailed from the Marquesas without me, for I was bent on finding another Fayaway and another Kory-Kory. I doubt that the captain read desertion in my eye. Perhaps even the berth of cabin-boy was already filled. At any rate, I did not get it.

Then came the rush of years, filled brimming with projects, achievements, and failures; but Typee was not forgotten, and here I was now, gazing at its misty outlines till the squall swooped down and the *Snark* dashed on into the driving smother. Ahead, we caught a glimpse and took the compass bearing of Sentinel Rock, wreathed with pounding surf. Then it, too, was effaced by the rain and darkness. We steered straight for it, trusting to hear the sound of breakers in time to sheer clear. We had to steer for it. We had naught but a compass bearing with which to orientate ourselves, and if we missed Sentinel Rock, we missed Taiohae Bay, and we would have to throw the *Snark* up to the wind and lie off and on the whole night—no pleasant prospect for voyagers weary from a sixty days' traverse of the vast Pacific solitude, and land-hungry, and fruit-hungry, and hungry with an appetite of years for the sweet vale of Typee.

Abruptly, with a roar of sound, Sentinel Rock loomed through the rain dead ahead. We altered our course, and, with mainsail and spinnaker bellying to the squall, drove past. Under the lea of the rock the wind dropped us, and we rolled in an absolute calm. Then a puff of air struck us, right in our teeth, out of Taiohae Bay. It was in spinnaker, up mizzen, all sheets by the wind, and we were moving slowly ahead, heaving the lead and straining our eyes for the fixed red light on the ruined fort that would give us our bearings to anchorage. The air was light and baffling, now east, now west, now north, now south; while from either hand came the roar of unseen breakers. From the looming cliffs arose the blatting of wild goats, and overhead the first stars were peeping mistily through the ragged train of the passing squall. At the end of two hours, having come a mile into the bay, we dropped anchor in eleven fathoms. And so we came to Taiohae.

In the morning we awoke in fairyland. The *Snark* rested in a placid harbour that nestled in a vast amphitheatre, the towering, vine-clad walls of which seemed to rise directly from the water. Far up, to the east, we glimpsed the thin line of a trail, visible in one place, where it scoured across the face of the wall.

"The path by which Toby escaped from Typee!" we cried.

We were not long in getting ashore and astride horses, though the consummation of our pilgrimage had to be deferred for a day. Two months at sea, bare-footed all the time, without space in which to exercise one's limbs, is not the best preliminary to leather shoes and walking. Besides, the land had to cease its nauseous rolling before we could feel fit for riding goat-like horses over giddy trails. So we took a short ride to break in, and crawled through thick jungle to make the acquaintance of a venerable moss-grown idol, where had foregathered a German trader and a Norwegian captain to estimate the weight of said idol, and to speculate upon depreciation in value caused by sawing him in half. They treated the old fellow sacrilegiously, digging their knives into him to see how hard he was and how deep his mossy mantle, and commanding him to rise up and save them trouble by walking down to the ship himself. In lieu of which, nineteen Kanakas slung him on a frame of timbers and toted him to the ship, where, battened down under hatches, even now he is cleaving the South Pacific Hornward and toward Europe—the ultimate abiding-place for all good heathen idols, save for the few in America and one in particular who grins beside me as I write, and who, barring shipwreck, will grin somewhere in my neighbourhood until I die. And he will win out. He will be grinning when I am dust.

Also, as a preliminary, we attended a feast, where one Taiara Tamarii, the son of an Hawaiian sailor who deserted from a whaleship, commemorated the death of his Marquesan mother by roasting fourteen whole hogs and inviting in the village. So we came along, welcomed by a native herald, a young girl, who stood on a great rock and chanted the information that the banquet was made perfect by our presence—which information she extended impartially to every arrival. Scarcely were we seated, however, when she changed her tune, while the company manifested intense excitement. Her cries became eager and piercing. From a distance came answering cries, in men's voices, which blended into a wild, barbaric chant that sounded incredibly savage, smacking of blood and war. Then, through vistas of tropical foliage appeared a procession of savages, naked save for gaudy loin-cloths. They advanced slowly, uttering deep guttural cries of triumph and exaltation. Slung from young saplings carried on their shoulders were mysterious objects of considerable weight, hidden from view by wrappings of green leaves.

Nothing but pigs, innocently fat and roasted to a turn, were inside those wrappings, but the men were carrying them into camp in imitation of old times when they carried in "long-pig." Now long-pig is not pig. Long-pig is the Polynesian euphemism for human flesh; and these descendants of man-eaters, a king's son at their head, brought in the pigs to table as of old their grandfathers had brought in their slain enemies. Every now and then the procession halted in order that the bearers should have every advantage in uttering particularly ferocious shouts of victory, of contempt for their enemies, and of gustatory desire. So Melville, two generations ago, witnessed the bodies of slain Happar warriors, wrapped in palm-leaves, carried to banquet at the Ti. At another time, at the Ti, he "observed a curiously carved vessel of wood," and on looking into it his eyes "fell upon the disordered members of a human skeleton, the bones still fresh with moisture, and with particles of flesh clinging to them here and there."

Cannibalism has often been regarded as a fairy story by ultra-civilized men who dislike, perhaps, the notion that their own savage forebears have somewhere in the past been addicted to similar practices. Captain Cook was rather sceptical upon the subject, until, one day, in a harbour of New Zealand, he deliberately tested the matter. A native happened to have brought on board, for sale, a nice, sun-dried head. At Cook's orders strips of the flesh were cut away and handed to the native, who greedily devoured them. To say the least, Captain Cook was a rather thorough-going empiricist. At any rate, by that act he supplied one ascertained fact of which science had been badly in need. Little did he dream of the existence of a certain group of islands, thousands of miles away, where in subsequent days there would arise a curious suit at law, when an old chief of Maui would be charged with defamation of character because he persisted in asserting that his body was the living repository of Captain Cook's great toe. It is said that the plaintiffs failed to prove that the old chief was not the tomb of the navigator's great toe, and that the suit was dismissed.

I suppose I shall not have the chance in these degenerate days to see any long-pig eaten, but at least I am already the possessor of a duly certified Marquesan calabash, oblong in shape, curiously carved, over a century old, from which has been drunk the blood of two shipmasters. One of those captains was a mean man. He sold a decrepit whale-boat, as good as new what of the fresh white paint, to a Marquesan chief. But no sooner had the captain sailed away than the whale-boat dropped to pieces. It was his fortune, some time afterwards, to be wrecked, of all places, on that particular island. The Marquesan chief was ignorant of rebates and discounts; but he had a primitive sense of equity and an equally primitive conception of the economy of nature, and he balanced the account by eating the man who had cheated him.

We started in the cool dawn for Typee, astride ferocious little stallions that pawed and screamed and bit and fought one another quite oblivious of the fragile humans on their backs and of the slippery boulders, loose rocks, and yawning gorges. The way led up an ancient road through a jungle of hau trees. On every side were the vestiges of a one-time dense population. Wherever the eye could penetrate the thick growth, glimpses were caught of stone walls and of stone foundations, six to eight feet in height, built solidly throughout, and many yards in width and depth. They formed great stone platforms, upon which, at one time, there had been houses. But the houses and the people were gone, and huge trees sank their roots through the platforms and towered over the underrunning jungle. These foundations are called pae-paes—the pi-pis of Melville, who spelled phonetically.

The Marquesans of the present generation lack the energy to hoist and place such huge stones. Also, they lack incentive. There are plenty of pae-paes to go around, with a few thousand unoccupied ones left over. Once or twice, as we ascended the valley, we saw magnificent pae-paes bearing on their general surface pitiful little straw huts, the proportions being similar to a voting booth perched on the broad foundation of the Pyramid of Cheops. For the Marquesans are perishing, and, to judge from conditions at Taiohae, the one thing that retards their destruction is the infusion of fresh blood. A pure Marquesan is a rarity. They seem to be all half-breeds and strange conglomerations of dozens of different races. Nineteen able labourers are all the trader at Taiohae can muster for the loading of copra on shipboard, and in their veins runs the blood of English, American, Dane, German, French, Corsican, Spanish, Portuguese, Chinese, Hawaiian, Paumotan, Tahitian, and Easter Islander. There are more races than there are persons, but it is a wreckage of races at best. Life faints and stumbles and gasps itself away. In this warm, equable clime—a truly terrestrial paradise—where are never extremes of temperature and where the air is like balm, kept ever pure by the ozone-laden southeast trade, asthma, phthisis, and tuberculosis flourish as luxuriantly as the vegetation. Everywhere, from the few grass huts, arises the racking cough or exhausted groan of wasted lungs. Other horrible diseases prosper as well, but the most deadly of all are those that attack the lungs. There is a form of consumption called "galloping," which is especially dreaded. In two months' time it reduces the strongest man to a skeleton under a grave-cloth. In valley after valley the last inhabitant has passed and the fertile soil has relapsed to jungle. In Melville's day the valley of Hapaa (spelled by him "Happar") was peopled by a strong and warlike tribe. A generation later, it contained but two hundred persons. To-day it is an untenanted, howling, tropical wilderness.

We climbed higher and higher in the valley, our unshod stallions picking their steps on the disintegrating trail, which led in and out through the abandoned pae-paes and insatiable jungle. The sight of red mountain apples, the ohias, familiar to us from Hawaii, caused a native to be sent climbing after them. And again he climbed for cocoa-nuts. I have drunk the cocoanuts of Jamaica and of Hawaii, but I never knew how delicious such draught could be till I drank it here in the Marquesas. Occasionally we rode under wild limes and oranges—great trees which had survived the wilderness longer than the motes of humans who had cultivated them.

We rode through endless thickets of yellow-pollened cassi—if riding it could be called; for those fragrant thickets were inhabited by wasps. And such wasps! Great yellow fellows the size of small canary birds, darting through the air with behind them drifting a bunch of legs a couple of inches long. A stallion abruptly stands on his forelegs and thrusts his hind legs skyward. He withdraws them from the sky long enough to make one wild jump ahead, and then returns them to their index position. It is nothing. His thick hide has merely been punctured by a flaming lance of wasp virility. Then a second and a third stallion, and all the stallions, begin to cavort on their forelegs over the precipitous landscape. Swat! A white-hot poniard penetrates my cheek. Swat again!! I am stabbed in the neck. I am bringing up the rear and getting more than my share. There is no retreat, and the plunging horses ahead, on a precarious trail, promise little safety. My horse overruns Charmian's horse, and that sensitive creature, fresh-stung at the psychological moment, planks one of his hoofs into my horse and the other hoof into me. I thank my stars that he is not steel-shod, and half-arise from the saddle at the impact of another flaming dagger. I am certainly getting more than my share, and so is my poor horse, whose pain and panic are only exceeded by mine.

"Get out of the way! I'm coming!" I shout, frantically dashing my cap at the winged vipers around me.

On one side of the trail the landscape rises straight up. On the other side it sinks straight down. The only way to get out of my way is to keep on going. How that string of horses kept their feet is a miracle; but they dashed ahead, over-running one another, galloping, trotting, stumbling, jumping, scrambling, and kicking methodically skyward every time a wasp landed on them. After a while we drew breath and counted our injuries. And this happened not once, nor twice, but time after time. Strange to say, it never grew monotonous. I know that I, for one, came through each brush with the undiminished zest of a man flying from sudden death. No; the pilgrim from Taiohae to Typee will never suffer from ennui on the way.

At last we arose above the vexation of wasps. It was a matter of altitude, however, rather than of fortitude. All about us lay the jagged back-bones of ranges, as far as the eye could see, thrusting their pinnacles into the trade-wind clouds. Under us, from the way we had come, the *Snark* lay like a tiny toy on the calm water of Taiohae Bay. Ahead we could see the inshore indentation of Comptroller Bay. We dropped down a thousand feet, and Typee lay beneath us. "Had a glimpse of the gardens of paradise been revealed to me I could scarcely have been more ravished with the sight"—so said Melville on the moment of his first view of the valley. He saw a garden. We saw a wilderness. Where were the hundred groves of the breadfruit tree he saw? We saw jungle, nothing but jungle, with the exception of two grass huts and several clumps of cocoanuts breaking the primordial green mantle. Where was the Ti of Mehevi, the bachelors' hall, the palace where women were taboo, and where he ruled with his lesser chieftains, keeping the half-dozen dusty and torpid ancients to remind them of the valorous past? From the swift stream no sounds arose of maids and matrons pounding tapa. And where was the hut that old Narheyo eternally builded? In vain I looked for him perched ninety feet from the ground in some tall cocoanut, taking his morning smoke.

We went down a zigzag trail under overarching, matted jungle, where great butterflies drifted by in the silence. No tattooed savage with club and javelin guarded the path; and when we forded the stream, we were free to roam where we pleased. No longer did the taboo, sacred and merciless, reign in that sweet vale. Nay, the taboo still did reign, a new taboo, for when we approached too near the several wretched native women, the taboo was uttered warningly. And it was well. They were lepers. The man who warned us was afflicted horribly with elephantiasis. All were suffering from lung trouble. The valley of Typee was the abode of death, and the dozen survivors of the tribe were gasping feebly the last painful breaths of the race.

Certainly the battle had not been to the strong, for once the Typeans were very strong, stronger than the Happars, stronger than the Taiohaeans, stronger than all the tribes of Nuku-hiva. The word "typee," or, rather, "taipi," originally signified an eater of human flesh. But since all the Marquesans were human-flesh eaters, to be so designated was the token that the Typeans were the human-flesh eaters par excellence. Not alone to Nuku-hiva did the Typean reputation for bravery and ferocity extend. In all the islands of the Marquesas the Typeans were named with dread. Man could not conquer them. Even the French fleet that took possession of the Marquesas left the Typeans alone. Captain Porter, of the frigate Essex, once invaded the valley. His sailors and marines were reinforced by two thousand warriors of Happar and Taiohae. They penetrated quite a distance into the valley, but met with so fierce a resistance that they were glad to retreat and get away in their flotilla of boats and war-canoes.

Of all inhabitants of the South Seas, the Marquesans were adjudged the strongest and the most beautiful. Melville said of them: "I was especially struck by the physical strength and beauty they displayed . . . In beauty of form they surpassed anything I had ever seen. Not a single instance of natural deformity was observable in all the throng attending the revels. Every individual appeared free from those blemishes which sometimes mar the effect of an otherwise perfect form. But their physical excellence did not merely consist in an exemption from these evils; nearly every individual of the number might have been taken for a sculptor's model." Mendana, the discoverer of the Marquesas, described the natives as wondrously beautiful to behold. Figueroa, the chronicler of his voyage, said of them: "In complexion they were nearly white; of good stature and finely formed." Captain Cook called the Marquesans the most splendid islanders in the South Seas. The men were described, as "in almost every instance of lofty stature, scarcely ever less than six feet in height."

And now all this strength and beauty has departed, and the valley of Typee is the abode of some dozen wretched creatures, afflicted by leprosy, elephantiasis, and tuberculosis. Melville estimated the population at two thousand, not taking into consideration the small adjoining valley of Ho-o-u-mi. Life has rotted away in this wonderful garden spot, where the climate is as delightful and healthful as any to be found in the world. Not alone were the Typeans physically magnificent; they were pure. Their air did not contain the bacilli and germs and microbes of disease that fill our own air. And when the white men imported in their ships these various micro-organisms or disease, the Typeans crumpled up and went down before them.

When one considers the situation, one is almost driven to the conclusion that the white race flourishes on impurity and corruption. Natural selection, however, gives the explanation. We of the white race are the survivors and the descendants of the thousands of generations of survivors in the war with the microorganisms. Whenever one of us was born with a constitution peculiarly receptive to these minute enemies, such a one promptly died. Only those of us survived who could withstand them. We who are alive are the immune, the fit—the ones best constituted to live in a world of hostile micro-organisms. The poor Marquesans had undergone no such selection. They were not immune. And they, who had made a custom of eating their enemies, were now eaten by enemies so microscopic as to be invisible, and against whom no war of dart and javelin was possible. On the other hand, had there been a few hundred thousand Marquesans to begin with, there might have been sufficient survivors to lay the foundation for a new race—a regenerated race, if a plunge into a festering bath of organic poison can be called regeneration.

We unsaddled our horses for lunch, and after we had fought the stallions apart—mine with several fresh chunks bitten out of his back—and after we had vainly fought the sand-flies, we ate bananas and tinned meats, washed down by generous draughts of cocoanut milk. There was little to be seen. The jungle had rushed back and engulfed the puny works of man. Here and there pai-pais were to be stumbled upon, but there were no inscriptions, no hieroglyphics, no clues to the past they attested—only dumb stones, builded and carved by hands that were forgotten dust. Out of the pai-pais grew great trees, jealous of the wrought work of man, splitting and scattering the stones back into the primeval chaos.

We gave up the jungle and sought the stream with the idea of evading the sand-flies. Vain hope! To go in swimming one must take off his clothes. The sand-flies are aware of the fact, and they lurk by the river bank in countless myriads. In the native they are called the nau-nau, which is pronounced "now-now." They are certainly well named, for they are the insistent present. There is no past nor future when they fasten upon one's epidermis, and I am willing to wager that Omar Khayyam could never have written *The Rubaiyat* in the valley of Typee—it would have been psychologically impossible. I made the strategic mistake of undressing on the edge of a steep bank where I could dive in but could not climb out. When I was ready to dress, I had a hundred yards' walk on the bank before I could reach my clothes. At the first step, fully ten thousand nau-naus landed upon me. At the second step I was walking in a cloud. By the third step the sun was dimmed in the sky. After that I don't know what happened. When I arrived at my clothes, I was a maniac. And here enters my grand tactical error. There is only one rule of conduct in dealing with nau-naus. Never swat them. Whatever you do, don't swat them. They are so vicious that in the instant of annihilation they eject their last atom of poison into your carcass. You must pluck them delicately, between thumb and forefinger, and persuade them gently to remove their proboscides from your quivering flesh. It is like pulling teeth. But the difficulty was that the teeth sprouted faster than I could pull them, so I swatted, and, so doing, filled myself full with their poison. This was a week ago. At the present moment I resemble a sadly neglected smallpox convalescent.

Ho-o-u-mi is a small valley, separated from Typee by a low ridge, and thither we started when we had knocked our indomitable and insatiable riding-animals into submission. As it was, Warren's mount, after a mile run, selected the most dangerous part of the trail for an exhibition that kept us all on the anxious seat for fully five minutes. We rode by the mouth of Typee valley and gazed down upon the beach from which Melville escaped. There was where the whale-boat lay on its oars close in to the surf; and there was where Karakoee, the taboo Kanaka, stood in the water and trafficked for the sailor's life. There, surely, was where Melville gave Fayaway the parting embrace ere he dashed for the boat. And there was the point of land from which Mehevi and Mow-mow and their following swam off to intercept the boat, only to have their wrists gashed by sheath-knives when they laid hold of the gunwale, though it was reserved for Mow-mow to receive the boat-hook full in the throat from Melville's hands.

We rode on to Ho-o-u-mi. So closely was Melville guarded that he never dreamed of the existence of this valley, though he must continually have met its inhabitants, for they belonged to Typee. We rode through the same abandoned pae-paes, but as we neared the sea we found a profusion of cocoanuts, breadfruit trees and taro patches, and fully a dozen grass dwellings. In one of these we arranged to pass the night, and preparations were immediately put on foot for a feast. A young pig was promptly despatched, and while he was being roasted among hot stones, and while chickens were stewing in cocoanut milk, I persuaded one of the cooks to climb an unusually tall cocoanut palm. The cluster of nuts at the top was fully one hundred and twenty-five feet from the ground, but that native strode up to the tree, seized it in both hands, jack-knived at the waist so that the soles of his feet rested flatly against the trunk, and then he walked right straight up without stopping. There were no notches in the tree. He had no ropes to help him. He merely walked up the tree, one hundred and twenty-five feet in the air, and cast down the nuts from the summit. Not every man there had the physical stamina for such a feat, or the lungs, rather, for most of them were coughing their lives away. Some of the women kept up a ceaseless moaning and groaning, so badly were their lungs wasted. Very few of either sex were full-blooded Marquesans. They were mostly half-breeds and three-quarter-breeds of French, English, Danish, and Chinese extraction. At the best, these infusions of fresh blood merely delayed the passing, and the results led one to wonder whether it was worthwhile.

The feast was served on a broad pae-pae, the rear portion of which was occupied by the house in which we were to sleep. The first course was raw fish and poi-poi, the latter sharp and more acrid of taste than the poi of Hawaii, which is made from taro. The poi-poi of the Marquesas is made from breadfruit. The ripe fruit, after the core is removed, is placed in a calabash and pounded with a stone pestle into a stiff, sticky paste. In this stage of the process, wrapped in leaves, it can be buried in the ground, where it will keep for years. Before it can be eaten, however, further processes are necessary. A leaf-covered package is placed among hot stones, like the pig, and thoroughly baked. After that it is mixed with cold water and thinned out—not thin enough to run, but thin enough to be eaten by sticking one's first and second fingers into it. On close acquaintance it proves a pleasant and most healthful food. And breadfruit, ripe and well boiled or roasted! It is delicious. Breadfruit and taro are kingly vegetables, the pair of them, though the former is patently a misnomer and more resembles a sweet potato than anything else, though it is not mealy like a sweet potato, nor is it so sweet.

The feast ended, we watched the moon rise over Typee. The air was like balm, faintly scented with the breath of flowers. It was a magic night, deathly still, without the slightest breeze to stir the foliage; and one caught one's breath and felt the pang that is almost hurt, so exquisite was the beauty of it. Faint and far could be heard the thin thunder of the surf upon the beach. There were no beds; and we drowsed and slept wherever we thought the floor softest. Near by, a woman panted and moaned in her sleep, and all about us the dying islanders coughed in the night.

Chapter 20
Nature Man

I first met him on Market Street in San Francisco. It was a wet and drizzly afternoon, and he was striding along, clad solely in a pair of abbreviated knee-trousers and an abbreviated shirt, his bare feet going slick-slick through the pavement-slush. At his heels trooped a score of excited gamins. Every head—and there were thousands—turned to glance curiously at him as he went by. And

I turned, too. Never had I seen such lovely sunburn. He was all sunburn, of the sort a blond takes on when his skin does not peel. His long yellow hair was burnt, so was his beard, which sprang from a soil unploughed by any razor. He was a tawny man, a golden-tawny man, all glowing and radiant with the sun. Another prophet, thought I, come up to town with a message that will save the world.

A few weeks later I was with some friends in their bungalow in the Piedmont hills overlooking San Francisco Bay. "We've got him, we've got him," they barked. "We caught him up a tree; but he's all right now, he'll feed from the hand. Come on and see him." So I accompanied them up a dizzy hill, and in a rickety shack in the midst of a eucalyptus grove found my sunburned prophet of the city pavements.

He hastened to meet us, arriving in the whirl and blur of a handspring. He did not shake hands with us; instead, his greeting took the form of stunts. He turned more handsprings. He twisted his body sinuously, like a snake, until, having sufficiently limbered up, he bent from the hips, and, with legs straight and knees touching, beat a tattoo on the ground with the palms of his hands. He whirligigged and pirouetted, dancing and cavorting round like an inebriated ape. All the sun-warmth of his ardent life beamed in his face. I am so happy, was the song without words he sang.

He sang it all evening, ringing the changes on it with an endless variety of stunts. "A fool! a fool! I met a fool in the forest!" thought I, and a worthy fool he proved. Between handsprings and whirligigs he delivered his message that would save the world. It was twofold. First, let suffering humanity strip off its clothing and run wild in the mountains and valleys; and, second, let the very miserable world adopt phonetic spelling. I caught a glimpse of the great social problems being settled by the city populations swarming naked over the landscape, to the popping of shot-guns, the barking of ranch-dogs, and countless assaults with pitchforks wielded by irate farmers.

The years passed, and, one sunny morning, the *Snark* poked her nose into a narrow opening in a reef that smoked with the crashing impact of the trade-wind swell, and beat slowly up Papeete harbour.

Coming off to us was a boat, flying a yellow flag. We knew it contained the port doctor. But quite a distance off, in its wake, was a tiny out rigger canoe that puzzled us. It was flying a red flag. I studied it through the glasses, fearing that it marked some hidden danger to navigation, some recent wreck or some buoy or beacon that had been swept away. Then the doctor came on board. After he had examined the state of our health and been assured that we had no live rats hidden away in the *Snark,* I asked him the meaning of the red flag. "Oh, that is Darling," was the answer.

And then Darling, Ernest Darling flying the red flag that is indicative of the brotherhood of man, hailed us. "Hello, Jack!" he called. "Hello, Charmian! He paddled swiftly nearer, and I saw that he was the tawny prophet of the Piedmont hills. He came over the side, a sun-god clad in a scarlet loin-cloth, with presents of Arcady and greeting in both his hands—a bottle of golden honey and a leaf-basket filled WITH great golden mangoes, golden bananas specked with freckles of deeper gold, golden pine-apples and golden limes, and juicy oranges minted from the same precious ore of sun and soil. And in this fashion under the southern sky, I met once more Darling, the Nature Man.

Tahiti is one of the most beautiful spots in the world, inhabited by thieves and robbers and liars, also by several honest and truthful men and women. Wherefore, because of the blight cast upon Tahiti's wonderful beauty by the spidery human vermin that infest it, I am minded to write, not of Tahiti, but of the Nature Man. He, at least, is refreshing and wholesome. The spirit that emanates from him is so gentle and sweet that it would harm nothing, hurt nobody's feelings save the feelings of a predatory and plutocratic capitalist.

"What does this red flag mean?" I asked.

"Socialism, of course."

"Yes, yes, I know that," I went on; "but what does it mean in your hands?"

"Why, that I've found my message."

"And that you are delivering it to Tahiti?" I demanded incredulously.

"Sure," he answered simply; and later on I found that he was, too.

When we dropped anchor, lowered a small boat into the water, and started ashore, the Nature Man joined us. Now, thought I, I shall be pestered to death by this crank. Waking or sleeping I shall never be quit of him until I sail away from here.

But never in my life was I more mistaken. I took a house and went to live and work in it, and the Nature Man never came near me. He was waiting for the invitation. In the meantime he went aboard the *Snark* and took possession of her library, delighted by the quantity of scientific books, and shocked, as I learned afterwards, by the inordinate amount of fiction. The Nature Man never wastes time on fiction.

After a week or so, my conscience smote me, and I invited him to dinner at a downtown hotel.

He arrived, looking unwontedly stiff and uncomfortable in a cotton jacket. When invited to peel it off, he beamed his gratitude and joy, and did so, revealing his sun-gold skin, from waist to shoulder, covered only by a piece of fish-net of coarse twine and large of mesh. A scarlet loin-cloth completed his costume. I began my acquaintance with him that night, and during my long stay in Tahiti that acquaintance ripened into friendship.

"So you write books," he said, one day when, tired and sweaty, I finished my morning's work.

"I, too, write books," he announced.

Aha, thought I, now at last is he going to pester me with his literary efforts. My soul was in revolt. I had not come all the way to the South Seas to be a literary bureau.

"This is the book I write," he explained, smashing himself a resounding blow on the chest with his clenched fist. "The gorilla in the African jungle pounds his chest till the noise of it can be heard half a mile away."

"A pretty good chest," quoth I, admiringly; "it would even make a gorilla envious."

And then, and later, I learned the details of the marvellous book Ernest Darling had written. Twelve years ago he lay close to death. He weighed but ninety pounds, and was too weak to speak. The doctors had given him up. His father, a practising physician, had given him up. Consultations with other physicians had been held upon him. There was no hope for him. Overstudy (as a school-teacher and as a university student) and two successive attacks of pneumonia were responsible for his breakdown. Day by day he was losing strength. He could extract no nutrition from the heavy foods they gave him; nor could pellets and powders help his stomach to do the work of digestion. Not only was he a physical wreck, but he was a mental wreck. His mind was overwrought. He was sick and tired of medicine, and he was sick and tired of persons. Human speech jarred upon him. Human attentions drove him frantic. The thought came to him that since he was going to die, he might as well die in the open, away from all the bother and irritation. And behind this idea lurked a sneaking idea that perhaps he would not die after all if only he could escape from the heavy foods, the medicines, and the well-intentioned persons who made him frantic.

So Ernest Darling, a bag of bones and a death's-head, a perambulating corpse, with just the dimmest flutter of life in it to make it perambulate, turned his back upon men and the habitations of men and dragged himself for five miles through the brush, away from the city of Portland, Oregon. Of course he was crazy. Only a lunatic would drag himself out of his death-bed.

But in the brush, Darling found what he was looking for—rest. Nobody bothered him with beefsteaks and pork. No physicians lacerated his tired nerves by feeling his pulse, nor tormented his tired stomach with pellets and powders. He began to feel soothed. The sun was shining warm, and he basked in it. He had the feeling that the sunshine was an elixir of health. Then it seemed to him that his whole wasted wreck of a body was crying for the sun. He stripped off his clothes and bathed in the sunshine. He felt better. It had done him good—the first relief in weary months of pain.

As he grew better, he sat up and began to take notice. All about him were the birds fluttering and chirping, the squirrels chattering and playing. He envied them their health and spirits, their happy, care-free existence. That he should contrast their condition with his was inevitable; and that he should question why they were splendidly vigorous while he was a feeble, dying wraith of a man, was likewise inevitable. His conclusion was the very obvious one, namely, that they lived naturally, while he lived most unnaturally, therefore, if he intended to live, he must return to nature.

Alone, there in the brush, he worked out his problem and began to apply it. He stripped off his clothing and leaped and gambolled about, running on all fours, climbing trees; in short, doing physical stunts,—and all the time soaking in the sunshine. He imitated the animals. He built a nest of dry leaves and grasses in which to sleep at night, covering it over with bark as a protection against the early fall rains. "Here is a beautiful exercise," he told me, once, flapping his arms mightily against his sides; "I learned it from watching the roosters crow." Another time I remarked the loud, sucking intake with which he drank cocoanut-milk. He explained that he had noticed the cows drinking that way and concluded there must be something in it. He tried it and found it good, and thereafter he drank only in that fashion.

He noted that the squirrels lived on fruits and nuts. He started on a fruit-and-nut diet, helped out by bread, and he grew stronger and put on weight. For three months he continued his primordial existence in the brush, and then the heavy Oregon rains drove him back to the habitations of men. Not in three months could a ninety-pound survivor of two attacks of pneumonia develop sufficient ruggedness to live through an Oregon winter in the open.

He had accomplished much, but he had been driven in. There was no place to go but back to his father's house, and there, living in close rooms with lungs that panted for all the air of the open sky, he was brought down by a third attack of pneumonia. He grew weaker even than before. In that tottering tabernacle of flesh, his brain collapsed. He lay like a corpse, too weak to stand the fatigue of speaking, too irritated and tired in his miserable brain to care to listen to the speech of others. The only act of will of which he was capable was to stick his fingers in his ears and resolutely to refuse to hear a single word that was spoken to him. They sent for the insanity experts. He was adjudged insane, and also the verdict was given that he would not live a month.

By one such mental expert he was carted off to a sanatorium on Mt. Tabor. Here, when they learned that he was harmless, they gave him his own way. They no longer dictated as to the food he ate, so he resumed his fruits and nuts—olive oil, peanut butter, and bananas the chief articles of his diet. As he regained his strength he made up his mind to live thenceforth his own life. If he lived like others, according to social conventions, he would surely die. And he did not want to die. The fear of death was one of the strongest factors in the genesis of the Nature Man. To live, he must have a natural diet, the open air, and the blessed sunshine.

Now an Oregon winter has no inducements for those who wish to return to Nature, so Darling started out in search of a climate. He mounted a bicycle and headed south for the sunlands. Stanford University claimed him for a year. Here he studied and worked his way, attending lectures in as scant garb as the authorities would allow and applying as much as possible the principles of living that he had learned in squirrel-town. His favourite method of study was to go off in the hills back of the University, and there to strip off his clothes and lie on the grass, soaking in sunshine and health at the same time that he soaked in knowledge.

But Central California has her winters, and the quest for a Nature Man's climate drew him on. He tried Los Angeles and Southern California, being arrested a few times and brought before the insanity commissions because, forsooth, his mode of life was not modelled after the mode of life of his fellow-men. He tried Hawaii, where, unable to prove him insane, the authorities deported him. It was not exactly a deportation. He could have remained by serving a year in prison. They gave him his choice. Now prison is death to the Nature Man, who thrives only in the open air and in God's sunshine. The authorities of Hawaii are not to be blamed. Darling was an undesirable citizen. Any man is undesirable who disagrees with one. And that any man should disagree to the extent Darling did in his philosophy of the simple life is ample vindication of the Hawaiian authorities verdict of his undesirableness.

So Darling went thence in search of a climate which would not only be desirable, but wherein he would not be undesirable. And he found it in Tahiti, the garden-spot of garden-spots. And so it was, according to the narrative as given, that he wrote the pages of his book. He wears only a loin-cloth and a sleeveless fish-net shirt. His stripped weight is one hundred and sixty-five pounds. His health is perfect. His eyesight, that at one time was considered ruined, is excellent. The lungs that were practically destroyed by three attacks of pneumonia have not only recovered, but are stronger than ever before.

I shall never forget the first time, while talking to me, that he squashed a mosquito. The stinging pest had settled in the middle of his back between his shoulders. Without interrupting the flow of conversation, without dropping even a syllable, his clenched fist shot up in the air, curved backward, and smote his back between the shoulders, killing the mosquito and making his frame resound like a bass drum. It reminded me of nothing so much as of horses kicking the woodwork in their stalls.

"The gorilla in the African jungle pounds his chest until the noise of it can be heard half a mile away," he will announce suddenly, and thereat beat a hair-raising, devil's tattoo on his own chest.

One day he noticed a set of boxing-gloves hanging on the wall, and promptly his eyes brightened.

"Do you box?" I asked.

"I used to give lessons in boxing when I was at Stanford," was the reply.

And there and then we stripped and put on the gloves. Bang! a long, gorilla arm flashed out, landing the gloved end on my nose. Biff! he caught me, in a duck, on the side of the head nearly knocking me over sidewise. I carried the lump raised by that blow for a week. I ducked under a straight left, and landed a straight right on his stomach. It was a fearful blow. The whole weight of my body was behind it, and his body had been met as it lunged forward. I looked for him to crumple up and go down. Instead of which his face beamed approval, and he said, "That was beautiful." The next instant I was covering up and striving to protect myself from a hurricane of hooks, jolts, and uppercuts. Then I watched my chance and drove in for the solar plexus. I hit the mark. The Nature Man dropped his arms, gasped, and sat down suddenly.

"I'll be all right," he said. "Just wait a moment."

And inside thirty seconds he was on his feet—ay, and returning the compliment, for he hooked me in the solar plexus, and I gasped, dropped my hands, and sat down just a trifle more suddenly than he had.

All of which I submit as evidence that the man I boxed with was a totally different man from the poor, ninety-pound weight of eight years before, who, given up by physicians and alienists, lay gasping his life away in a closed room in Portland, Oregon. The book that Ernest Darling has written is a good book, and the binding is good, too.

Hawaii has wailed for years her need for desirable immigrants. She has spent much time, and thought, and money, in importing desirable citizens, and she has, as yet, nothing much to show for it. Yet Hawaii deported the Nature Man. She refused to give him a chance. So it is, to chasten Hawaii's proud spirit, that I take this opportunity to show her what she has lost in the Nature Man. When he arrived in Tahiti, he proceeded to seek out a piece of land on which to grow the food he ate. But land was difficult to find—that is, inexpensive land. The Nature Man was not rolling in wealth. He spent weeks in wandering over the steep hills, until, high up the mountain, where clustered several tiny canyons, he found eighty acres of brush-jungle which were apparently unrecorded as the property of any one. The government officials told him that if he would clear the land and till it for thirty years he would be given a title for it.

Immediately he set to work. And never was there such work. Nobody farmed that high up. The land was covered with matted jungle and overrun by wild pigs and countless rats. The view of Papeete and the sea was magnificent, but the outlook was not encouraging. He spent weeks in building a road in order to make the plantation accessible. The pigs and the rats ate up whatever he planted as fast as it sprouted. He shot the pigs and trapped the rats. Of the latter, in two weeks he caught fifteen hundred. Everything had to be carried up on his back. He usually did his packhorse work at night.

Gradually he began to win out. A grass-walled house was built. On the fertile, volcanic soil he had wrested from the jungle and jungle beasts were growing five hundred cocoanut trees, five hundred papaia trees, three hundred mango trees, many breadfruit trees and alligator-pear trees, to say nothing of vines, bushes, and vegetables. He developed the drip of the hills in the canyons and worked out an efficient irrigation scheme, ditching the water from canyon to canyon and paralleling the ditches at different altitudes. His narrow canyons became botanical gardens. The arid shoulders of the hills, where formerly the blazing sun had parched the jungle and beaten it close to earth, blossomed into trees and shrubs and flowers. Not only had the Nature Man become self-supporting, but he was now a prosperous agriculturist with produce to sell to the city-dwellers of Papeete.

Then it was discovered that his land, which the government officials had informed him was without an owner, really had an owner, and that deeds, descriptions, etc., were on record. All his work bade fare to be lost. The land had been valueless when he took it up, and the owner, a large landholder, was unaware of the extent to which the Nature Man had developed it. A just price was agreed upon, and Darling's deed was officially filed.

Next came a more crushing blow. Darling's access to market was destroyed. The road he had built was fenced across by triple barb-wire fences. It was one of those jumbles in human affairs that is so common in this absurdest of social systems. Behind it was the fine hand of the same conservative element that haled the Nature Man before the Insanity Commission in Los Angeles and that deported him from Hawaii. It is so hard for self-satisfied men to understand any man whose satisfactions are fundamentally different. It seems clear that the officials have connived with the conservative element, for to this day the road the Nature Man built is closed; nothing has been done about it, while an adamant unwillingness to do anything about it is evidenced on every hand. But the Nature Man dances and sings along his way. He does not sit up nights thinking about the wrong which has been done him; he leaves the worrying to the doers of the wrong. He has no time for bitterness. He believes he is in the world for the purpose of being happy, and he has not a moment to waste in any other pursuit.

The road to his plantation is blocked. He cannot build a new road, for there is no ground on which he can build it. The government has restricted him to a wild-pig trail which runs precipitously up the mountain. I climbed the trail with him, and we had to climb with hands and feet in order to get up. Nor can that wild-pig trail be made into a road by any amount of toil less than that of an engineer, a steam-engine, and a steel cable. But what does the Nature Man care? In his gentle ethics the evil men do him he requites with goodness. And who shall say he is not happier than they?

"Never mind their pesky road," he said to me as we dragged ourselves up a shelf of rock and sat down, panting, to rest. "I'll get an air machine soon and fool them. I'm clearing a level space for a landing stage for the airships, and next time you come to Tahiti you will alight right at my door."

Yes, the Nature Man has some strange ideas besides that of the gorilla pounding his chest in the African jungle. The Nature Man has ideas about levitation. "Yes, sir," he said to me, "levitation is not impossible. And think of the glory of it—lifting one's self from the ground by an act of will. Think of it! The astronomers tell us that our whole solar system is dying; that, barring accidents, it will all be so cold that no life can live upon it. Very well. In that day all men will be accomplished levitationists, and they will leave this perishing planet and seek more hospitable worlds. How can levitation be accomplished? By progressive fasts. Yes, I have tried them, and toward the end I could feel myself actually getting lighter."

The man is a maniac, thought I.

"Of course," he added, "these are only theories of mine. I like to speculate upon the glorious future of man. Levitation may not be possible, but I like to think of it as possible."

One evening, when he yawned, I asked him how much sleep he allowed himself.

"Seven hours," was the answer. "But in ten years I'll be sleeping only six hours, and in twenty years only five hours. You see, I shall cut off an hour's sleep every ten years."

"Then when you are a hundred you won't be sleeping at all," I interjected.

"Just that. Exactly that. When I am a hundred I shall not require sleep. Also, I shall be living on air. There are plants that live on air, you know."

"But has any man ever succeeded in doing it?"

He shook his head.

"I never heard of him if he did. But it is only a theory of mine, this living on air. It would be fine, wouldn't it? Of course it may be impossible—most likely it is. You see, I am not unpractical. I never forget the present. When I soar ahead into the future, I always leave a string by which to find my way back again."

I fear me the Nature Man is a joker. At any rate he lives the simple life. His laundry bill cannot be large. Up on his plantation he lives on fruit the labour cost of which, in cash, he estimates at five cents a day. At present, because of his obstructed road and because he is head over heels in the propaganda of socialism, he is living in town, where his expenses, including rent, are twenty-five cents a day. In order to pay those expenses he is running a night school for Chinese.

The Nature Man is not bigoted. When there is nothing better to eat than meat, he eats meat, as, for instance, when in jail or on shipboard and the nuts and fruits give out. Nor does he seem to crystallize into anything except sunburn.

"Drop anchor anywhere and the anchor will drag—that is, if your soul is a limitless, fathomless sea, and not dog-pound," he quoted to me, then added: "You see, my anchor is always dragging. I live for human health and progress, and I strive to drag my anchor always in that direction. To me, the two are identical. Dragging anchor is what has saved me. My anchor did not hold me to my death-bed. I dragged anchor into the brush and fooled the doctors. When I recovered health and strength, I started, by preaching and by example, to teach the people to become nature men and nature women.

But they had deaf ears. Then, on the steamer coming to Tahiti, a quarter-master expounded socialism to me. He showed me that an economic square deal was necessary before men and women could live naturally. So I dragged anchor once more, and now I am working for the co-operative commonwealth. When that arrives, it will be easy to bring about nature living."

"I had a dream last night," he went on thoughtfully, his face slowly breaking into a glow. "It seemed that twenty-five nature men and nature women had just arrived on the steamer from California, and that I was starting to go with them up the wild-pig trail to the plantation."

Ah, me, Ernest Darling, sun-worshipper and nature man, there are times when I am compelled to envy you and your carefree existence. I see you now, dancing up the steps and cutting antics on the veranda; your hair dripping from a plunge in the salt sea, your eyes sparkling, your sun-gilded body flashing, your chest resounding to the devil's own tattoo as you chant: "The gorilla in the African jungle pounds his chest until the noise of it can be heard half a mile away." And I shall see you always as I saw you that last day, when the *Snark* poked her nose once more through the passage in the smoking reef, outward bound, and I waved good-bye to those on shore. Not least in goodwill and affection was the wave I gave to the golden sun-god in the scarlet loin-cloth, standing upright in his tiny outrigger canoe.

Chapter 21
The High Sea of Abundance

On the arrival of strangers, every man endeavoured to obtain one as a friend and carry him off to his own habitation, where he is treated with the greatest kindness by the inhabitants of the district; they place him on a high seat and feed him with abundance of the finest food.

—*Polynesian Researches*

The *Snark* was lying at anchor at Raiatea, just off the village of Uturoa. She had arrived the night before, after dark, and we were preparing to pay our first visit ashore. Early in the morning I had noticed a tiny outrigger canoe, with an impossible spritsail, skimming the surface of the lagoon. The canoe itself was coffin-shaped, a mere dugout, fourteen feet long, a scant twelve inches wide, and maybe twenty-four inches deep. It had no lines, except in so far that it was sharp at both ends. Its sides were perpendicular. Shorn of the outrigger, it would have capsized of itself inside a tenth of a second. It was the outrigger that kept it right side up.

I have said that the sail was impossible. It was. It was one of those things, not that you have to see to believe, but that you cannot believe after you have seen it. The hoist of it and the length of its boom were sufficiently appalling; but, not content with that, its artificer had given it a tremendous head. So large was the head that no common sprit could carry the strain of it in an ordinary breeze. So a spar had been lashed to the canoe, projecting aft over the water. To this had been made fast a sprit guy: thus, the foot of the sail was held by the main-sheet, and the peak by the guy to the sprit.

It was not a mere boat, not a mere canoe, but a sailing machine. And the man in it sailed it by his weight and his nerve—principally by the latter. I watched the canoe beat up from leeward and run in toward the village, its sole occupant far out on the outrigger and luffing up and spilling the wind in the puffs.

"Well, I know one thing," I announced; "I don't leave Raiatea till I have a ride in that canoe."

A few minutes later Warren called down the companionway, "Here's that canoe you were talking about."

Promptly I dashed on deck and gave greeting to its owner, a tall, slender Polynesian, ingenuous of face, and with clear, sparkling, intelligent eyes. He was clad in a scarlet loin-cloth and a straw hat. In his hands were presents—a fish, a bunch of greens, and several enormous yams. All of which acknowledged by smiles (which are coinage still in isolated spots of Polynesia) and by frequent repetitions of mauruuru (which is the Tahitian "thank you"), I proceeded to make signs that I desired to go for a sail in his canoe.

His face lighted with pleasure and he uttered the single word, "Tahaa," turning at the same time and pointing to the lofty, cloud-draped peaks of an island three miles away—the island of Tahaa. It was fair wind over, but a head-beat back. Now I did not want to go to Tahaa. I had letters to deliver in Raiatea, and officials to see, and there was Charmian down below getting ready to go ashore. By insistent signs I indicated that I desired no more than a short sail on the lagoon. Quick was the disappointment in his face, yet smiling was the acquiescence.

"Come on for a sail," I called below to Charmian. "But put on your swimming suit. It's going to be wet."

It wasn't real. It was a dream. That canoe slid over the water like a streak of silver. I climbed out on the outrigger and supplied the weight to hold her down, while Tehei (pronounced Tayhayee) supplied the nerve. He, too, in the puffs, climbed part way out on the outrigger, at the same time steering with both hands on a large paddle and holding the mainsheet with his foot.

"Ready about!" he called.

I carefully shifted my weight inboard in order to maintain the equilibrium as the sail emptied.

"Hard a-lee!" he called, shooting her into the wind.

I slid out on the opposite side over the water on a spar lashed across the canoe, and we were full and away on the other tack.

"All right," said Tehei.

Those three phrases, "Ready about," "Hard a-lee," and "All right," comprised Tehei's English vocabulary and led me to suspect that at some time he had been one of a Kanaka crew under an American captain. Between the puffs I made signs to him and repeatedly and interrogatively uttered the word SAILOR. Then I tried it in atrocious French. MARIN conveyed no meaning to him; nor did MATELOT. Either my French was bad, or else he was not up in it. I have since concluded that both conjectures were correct. Finally, I began naming over the adjacent islands. He nodded that he had been to them. By the time my quest reached Tahiti, he caught my drift. His thought-processes were almost visible, and it was a joy to watch him think. He nodded his head vigorously.

Yes, he had been to Tahiti, and he added himself names of islands such as Tikihau, Rangiroa, and Fakarava, thus proving that he had sailed as far as the Paumotus—undoubtedly one of the crew of a trading schooner.

After our short sail, when he had returned on board, he by signs inquired the destination of the *Snark*, and when I had mentioned Samoa, Fiji, New Guinea, France, England, and California in their geographical sequence, he said "Samoa," and by gestures intimated that he wanted to go along. Whereupon I was hard put to explain that there was no room for him. "Petit bateau" finally solved it, and again the disappointment in his face was accompanied by smiling acquiescence, and promptly came the renewed invitation to accompany him to Tahaa.

Charmian and I looked at each other. The exhilaration of the ride we had taken was still upon us. Forgotten were the letters to Raiatea, the officials we had to visit. Shoes, a shirt, a pair of trousers, cigarettes matches, and a book to read were hastily crammed into a biscuit tin and wrapped in a rubber blanket, and we were over the side and into the canoe.

"When shall we look for you?" Warren called, as the wind filled the sail and sent Tehei and me scurrying out on the outrigger.

"I don't know," I answered. "When we get back, as near as I can figure it."

And away we went. The wind had increased, and with slacked sheets we ran off before it. The freeboard of the canoe was no more than two and a half inches, and the little waves continually lapped over the side. This required bailing. Now bailing is one of the principal functions of the vahine. Vahine is the Tahitian for woman, and Charmian being the only vahine aboard, the bailing fell appropriately to her. Tehei and I could not very well do it, the both of us being perched part way out on the outrigger and busied with keeping the canoe bottom-side down. So Charmian bailed, with a wooden scoop of primitive design, and so well did she do it that there were occasions when she could rest off almost half the time.

Raiatea and Tahaa are unique in that they lie inside the same encircling reef. Both are volcanic islands, ragged of sky-line, with

heaven-aspiring peaks and minarets. Since Raiatea is thirty miles in circumference, and Tahaa fifteen miles, some idea may be gained of the magnitude of the reef that encloses them. Between them and the reef stretches from one to two miles of water, forming a beautiful lagoon. The huge Pacific seas, extending in unbroken lines sometimes a mile or half as much again in length, hurl themselves upon the reef, overtowering and falling upon it with tremendous crashes, and yet the fragile coral structure withstands the shock and protects the land. Outside lies destruction to the mightiest ship afloat. Inside reigns the calm of untroubled water, whereon a canoe like ours can sail with no more than a couple of inches of free-board.

We flew over the water. And such water!—clear as the clearest spring-water, and crystalline in its clearness, all intershot with a maddening pageant of colours and rainbow ribbons more magnificently gorgeous than any rainbow. Jade green alternated with turquoise, peacock blue with emerald, while now the canoe skimmed over reddish purple pools, and again over pools of dazzling, shimmering white where pounded coral sand lay beneath and upon which oozed monstrous sea-slugs. One moment we were above wonder-gardens of coral, wherein coloured fishes disported, fluttering like marine butterflies; the next moment we were dashing across the dark surface of deep channels, out of which schools of flying fish lifted their silvery flight; and a third moment we were above other gardens of living coral, each more wonderful than the last. And above all was the tropic, trade-wind sky with its fluffy clouds racing across the zenith and heaping the horizon with their soft masses.

Before we were aware, we were close in to Tahaa (pronounced Tah-hah-ah, with equal accents), and Tehei was grinning approval of the vahine's proficiency at bailing. The canoe grounded on a shallow shore, twenty feet from land, and we waded out on a soft bottom where big slugs curled and writhed under our feet and where small octopuses advertised their existence by their superlative softness when stepped upon. Close to the beach, amid cocoanut palms and banana trees, erected on stilts, built of bamboo, with a grass-thatched roof, was Tehei's house. And out of the house came Tehei's vahine, a slender mite of a woman, kindly eyed and Mongolian of feature—when she was not North American Indian. "Bihaura," Tehei called her, but he did not pronounce it according to English notions of spelling. Spelled "Bihaura," it sounded like Bee-ah-oo-rah, with every syllable sharply emphasized.

She took Charmian by the hand and led her into the house, leaving Tehei and me to follow. Here, by sign-language unmistakable, we were informed that all they possessed was ours. No hidalgo was ever more generous in the expression of giving, while I am sure that few hidalgos were ever as generous in the actual practice. We quickly discovered that we dare not admire their possessions, for whenever we did admire a particular object it was immediately presented to us. The two vahines, according to the way of vahines, got together in a discussion and examination of feminine fripperies, while Tehei and I, manlike, went over fishing-tackle and wild-pig-hunting, to say nothing of the device whereby bonitas are caught on forty-foot poles from double canoes. Charmian admired a sewing basket—the best example she had seen of Polynesian basketry; it was hers. I admired a bonita hook, carved in one piece from a pearl-shell; it was mine. Charmian was attracted by a fancy braid of straw sennit, thirty feet of it in a roll, sufficient to make a hat of any design one wished; the roll of sennit was hers. My gaze lingered upon a poi-pounder that dated back to the old stone days; it was mine. Charmian dwelt a moment too long on a wooden poi-bowl, canoe-shaped, with four legs, all carved in one piece of wood; it was hers. I glanced a second time at a gigantic cocoanut calabash; it was mine. Then Charmian and I held a conference in which we resolved to admire no more—not because it did not pay well enough, but because it paid too well. Also, we were already racking our brains over the contents of the *Snark* for suitable return presents. Christmas is an easy problem compared with a Polynesian giving-feast.

We sat on the cool porch, on Bihaura's best mats while dinner was preparing, and at the same time met the villagers. In twos and threes and groups they strayed along, shaking hands and uttering the Tahitian word of greeting—Ioarana, pronounced YO-rah-nah. The men, big strapping fellows, were in loin-cloths, with here and there no shirt, while the women wore the universal ahu, a sort of adult pinafore that flows in graceful lines from the shoulders to the ground. Sad to see was the elephantiasis that afflicted some of them. Here would be a comely woman of magnificent proportions, with the port of a queen, yet marred by one arm four times—or a dozen times—the size of the other. Beside her might stand a six-foot man, erect, mighty-muscled, bronzed, with the body of a god, yet with feet and calves so swollen that they ran together, forming legs, shapeless, monstrous, that were for all the world like elephant legs.

No one seems really to know the cause of the South Sea elephantiasis. One theory is that it is caused by the drinking of polluted water. Another theory attributes it to inoculation through mosquito bites. A third theory charges it to predisposition plus the process of acclimatization. On the other hand, no one that stands in finicky dread of it and similar diseases can afford to travel in the South Seas. There will be occasions when such a one must drink water. There may be also occasions when the mosquitoes let up biting. But every precaution of the finicky one will be useless. If he runs barefoot across the beach to have a swim, he will tread where an elephantiasis case trod a few minutes before. If he closets himself in his own house, yet every bit of fresh food on his table will have been subjected to the contamination, be it flesh, fish, fowl, or vegetable. In the public market at Papeete two known lepers run stalls, and heaven alone knows through what channels arrive at that market the daily supplies of fish, fruit, meat, and vegetables. The only happy way to go through the South Seas is with a careless poise, without apprehension, and with a Christian Science-like faith in the resplendent fortune of your own particular star. When you see a woman, afflicted with elephantiasis wringing out cream from cocoanut meat with her naked hands, drink and reflect how good is the cream, forgetting the hands that pressed it out. Also, remember that diseases such as elephantiasis and leprosy do not seem to be caught by contact.

We watched a Raratongan woman, with swollen, distorted limbs, prepare our cocoanut cream, and then went out to the cook-shed where Tehei and Bihaura were cooking dinner. And then it was served to us on a dry-goods box in the house. Our hosts waited until we were done and then spread their table on the floor. But our table! We were certainly in the high seat of abundance. First, there was glorious raw fish, caught several hours before from the sea and steeped the intervening time in lime-juice diluted with water. Then came roast chicken. Two cocoanuts, sharply sweet, served for drink. There were bananas that tasted like strawberries and that melted in the mouth, and there was banana-poi that made one regret that his Yankee forebears ever attempted puddings. Then there was boiled yam, boiled taro, and roasted feis, which last are nothing more or less than large mealy, juicy, red-coloured cooking bananas. We marvelled at the abundance, and, even as we marvelled, a pig was brought on, a whole pig, a sucking pig, swathed in green leaves and roasted upon the hot stones of a native oven, the most honourable and triumphant dish in the Polynesian cuisine. And after that came coffee, black coffee, delicious coffee, native coffee grown on the hillsides of Tahaa.

Tehei's fishing-tackle fascinated me, and after we arranged to go fishing, Charmian and I decided to remain all night. Again Tehei broached Samoa, and again my petit bateau brought the disappointment and the smile of acquiescence to his face. Bora Bora was my next port. It was not so far away but that cutters made the passage back and forth between it and Raiatea. So I invited Tehei to go that far with us on the *Snark*. Then I learned that his wife had been born on Bora Bora and still owned a house there. She likewise was invited, and immediately came the counter invitation to stay with them in their house in Born Bora. It was Monday. Tuesday we would go fishing and return to Raiatea. Wednesday we would sail by Tahaa and off a certain point, a mile away, pick up Tehei and Bihaura and go on to Bora Bora. All this we arranged in detail, and talked over scores of other things as well, and yet Tehei knew three phrases in English, Charmian and I knew possibly a dozen Tahitian words, and among the four of us there were a dozen or so French words that all understood. Of course, such polyglot conversation was slow, but, eked out with a pad, a lead pencil, the face of a clock Charmian drew on the back of a pad, and with ten thousand and one gestures, we managed to get on very nicely.

At the first moment we evidenced an inclination for bed the visiting natives, with soft Iaoranas, faded away, and Tehei and Bihaura likewise faded away. The house consisted of one large room, and it was given over to us, our hosts going elsewhere to sleep. In truth, their castle was ours. And right here, I want to say that of all the entertainment I have received in this world at the hands of all sorts of races in all sorts of places, I have never received entertainment that equalled this at the hands of this brown-skinned couple of Tahaa. I do not refer to the presents, the free-handed generousness, the high abundance, but to the fineness of courtesy and consideration and tact, and to the sympathy that was real sympathy in that it was understanding. They did nothing they thought ought to be done for us, according to their standards, but they did what they divined we waited to be done for us, while their divination was most successful. It would be impossible to enumerate the hundreds of little acts of consideration they performed during the few days of our intercourse. Let it suffice for me to say that of all hospitality and entertainment I have known, in no case was theirs not only not excelled, but in no case was it quite equalled. Perhaps the most delightful feature of it was that it was due to no training, to no complex social ideals, but that it was the untutored and spontaneous outpouring from their hearts.

The next morning we went fishing, that is, Tehei, Charmian, and I did, in the coffin-shaped canoe; but this time the enormous sail was left behind. There was no room for sailing and fishing at the same time in that tiny craft. Several miles away, inside the reef, in a channel twenty fathoms deep, Tehei dropped his baited hooks and rock-sinkers. The bait was chunks of octopus flesh, which he bit out of a live octopus that writhed in the bottom of the canoe. Nine of these lines he set, each line attached to one end of a short length of bamboo floating on the surface. When a fish was hooked, the end of the bamboo was drawn under the water. Naturally, the other end rose up in the air, bobbing and waving frantically for us to make haste. And make haste we did, with whoops and yells and driving paddles, from one signalling bamboo to another, hauling up from the depths great glistening beauties from two to three feet in length.

Steadily, to the eastward, an ominous squall had been rising and blotting out the bright trade-wind sky. And we were three miles to leeward of home. We started as the first wind-gusts whitened the water. Then came the rain, such rain as only the tropics afford, where every tap and main in the sky is open wide, and when, to top it all, the very reservoir itself spills over in blinding deluge. Well, Charmian was in a swimming suit, I was in pyjamas, and Tehei wore only a loin-cloth. Bihaura was on the beach waiting for us, and she led Charmian into the house in much the same fashion that the mother leads in the naughty little girl who has been playing in mud-puddles.

It was a change of clothes and a dry and quiet smoke while kai-kai was preparing. Kai-kai, by the way, is the Polynesian for "food" or "to eat," or, rather, it is one form of the original root, whatever it may have been, that has been distributed far and wide over the vast area of the Pacific. It is kai in the Marquesas, Raratonga, Manahiki, Niue, Fakaafo, Tonga, New Zealand, and Vate. In Tahiti "to eat" changes to amu, in Hawaii and Samoa to ai, in Ban to kana, in Nina to kana, in Nongone to kaka, and in New Caledonia to ki. But by whatsoever sound or symbol, it was welcome to our ears after that long paddle in the rain. Once more we sat in the high seat of abundance until we regretted that we had been made unlike the image of the giraffe and the camel.

Again, when we were preparing to return to the *Snark*, the sky to windward turned black and another squall swooped down. But this time it was little rain and all wind. It blew hour after hour, moaning and screeching through the palms, tearing and wrenching and shaking the frail bamboo dwelling, while the outer reef set no a mighty thundering as it broke the force of the swinging seas. Inside the reef, the lagoon, sheltered though it was, was white with fury, and not even Tehei's seamanship could have enabled his slender canoe to live in such a welter.

By sunset, the back of the squall had broken though it was still too rough for the canoe. So I had Tehei find a native who was willing to venture his cutter across to Raiatea for the outrageous sum of two dollars, Chili, which is equivalent in our money to ninety cents. Half the village was told off to carry presents, with which Tehei and Bihaura speeded their parting guests—captive chickens, fishes dressed and swathed in wrappings of green leaves, great golden bunches of bananas, leafy baskets spilling over with oranges and limes, alligator pears (the butter-fruit, also called the avoca), huge baskets of yams, bunches of taro and cocoanuts, and last of all, large branches and trunks of trees—firewood for the *Snark*.

While on the way to the cutter we met the only white man on Tahaa, and of all men, George Lufkin, a native of New England! Eighty-six years of age he was, sixty-odd of which, he said, he had spent in the Society Islands, with occasional absences, such as the gold rush to Eldorado in '49 and a short period of ranching in California near Tulare. Given no more than three months by the doctors to live, he had returned to his South Seas and lived to eighty-six and to chuckle over the doctors aforesaid, who were all in their graves. Fee-fee he had, which is the native for elephantiasis and which is pronounced fay-fay. A quarter of a century before, the disease had fastened upon him, and it would remain with him until he died. We asked him about kith and kin. Beside him sat a sprightly damsel of sixty, his daughter. "She is all I have," he murmured plaintively, "and she has no children living."

The cutter was a small, sloop-rigged affair, but large it seemed alongside Tehei's canoe. On the other hand, when we got out on the lagoon and were struck by another heavy wind-squall, the cutter became liliputian, while the *Snark*, in our imagination, seemed to promise all the stability and permanence of a continent. They were good boatmen. Tehei and Bihaura had come along to see us home, and the latter proved a good boatwoman herself. The cutter was well ballasted, and we met the squall under full sail. It was getting dark, the lagoon was full of coral patches, and we were carrying on. In the height of the squall we had to go about, in order to make a short leg to windward to pass around a patch of coral no more than a foot under the surface. As the cutter filled on the other tack, and while she was in that "dead" condition that precedes gathering way, she was knocked flat. Jib-sheet and main-sheet were let go, and she righted into the wind. Three times she was knocked down, and three times the sheets were flung loose, before she could get away on that tack.

By the time we went about again, darkness had fallen. We were now to windward of the *Snark*, and the squall was howling. In came the jib, and down came the mainsail, all but a patch of it the size of a pillow-slip. By an accident we missed the *Snark*, which was riding it out to two anchors, and drove aground upon the inshore coral. Running the longest line on the *Snark* by means of the launch, and after an hour's hard work, we heaved the cutter off and had her lying safely astern.

The day we sailed for Bora Bora the wind was light, and we crossed the lagoon under power to the point where Tehei and Bihaura were to meet us. As we made in to the land between the coral banks, we vainly scanned the shore for our friends. There was no sign of them.

"We can't wait," I said. "This breeze won't fetch us to Bora Bora by dark, and I don't want to use any more gasolene than I have to."

You see, gasolene in the South Seas is a problem. One never knows when he will be able to replenish his supply.

But just then Tehei appeared through the trees as he came down to the water. He had peeled off his shirt and was wildly waving it. Bihaura apparently was not ready. Once aboard, Tehei informed us by signs that we must proceed along the land till we got opposite to his house. He took the wheel and conned the *Snark* through the coral, around point after point till we cleared the last point of all. Cries of welcome went up from the beach, and Bihaura, assisted by several of the villagers, brought off two canoe-loads of abundance. There were yams, taro, feis, breadfruit, cocoanuts, oranges, limes, pineapples, watermelons, alligator pears, pomegranates, fish, chickens galore crowing and cackling and laying eggs on our decks, and a live pig that squealed infernally and all the time in apprehension of imminent slaughter.

Under the rising moon we came in through the perilous passage of the reef of Bora Bora and dropped anchor off Vaitape village. Bihaura, with housewifely anxiety, could not get ashore too quickly to her house to prepare more abundance for us. While the launch was taking her and Tehei to the little jetty, the sound of music and of singing drifted across the quiet lagoon. Throughout the Society Islands we had been continually informed that we would find the Bora Borans very jolly. Charmian and I went ashore to see, and on the village green, by forgotten graves on the beach, found the youths and maidens dancing, flower-garlanded and flower-bedecked, with strange phosphorescent flowers in their hair that pulsed and dimmed and glowed in the moonlight. Farther along the beach we came upon a huge grass house, oval-shaped seventy feet in length, where the elders of the village were singing himines. They, too, were flower-garlanded and jolly, and they welcomed us into the fold as little lost sheep straying along from outer darkness.

Early next morning Tehei was on board, with a string of fresh-caught fish and an invitation to dinner for that evening. On the way to dinner, we dropped in at the himine house. The same elders were singing, with here or there a youth or maiden that we had not seen the previous night. From all the signs, a feast was in preparation. Towering up from the floor was a mountain of fruits and vegetables, flanked on either side by numerous chickens tethered by cocoanut strips. After several himines had been sung, one of the men arose and made oration. The oration was made to us, and though it was Greek to us, we knew that in some way it connected us with that mountain of provender.

"Can it be that they are presenting us with all that?" Charmian whispered.

"Impossible," I muttered back. "Why should they be giving it to us? Besides, there is no room on the *Snark* for it. We could not eat a tithe of it. The rest would spoil. Maybe they are inviting us to the feast. At any rate, that they should give all that to us is impossible."

Nevertheless we found ourselves once more in the high seat of abundance. The orator, by gestures unmistakable, in detail presented every item in the mountain to us, and next he presented it to us in toto. It was an embarrassing moment. What would you do if you lived in a hall bedroom and a friend gave you a white elephant? Our *Snark* was no more than a hall bedroom, and already she was loaded down with the abundance of Tahaa. This new supply was too much. We blushed, and stammered, and mauruuru'd. We mauruuru'd with repeated nui's which conveyed the largeness and overwhelmingness of our thanks. At the same time, by signs, we committed the awful breach of etiquette of not accepting the present. The himine singers' disappointment was plainly betrayed, and that evening, aided by Tehei, we compromised by accepting one chicken, one bunch of bananas, one bunch of taro, and so on down the list.

But there was no escaping the abundance. I bought a dozen chickens from a native out in the country, and the following day he delivered thirteen chickens along with a canoe-load of fruit. The French storekeeper presented us with pomegranates and lent us his finest horse. The gendarme did likewise, lending us a horse that was the very apple of his eye. And everybody sent us flowers. The *Snark* was a fruit-stand and a greengrocer's shop masquerading under the guise of a conservatory. We went around flower-garlanded all the time. When the himine singers came on board to sing, the maidens kissed us welcome, and the crew, from captain to cabin-boy, lost its heart to the maidens of Bora Bora. Tehei got up a big fishing expedition in our honour, to which we went in a double canoe, paddled by a dozen strapping Amazons. We were relieved that no fish were caught, else the *Snark* would have sunk at her moorings.

The days passed, but the abundance did not diminish. On the day of departure, canoe after canoe put off to us. Tehei brought cucumbers and a young papaia tree burdened with splendid fruit. Also, for me he brought a tiny, double canoe with fishing apparatus complete. Further, he brought fruits and vegetables with the same lavishness as at Tahaa. Bihaura brought various special presents for Charmian, such as silk-cotton pillows, fans, and fancy mats. The whole population brought fruits, flowers, and chickens. And Bihaura added a live sucking pig. Natives whom I did not remember ever having seen before strayed over the rail and presented me with such things as fish-poles, fish-lines, and fish-hooks carved from pearl-shell.

As the *Snark* sailed out through the reef, she had a cutter in tow. This was the craft that was to take Bihaura back to Tahaa—but not Tehei. I had yielded at last, and he was one of the crew of the *Snark*. When the cutter cast off and headed east, and the *Snark*'s bow turned toward the west, Tehei knelt down by the cockpit and breathed a silent prayer, the tears flowing down his cheeks. A week later, when Martin got around to developing and printing, he showed Tehei some of the photographs. And that brown-skinned son of Polynesia, gazing on the pictured lineaments of his beloved Bihaura broke down in tears.

But the abundance! There was so much of it. We could not work the *Snark* for the fruit that was in the way. She was festooned with fruit. The life-boat and launch were packed with it. The awning guys groaned under their burdens. But once we struck the full trade-wind sea, the disburdening began. At every roll the *Snark* shook overboard a bunch or so of bananas and cocoanuts, or a basket of limes. A golden flood of limes washed about in the lee-scuppers. The big baskets of yams burst, and pineapples and pomegranates rolled back and forth. The chickens had got loose and were everywhere, roosting on the awnings, fluttering and squawking out on the jib-boom, and essaying the perilous feat of balancing on the spinnaker-boom. They were wild chickens, accustomed to flight. When attempts were made to catch them, they flew out over the ocean, circled about, and came lack. Sometimes they did not come back. And in the confusion, unobserved, the little sucking pig got loose and slipped overboard.

"On the arrival of strangers, every man endeavoured to obtain one as a friend and carry him off to his own habitation, where he is treated with the greatest kindness by the inhabitants of the district: they place him on a high seat and feed him with abundance of the finest foods."

Chapter 22
Cruising in the Solomons

"Why not come along now?" said Captain Jansen to us, at Penduffryn, on the island of Guadalcanar.

Charmian and I looked at each other and debated silently for half a minute. Then we nodded our heads simultaneously. It is a way we have of making up our minds to do things; and a very good way it is when one has no temperamental tears to shed over the last tin-of condensed milk when it has capsized. (We are living on tinned goods these days, and since mind is rumoured to be an emanation of matter, our similes are naturally of the packing-house variety.)

"You'd better bring your revolvers along, and a couple of rifles," said Captain Jansen. "I've got five rifles aboard, though the one Mauser is without ammunition. Have you a few rounds to spare?"

We brought our rifles on board, several handfuls of Mauser cartridges, and Wada and Nakata, the *Snark*'s cook and cabin-boy respectively. Wada and Nakata were in a bit of a funk. To say the least, they were not enthusiastic, though never did Nakata show the white feather in the face of danger. The Solomon Islands had not dealt kindly with them. In the first place, both had suffered from Solomon sores. So had the rest of us (at the time, I was nursing two fresh ones on a diet of corrosive sublimate); but the two Japanese had had more than their share. And the sores are not nice. They may be described as excessively active ulcers. A mosquito bite, a cut, or the slightest abrasion, serves for lodgment of the poison with which the air seems to be filled. Immediately the ulcer commences to eat. It eats in every direction, consuming skin and muscle with astounding rapidity. The pin-point ulcer of the first day is the size of a dime by the second day, and by the end of the week a silver dollar will not cover it.

Worse than the sores, the two Japanese had been afflicted with Solomon Island fever. Each had been down repeatedly with it, and in their weak, convalescent moments they were wont to huddle together on the portion of the *Snark* that happened to be nearest to faraway Japan, and to gaze yearningly in that direction.

But worst of all, they were now brought on board the *Minota* for a recruiting cruise along the savage coast of Malaita. Wada, who had the worse funk, was sure that he would never see Japan again, and with bleak, lack-lustre eyes he watched our rifles and ammunition going on board the *Minota*. He knew about the *Minota* and her Malaita cruises. He knew that she had been captured six months before on the Malaita coast, that her captain had been chopped to pieces with tomahawks, and that, according to the barbarian sense of equity on that sweet isle, she owed two more heads. Also, a labourer on Penduffryn Plantation, a Malaita boy, had just died of dysentery, and Wada knew that Penduffryn had been put in the debt of Malaita by one more head. Furthermore, in stowing our luggage away in the skipper's tiny cabin, he saw the axe gashes on the door where the triumphant bushmen had cut their way in. And, finally, the galley stove was without a pipe—said pipe having been part of the loot.

The *Minota* was a teak-built, Australian yacht, ketch-rigged, long and lean, with a deep fin-keel, and designed for harbour racing rather than for recruiting blacks. When Charmian and I came on board, we found her crowded. Her double boat's crew, including substitutes, was fifteen, and she had a score and more of "return" boys, whose time on the plantations was served and who were bound back to their bush villages. To look at, they were certainly true head-hunting cannibals. Their perforated nostrils were thrust through with bone and wooden bodkins the size of lead-pencils. Numbers of them had punctured the extreme meaty point of the nose, from which protruded, straight out, spikes of turtle-shell or of beads strung on stiff wire. A few had further punctured their noses with rows of holes following the curves of the nostrils from lip to point. Each ear of every man had from two to a dozen holes in it—holes large enough to carry wooden plugs three inches in diameter down to tiny holes in which were carried clay-pipes and similar trifles. In fact, so many holes did they possess that they lacked ornaments to fill them; and when, the following day, as we neared Malaita, we tried out our rifles to see that they were in working order, there was a general scramble for the empty cartridges, which were thrust forthwith into the many aching voids in our passengers' ears.

At the time we tried out our rifles we put up our barbed wire railings. The *Minota*, crown-decked, without any house, and with a rail six inches high, was too accessible to boarders. So brass stanchions were screwed into the rail and a double row of barbed wire stretched around her from stem to stern and back again. Which was all very well as a protection from savages, but it was mighty uncomfortable to those on board when the *Minota* took to jumping and plunging in a sea-way. When one dislikes sliding down upon the lee-rail barbed wire, and when he dares not catch hold of the weather-rail barbed wire to save himself from sliding, and when, with these various disinclinations, he finds himself on a smooth flush-deck that is heeled over at an angle of forty-five degrees, some of the delights of Solomon Islands cruising may be comprehended. Also, it must be remembered, the penalty of a fall into the barbed wire is more than the mere scratches, for each scratch is practically certain to become a venomous ulcer. That caution will not save one from the wire was evidenced one fine morning when we were running along the Malaita coast with the breeze on our quarter. The wind was fresh, and a tidy sea was making. A black boy was at the wheel. Captain Jansen, Mr. Jacobsen (the mate), Charmian, and I had just sat down on deck to breakfast. Three unusually large seas caught us. The boy at the wheel lost his head. Three times the *Minota* was swept. The breakfast was rushed over the lee-rail. The knives and forks went through the scuppers; a boy aft went clean overboard and was dragged back; and our doughty skipper lay half inboard and half out, jammed in the barbed wire. After that, for the rest of the cruise, our joint use of the several remaining eating utensils was a splendid example of primitive communism. On the *Eugenie*, however, it was even worse, for we had but one teaspoon among four of us—but the *Eugenie* is another story.

Our first port was Su'u on the west coast of Malaita. The Solomon Islands are on the fringe of things. It is difficult enough sailing on dark nights through reef-spiked channels and across erratic currents where there are no lights to guide (from northwest to southeast the Solomons extend across a thousand miles of sea, and on all the thousands of miles of coasts there is not one lighthouse); but the difficulty is seriously enhanced by the fact that the land itself is not correctly charted. Su'u is an example. On the Admiralty chart of Malaita the coast at this point runs a straight, unbroken line. Yet across this straight, unbroken line the *Minota* sailed in twenty fathoms of water. Where the land was alleged to be, was a deep indentation. Into this we sailed, the mangroves closing about us, till we dropped anchor in a mirrored pond. Captain Jansen did not like the anchorage. It was the first time he had been there, and Su'u had a bad reputation. There was no wind with which to get away in case of attack, while the crew could be bushwhacked to a man if they attempted to tow out in the whale-boat. It was a pretty trap, if trouble blew up.

"Suppose the *Minota* went ashore—what would you do?" I asked.

"She's not going ashore," was Captain Jansen's answer.

"But just in case she did?" I insisted. He considered for a moment and shifted his glance from the mate buckling on a revolver to the boat's crew climbing into the whale-boat each man with a rifle.

"We'd get into the whale-boat, and get out of here as fast as God'd let us," came the skipper's delayed reply.

He explained at length that no white man was sure of his Malaita crew in a tight place; that the bushmen looked upon all wrecks as their personal property; that the bushmen possessed plenty of Snider rifles; and that he had on board a dozen "return" boys for Su'u who were certain to join in with their friends and relatives ashore when it came to looting the *Minota.*

The first work of the whale-boat was to take the "return" boys and their trade-boxes ashore. Thus one danger was removed. While this was being done, a canoe came alongside manned by three naked savages. And when I say naked, I mean naked. Not one vestige of clothing did they have on, unless nose-rings, ear-plugs, and shell armlets be accounted clothing. The head man in the canoe was an old chief, one-eyed, reputed to be friendly, and so dirty that a boat-scraper would have lost its edge on him. His mission was to warn the skipper against allowing any of his people to go ashore. The old fellow repeated the warning again that night.

In vain did the whale-boat ply about the shores of the bay in quest of recruits. The bush was full of armed natives; all willing enough to talk with the recruiter, but not one would engage to sign on for three years' plantation labour at six pounds per year. Yet they were anxious enough to get our people ashore. On the second day they raised a smoke on the beach at the head of the bay. This being the customary signal of men desiring to recruit, the boat was sent. But nothing resulted. No one recruited, nor were any of our men lured ashore. A little later we caught glimpses of a number of armed natives moving about on the beach.

Outside of these rare glimpses, there was no telling how many might be lurking in the bush. There was no penetrating that primeval jungle with the eye. In the afternoon, Captain Jansen, Charmian, and I went dynamiting fish. Each one of the boat's crew carried a Lee-Enfield. "Johnny," the native recruiter, had a Winchester beside him at the steering sweep. We rowed in close to a portion of the shore that looked deserted. Here the boat was turned around and backed in; in case of attack, the boat would be ready to dash away. In all the time I was on Malaita I never saw a boat land bow on. In fact, the recruiting vessels use two boats—one to go in on the beach, armed, of course, and the other to lie off several hundred feet and "cover" the first boat. The *Minota*, however, being a small vessel, did not carry a covering boat.

We were close in to the shore and working in closer, stern-first, when a school of fish was sighted. The fuse was ignited and the stick of dynamite thrown. With the explosion, the surface of the water was broken by the flash of leaping fish. At the same instant the woods broke into life. A score of naked savages, armed with bows and arrows, spears, and Sniders, burst out upon the shore. At the same moment our boat's crew, lifted their rifles. And thus the opposing parties faced each other, while our extra boys dived over after the stunned fish.

Three fruitless days were spent at Su'u. The *Minota* got no recruits from the bush, and the bushmen got no heads from the *Minota.* In fact, the only one who got anything was Wade, and his was a nice dose of fever. We towed out with the whale-boat, and ran along the coast to Langa Langa, a large village of salt-water people, built with prodigious labour on a lagoon sand-bank—literally BUILT up, an artificial island reared as a refuge from the blood-thirsty bushmen. Here, also, on the shore side of the lagoon, was Binu, the place where the *Minota* was captured half a year previously and her captain killed by the bushmen. As we sailed in through the narrow entrance, a canoe came alongside with the news that the man-of-war had just left that morning after having burned three villages, killed some thirty pigs, and drowned a baby. This was the Cambrian, Captain Lewes commanding. He and I had first met in Korea during the Japanese-Russian War, and we had been crossing each ether's trail ever since without ever a meeting. The day the *Snark* sailed into Suva, in the Fijis, we made out the Cambrian going out. At Vila, in the New Hebrides, we missed each other by one day. We passed each other in the night-time off the island of Santo. And the day the Cambrian arrived at Tulagi, we sailed from Penduffryn, a dozen miles away. And here at Langa Langa we had missed by several hours.

The Cambrian had come to punish the murderers of the *Minota*'s captain, but what she had succeeded in doing we did not learn until later in the day, when a Mr. Abbot, a missionary, came alongside in his whale-boat. The villages had been burned and the pigs killed. But the natives had escaped personal harm. The murderers had not been captured, though the *Minota*'s flag and other of her gear had been recovered. The drowning of the baby had come about through a misunderstanding. Chief Johnny, of Binu, had declined to guide the landing party into the bush, nor could any of his men be induced to perform that office. Whereupon Captain Lewes, righteously indignant, had told Chief Johnny that he deserved to have his village burned. Johnny's beche de mer English did not include the word "deserve." So his understanding of it was that his village was to be burned anyway. The immediate stampede of the inhabitants was so hurried that the baby was dropped into the water. In the meantime Chief Johnny hastened to Mr. Abbot. Into his hand he put fourteen sovereigns and requested him to go on board the Cambrian and buy Captain Lewes off. Johnny's village was not burned. Nor did Captain Lewes get the fourteen sovereigns, for I saw them later in Johnny's possession when he boarded the *Minota*. The excuse Johnny gave me for not guiding the landing party was a big boil which he proudly revealed. His real reason, however, and a perfectly valid one, though he did not state it, was fear of revenge on the part of the bushmen. Had he, or any of his men, guided the marines, he could have looked for bloody reprisals as soon as the Cambrian weighed anchor.

As an illustration of conditions in the Solomons, Johnny's business on board was to turn over, for a tobacco consideration, the sprit, mainsail, and jib of a whale-boat. Later in the day, a Chief Billy came on board and turned over, for a tobacco consideration, the mast and boom. This gear belonged to a whale-boat which Captain Jansen had recovered the previous trip of the *Minota*. The whale-boat belonged to Meringe Plantation on the island of Ysabel. Eleven contract labourers, Malaita men and bushmen at that, had decided to run away. Being bushmen, they knew nothing of salt water nor of the way of a boat in the sea. So they persuaded two natives of San Cristoval, salt-water men, to run away with them. It served the San Cristoval men right. They should have known better. When they had safely navigated the stolen boat to Malaita, they had their heads hacked off for their pains. It was this boat and gear that Captain Jansen had recovered.

Not for nothing have I journeyed all the way to the Solomons. At last I have seen Charmian's proud spirit humbled and her imperious queendom of femininity dragged in the dust. It happened at Langa Langa, ashore, on the manufactured island which one cannot see for the houses. Here, surrounded by hundreds of unblushing naked men, women, and children, we wandered about and saw the sights. We had our revolvers strapped on, and the boat's crew, fully armed, lay at the oars, stern in; but the lesson of the man-of-war was too recent for us to apprehend trouble. We walked about everywhere and saw everything until at last we approached a large tree trunk that served as a bridge across a shallow estuary. The blacks formed a wall in front of us and refused to let us pass. We wanted to know why we were stopped. The blacks said we could go on. We misunderstood, and started. Explanations became more definite. Captain Jansen and I, being men, could go on. But no Mary was allowed to wade around that bridge, much less cross it. "Mary" is beche de mer for woman. Charmian was a Mary. To her the bridge was tambo, which is the native for taboo. Ah, how my chest expanded! At last my manhood was vindicated. In truth I belonged to the lordly sex. Charmian could traipse along at our heels, but we were MEN, and we could go right over that bridge while she would have to go around by whale-boat.

Now I should not care to be misunderstood by what follows; but it is a matter of common knowledge in the Solomons that attacks of fever are often brought on by shock. Inside half an hour after Charmian had been refused the right of way, she was being rushed aboard the *Minota*, packed in blankets, and dosed with quinine. I don't know what kind of shock had happened to Wada and Nakata, but at any rate they were down with fever as well. The Solomons might be healthfuller.

Also, during the attack of fever, Charmian developed a Solomon sore. It was the last straw. Every one on the *Snark* had been afflicted except her. I had thought that I was going to lose my foot at the ankle by one exceptionally malignant boring ulcer. Henry and Tehei, the Tahitian sailors, had had numbers of them. Wada had been able to count his by the score. Nakata had had single ones three inches in length. Martin had been quite certain that necrosis of his shinbone had set in from the roots of the amazing colony he elected to cultivate in that locality. But Charmian had escaped. Out of her long immunity had been bred contempt for the rest of us. Her ego was flattered to such an extent that one day she shyly informed me that it was all a matter of pureness of blood. Since all the rest of us cultivated the sores, and since she did not—well, anyway, hers was the size of a silver dollar, and the pureness of her blood enabled her to cure it after several weeks of strenuous nursing. She pins her faith to corrosive sublimate. Martin swears by iodoform. Henry uses lime-juice undiluted. And I believe that when corrosive sublimate is slow in taking hold, alternate dressings of peroxide of hydrogen are just the thing. There are white men in the Solomons who stake all upon boracic acid, and others who are prejudiced in favour of lysol. I also have the weakness of a panacea. It is California. I defy any man to get a Solomon Island sore in California.

We ran down the lagoon from Langa Langa, between mangrove swamps, through passages scarcely wider than the *Minota*, and past the reef villages of Kaloka and Auki. Like the founders of Venice, these salt-water men were originally refugees from the mainland. Too weak to hold their own in the bush, survivors of village massacres, they fled to the sand-banks of the lagoon. These sand-banks they built up into islands. They were compelled to seek their provender from the sea, and in time they became salt-water men. They learned the ways of the fish and the shellfish, and they invented hooks and lines, nets and fish-traps. They developed canoe-bodies. Unable to walk about, spending all their time in the canoes, they became thick-armed and broad-shouldered, with narrow waists and frail spindly legs. Controlling the sea-coast, they became wealthy, trade with the interior passing largely through their hands. But perpetual enmity exists between them and the bushmen. Practically their only truces are on market-days, which occur at stated intervals, usually twice a week. The bushwomen and the salt-water women do the bartering. Back in the bush, a hundred yards away, fully armed, lurk the bushmen, while to seaward, in the canoes, are the salt-water men. There are very rare instances of the market-day truces being broken. The bushmen like their fish too well, while the salt-water men have an organic craving for the vegetables they cannot grow on their crowded islets.

Thirty miles from Langa Langa brought us to the passage between Bassakanna Island and the mainland. Here, at nightfall, the wind left us, and all night, with the whale-boat towing ahead and the crew on board sweating at the sweeps, we strove to win through. But the tide was against us. At midnight, midway in the passage, we came up with the *Eugenie,* a big recruiting schooner, towing with two whale-boats. Her skipper, Captain Keller, a sturdy young German of twenty-two, came on board for a "gam," and the latest news of Malaita was swapped back and forth. He had been in luck, having gathered in twenty recruits at the village of Fiu. While lying there, one of the customary courageous killings had taken place. The murdered boy was what is called a salt-water bushman—that is, a salt-water man who is half bushman and who lives by the sea but does not live on an islet. Three bushmen came down to this man where he was working in his garden. They behaved in friendly fashion, and after a time suggested kai-kai. Kai-kai means food. He built a fire and started to boil some taro. While bending over the pot, one of the bushmen shot him through the head. He fell into the flames, whereupon they thrust a spear through his stomach, turned it around, and broke it off.

"My word," said Captain Keller, "I don't want ever to be shot with a Snider. Spread! You could drive a horse and carriage through that hole in his head."

Another recent courageous killing I heard of on Malaita was that of an old man. A bush chief had died a natural death. Now the bushmen don't believe in natural deaths. No one was ever known to die a natural death. The only way to die is by bullet, tomahawk, or spear thrust. When a man dies in any other way, it is a clear case of having been charmed to death. When the bush chief died naturally, his tribe placed the guilt on a certain family. Since it did not matter which one of the family was killed, they selected this old man who lived by himself. This would make it easy. Furthermore, he possessed no Snider. Also, he was blind. The old fellow got an inkling of what was coming and laid in a large supply of arrows. Three brave warriors, each with a Snider, came down upon him in the night time. All night they fought valiantly with him. Whenever they moved in the bush and made a noise or a rustle, he discharged an arrow in that direction. In the morning, when his last arrow was gone, the three heroes crept up to him and blew his brains out.

Morning found us still vainly toiling through the passage. At last, in despair, we turned tail, ran out to sea, and sailed clear round Bassakanna to our objective, Malu. The anchorage at Malu was very good, but it lay between the shore and an ugly reef, and while easy to enter, it was difficult to leave. The direction of the southeast trade necessitated a beat to windward; the point of the reef was widespread and shallow; while a current bore down at all times upon the point.

Mr. Caulfeild, the missionary at Malu, arrived in his whale-boat from a trip down the coast. A slender, delicate man he was, enthusiastic in his work, level-headed and practical, a true twentieth-century soldier of the Lord. When he came down to this station on Malaita, as he said, he agreed to come for six months. He further agreed that if he were alive at the end of that time, he would continue on. Six years had passed and he was still continuing on. Nevertheless he was justified in his doubt as to living longer than six months. Three missionaries had preceded him on Malaita, and in less than that time two had died of fever and the third had gone home a wreck.

"What murder are you talking about?" he asked suddenly, in the midst of a confused conversation with Captain Jansen.

Captain Jansen explained.

"Oh, that's not the one I have reference to," quoth Mr. Caulfeild. "That's old already. It happened two weeks ago."

It was here at Malu that I atoned for all the exulting and gloating I had been guilty of over the Solomon sore Charmian had collected at Langa Langa. Mr. Caulfeild was indirectly responsible for my atonement. He presented us with a chicken, which I pursued into the bush with a rifle. My intention was to clip off its head. I succeeded, but in doing so fell over a log and barked my shin. Result:

three Solomon sores. This made five all together that were adorning my person. Also, Captain Jansen and Nakata had caught gari-gari. Literally translated, gari-gari is scratch-scratch. But translation was not necessary for the rest of us. The skipper's and Nakata's gymnastics served as a translation without words.

(No, the Solomon Islands are not as healthy as they might be. I am writing this article on the island of Ysabel, where we have taken the *Snark* to careen and clean her cooper. I got over my last attack of fever this morning, and I have had only one free day between attacks. Charmian's are two weeks apart. Wada is a wreck from fever. Last night he showed all the symptoms of coming down with pneumonia. Henry, a strapping giant of a Tahitian, just up from his last dose of fever, is dragging around the deck like a last year's crab-apple. Both he and Tehei have accumulated a praiseworthy display of Solomon sores. Also, they have caught a new form of gari-gari, a sort of vegetable poisoning like poison oak or poison ivy. But they are not unique in this. A number of days ago Charmian, Martin, and I went pigeon-shooting on a small island, and we have had a foretaste of eternal torment ever since. Also, on that small island, Martin cut the soles of his feet to ribbons on the coral whilst chasing a shark—at least, so he says, but from the glimpse I caught of him I thought it was the other way about. The coral-cuts have all become Solomon sores. Before my last fever I knocked the skin off my knuckles while heaving on a line, and I now have three fresh sores. And poor Nakata! For three weeks he has been unable to sit down. He sat down yesterday for the first time, and managed to stay down for fifteen minutes. He says cheerfully that he expects to be cured of his gari-gari in another month. Furthermore, his gari-gari, from too enthusiastic scratch-scratching, has furnished footholds for countless Solomon sores. Still furthermore, he has just come down with his seventh attack of fever. If I were king, the worst punishment I could inflict on my enemies would be to banish them to the Solomons. On second thought, king or no king, I don't think I'd have the heart to do it.)

Recruiting plantation labourers on a small, narrow yacht, built for harbour sailing, is not any too nice. The decks swarm with recruits and their families. The main cabin is packed with them. At night they sleep there. The only entrance to our tiny cabin is through the main cabin, and we jam our way through them or walk over them. Nor is this nice. One and all, they are afflicted with every form of malignant skin disease. Some have ringworm, others have bukua. This latter is caused by a vegetable parasite that invades the skin and eats it away. The itching is intolerable. The afflicted ones scratch until the air is filled with fine dry flakes. Then there are yaws and many other skin ulcerations. Men come aboard with Solomon sores in their feet so large that they can walk only on their toes, or with holes in their legs so terrible that a fist could be thrust in to the bone. Blood-poisoning is very frequent, and Captain Jansen, with sheath-knife and sail needle, operates lavishly on one and all. No matter how desperate the situation, after opening and cleansing, he claps on a poultice of sea-biscuit soaked in water. Whenever we see a particularly horrible case, we retire to a corner and deluge our own sores with corrosive sublimate. And so we live and eat and sleep on the *Minota*, taking our chance and "pretending it is good."

At Suava, another artificial island, I had a second crow over Charmian. A big fella marster belong Suava (which means the high chief of Suava) came on board. But first he sent an emissary to Captain Jansen for a fathom of calico with which to cover his royal nakedness. Meanwhile he lingered in the canoe alongside. The regal dirt on his chest I swear was half an inch thick, while it was a good wager that the underneath layers were anywhere from ten to twenty years of age. He sent his emissary on board again, who explained that the big fella marster belong Suava was condescendingly willing enough to shake hands with Captain Jansen and me and cadge a stick or so of trade tobacco, but that nevertheless his high-born soul was still at so lofty an altitude that it could not sink itself to such a depth of degradation as to shake hands with a mere female woman. Poor Charmian! Since her Malaita experiences she has become a changed woman. Her meekness and humbleness are appallingly becoming, and I should not be surprised, when we return to civilization and stroll along a sidewalk, to see her take her station, with bowed head, a yard in the rear.

Nothing much happened at Suava. Bichu, the native cook, deserted. The *Minota* dragged anchor. It blew heavy squalls of wind and rain. The mate, Mr. Jacobsen, and Wada were prostrated with fever. Our Solomon sores increased and multiplied. And the cockroaches on board held a combined Fourth of July and Coronation Parade. They selected midnight for the time, and our tiny cabin for the place. They were from two to three inches long; there were hundreds of them, and they walked all over us. When we attempted to pursue them, they left solid footing, rose up in the air, and fluttered about like humming-birds. They were much larger than ours on the *Snark*. But ours are young yet, and haven't had a chance to grow. Also, the *Snark* has centipedes, big ones, six inches long. We kill them occasionally, usually in Charmian's bunk. I've been bitten twice by them, both times foully, while I was asleep. But poor Martin had worse luck. After being sick in bed for three weeks, the first day he sat up he sat down on one. Sometimes I think they are the wisest who never go to Carcassonne.

Later on we returned to Malu, picked up seven recruits, hove up anchor, and started to beat out the treacherous entrance. The wind was chopping about, the current upon the ugly point of reef setting strong. Just as we were on the verge of clearing it and gaining open sea, the wind broke off four points. The *Minota* attempted to go about, but missed stays. Two of her anchors had been lost at Tulagi. Her one remaining anchor was let go. Chain was let out to give it a hold on the coral. Her fin keel struck bottom, and her main topmast lurched and shivered as if about to come down upon our heads. She fetched up on the slack of the anchors at the moment a big comber smashed her shoreward. The chain parted. It was our only anchor. The *Minota* swung around on her heel and drove headlong into the breakers.

Bedlam reigned. All the recruits below, bushmen and afraid of the sea, dashed panic-stricken on deck and got in everybody's way. At the same time the boat's crew made a rush for the rifles. They knew what going ashore on Malaita meant—one hand for the ship and the other hand to fight off the natives. What they held on with I don't know, and they needed to hold on as the *Minota* lifted, rolled, and pounded on the coral. The bushmen clung in the rigging, too witless to watch out for the topmast. The whale-boat was run out with a tow-line endeavouring in a puny way to prevent the *Minota* from being flung farther in toward the reef, while Captain Jansen and the mate, the latter pallid and weak with fever, were resurrecting a scrap-anchor from out the ballast and rigging up a stock for it. Mr. Caulfeild, with his mission boys, arrived in his whale-boat to help.

When the *Minota* first struck, there was not a canoe in sight; but like vultures circling down out of the blue, canoes began to arrive from every quarter. The boat's crew, with rifles at the ready, kept them lined up a hundred feet away with a promise of death if they ventured nearer. And there they clung, a hundred feet away, black and ominous, crowded with men, holding their canoes with their paddles on the perilous edge of the breaking surf. In the meantime the bushmen were flocking down from the hills armed with spears, Sniders, arrows, and clubs, until the beach was massed with them. To complicate matters, at least ten of our recruits had been enlisted from the very bushmen ashore who were waiting hungrily for the loot of the tobacco and trade goods and all that we had on board.

The *Minota* was honestly built, which is the first essential for any boat that is pounding on a reef. Some idea of what she endured may be gained from the fact that in the first twenty-four hours she parted two anchor-chains and eight hawsers. Our boat's crew was kept busy diving for the anchors and bending new lines. There were times when she parted the chains reinforced with hawsers. And yet she held together. Tree trunks were brought from ashore and worked under her to save her keel and bilges, but the trunks were gnawed and splintered and the ropes that held them frayed to fragments, and still she pounded and held together. But we were luckier than the Ivanhoe, a big recruiting schooner, which had gone ashore on Malaita several months previously and been promptly rushed by the natives. The captain and crew succeeded in getting away in the whale-boats, and the bushmen and salt-water men looted her clean of everything portable.

Squall after squall, driving wind and blinding rain, smote the *Minota*, while a heavier sea was making. The *Eugenie* lay at anchor five miles to windward, but she was behind a point of land and could not know of our mishap. At Captain Jansen's suggestion, I wrote a note to Captain Keller, asking him to bring extra anchors and gear to our aid. But not a canoe could be persuaded to carry the letter. I offered half a case of tobacco, but the blacks grinned and held their canoes bow-on to the breaking seas. A half a case of tobacco was worth three pounds. In two hours, even against the strong wind and sea, a man could have carried the letter and received in payment what he would have laboured half a year for on a plantation. I managed to get into a canoe and paddle out to where Mr. Caulfeild was running an anchor with his whale-boat. My idea was that he would have more influence over the natives. He called the canoes up to him, and a score of them clustered around and heard the offer of half a case of tobacco. No one spoke.

"I know what you think," the missionary called out to them. "You think plenty tobacco on the schooner and you're going to get it. I tell you plenty rifles on schooner. You no get tobacco, you get bullets."

At last, one man, alone in a small canoe, took the letter and started. Waiting for relief, work went on steadily on the *Minota*. Her water-tanks were emptied, and spars, sails, and ballast started shoreward. There were lively times on board when the *Minota* rolled one bilge down and then the other, a score of men leaping for life and legs as the trade-boxes, booms, and eighty-pound pigs of iron ballast rushed across from rail to rail and back again. The poor pretty harbour yacht! Her decks and running rigging were a raffle. Down below everything was disrupted. The cabin floor had been torn up to get at the ballast, and rusty bilge-water swashed and splashed. A bushel of limes, in a mess of flour and water, charged about like so many sticky dumplings escaped from a half-cooked stew. In the inner cabin, Nakata kept guard over our rifles and ammunition.

Three hours from the time our messenger started, a whale-boat, pressing along under a huge spread of canvas, broke through the thick of a shrieking squall to windward. It was Captain Keller, wet with rain and spray, a revolver in belt, his boat's crew fully armed, anchors and hawsers heaped high amidships, coming as fast as wind could drive—the white man, the inevitable white man, coming to a white man's rescue.

The vulture line of canoes that had waited so long broke and disappeared as quickly as it had formed. The corpse was not dead after all. We now had three whale-boats, two plying steadily between the vessel and shore, the other kept busy running out anchors, rebending parted hawsers, and recovering the lost anchors. Later in the afternoon, after a consultation, in which we took into consideration that a number of our boat's crew, as well as ten of the recruits, belonged to this place, we disarmed the boat's crew. This, incidently, gave them both hands free to work for the vessel. The rifles were put in the charge of five of Mr. Caulfeild's mission boys. And down below in the wreck of the cabin the missionary and his converts prayed to God to save the *Minota.* It was an impressive scene! the unarmed man of God praying with cloudless faith, his savage followers leaning on their rifles and mumbling amens. The cabin walls reeled about them. The vessel lifted and smashed upon the coral with every sea. From on deck came the shouts of men heaving and toiling, praying, in another fashion, with purposeful will and strength of arm.

That night Mr. Caulfeild brought off a warning. One of our recruits had a price on his head of fifty fathoms of shell-money and forty pigs. Baffled in their desire to capture the vessel, the bushmen decided to get the head of the man. When killing begins, there is no telling where it will end, so Captain Jansen armed a whale-boat and rowed in to the edge of the beach. Ugi, one of his boat's crew, stood up and orated for him. Ugi was excited. Captain Jansen's warning that any canoe sighted that night would be pumped full of lead, Ugi turned into a bellicose declaration of war, which wound up with a peroration somewhat to the following effect: "You kill my captain, I drink his blood and die with him!"

The bushmen contented themselves with burning an unoccupied mission house, and sneaked back to the bush. The next day the *Eugenie* sailed in and dropped anchor. Three days and two nights the *Minota* pounded on the reef; but she held together, and the shell of her was pulled off at last and anchored in smooth water. There we said good-bye to her and all on board, and sailed away on the *Eugenie,* bound for Florida Island.

Chapter 23
Amateur M.D.

When we sailed from San Francisco on the *Snark* I knew as much about sickness as the Admiral of the Swiss Navy knows about salt water. And here, at the start, let me advise anyone who meditates going to out-of-the-way tropic places. Go to a first-class druggist—the sort that have specialists on their salary list who know everything. Talk the matter over with such an one. Note carefully all that he says. Have a list made of all that he recommends. Write out a cheque for the total cost, and tear it up.

I wish I had done the same. I should have been far wiser, I know now, if I had bought one of those ready-made, self-acting, fool-proof medicine chests such as are favoured by fourth-rate ship-masters. In such a chest each bottle has a number. On the inside of the lid is placed a simple table of directions: No. 1, toothache; No. 2, smallpox; No. 3, stomachache; No. 4, cholera; No. 5, rheumatism;

and so on, through the list of human ills. And I might have used it as did a certain venerable skipper, who, when No. 3 was empty, mixed a dose from No. 1 and No. 2, or, when No. 7 was all gone, dosed his crew with 4 and 3 till 3 gave out, when he used 5 and 2.

So far, with the exception of corrosive sublimate (which was recommended as an antiseptic in surgical operations, and which I have not yet used for that purpose), my medicine-chest has been useless. It has been worse than useless, for it has occupied much space which I could have used to advantage.

With my surgical instruments it is different. While I have not yet had serious use for them, I do not regret the space they occupy. The thought of them makes me feel good. They are so much life insurance, only, fairer than that last grim game, one is not supposed to die in order to win. Of course, I don't know how to use them, and what I don't know about surgery would set up a dozen quacks in prosperous practice. But needs must when the devil drives, and we of the *Snark* have no warning when the devil may take it into his head to drive, ay, even a thousand miles from land and twenty days from the nearest port.

I did not know anything about dentistry, but a friend fitted me out with forceps and similar weapons, and in Honolulu I picked up a book upon teeth. Also, in that sub-tropical city I managed to get hold of a skull, from which I extracted the teeth swiftly and painlessly. Thus equipped, I was ready, though not exactly eager, to tackle any tooth that get in my way. It was in Nuku-hiva, in the Marquesas, that my first case presented itself in the shape of a little, old Chinese. The first thing I did was to get the buck fever, and I leave it to any fair-minded person if buck fever, with its attendant heart-palpitations and arm-tremblings, is the right condition for a man to be in who is endeavouring to pose as an old hand at the business. I did not fool the aged Chinaman. He was as frightened as I and a bit more shaky. I almost forgot to be frightened in the fear that he would bolt. I swear, if he had tried to, that I would have tripped him up and sat on him until calmness and reason returned.

I wanted that tooth. Also, Martin wanted a snap-shot of me getting it. Likewise Charmian got her camera. Then the procession started. We were stopping at what had been the club-house when Stevenson was in the Marquesas on the Casco. On the veranda, where he had passed so many pleasant hours, the light was not good—for snapshots, I mean. I led on into the garden, a chair in one hand, the other hand filled with forceps of various sorts, my knees knocking together disgracefully. The poor old Chinaman came second, and he was shaking, too. Charmian and Martin brought up the rear, armed with kodaks. We dived under the avocado trees, threaded our way through the cocoanut palms, and came on a spot that satisfied Martin's photographic eye.

I looked at the tooth, and then discovered that I could not remember anything about the teeth I had pulled from the skull five months previously. Did it have one prong? two prongs? or three prongs? What was left of the part that showed appeared very crumbly, and I knew that I should have take hold of the tooth deep down in the gum. It was very necessary that I should know how many prongs that tooth had. Back to the house I went for the book on teeth. The poor old victim looked like photographs I had seen of fellow-countrymen of his, criminals, on their knees, waiting the stroke of the beheading sword.

"Don't let him get away," I cautioned to Martin. "I want that tooth."

"I sure won't," he replied with enthusiasm, from behind his camera. "I want that photograph."

For the first time I felt sorry for the Chinaman. Though the book did not tell me anything about pulling teeth, it was all right, for on one page I found drawings of all the teeth, including their prongs and how they were set in the jaw. Then came the pursuit of the forceps. I had seven pairs, but was in doubt as to which pair I should use. I did not want any mistake. As I turned the hardware over with rattle and clang, the poor victim began to lose his grip and to turn a greenish yellow around the gills. He complained about the sun, but that was necessary for the photograph, and he had to stand it. I fitted the forceps around the tooth, and the patient shivered and began to wilt.

"Ready?" I called to Martin.

"All ready," he answered.

I gave a pull. Ye gods! The tooth, was loose! Out it came on the instant. I was jubilant as I held it aloft in the forceps.

"Put it back, please, oh, put it back," Martin pleaded. "You were too quick for me."

And the poor old Chinaman sat there while I put the tooth back and pulled over. Martin snapped the camera. The deed was done. Elation? Pride? No hunter was ever prouder of his first pronged buck than I was of that tree-pronged tooth. I did it! I did it! With my of own hands and a pair of forceps I did it, to say nothing of the forgotten memories of the dead man's skull.

My next case was a Tahitian sailor. He was a small man, in a state of collapse from long days and nights of jumping toothache. I lanced the gums first. I didn't know how to lance them, but I lanced them just the same. It was a long pull and a strong pull. The man was a hero. He groaned and moaned, and I thought he was going to faint. But he kept his mouth open and let me pull. And then it came.

After that I was ready to meet all comers—just the proper state of mind for a Waterloo. And it came. Its name was Tomi. He was a strapping giant of a heathen with a bad reputation. He was addicted to deeds of violence. Among other things he had beaten two of his wives to death with his fists. His father and mother had been naked cannibals. When he sat down and I put the forceps into his mouth, he was nearly as tall as I was standing up. Big men, prone to violence, very often have a streak of fat in their make-up, so I was doubtful of him. Charmian grabbed one arm and Warren grabbed the other. Then the tug of war began. The instant the forceps closed down on the tooth, his jaws closed down on the forceps. Also, both his hands flew up and gripped my pulling hand. I held on, and he held on. Charmian and Warren held on. We wrestled all about the shop.

It was three against one, and my hold on an aching tooth was certainly a foul one; but in spite of the handicap he got away with us. The forceps slipped off, banging and grinding along against his upper teeth with a nerve-scraping sound. Out of his month flew the forceps, and he rose up in the air with a blood-curdling yell. The three of us fell back. We expected to be massacred. But that howling savage of sanguinary reputation sank back in the chair. He held his head in both his hands, and groaned and groaned and groaned. Nor would he listen to reason. I was a quack. My painless tooth-extraction was a delusion and a snare and a low advertising dodge. I was so anxious to get that tooth that I was almost ready to bribe him. But that went against my professional pride and I let him depart with the tooth still intact, the only case on record up to date of failure on my part when once I had got a grip. Since then I have never let a tooth go by me. Only the other day I volunteered to beat up three days to windward to pull a woman missionary's tooth. I expect, before the voyage of the *Snark* is finished, to be doing bridge work and putting on gold crowns.

I don't know whether they are yaws or not—a physician in Fiji told me they were, and a missionary in the Solomons told me they were not; but at any rate I can vouch for the fact that they are most uncomfortable. It was my luck to ship in Tahiti a French-sailor, who, when we got to sea, proved to be afflicted with a vile skin disease. The *Snark* was too small and too much of a family party to permit retaining him on board; but perforce, until we could reach land and discharge him, it was up to me to doctor him. I read up the books and proceeded to treat him, taking care afterwards always to use a thorough antiseptic wash. When we reached Tutuila, far from getting rid of him, the port doctor declared a quarantine against him and refused to allow him ashore. But at Apia, Samoa, I managed to ship him off on a steamer to New Zealand. Here at Apia my ankles were badly bitten by mosquitoes, and I confess to having scratched the bites—as I had a thousand times before. By the time I reached the island of Savaii, a small sore had developed on the hollow of my instep. I thought it was due to chafe and to acid fumes from the hot lava over which I tramped. An application of salve would cure it—so I thought. The salve did heal it over, whereupon an astonishing inflammation set in, the new skin came off, and a larger sore was exposed. This was repeated many times. Each time new skin formed, an inflammation followed, and the circumference of the sore increased. I was puzzled and frightened. All my life my skin had been famous for its healing powers, yet here was something that would not heal. Instead, it was daily eating up more skin, while it had eaten down clear through the skin and was eating up the muscle itself.

By this time the *Snark* was at sea on her way to Fiji. I remembered the French sailor, and for the first time became seriously alarmed. Four other similar sores had appeared—or ulcers, rather, and the pain of them kept me awake at night. All my plans were made to lay up the *Snark* in Fiji and get away on the first steamer to Australia and professional M.D.s. In the meantime, in my amateur M.D. way, I did my best. I read through all the medical works on board. Not a line nor a word could I find descriptive of my affliction. I brought common horse-sense to bear on the problem. Here were malignant and excessively active ulcers that were eating me up. There was an organic and corroding poison at work. Two things I concluded must be done. First, some agent must be found to destroy the poison. Secondly, the ulcers could not possibly heal from the outside in; they must heal from the inside out. I decided to fight the poison with corrosive sublimate. The very name of it struck me as vicious. Talk of fighting fire with fire! I was being consumed by a corrosive poison, and it appealed to my fancy to fight it with another corrosive poison. After several days I alternated dressings of corrosive sublimate with dressings of peroxide of hydrogen. And behold, by the time we reached Fiji four of the five ulcers were healed, while the remaining one was no bigger than a pea.

I now felt fully qualified to treat yaws. Likewise I had a wholesome respect for them. Not so the rest of the crew of the *Snark*. In their case, seeing was not believing. One and all, they had seen my dreadful predicament; and all of them, I am convinced, had a subconscious certitude that their own superb constitutions and glorious personalities would never allow lodgment of so vile a poison in their carcasses as my anaemic constitution and mediocre personality had allowed to lodge in mine. At Port Resolution, in the New Hebrides, Martin elected to walk barefooted in the bush and returned on board with many cuts and abrasions, especially on his shins.

"You'd better be careful," I warned him. "I'll mix up some corrosive sublimate for you to wash those cuts with. An ounce of prevention, you know."

But Martin smiled a superior smile. Though he did not say so, I nevertheless was given to understand that he was not as other men (I was the only man he could possibly have had reference to), and that in a couple of days his cuts would be healed. He also read me a dissertation upon the peculiar purity of his blood and his remarkable healing powers. I felt quite humble when he was done with me. Evidently I was different from other men in so far as purity of blood was concerned.

Nakata, the cabin-boy, while ironing one day, mistook the calf of his leg for the ironing-block and accumulated a burn three inches in length and half an inch wide. He, too, smiled the superior smile when I offered him corrosive sublimate and reminded him of my own cruel experience. I was given to understand, with all due suavity and courtesy, that no matter what was the matter with my blood, his number-one, Japanese, Port-Arthur blood was all right and scornful of the festive microbe.

Wada, the cook, took part in a disastrous landing of the launch, when he had to leap overboard and fend the launch off the beach in a smashing surf. By means of shells and coral he cut his legs and feet up beautifully. I offered him the corrosive sublimate bottle. Once again I suffered the superior smile and was given to understand that his blood was the same blood that had licked Russia and was going to lick the United States some day, and that if his blood wasn't able to cure a few trifling cuts, he'd commit hari-kari in sheer disgrace.

From all of which I concluded that an amateur M.D. is without honour on his own vessel, even if he has cured himself. The rest of the crew had begun to look upon me as a sort of mild mono-maniac on the question of sores and sublimate. Just because my blood was impure was no reason that I should think everybody else's was. I made no more overtures. Time and microbes were with me, and all I had to do was wait.

"I think there's some dirt in these cuts," Martin said tentatively, after several days. "I'll wash them out and then they'll be all right," he added, after I had refused to rise to the bait.

Two more days passed, but the cuts did not pass, and I caught Martin soaking his feet and legs in a pail of hot water.

"Nothing like hot water," he proclaimed enthusiastically. "It beats all the dope the doctors ever put up. These sores will be all right in the morning."

But in the morning he wore a troubled look, and I knew that the hour of my triumph approached.

"I think I WILL try some of that medicine," he announced later on in the day. "Not that I think it'll do much good," he qualified, "but I'll just give it a try anyway."

Next came the proud blood of Japan to beg medicine for its illustrious sores, while I heaped coals of fire on all their houses by explaining in minute and sympathetic detail the treatment that should be given. Nakata followed instructions implicitly, and day by day his sores grew smaller. Wada was apathetic, and cured less readily. But Martin still doubted, and because he did not cure immediately, he developed the theory that while doctor's dope was all right, it did not follow that the same kind of dope was efficacious with everybody. As for himself, corrosive sublimate had no effect. Besides, how did I know that it was the right stuff? I had had no experience. Just because I happened to get well while using it was not proof that it had played any part in the cure. There were such things as coincidences. Without doubt there was a dope that would cure the sores, and when he ran across a real doctor he would find what that dope was and get some of it.

About this time we arrived in the Solomon Islands. No physician would ever recommend the group for invalids or sanitoriums. I spent but little time there ere I really and for the first time in my life comprehended how frail and unstable is human tissue. Our first anchorage was Port Mary, on the island of Santa Anna. The one lone white man, a trader, came alongside. Tom Butler was his name, and he was a beautiful example of what the Solomons can do to a strong man. He lay in his whale-boat with the helplessness of a dying man. No smile and little intelligence illumined his face. He was a sombre death's-head, too far gone to grin. He, too, had yaws, big ones. We were compelled to drag him over the rail of the *Snark*. He said that his health was good, that he had not had the fever for some time, and that with the exception of his arm he was all right and trim. His arm appeared to be paralysed. Paralysis he rejected with scorn. He had had it before, and recovered. It was a common native disease on Santa Anna, he said, as he was helped down the companion ladder, his dead arm dropping, bump-bump, from step to step. He was certainly the ghastliest guest we ever entertained, and we've had not a few lepers and elephantiasis victims on board.

Martin inquired about yaws, for here was a man who ought to know. He certainly did know, if we could judge by his scarred arms and legs and by the live ulcers that corroded in the midst of the scars. Oh, one got used to yaws, quoth Tom Butler. They were never really serious until they had eaten deep into the flesh. Then they attacked the walls of the arteries, the arteries burst, and there was a funeral. Several of the natives had recently died that way ashore. But what did it matter? If it wasn't yaws, it was something else in the Solomons.

I noticed that from this moment Martin displayed a swiftly increasing interest in his own yaws. Dosings with corrosive sublimate were more frequent, while, in conversation, he began to revert with growing enthusiasm to the clean climate of Kansas and all other things Kansan. Charmian and I thought that California was a little bit of all right. Henry swore by Rapa, and Tehei staked all on Bora Bora for his own blood's sake; while Wada and Nakata sang the sanitary paean of Japan.

One evening, as the *Snark* worked around the southern end of the island of Ugi, looking for a reputed anchorage, a Church of England missionary, a Mr. Drew, bound in his whaleboat for the coast of San Cristoval, came alongside and stopped for dinner. Martin, his legs swathed in Red Cross bandages till they looked like a mummy's, turned the conversation upon yaws. Yes, said Mr. Drew, they were quite common in the Solomons. All white men caught them.

"And have you had them?" Martin demanded, in the soul of him quite shocked that a Church of England missionary could possess so vulgar an affliction.

Mr. Drew nodded his head and added that not only had he had them, but at that moment he was doctoring several.

"What do you use on them?" Martin asked like a flash.

My heart almost stood still waiting the answer. By that answer my professional medical prestige stood or fell. Martin, I could see, was quite sure it was going to fall. And then the answer—O blessed answer!

"Corrosive sublimate," said Mr. Drew.

Martin gave in handsomely, I'll admit, and I am confident that at that moment, if I had asked permission to pull one of his teeth, he would not have denied me.

All white men in the Solomons catch yaws, and every cut or abrasion practically means another yaw. Every man I met had had them, and nine out of ten had active ones. There was but one exception, a young fellow who had been in the islands five months, who had come down with fever ten days after he arrived, and who had since then been down so often with fever that he had had neither time nor opportunity for yaws.

Everyone on the *Snark* except Charmian came down with yaws. Hers was the same egotism that Japan and Kansas had displayed. She ascribed her immunity to the pureness of her blood, and as the days went by she ascribed it more often and more loudly to the pureness of her blood. Privately I ascribed her immunity to the fact that, being a woman, she escaped most of the cuts and abrasions to which we hard-working men were subject in the course of working the *Snark* around the world. I did not tell her so. You see, I did not wish to bruise her ego with brutal facts. Being an M.D., if only an amateur one, I knew more about the disease than she, and I knew that time was my ally. But alas, I abused my ally when it dealt a charming little yaw on the shin. So quickly did I apply antiseptic treatment, that the yaw was cured before she was convinced that she had one. Again, as an M.D., I was without honour on my own vessel; and, worse than that, I was charged with having tried to mislead her into the belief that she had had a yaw. The pureness of her blood was more rampant than ever, and I poked my nose into my navigation books and kept quiet. And then came the day. We were cruising along the coast of Malaita at the time.

"What's that abaft your ankle-bone?" said I.

"Nothing," said she.

"All right," said I; "but put some corrosive sublimate on it just the same. And some two or three weeks from now, when it is well and you have a scar that you will carry to your grave, just forget about the purity of your blood and your ancestral history and tell me what you think about yaws anyway."

It was as large as a silver dollar, that yaw, and it took all of three weeks to heal. There were times when Charmian could not walk because of the hurt of it; and there were times upon times when she explained that abaft the ankle-bone was the most painful place to have a yaw. I explained, in turn, that, never having experienced a yaw in that locality, I was driven to conclude the hollow of the instep was the most painful place for yaw-culture. We left it to Martin, who disagreed with both of us and proclaimed passionately that the only truly painful place was the shin. No wonder horse-racing is so popular.

But yaws lose their novelty after a time. At the present moment of writing I have five yaws on my hands and three more on my shin. Charmian has one on each side of her right instep. Tehei is frantic with his. Martin's latest shin-cultures have eclipsed his earlier ones. And Nakata has several score casually eating away at his tissue. But the history of the *Snark* in the Solomons has been the history of every ship since the early discoverers. From the "Sailing Directions" I quote the following:

"The crews of vessels remaining any considerable time in the Solomons find wounds and sores liable to change into malignant ulcers."

Nor on the question of fever were the "Sailing Directions" any more encouraging, for in them I read:

"New arrivals are almost certain sooner or later to suffer from fever. The natives are also subject to it. The number of deaths among the whites in the year 1897 amounted to 9 among a population of 50."

Some of these deaths, however, were accidental.

Nakata was the first to come down with fever. This occurred at Penduffryn. Wada and Henry followed him. Charmian surrendered next. I managed to escape for a couple of months; but when

I was bowled over, Martin sympathetically joined me several days later. Out of the seven of us all told Tehei is the only one who has escaped; but his sufferings from nostalgia are worse than fever. Nakata, as usual, followed instructions faithfully, so that by the end of his third attack he could take a two hours' sweat, consume thirty or forty grains of quinine, and be weak but all right at the end of twenty-four hours.

Wada and Henry, however, were tougher patients with which to deal. In the first place, Wada got in a bad funk. He was of the firm conviction that his star had set and that the Solomons would receive his bones. He saw that life about him was cheap. At Penduffryn he saw the ravages of dysentery, and, unfortunately for him, he saw one victim carried out on a strip of galvanized sheet-iron and dumped without coffin or funeral into a hole in the ground. Everybody had fever, everybody had dysentery, everybody had everything. Death was common. Here to-day and gone to-morrow—and Wada forgot all about to-day and made up his mind that to-morrow had come.

He was careless of his ulcers, neglected to sublimate them, and by uncontrolled scratching spread them all over his body. Nor would he follow instructions with fever, and, as a result, would be down five days at a time, when a day would have been sufficient. Henry, who is a strapping giant of a man, was just as bad. He refused point blank to take quinine, on the ground that years before he had had fever and that the pills the doctor gave him were of different size and colour from the quinine tablets I offered him. So Henry joined Wada.

But I fooled the pair of them, and dosed them with their own medicine, which was faith-cure. They had faith in their funk that they were going to die. I slammed a lot of quinine down their throats and took their temperature. It was the first time I had used my medicine-chest thermometer, and I quickly discovered that it was worthless, that it had been produced for profit and not for service. If I had let on to my two patients that the thermometer did not work, there would have been two funerals in short order. Their temperature I swear was 105 degrees. I solemnly made one and then the other smoke the thermometer, allowed an expression of satisfaction to irradiate my countenance, and joyfully told them that their temperature was 94 degrees. Then I slammed more quinine down their throats, told them that any sickness or weakness they might experience would be due to the quinine, and left them to get well. And they did get well, Wada in spite of himself. If a man can die through a misapprehension, is there any immorality in making him live through a misapprehension?

Commend me the white race when it comes to grit and surviving. One of our two Japanese and both our Tahitians funked and had to be slapped on the back and cheered up and dragged along by main strength toward life. Charmian and Martin took their afflictions cheerfully, made the least of them, and moved with calm certitude along the way of life. When Wada and Henry were convinced that they were going to die, the funeral atmosphere was too much for Tehei, who prayed dolorously and cried for hours at a time. Martin, on the other hand, cursed and got well, and Charmian groaned and made plans for what she was going to do when she got well again.

Charmian had been raised a vegetarian and a sanitarian. Her Aunt Netta, who brought her up and who lived in a healthful climate, did not believe in drugs. Neither did Charmian. Besides, drugs disagreed with her. Their effects were worse than the ills they were supposed to alleviate. But she listened to the argument in favour of quinine, accepted it as the lesser evil, and in consequence had shorter, less painful, and less frequent attacks of fever. We encountered a Mr. Caulfeild, a missionary, whose two predecessors had died after less than six months' residence in the Solomons. Like them he had been a firm believer in homeopathy, until after his first fever, whereupon, unlike them, he made a grand slide back to allopathy and quinine, catching fever and carrying on his Gospel work.

But poor Wada! The straw that broke the cook's back was when Charmian and I took him along on a cruise to the cannibal island of Malaita, in a small yacht, on the deck of which the captain had been murdered half a year before. Kai-kai means to eat, and Wada was sure he was going to be kai-kai'd. We went about heavily armed, our vigilance was unremitting, and when we went for a bath in the mouth of a fresh-water stream, black boys, armed with rifles, did sentry duty about us. We encountered English war vessels burning and shelling villages in punishment for murders. Natives with prices on their heads sought shelter on board of us. Murder stalked abroad in the land. In out-of-they-way places we received warnings from friendly savages of impending attacks. Our vessel owed two heads to Malaita, which were liable to be collected any time. Then to cap it all, we were wrecked on a reef, and with rifles in one hand warned the canoes of wreckers off while with the other hand we toiled to save the ship. All of which was too much for Wada, who went daffy, and who finally quitted the *Snark* on the island of Ysabel, going ashore for good in a driving rain-storm, between two attacks of fever, while threatened with pneumonia. If he escapes being kai-kai'd, and if he can survive sores and fever which are riotous ashore, he can expect, if he is reasonably lucky, to get away from that place to the adjacent island in anywhere from six to eight weeks. He never did think much of my medicine, despite the fact that I successfully and at the first trail pulled two aching teeth for him.

The *Snark* has been a hospital for months, and I confess that we are getting used to it. At Meringe Lagoon, where we careened and cleaned the *Snark's* copper, there were times when only one man of us was able to go into the water, while the three white men on the plantation ashore were all down with fever. At the moment of writing this we are lost at sea somewhere northeast of Ysabel and trying vainly to find Lord Howe Island, which is an atoll that cannot be sighted unless one is on top of it. The chronometer has gone wrong. The sun does not shine anyway, nor can I get a star observation at night, and we have had nothing but squalls and rain for days and days. The cook is gone. Nakata, who has been trying to be both cook and cabin boy, is down on his back with fever. Martin is just up from fever, and going down again. Charmian, whose fever has become periodical, is looking up in her date book to find when the next attack will be. Henry has begun to eat quinine in an expectant mood. And, since my attacks hit me with the suddenness of bludgeon-blows I do not know from moment to moment when I shall be brought down. By a mistake we gave our last flour away to some white men who did not have any flour. We don't know when we'll make land. Our Solomon sores are worse than ever, and more numerous. The corrosive sublimate was accidentally left ashore at Penduffryn; the peroxide of hydrogen is exhausted; and I am experimenting with boracic acid, lysol, and antiphlogystine. At any rate, if I fail in becoming a reputable M.D., it won't be from lack of practice.

P.S. It is now two weeks since the foregoing was written, and Tehei, the only immune on board has been down ten days with far severer fever than any of us and is still down. His temperature has been repeatedly as high as 104, and his pulse 115.

P.S. At sea, between Tasman atoll and Manning Straits. Tehei's attack developed into black water fever—the severest form of malarial fever, which, the doctor-book assures me, is due to some outside infection as well. Having pulled him through his fever, I am now at my wit's end, for he has lost his wits altogether. I am rather recent in practice to take up the cure of insanity. This makes the second lunacy case on this short voyage.

P.S. Some day I shall write a book (for the profession), and entitle it, "Around the World on the Hospital Ship *Snark*." Even our pets have not escaped. We sailed from Meringe Lagoon with two, an Irish terrier and a white cockatoo. The terrier fell down the cabin companionway and lamed its nigh hind leg, then repeated the manoeuvre and lamed its off fore leg. At the present moment it has but two legs to walk on. Fortunately, they are on opposite sides and ends, so that she can still dot and carry two. The cockatoo was crushed under the cabin skylight and had to be killed. This was our first funeral—though for that matter, the several chickens we had, and which would have made welcome broth for the convalescents, flew overboard and were drowned. Only the cockroaches flourish. Neither illness nor accident ever befalls them, and they grow larger and more carnivorous day by day, gnawing our finger-nails and toe-nails while we sleep.

P.S. Charmian is having another bout with fever. Martin, in despair, has taken to horse-doctoring his yaws with bluestone and to blessing the Solomons. As for me, in addition to navigating, doctoring, and writing short stories, I am far from well. With the exception of the insanity cases, I'm the worst off on board. I shall catch the next steamer to Australia and go on the operating table. Among my minor afflictions, I may mention a new and mysterious one. For the past week my hands have been swelling as with dropsy. It is only by a painful effort that I can close them. A pull on a rope is excruciating. The sensations are like those that accompany severe chilblains. Also, the skin is peeling off both hands at an alarming rate, besides which the new skin underneath is growing hard and thick. The doctor-book fails to mention this disease. Nobody knows what it is.

P.S. Well, anyway, I've cured the chronometer. After knocking about the sea for eight squally, rainy days, most of the time hove to, I succeeded in catching a partial observation of the sun at midday. From this I worked up my latitude, then headed by log to the latitude of Lord Howe, and ran both that latitude and the island down together. Here I tested the chronometer by longitude sights and found it something like three minutes out. Since each minute is equivalent to fifteen miles, the total error can be appreciated. By repeated observations at Lord Howe I rated the chronometer, finding it to have a daily losing error of seven-tenths of a second. Now it happens that a year ago, when we sailed from Hawaii, that selfsame chronometer had that selfsame losing error of seven-tenths of a second. Since that error was faithfully added every day, and since that error, as proved by my observations at Lord Howe, has not changed, then what under the sun made that chronometer all of a sudden accelerate and catch up with itself three minutes? Can such things be? Expert watchmakers say no; but I say that they have never done any expert watch-making and watch-rating in the Solomons. That it is the climate is my only diagnosis. At any rate, I have successfully doctored the chronometer, even if I have failed with the lunacy cases and with Martin's yaws.

P.S. Martin has just tried burnt alum, and is blessing the Solomons more fervently than ever.

P.S. Between Manning Straits and Pavuvu Islands.

Henry has developed rheumatism in his back, ten skins have peeled off my hands and the eleventh is now peeling, while Tehei is more lunatic than ever and day and night prays God not to kill him. Also, Nakata and I are slashing away at fever again. And finally up to date, Nakata last evening had an attack of ptomaine poisoning, and we spent half the night pulling him through.

Chapter 24
Back Word

The *Snark* was forty-three feet on the water-line and fifty-five over all, with fifteen feet beam (tumble-home sides) and seven feet eight inches draught. She was ketch-rigged, carrying flying-jib, jib, fore-staysail, main-sail, mizzen, and spinnaker. There were six feet of head-room below, and she was crown-decked and flush-decked.

There were four alleged WATER-TIGHT compartments. A seventy-horse power auxiliary gas-engine sporadically furnished locomotion at an approximate cost of twenty dollars per mile. A five-horse power engine ran the pumps when it was in order, and on two occasions proved capable of furnishing juice for the search-light. The storage batteries worked four or five times in the course of two years. The fourteen-foot launch was rumoured to work at times, but it invariably broke down whenever I stepped on board.

But the *Snark* sailed. It was the only way she could get anywhere. She sailed for two years, and never touched rock, reef, nor shoal. She had no inside ballast, her iron keel weighed five tons, but her deep draught and high freeboard made her very stiff. Caught under full sail in tropic squalls, she buried her rail and deck many times, but stubbornly refused to turn turtle. She steered easily, and she could run day and night, without steering, close-by, full-and-by, and with the wind abeam. With the wind on her quarter and the sails properly trimmed, she steered herself within two points, and with the wind almost astern she required scarcely three points for self-steering.

The *Snark* was partly built in San Francisco. The morning her iron keel was to be cast was the morning of the great earthquake. Then came anarchy. Six months overdue in the building, I sailed the shell of her to Hawaii to be finished, the engine lashed to the bottom, building materials lashed on deck. Had I remained in San Francisco for completion, I'd still be there. As it was, partly built, she cost four times what she ought to have cost.

The *Snark* was born unfortunately. She was libelled in San Francisco, had her cheques protested as fraudulent in Hawaii, and was fined for breach of quarantine in the Solomons. To save themselves, the newspapers could not tell the truth about her. When I discharged an incompetent captain, they said I had beaten him to a pulp. When one young man returned home to continue at college, it was reported that I was a regular Wolf Larsen, and that my whole crew had deserted because I had beaten it to a pulp. In fact the only blow struck on the *Snark* was when the cook was manhandled by a captain who had shipped with me under false pretences, and whom

I discharged in Fiji. Also, Charmian and I boxed for exercise; but neither of us was seriously maimed.

The voyage was our idea of a good time. I built the *Snark* and paid for it, and for all expenses. I contracted to write thirty-five thousand words descriptive of the trip for a magazine which was to pay me the same rate I received for stories written at home. Promptly the magazine advertised that it was sending me especially around the world for itself. It was a wealthy magazine. And every man who had business dealings with the *Snark* charged three prices because forsooth the magazine could afford it. Down in the uttermost South Sea isle this myth obtained, and I paid accordingly. To this day everybody believes that the magazine paid for everything and that I made a fortune out of the voyage. It is hard, after such advertising, to hammer it into the human understanding that the whole voyage was done for the fun of it.

I went to Australia to go into hospital, where I spent five weeks. I spent five months miserably sick in hotels. The mysterious malady that afflicted my hands was too much for the Australian specialists. It was unknown in the literature of medicine. No case like it had ever been reported. It extended from my hands to my feet so that at times I was as helpless as a child. On occasion my hands were twice their natural size, with seven dead and dying skins peeling off at the same time. There were times when my toe-nails, in twenty-four hours, grew as thick as they were long. After filing them off, inside another twenty-four hours they were as thick as before.

The Australian specialists agreed that the malady was non-parasitic, and that, therefore, it must be nervous. It did not mend, and it was impossible for me to continue the voyage. The only way I could have continued it would have been by being lashed in my bunk, for in my helpless condition, unable to clutch with my hands, I could not have moved about on a small rolling boat. Also, I said to myself that while there were many boats and many voyages, I had but one pair of hands and one set of toe-nails. Still further, I reasoned that in my own climate of California I had always maintained a stable nervous equilibrium. So back I came.

Since my return I have completely recovered. And I have found out what was the matter with me. I encountered a book by Lieutenant-Colonel Charles E. Woodruff of the United States Army entitled "Effects of Tropical Light on White Men." Then I knew. Later, I met Colonel Woodruff, and learned that he had been similarly afflicted. Himself an Army surgeon, seventeen Army surgeons sat on his case in the Philippines, and, like the Australian specialists, confessed themselves beaten. In brief, I had a strong predisposition toward the tissue-destructiveness of tropical light. I was being torn to pieces by the ultra-violet rays just as many experimenters with the X-ray have been torn to pieces.

In passing, I may mention that among the other afflictions that jointly compelled the abandonment of the voyage, was one that is variously called the healthy man's disease, European Leprosy, and Biblical Leprosy. Unlike True Leprosy, nothing is known of this mysterious malady. No doctor has ever claimed a cure for a case of it, though spontaneous cures are recorded. It comes, they know not how. It is, they know not what. It goes, they know not why. Without the use of drugs, merely by living in the wholesome California climate, my silvery skin vanished. The only hope the doctors had held out to me was a spontaneous cure, and such a cure was mine.

A last word: the test of the voyage. It is easy enough for me or any man to say that it was enjoyable. But there is a better witness, the one woman who made it from beginning to end. In hospital when I broke the news to Charmian that I must go back to California, the tears welled into her eyes. For two days she was wrecked and broken by the knowledge that the happy, happy voyage was abandoned.

Part Three
John Barleycorn

I am a seasoned drinker. I have no constitutional predisposition for alcohol. I am not stupid. I am not a swine. I know the drinking game from A to Z, and I have used my judgment in drinking. I never have to be put to bed. Nor do I stagger. In short, I am a normal, average man; and I drink in the normal, average way, as drinking goes. And this is the very point: I am writing of the effects of alcohol on the normal, average man. I have no word to say for or about the microscopically unimportant excessivist, the dipsomaniac.

There are, broadly speaking, two types of drinkers. There is the man whom we all know, stupid, unimaginative, whose brain is bitten numbly by numb maggots; who walks generously with wide-spread, tentative legs, falls frequently in the gutter, and who sees, in the extremity of his ecstasy, blue mice and pink elephants. He is the type that gives rise to the jokes in the funny papers.

The other type of drinker has imagination, vision. Even when most pleasantly jingled, he walks straight and naturally, never staggers nor falls, and knows just where he is and what he is doing. It is not his body but his brain that is drunken. He may bubble with wit, or expand with good fellowship. Or he may see intellectual spectres and phantoms that are cosmic and logical and that take the forms of syllogisms. It is when in this condition that he strips away the husks of life's healthiest illusions and gravely considers the iron collar of necessity welded about the neck of his soul. This is the hour of John Barleycorn's subtlest power. It is easy for any man to roll in the gutter. But it is a terrible ordeal for a man to stand upright on his two legs unswaying, and decide that in all the universe he finds for himself but one freedom—namely, the anticipating of the day of his death. With this man this is the hour of the white logic (of which more anon), when he knows that he may know only the laws of things—the meaning of things never. This is a is danger hour. His feet are taking hold of the pathway that leads down into the grave.

All is clear to him. All these baffling head-reaches after immortality are but the panics of souls frightened by the fear of death, and cursed with the thrice-cursed gift of imagination. They have not the instinct for death; they lack the will to die when the time to die is at hand. They trick themselves into believing they will outwit the game and win to a future, leaving the other animals to the darkness of the grave or the annihilating heats of the crematory. But he, this man in the hour of his white logic, knows that they trick and outwit themselves. The one event happeneth to all alike. There is no new thing under the sun, not even that yearned-for bauble of feeble souls—immortality. But he knows, HE knows, standing upright on his two legs unswaying. He is compounded of meat and wine and sparkle, of sun-mote and world-dust, a frail mechanism made to run for a span, to be tinkered at by doctors of divinity and doctors of physic, and to be flung into the scrap-heap at the end.

I was five years old the first time I got drunk. It was on a hot day, and my father was ploughing in the field. I was sent from the house, half a mile away, to carry to him a pail of beer. "And be sure you don't spill it," was the parting injunction.

It was, as I remember it, a lard pail, very wide across the top, and without a cover. As I toddled along, the beer slopped over the rim upon my legs. And as I toddled, I pondered. Beer was a very precious thing. Come to think of it, it must be wonderfully good. Else why was I never permitted to drink of it in the house? Other things kept from me by the grown-ups I had found good. Then this, too, was good. Trust the grown-ups. They knew. And, anyway, the pail was too full. I was slopping it against my legs and spilling it on the ground. Why waste it? And no one would know whether I had drunk or spilled it.

I was so small that, in order to negotiate the pail, I sat down and gathered it into my lap. First I sipped the foam. I was disappointed. The preciousness evaded me. Evidently it did not reside in the foam. Besides, the taste was not good. Then I remembered seeing the grown-ups blow the foam away before they drank. I buried my face in the foam and lapped the solid liquid beneath. It wasn't good at all. But still I drank. The grown-ups knew what they were about. Considering my diminutiveness, the size of the pail in my lap, and my drinking out of it my breath held and my face buried to the ears in foam, it was rather difficult to estimate how much I drank. Also, I was gulping it down like medicine, in nauseous haste to get the ordeal over.

I shuddered when I started on, and decided that the good taste would come afterward. I tried several times more in the course of that long half-mile. Then, astounded by the quantity of beer that was lacking, and remembering having seen stale beer made to foam afresh, I took a stick and stirred what was left till it foamed to the brim.

And my father never noticed. He emptied the pail with the wide thirst of the sweating ploughman, returned it to me, and started up the plough. I endeavoured to walk beside the horses. I remember tottering and falling against their heels in front of the shining share, and that my father hauled back on the lines so violently that the horses nearly sat down on me. He told me afterward that it was by only a matter of inches that I escaped disembowelling. Vaguely, too, I remember, my father carried me in his arms to the trees on the edge of the field, while all the world reeled and swung about me, and I was aware of deadly nausea mingled with an appalling conviction of sin.

I slept the afternoon away under the trees, and when my father roused me at sundown it was a very sick little boy that got up and dragged wearily homeward. I was exhausted, oppressed by the weight of my limbs, and in my stomach was a harp-like vibrating that extended to my throat and brain. My condition was like that of one who had gone through a battle with poison. In truth, I had been poisoned.

In the weeks and months that followed I had no more interest in beer than in the kitchen stove after it had burned me. The grown-ups were right. Beer was not for children. The grown-ups didn't mind it; but neither did they mind taking pills and castor oil. As for me, I could manage to get along quite well without beer. Yes, and to the day of my death I could have managed to get along quite well without it. But circumstance decreed otherwise. At every turn in the world in which I lived, John Barleycorn beckoned. There was no escaping him. All paths led to him. And it took twenty years of contact, of exchanging greetings and passing on with my tongue in my cheek, to develop in me a sneaking liking for the rascal.

* * *

And yet, despite my physical loathing for alcohol, the brightest spots in my child life were the saloons. Sitting on the heavy potato wagons, wrapped in fog, feet stinging from inactivity, the horses plodding slowly along the deep road through the sandhills, one bright vision made the way never too long. The bright vision was the saloon at Colma, where my father, or whoever drove, always got out to get a drink. And I got out to warm by the great stove and get a soda cracker. Just one soda cracker, but a fabulous luxury. Saloons were good for something. Back behind the plodding horses, I would take an hour in consuming that one cracker. I took the smallest nibbles, never losing a crumb, and chewed the nibble till it became the thinnest and most delectable of pastes. I never voluntarily swallowed this paste. I just tasted it, and went on tasting it, turning it over with my tongue, spreading it on the inside of this cheek, then on the inside of the other cheek, until, at the end, it eluded me and in tiny drops and oozelets, slipped and dribbled down my throat. Horace Fletcher had nothing on me when it came to soda crackers.

I liked saloons. Especially I liked the San Francisco saloons. They had the most delicious dainties for the taking—strange breads and crackers, cheeses, sausages, sardines—wonderful foods that I never saw on our meagre home-table. And once, I remember, a barkeeper mixed me a sweet temperance drink of syrup and soda-water. My father did not pay for it. It was the barkeeper's treat, and he became my ideal of a good, kind man. I dreamed day-dreams of him for years. Although I was seven years old at the time, I can see him now with undiminished clearness, though I never laid eyes on him but that one time. The saloon was south of Market Street in San Francisco. It stood on the west side of the street. As you entered, the bar was on the left. On the right, against the wall, was the free lunch counter. It was a long, narrow room, and at the rear, beyond the beer kegs on tap, were small, round tables and chairs. The barkeeper was blue-eyed, and had fair, silky hair peeping out from under a black silk skull-cap. I remember he wore a brown Cardigan jacket, and I know precisely the spot, in the midst of the array of bottles, from which he took the bottle of red-coloured syrup. He and my father talked long, and I sipped my sweet drink and worshipped him. And for years afterward I worshipped the memory of him.

* * *

By the time I was ten years old, my family had abandoned ranching and gone to live in the city. And here, at ten, I began on the streets as a newsboy. One of the reasons for this was that we needed the money. Another reason was that I needed the exercise. I had found my way to the free public library, and was reading myself into nervous prostration. On the poor ranches on which I had lived there had been no books. In ways truly miraculous, I had been lent four books, marvellous books, and them I had devoured. One was the life of Garfield; the second, Paul du Chaillu's African travels; the third, a novel by Ouida with the last forty pages missing; and the fourth, Irving's "Alhambra." This last had been lent me by a school-teacher. I was not a forward child. Unlike Oliver Twist, I was incapable of asking for more. When I returned the "Alhambra" to the teacher I hoped she would lend me another book. And because she did not—most likely she deemed me unappreciative—I cried all the way home on the three-mile tramp from the school to the ranch. I waited and yearned for her to lend me another book. Scores of times I nerved myself almost to the point of asking her, but never quite reached the necessary pitch of effrontery.

And then came the city of Oakland, and on the shelves of that free library I discovered all the great world beyond the skyline. Here were thousands of books as good as my four wonder-books, and some were even better. Libraries were not concerned with children in those days, and I had strange adventures. I remember, in the catalogue, being impressed by the title, "The Adventures of Peregrine Pickle." I filled an application blank and the librarian handed me the collected and entirely unexpurgated works of Smollett in one huge volume. I read everything, but principally history and adventure, and all the old travels and voyages. I read mornings, afternoons, and nights. I read in bed, I read at table, I read as I walked to and from school, and I read at recess while the other boys were playing. I began to get the "jerks." To everybody I replied: "Go away. You make me nervous."

And so, at ten, I was out on the streets, a newsboy. I had no time to read. I was busy getting exercise and learning how to fight, busy learning forwardness, and brass and bluff. I had an imagination and a curiosity about all things that made me plastic. Not least among the things I was curious about was the saloon. And I was in and out of many a one. I remember, in those days, on the east side of Broadway, between Sixth and Seventh, from corner to corner, there was a solid block of saloons.

In the saloons life was different. Men talked with great voices, laughed great laughs, and there was an atmosphere of greatness. Here was something more than common every-day where nothing happened. Here life was always very live, and, sometimes, even lurid, when blows were struck, and blood was shed, and big policemen came shouldering in. Great moments, these, for me, my head filled with all the wild and valiant fighting of the gallant adventurers on sea and land. There were no big moments when I trudged along the street throwing my papers in at doors. But in the saloons, even the sots, stupefied, sprawling across the tables or in the sawdust, were objects of mystery and wonder.

And more, the saloons were right. The city fathers sanctioned them and licensed them. They were not the terrible places I heard boys deem them who lacked my opportunities to know. Terrible they might be, but then that only meant they were terribly wonderful, and it is the terribly wonderful that a boy desires to know. In the same way pirates, and shipwrecks, and battles were terrible; and what healthy boy wouldn't give his immortal soul to participate in such affairs?

Besides, in saloons I saw reporters, editors, lawyers, judges, whose names and faces I knew. They put the seal of social approval on the saloon. They verified my own feeling of fascination in the saloon. They, too, must have found there that something different, that something beyond, which I sensed and groped after.

What it was, I did not know; yet there it must be, for there men focused like buzzing flies about a honey pot. I had no sorrows, and the world was very bright, so I could not guess that what these men sought was forgetfulness of jaded toil and stale grief.

Not that I drank at that time. From ten to fifteen I rarely tasted liquor, but I was intimately in contact with drinkers and drinking places. The only reason I did not drink was because I didn't like the stuff. As the time passed, I worked as boy-helper on an ice-wagon, set up pins in a bowling alley with a saloon attached, and swept out saloons at Sunday picnic grounds.

Big jovial Josie Harper ran a road house at Telegraph Avenue and Thirty-ninth Street. Here for a year I delivered an evening paper, until my route was changed to the water-front and tenderloin of Oakland. The first month, when I collected Josie Harper's bill, she poured me a glass of wine. I was ashamed to refuse, so I drank it. But after that I watched the chance when she wasn't around so as to collect from her barkeeper.

The first day I worked in the bowling alley, the barkeeper, according to custom, called us boys up to have a drink after we had been setting up pins for several hours. The others asked for beer. I said I'd take ginger ale. The boys snickered, and I noticed the barkeeper favoured me with a strange, searching scrutiny. Nevertheless, he opened a bottle of ginger ale. Afterward, back in the alleys, in the pauses between games, the boys enlightened me. I had offended the barkeeper. A bottle of ginger ale cost the saloon ever so much more than a glass of steam beer; and it was up to me, if I wanted to hold my job, to drink beer. Besides, beer was food. I could work better on it. There was no food in ginger ale. After that, when I couldn't sneak out of it, I drank beer and wondered what men found in it that was so good. I was always aware that I was missing something.

What I really liked in those days was candy. For five cents I could buy five "cannon-balls"—big lumps of the most delicious lastingness. I could chew and worry a single one for an hour. Then there was a Mexican who sold big slabs of brown chewing taffy for five cents each. It required a quarter of a day properly to absorb one of them. And many a day I made my entire lunch off one of those slabs. In truth, I found food there, but not in beer.

* * *

When I was fourteen, my head filled with the tales of the old voyagers, my vision with tropic isles and far sea-rims, I was sailing a small centreboard skiff around San Francisco Bay and on the Oakland Estuary. I wanted to go to sea. I wanted to get away from monotony and the commonplace. I was in the flower of my adolescence, a-thrill with romance and adventure, dreaming of wild life in the wild man-world. Little I guessed how all the warp and woof of that man-world was entangled with alcohol.

So, one day, as I hoisted sail on my skiff, I met Scotty. He was a husky youngster of seventeen, a runaway apprentice, he told me, from an English ship in Australia. He had just worked his way on another ship to San Francisco; and now he wanted to see about getting a berth on a whaler. Across the estuary, near where the whalers lay, was lying the sloop-yacht *Idler*. The caretaker was a harpooner who intended sailing next voyage on the whale ship *Bonanza*. Would I take him, Scotty, over in my skiff to call upon the harpooner?

Would I! Hadn't I heard the stories and rumours about the *Idler*?—the big sloop that had come up from the Sandwich Islands where it had been engaged in smuggling opium. And the harpooner who was caretaker! How often had I seen him and envied him his freedom. He never had to leave the water. He slept aboard the *Idler* each night, while I had to go home upon the land to go to bed. The harpooner was only nineteen years old (and I have never had anything but his own word that he was a harpooner); but he had been too shining and glorious a personality for me ever to address as I paddled around the yacht at a wistful distance. Would I take Scotty, the runaway sailor, to visit the harpooner, on the opium-smuggler *Idler*? WOULD I!

The harpooner came on deck to answer our hail, and invited us aboard. I played the sailor and the man, fending off the skiff so that it would not mar the yacht's white paint, dropping the skiff astern on a long painter, and making the painter fast with two nonchalant half-hitches.

We went below. It was the first sea-interior I had ever seen. The clothing on the wall smelled musty. But what of that? Was it not the sea-gear of men?—leather jackets lined with corduroy, blue coats of pilot cloth, sou'westers, sea-boots, oilskins. And everywhere was in evidence the economy of space—the narrow bunks, the swinging tables, the incredible lockers. There were the tell-tale compass, the sea-lamps in their gimbals, the blue-backed charts carelessly rolled and tucked away, the signal-flags in alphabetical order, and a mariner's dividers jammed into the woodwork to hold a calendar. At last I was living. Here I sat, inside my first ship, a smuggler, accepted as a comrade by a harpooner and a runaway English sailor who said his name was Scotty.

The first thing that the harpooner, aged nineteen, and the sailor, aged seventeen, did to show that they were men was to behave like men. The harpooner suggested the eminent desirableness of a drink, and Scotty searched his pockets for dimes and nickels. Then the harpooner carried away a pink flask to be filled in some blind pig, for there were no licensed saloons in that locality. We drank the cheap rotgut out of tumblers. Was I any the less strong, any the less valiant, than the harpooner and the sailor? They were men. They proved it by the way they drank. Drink was the badge of manhood. So I drank with them, drink by drink, raw and straight, though the damned stuff couldn't compare with a stick of chewing taffy or a delectable "cannon-ball." I shuddered and swallowed my gorge with every drink, though I manfully hid all such symptoms.

Diverse times we filled the flask that afternoon. All I had was twenty cents, but I put it up like a man, though with secret regret at the enormous store of candy it could have bought. The liquor mounted in the heads of all of us, and the talk of Scotty and the harpooner was upon running the Easting down, gales off the Horn and pamperos off the Plate, lower topsail breezes, southerly busters, North Pacific gales, and of smashed whaleboats in the Arctic ice.

"You can't swim in that ice water," said the harpooner confidentially to me. "You double up in a minute and go down. When a whale smashes your boat, the thing to do is to get your belly across an oar, so that when the cold doubles you you'll float."

"Sure," I said, with a grateful nod and an air of certitude that I, too, would hunt whales and be in smashed boats in the Arctic Ocean. And, truly, I registered his advice as singularly valuable information, and filed it away in my brain, where it persists to this day.

But I couldn't talk—at first. Heavens! I was only fourteen, and had never been on the ocean in my life. I could only listen to the two sea-dogs, and show my manhood by drinking with them, fairly and squarely, drink and drink.

The liquor worked its will with me; the talk of Scotty and the harpooner poured through the pent space of the *Idler*'s cabin and through my brain like great gusts of wide, free wind; and in imagination I lived my years to come and rocked over the wild, mad, glorious world on multitudinous adventures.

We unbent. Our inhibitions and taciturnities vanished. We were as if we had known each other for years and years, and we pledged ourselves to years of future voyagings together. The harpooner told of misadventures and secret shames. Scotty wept over his poor old mother in Edinburgh—a lady, he insisted, gently born—who was in reduced circumstances, who had pinched herself to pay the lump sum to the ship-owners for his apprenticeship, whose sacrificing dream had been to see him a merchantman officer and a gentleman, and who was heartbroken because he had deserted his ship in Australia and joined another as a common sailor before the mast. And Scotty proved it. He drew her last sad letter from his pocket and wept over it as he read it aloud. The harpooner and I wept with him, and swore that all three of us would ship on the whaleship Bonanza, win a big pay-day, and, still together, make a pilgrimage to Edinburgh and lay our store of money in the dear lady's lap.

And, as John Barleycorn heated his way into my brain, thawing my reticence, melting my modesty, talking through me and with me and as me, my adopted twin brother and alter ego, I, too, raised my voice to show myself a man and an adventurer, and bragged in detail and at length of how I had crossed San Francisco Bay in my open skiff in a roaring southwester when even the schooner sailors doubted my exploit. Further, I—or John Barleycorn, for it was the same thing—told Scotty that he might be a deep-sea sailor and know the last rope on the great deep-sea ships, but that when it came to small-boat sailing I could beat him hands down and sail circles around him.

The best of it was that my assertion and brag were true. With reticence and modesty present, I could never have dared tell Scotty my small-boat estimate of him. But it is ever the way of John Barleycorn to loosen the tongue and babble the secret thought.

Scotty, or John Barleycorn, or the pair, was very naturally offended by my remarks. Nor was I loath. I could whip any runaway sailor seventeen years old. Scotty and I flared and raged like young cockerels, until the harpooner poured another round of drinks to enable us to forgive and make up. Which we did, arms around each other's necks, protesting vows of eternal friendship—just like Black Matt and Tom Morrisey, I remembered, in the ranch kitchen in San Mateo. And, remembering, I knew that I was at last a man—despite my meagre fourteen years—a man as big and manly as those two strapping

giants who had quarrelled and made up on that memorable Sunday morning of long ago.

By this time the singing stage was reached, and I joined Scotty and the harpooner in snatches of sea songs and chanties. It was here, in the cabin of the *Idler*, that I first heard "Blow the Man Down," "Flying Cloud," and "Whisky, Johnny, Whisky." Oh, it was brave. I was beginning to grasp the meaning of life. Here was no commonplace, no Oakland Estuary, no weary round of throwing newspapers at front doors, delivering ice, and setting up ninepins. All the world was mine, all its paths were under my feet, and John Barleycorn, tricking my fancy, enabled me to anticipate the life of adventure for which I yearned.

We were not ordinary. We were three tipsy young gods, incredibly wise, gloriously genial, and without limit to our powers. Ah!—and I say it now, after the years—could John Barleycorn keep one at such a height, I should never draw a sober breath again. But this is not a world of free freights. One pays according to an iron schedule—for every strength the balanced weakness; for every high a corresponding low; for every fictitious god-like moment an equivalent time in reptilian slime. For every feat of telescoping long days and weeks of life into mad magnificent instants, one must pay with shortened life, and, oft-times, with savage usury added.

Intenseness and duration are as ancient enemies as fire and water. They are mutually destructive. They cannot co-exist. And John Barleycorn, mighty necromancer though he be, is as much a slave to organic chemistry as we mortals are. We pay for every nerve marathon we run, nor can John Barleycorn intercede and fend off the just payment. He can lead us to the heights, but he cannot keep us there, else would we all be devotees. And there is no devotee but pays for the mad dances John Barleycorn pipes.

Yet the foregoing is all in after wisdom spoken. It was no part of the knowledge of the lad, fourteen years old, who sat in the *Idler*'s cabin between the harpooner and the sailor, the air rich in his nostrils with the musty smell of men's sea-gear, roaring in chorus: "Yankee ship come down de ribber—pull, my bully boys, pull!"

We grew maudlin, and all talked and shouted at once. I had a splendid constitution, a stomach that would digest scrap-iron, and I was still running my marathon in full vigour when Scotty began to fail and fade. His talk grew incoherent. He groped for words and could not find them, while the ones he found his lips were unable to form. His poisoned consciousness was leaving him. The brightness went out of his eyes, and he looked as stupid as were his efforts to talk. His face and body sagged as his consciousness sagged. (A man cannot sit upright save by an act of will.) Scotty's reeling brain could not control his muscles. All his correlations were breaking down. He strove to take another drink, and feebly dropped the tumbler on the floor. Then, to my amazement, weeping bitterly, he rolled into a bunk on his back and immediately snored off to sleep.

The harpooner and I drank on, grinning in a superior way to each other over Scotty's plight. The last flask was opened, and we drank it between us, to the accompaniment of Scotty's stertorous breathing. Then the harpooner faded away into his bunk, and I was left alone, unthrown, on the field of battle.

I was very proud, and John Barleycorn was proud with me. I could carry my drink. I was a man. I had drunk two men, drink for drink, into unconsciousness. And I was still on my two feet, upright, making my way on deck to get air into my scorching lungs. It was in this bout on the *Idler* that I discovered what a good stomach and a strong head I had for drink—a bit of knowledge that was to be a source of pride in succeeding years, and that ultimately I was to come to consider a great affliction. The fortunate man is the one who cannot take more than a couple of drinks without becoming intoxicated. The unfortunate wight is the one who can take many glasses without betraying a sign, who must take numerous glasses in order to get the "kick."

The sun was setting when I came on the *Idler*'s deck. There were plenty of bunks below. I did not need to go home. But I wanted to demonstrate to myself how much I was a man. There lay my skiff astern. The last of a strong ebb was running out in channel in the teeth of an ocean breeze of forty miles an hour. I could see the stiff whitecaps, and the suck and run of the current was plainly visible in the face and trough of each one.

I set sail, cast off, took my place at the tiller, the sheet in my hand, and headed across channel. The skiff heeled over and plunged into it madly. The spray began to fly. I was at the pinnacle of exaltation. I sang "Blow the Man Down" as I sailed. I was no boy of fourteen, living the mediocre ways of the sleepy town called Oakland. I was a man, a god, and the very elements rendered me allegiance as I bitted them to my will.

The tide was out. A full hundred yards of soft mud intervened between the boat-wharf and the water. I pulled up my centreboard, ran full tilt into the mud, took in sail, and, standing in the stern, as I had often done at low tide, I began to shove the skiff with an oar. It was then that my correlations began to break down. I lost my balance and pitched head-foremost into the ooze. Then, and for the first time, as I floundered to my feet covered with slime, the blood running down my arms from a scrape against a barnacled stake, I knew that I was drunk. But what of it? Across the channel two strong sailormen lay unconscious in their bunks where I had drunk them. I WAS a man. I was still on my legs, if they were knee-deep in mud. I disdained to get back into the skiff. I waded through the mud, shoving the skiff before me and yammering the chant of my manhood to the world.

I paid for it. I was sick for a couple of days, meanly sick, and my arms were painfully poisoned from the barnacle scratches. For a week I could not use them, and it was a torture to put on and take off my clothes.

I swore, "Never again!" The game wasn't worth it. The price was too stiff. I had no moral qualms. My revulsion was purely physical. No exalted moments were worth such hours of misery and wretchedness. When I got back to my skiff, I shunned the *Idler*. I would cross the opposite side of the channel to go around her. Scotty had disappeared. The harpooner was still about, but him I avoided. Once, when he landed on the boat-wharf, I hid in a shed so as to escape seeing him. I was afraid he would propose some more drinking, maybe have a flask full of whisky in his pocket.

And yet—and here enters the necromancy of John Barleycorn—that afternoon's drunk on the *Idler* had been a purple passage flung into the monotony of my days. It was memorable. My mind dwelt on it continually. I went over the details, over and over again. Among other things, I had got into the cogs and springs of men's actions. I had seen Scotty weep about his own worthlessness and the sad case of his Edinburgh mother who was a lady. The harpooner had told me terribly wonderful things of himself. I had caught a myriad enticing and inflammatory hints of a world beyond my world, and for which I was certainly as fitted as the two lads who had drunk with me. I had got behind men's souls. I had got behind my own soul and found unguessed potencies and greatnesses.

* * *

I was barely turned fifteen, and working long hours in a cannery. Month in and month out, the shortest day I ever worked was ten hours. When to ten hours of actual work at a machine is added the noon hour; the walking to work and walking home from work; the getting up in the morning, dressing, and eating; the eating at night, undressing, and going to bed, there remains no more than the nine hours out of the twenty-four required by a healthy youngster for sleep. Out of those nine hours, after I was in bed and ere my eyes drowsed shut, I managed to steal a little time for reading.

But many a night I did not knock off work until midnight. On occasion I worked eighteen and twenty hours on a stretch. Once I worked at my machine for thirty-six consecutive hours. And there were weeks on end when I never knocked off work earlier than eleven o'clock, got home and in bed at half after midnight, and was called at half-past five to dress, eat, walk to work, and be at my machine at seven o'clock whistle blow.

I asked myself if this were the meaning of life—to be a work-beast? I knew of no horse in the city of Oakland that worked the hours I worked. If this were living, I was entirely unenamoured of it. I remembered my skiff, lying idle and accumulating barnacles at the boat-wharf; I remembered the wind that blew every day on the bay, the sunrises and sunsets I never saw; the bite of the salt air in my nostrils, the bite of the salt water on my flesh when I plunged overside; I remembered all the beauty and the wonder and the sense-delights of the world denied me. There was only one way to escape my deadening toil. I must get out and away on the water. I must earn my bread on the water.

I wanted to be where the winds of adventure blew. And the winds of adventure blew the oyster pirate sloops up and down San Francisco Bay, from raided oyster-beds and fights at night on shoal and flat, to markets in the morning against city wharves, where peddlers and saloon-keepers came down to buy. Every raid on an oyster-bed was a felony. The penalty was State imprisonment, the stripes and the lockstep. And what of that? The men in stripes worked a shorter day than I at my machine. And there was vastly more romance in being an oyster pirate or a convict than in being a machine slave. And behind it all, behind all of me with youth abubble, whispered Romance, Adventure.

So I interviewed my Mammy Jennie, my old nurse at whose black breast I had suckled. She was more prosperous than my folks. She was nursing sick people at a good weekly wage. Would she lend her "white child" the money? WOULD SHE? What she had was mine.

Then I sought out French Frank, the oyster pirate, who wanted to sell, I had heard, his sloop, the *Razzle Dazzle*. I found him lying at anchor on the Alameda side of the estuary near the Webster Street bridge, with visitors aboard, whom he was entertaining with afternoon wine. He came on deck to talk business. He was willing to sell. But it was Sunday. Besides, he had guests. On the morrow he would make out the bill of sale and I could enter into possession. And in the meantime I must come below and meet his friends. They were two sisters, Mamie and Tess; a Mrs. Hadley, who chaperoned them; "Whisky" Bob, a youthful oyster pirate of sixteen; and "Spider" Healey, a black-whiskered wharf-rat of twenty. Mamie, who was Spider's niece, was called the Queen of the Oyster Pirates, and, on occasion, presided at their revels. French Frank was in love with her, though I did not know it at the time; and she steadfastly refused to marry him.

French Frank poured a tumbler of red wine from a big demijohn to drink to our transaction. I remembered the red wine of the Italian rancho, and shuddered inwardly. Whisky and beer were not quite so repulsive. But the Queen of the Oyster Pirates was looking at me, a part-emptied glass in her own hand. I had my pride. If I was only fifteen, at least I could not show myself any less a man than she. Besides, there were her sister, and Mrs. Hadley, and the young oyster pirate, and the whiskered wharf-rat, all with glasses in their hands. Was I a milk-and-water sop? No; a thousand times no, and a thousand glasses no. I downed the tumblerful like a man.

French Frank was elated by the sale, which I had bound with a twenty-dollar goldpiece. He poured more wine. I had learned my strong head and stomach, and I was certain I could drink with them in a temperate way and not poison myself for a week to come. I could stand as much as they; and besides, they had already been drinking for some time.

We got to singing. Spider sang "The Boston Burglar" and "Black Lulu." The Queen sang "Then I Wisht I Were a Little Bird." And her sister Tess sang "Oh, Treat My Daughter Kindly." The fun grew fast and furious. I found myself able to miss drinks without being noticed or called to account. Also, standing in the companionway, head and shoulders out and glass in hand, I could fling the wine overboard.

I reasoned something like this: It is a queerness of these people that they like this vile-tasting wine. Well, let them. I cannot quarrel with their tastes. My manhood, according to their queer notions, must compel me to appear to like this wine. Very well. I shall so appear. But I shall drink no more than is unavoidable.

And the Queen began to make love to me, the latest recruit to the oyster pirate fleet, and no mere hand, but a master and owner. She went upon deck to take the air, and took me with her. She knew, of course, but I never dreamed, how French Frank was raging down below. Then Tess joined us, sitting on the cabin; and Spider, and Bob; and at the last, Mrs. Hadley and French Frank. And we sat there, glasses in hand, and sang, while the big demijohn went around; and I was the only strictly sober one.

And I enjoyed it as no one of them was able to enjoy it. Here, in this atmosphere of bohemianism, I could not but contrast the scene with my scene of the day before, sitting at my machine, in the stifling, shut-in air, repeating, endlessly repeating, at top speed, my series of mechanical motions. And here I sat now, glass in hand, in warm-glowing camaraderie, with the oyster pirates, adventurers who refused to be slaves to petty routine, who flouted restrictions and the law, who carried their lives and their liberty in their hands. And it was through John Barleycorn that I came to join this glorious company of free souls, unashamed and unafraid.

And the afternoon seabreeze blew its tang into my lungs, and curled the waves in mid-channel. Before it came the scow schooners, wing-and-wing, blowing their horns for the drawbridges to open. Red-stacked tugs tore by, rocking the *Razzle Dazzle* in the waves of their wake. A sugar barque towed from the "boneyard" to sea. The sun-wash was on the crisping water, and life was big.

There it was, the smack and slap of the spirit of revolt, of adventure, of romance, of the things forbidden and done defiantly and grandly. And I knew that on the morrow I would not go back to my machine at the cannery. To-morrow I would be an oyster pirate, as free a freebooter as the century and the waters of San Francisco Bay would permit. Spider had already agreed to sail with me as my crew of one, and, also, as cook while I did the deck work. We would outfit our grub and water in the morning, hoist the big mainsail (which was a bigger piece of canvas than any I had ever sailed under), and beat our way out the estuary on the first of the seabreeze and the last of the ebb. Then we would slack sheets, and on the first of the flood run down the bay to the Asparagus Islands, where we would anchor miles off shore. And at last my dream would be realised: I would sleep upon the water. And next morning I would wake upon the water; and thereafter all my days and nights would be on the water.

And the Queen asked me to row her ashore in my skiff, when at sunset French Frank prepared to take his guests ashore. Nor did I catch the significance of his abrupt change of plan when he turned the task of rowing his skiff over to Whisky Bob, himself remaining on board the sloop. Nor did I understand Spider's grinning side-remark to me: "Gee! There's nothin' slow about YOU." How could it possibly enter my boy's head that a grizzled man of fifty should be jealous of me?

* * *

We met by appointment, early Monday morning, to complete the deal, in Johnny Heinhold's "Last Chance"—a saloon, of course, for the transactions of men. I paid the money over, received the bill of sale, and French Frank treated. This struck me as an evident custom, and a logical one—the seller, who receives the money, to wet a piece of it in the establishment where the trade was consummated.

But, to my surprise, French Frank treated the house. He and I drank, which seemed just; but why should Johnny Heinhold, who owned the saloon and waited behind the bar, be invited to drink? I figured it immediately that he made a profit on the very drink he drank. I could, in a way, considering that they were friends and shipmates, understand Spider and Whisky Bob being asked to drink; but why should the longshoremen, Bill Kelley and Soup Kennedy, be asked?

Then there was Pat, the Queen's brother, making a total of eight of us. It was early morning, and all ordered whisky. What could I do, here in this company of big men, all drinking whisky? "Whisky," I said, with the careless air of one who had said it a thousand times. And such whisky! I tossed it down. A-r-r-r-gh! I can taste it yet.

And I was appalled at the price French Frank had paid—eighty cents. EIGHTY CENTS! It was an outrage to my thrifty soul. Eighty cents—the equivalent of eight long hours of my toil at the machine, gone down our throats, and gone like that, in a twinkling, leaving only a bad taste in the mouth. There was no discussion that French Frank was a waster.

I was anxious to be gone, out into the sunshine, out over the water to my glorious boat. But all hands lingered. Even Spider, my crew, lingered. No hint broke through my obtuseness of why they lingered. I have often thought since of how they must have regarded me, the newcomer being welcomed into their company standing at bar with them, and not standing for a single round of drinks.

French Frank, who, unknown to me, had swallowed his chagrin since the day before, now that the money for the *Razzle Dazzle* was in his pocket, began to behave curiously toward me. I sensed the change in his attitude, saw the forbidding glitter in his eyes, and wondered. The more I saw of men, the queerer they became. Johnny Heinhold leaned across the bar and whispered in my ear, "He's got it in for you. Watch out."

I nodded comprehension of his statement, and acquiescence in it, as a man should nod who knows all about men. But secretly I was perplexed. Heavens! How was I, who had worked hard and read books of adventure, and who was only fifteen years old, who had not dreamed of giving the Queen of the Oyster Pirates a second thought, and who did not know that French Frank was madly and Latinly in love with her—how was I to guess that I had done him shame? And how was I to guess that the story of how the Queen had thrown him down on his own boat, the moment I hove in sight, was already the gleeful gossip of the water-front? And by the same token, how was I to guess that her brother Pat's offishness with me was anything else than temperamental gloominess of spirit?

Whisky Bob got me aside a moment. "Keep your eyes open," he muttered. "Take my tip. French Frank's ugly. I'm going up river with him to get a schooner for oystering. When he gets down on the beds, watch out. He says he'll run you down. After dark, any time he's around, change your anchorage and douse your riding light. Savve?"

Oh, certainly, I savve'd. I nodded my head, and, as one man to another, thanked him for his tip; and drifted back to the group at the bar. No; I did not treat. I never dreamed that I was expected to treat. I left with Spider, and my ears burn now as I try to surmise the things they must have said about me.

I asked Spider, in an off-hand way, what was eating French Frank. "He's crazy jealous of you," was the answer. "Do you think so?" I said, and dismissed the matter as not worth thinking about.

But I leave it to any one—the swell of my fifteen-years-old manhood at learning that French Frank, the adventurer of fifty, the sailor of all the seas of all the world, was jealous of me—and jealous over a girl most romantically named the Queen of the Oyster Pirates. I had read of such things in books, and regarded them as personal probabilities of a distant maturity. Oh, I felt a rare young devil, as we hoisted the big mainsail that morning, broke out anchor, and filled away close-hauled on the three-mile beat to windward out into the bay.

Such was my escape from the killing machine-toil, and my introduction to the oyster pirates. True, the introduction had begun with drink, and the life promised to continue with drink. But was I to stay away from it for such reason? Wherever life ran free and great, there men drank. Romance and Adventure seemed always to go down the street locked arm in arm with John Barleycorn. To know the two, I must know the third. Or else I must go back to my free library books and read of the deeds of other men and do no deeds of my own save slave for ten cents an hour at a machine in a cannery.

No; I was not to be deterred from this brave life on the water by the fact that the water-dwellers had queer and expensive desires for beer and wine and whisky. What if their notions of happiness included the strange one of seeing me drink? When they persisted in buying the stuff and thrusting it upon me, why, I would drink it. It was the price I would pay for their comradeship. And I didn't have to get drunk. I had not got drunk the Sunday afternoon I arranged to buy the *Razzle Dazzle*, despite the fact that not one of the rest was sober. Well, I could go on into the future that way, drinking the stuff when it gave them pleasure that I should drink it, but carefully avoiding over-drinking.

* * *

The more I saw of the life, the more I was enamoured of it. I can never forget my thrills the first night I took part in a concerted raid, when we assembled on board the *Annie*—rough men, big and unafraid, and weazened wharf-rats, some of them ex-convicts, all of them enemies of the law and meriting jail, in sea-boots and sea-gear, talking in gruff low voices, and "Big" George with revolvers strapped about his waist to show that he meant business.

Oh, I know, looking back, that the whole thing was sordid and silly. But I was not looking back in those days when I was rubbing shoulders with John Barleycorn and beginning to accept him. The life was brave and wild, and I was living the adventure I had read so much about.

Nelson, "Young Scratch" they called him, to distinguish him from "Old Scratch," his father, sailed in the sloop *Reindeer*, partners with one "Clam." Clam was a dare-devil, but Nelson was a reckless maniac. He was twenty years old, with the body of a Hercules. When he was shot in Benicia, a couple of years later, the coroner said he was the greatest-shouldered man he had ever seen laid on a slab.

Nelson could not read or write. He had been "dragged" up by his father on San Francisco Bay, and boats were second nature with him. His strength was prodigious, and his reputation along the water-front for violence was anything but savoury. He had Berserker rages and did mad, terrible things. I made his acquaintance the first cruise of the *Razzle Dazzle*, and saw him sail the *Reindeer* in a blow and dredge oysters all around the rest of us as we lay at two anchors, troubled with fear of going ashore.

He was some man, this Nelson; and when, passing by the Last Chance saloon, he spoke to me, I felt very proud. But try to imagine my pride when he promptly asked me in to have a drink. I stood at the bar and drank a glass of beer with him, and talked manfully of oysters, and boats, and of the mystery of who had put the load of buckshot through the *Annie*'s mainsail.

We talked and lingered at the bar. It seemed to me strange that we lingered. We had had our beer. But who was I to lead the way outside when great Nelson chose to lean against the bar? After a few minutes, to my surprise, he asked me to have another drink, which I did. And still we talked, and Nelson evinced no intention of leaving the bar.

Bear with me while I explain the way of my reasoning and of my innocence. First of all, I was very proud to be in the company of Nelson, who was the most heroic figure among the oyster pirates and bay adventurers. Unfortunately for my stomach and mucous membranes, Nelson had a strange quirk of nature that made him find happiness in treating me to beer. I had no moral disinclination for beer, and just because I didn't like the taste of it and the weight of it was no reason I should forgo the honour of his company. It was his whim to drink beer, and to have me drink beer with him. Very well, I would put up with the passing discomfort.

So we continued to talk at the bar, and to drink beer ordered and paid for by Nelson. I think, now, when I look back upon it, that Nelson was curious. He wanted to find out just what kind of a gink I was. He wanted to see how many times I'd let him treat without offering to treat in return.

After I had drunk half a dozen glasses, my policy of temperateness in mind, I decided that I had had enough for that time. So I mentioned that I was going aboard the *Razzle Dazzle*, then lying at the city wharf, a hundred yards away.

I said good-bye to Nelson, and went on down the wharf. But, John Barleycorn, to the extent of six glasses, went with me. My brain tingled and was very much alive. I was uplifted by my sense of manhood. I, a truly-true oyster pirate, was going aboard my own boat after hob-nobbing in the Last Chance with Nelson, the greatest oyster pirate of us all. Strong in my brain was the vision of us leaning against the bar and drinking beer. And curious it was, I decided, this whim of nature that made men happy in spending good money for beer for a fellow like me who didn't want it.

As I pondered this, I recollected that several times other men, in couples, had entered the Last Chance, and first one, then the other, had treated to drinks. I remembered, on the drunk on the *Idler*, how Scotty and the harpooner and myself had raked and scraped dimes and nickels with which to buy the whisky. Then came my boy code: when on a day a fellow gave another a "cannon-ball" or a chunk of taffy, on some other day he would expect to receive back a cannon-ball or a chunk of taffy.

That was why Nelson had lingered at the bar. Having bought a drink, he had waited for me to buy one. I HAD LET HIM BUY SIX DRINKS AND NEVER ONCE OFFERED TO TREAT. And he was the great Nelson! I could feel myself blushing with shame. I sat down on the stringer-piece of the wharf and buried my face in my hands. And the heat of my shame burned up my neck and into my cheeks and forehead. I have blushed many times in my life, but never have I experienced so terrible a blush as that one.

I retraced my steps up the wharf to the Last Chance, where Nelson still stood outside. "Come on and have a beer," I invited. Again we stood at the bar and drank and talked, but this time it was I who paid ten cents! a whole hour of my labour at a machine for a drink of something I didn't want and which tasted rotten. But it wasn't difficult. I had achieved a concept. Money no longer counted. It was comradeship that counted. "Have another?" I said. And we had another, and I paid for it. Nelson, with the wisdom of the skilled drinker, said to the barkeeper, "Make mine a small one, Johnny." Johnny nodded and gave him a glass that contained only a third as much as the glasses we had been drinking. Yet the charge was the same—five cents.

By this time I was getting nicely jingled, so such extravagance didn't hurt me much. Besides, I was learning. There was more in this buying of drinks than mere quantity. I got my finger on it.

There was a stage when the beer didn't count at all, but just the spirit of comradeship of drinking together. And, ha!—another thing! I, too, could call for small beers and minimise by two-thirds the detestable freightage with which comradeship burdened one.

"I had to go aboard to get some money," I remarked casually, as we drank, in the hope Nelson would take it as an explanation of why I had let him treat six consecutive times.

"Oh, well, you didn't have to do that," he answered. "Johnny'll trust a fellow like you—won't you, Johnny!"

"Sure," Johnny agreed, with a smile.

"How much you got down against me?" Nelson queried.

Johnny pulled out the book he kept behind the bar, found Nelson's page, and added up the account of several dollars. At once I became possessed with a desire to have a page in that book. Almost it seemed the final badge of manhood.

After a couple more drinks, for which I insisted on paying, Nelson decided to go. We parted true comradely, and I wandered down the wharf to the *Razzle Dazzle*. Spider was just building the fire for supper.

"Where'd you get it?" he grinned up at me through the open companion.

"Oh, I've been with Nelson," I said carelessly, trying to hide my pride.

Then an idea came to me. Here was another one of them. Now that I had achieved my concept, I might as well practise it thoroughly. "Come on," I said, "up to Johnny's and have a drink."

Going up the wharf, we met Clam coming down. Clam was Nelson's partner, and he was a fine, brave, handsome, moustached man of thirty—everything, in short, that his nickname did not connote. "Come on," I said, "and have a drink." He came. As we turned into the Last Chance, there was Pat, the Queen's brother, coming out.

"What's your hurry?" I greeted him. "We're having a drink. Come on along." "I've just had one," he demurred. "What of it?—we're having one now," I retorted. And Pat consented to join us, and I melted my way into his good graces with a couple of glasses of beer. Oh! I was learning things that afternoon about John Barleycorn. There was more in him than the bad taste when you swallowed him. Here, at the absurd cost of ten cents, a gloomy, grouchy individual, who threatened to become an enemy, was made into a good friend. He became even genial, his looks were kindly, and our voices mellowed together as we talked water-front and oyster-bed gossip.

"Small beer for me, Johnny," I said, when the others had ordered schooners. Yes, and I said it like the accustomed drinker, carelessly, casually, as a sort of spontaneous thought that had just occurred to me. Looking back, I am confident that the only one there who guessed I was a tyro at bar-drinking was Johnny Heinhold.

"Where'd he get it?" I overheard Spider confidentially ask Johnny.

"Oh, he's been sousin' here with Nelson all afternoon," was Johnny's answer.

I never let on that I'd heard, but PROUD? Aye, even the barkeeper was giving me a recommendation as a man. "HE'S BEEN SOUSIN' HERE WITH NELSON ALL AFTERNOON." Magic words! The accolade delivered by a barkeeper with a beer glass!

* * *

My reputation grew. When the story went around the water-front of how French Frank had tried to run me down with his schooner, and of how I had stood on the deck of the *Razzle Dazzle*, a cocked double-barrelled shotgun in my hands, steering with my feet and holding her to her course, and compelled him to put up his wheel and keep away, the water-front decided that there was something in me despite my youth. And I continued to show what was in me. There were the times I brought the *Razzle Dazzle* in with a bigger load of oysters than any other two-man craft; there was the time when we raided far down in Lower Bay, and mine was the only craft back at daylight to the anchorage off Asparagus Island; there was the Thursday night we raced for market and I brought the *Razzle Dazzle* in without a rudder, first of the fleet, and skimmed the cream of the Friday morning trade; and there was the time I brought her in from Upper Bay under a jib, when Scotty burned my mainsail. (Yes; it was Scotty of the *Idler* adventure. Irish had followed Spider on board the *Razzle Dazzle*, and Scotty, turning up, had taken Irish's place.)

But the things I did on the water only partly counted. What completed everything, and won for me the title of "Prince of the Oyster Beds," was that I was a good fellow ashore with my money, buying drinks like a man. I little dreamed that the time would come when the Oakland water-front, which had shocked me at first would be shocked and annoyed by the devilry of the things I did.

But always the life was tied up with drinking. The saloons are poor men's clubs. Saloons are congregating places. We engaged to meet one another in saloons. We celebrated our good fortune or wept our grief in saloons. We got acquainted in saloons.

Can I ever forget the afternoon I met "Old Scratch," Nelson's father? It was in the Last Chance. Johnny Heinhold introduced us. That Old Scratch was Nelson's father was noteworthy enough. But there was more in it than that. He was owner and master of the scow-schooner *Annie Mine*, and some day I might ship as a sailor with him. Still more, he was romance. He was a blue-eyed, yellow-haired, raw-boned Viking, big-bodied and strong-muscled despite his age. And he had sailed the seas in ships of all nations in the old savage sailing days.

I had heard many weird tales about him, and worshipped him from a distance. It took the saloon to bring us together. Even so, our acquaintance might have been no more than a hand-grip and a word—he was a laconic old fellow—had it not been for the drinking.

"Have a drink," I said, with promptitude, after the pause which I had learned good form in drinking dictates. Of course, while we drank our beer, which I had paid for, it was incumbent on him to listen to me and to talk to me. And Johnny, like a true host, made the tactful remarks that enabled us to find mutual topics of conversation. And of course, having drunk my beer, Captain Nelson must now buy beer in turn. This led to more talking, and Johnny drifted out of the conversation to wait on other customers.

The more beer Captain Nelson and I drank, the better we got acquainted. In me he found an appreciative listener, who, by virtue of book-reading, knew much about the sea-life he had lived. So he drifted back to his wild young days, and spun many a rare yarn for me, while we downed beer, treat by treat, all through a blessed summer afternoon. And it was only John Barleycorn that made possible that long afternoon with the old sea-dog.

It was Johnny Heinhold who secretly warned me across the bar that I was getting pickled and advised me to take small beers. But as long as Captain Nelson drank large beers, my pride forbade anything else than large beers. And not until the skipper ordered his first small beer did I order one for myself. Oh, when we came to a lingering fond farewell, I was drunk. But I had the satisfaction of seeing Old Scratch as drunk as I. My youthful modesty scarcely let me dare believe that the hardened old buccaneer was even more drunk.

And afterwards, from Spider, and Pat, and Clam, and Johnny Heinhold, and others, came the tips that Old Scratch liked me and had nothing but good words for the fine lad I was. Which was the more remarkable, because he was known as a savage, cantankerous old cuss who never liked anybody. (His very nickname, "Scratch," arose from a Berserker trick of his, in fighting, of tearing off his opponent's face.) And that I had won his friendship, all thanks were due to John Barleycorn.

* * *

In ways, the accidental drunks were the best. Stranger and more exciting things happened at such times. As, for instance, the Sunday when Nelson and French Frank and Captain Spink stole the stolen salmon boat from Whisky Bob and Nicky the Greek. Changes had taken place in the personnel of the oyster boats. Nelson had got into a fight with Bill Kelley on the Annie and was carrying a bullet-hole through his left hand. Also, having quarrelled with Clam and broken partnership, Nelson had sailed the *Reindeer*, his arm in a sling, with a crew of two deep-water sailors, and he had sailed so madly as to frighten them ashore. Such was the tale of his recklessness they spread, that no one on the water-front would go out with Nelson. So the *Reindeer*, crewless, lay across the estuary at the sandspit. Beside her lay the *Razzle Dazzle* with a burned mainsail and Scotty and me on board. Whisky Bob had fallen out with French Frank and gone on a raid "up river" with Nicky the Greek.

The result of this raid was a brand-new Columbia River salmon boat, stolen from an Italian fisherman. We oyster pirates were all visited by the searching Italian, and we were convinced, from what we knew of their movements, that Whisky Bob and Nicky the Greek were the guilty parties. But where was the salmon boat? Hundreds of Greek and Italian fishermen, up river and down bay, had searched every slough and tule patch for it. When the owner despairingly offered a reward of fifty dollars, our interest increased and the mystery deepened.

One Sunday morning old Captain Spink paid me a visit. The conversation was confidential. He had just been fishing in his skiff in the old Alameda ferry slip. As the tide went down, he had noticed a rope tied to a pile under water and leading downward. In vain he had tried to heave up what was fast on the other end. Farther along, to another pile, was a similar rope, leading downward and unheavable. Without doubt, it was the missing salmon boat. If we restored it to its rightful owner there was fifty dollars in it for us. But I had queer ethical notions about honour amongst thieves, and declined to have anything to do with the affair.

But French Frank had quarrelled with Whisky Bob, and Nelson was also an enemy. (Poor Whisky Bob!—without viciousness, good-natured, generous, born weak, raised poorly, with an irresistible chemical demand for alcohol, still prosecuting his vocation of bay pirate, his body was picked up, not long afterward, beside a dock where it had sunk full of gunshot wounds.) Within an hour after I had rejected Captain Spink's proposal, I saw him sail down the estuary on board the *Reindeer* with Nelson. Also, French Frank went by on his schooner.

It was not long ere they sailed back up the estuary, curiously side by side. As they headed in for the sandspit, the submerged salmon boat could be seen, gunwales awash and held up from sinking by ropes fast to the schooner and the sloop. The tide was half out, and they sailed squarely in on the sand, grounding in a row, with the salmon boat in the middle.

Immediately Hans, one of French Frank's sailors, was into a skiff and pulling rapidly for the north shore. The big demijohn in the stern-sheets told his errand. They couldn't wait a moment to celebrate the fifty dollars they had so easily earned. It is the way of the devotees of John Barleycorn. When good fortune comes, they drink. When they have no fortune, they drink to the hope of good fortune. If fortune be ill, they drink to forget it. If they meet a friend, they drink. If they quarrel with a friend and lose him, they drink. If their love-making be crowned with success, they are so happy they needs must drink. If they be jilted, they drink for the contrary reason. And if they haven't anything to do at all, why, they take a drink, secure in the knowledge that when they have taken a sufficient number of drinks the maggots will start crawling in their brains and they will have their hands full with things to do. When they are sober they want to drink; and when they have drunk they want to drink more.

Of course, as fellow comrades, Scotty and I were called in for the drinking. We helped to make a hole in that fifty dollars not yet received. The afternoon, from just an ordinary common summer Sunday afternoon, became a gorgeous, purple afternoon. We all talked and sang and ranted and bragged, and ever French Frank and Nelson sent more drinks around. We lay in full sight of the Oakland water-front, and the noise of our revels attracted friends. Skiff after skiff crossed the estuary and hauled up on the sandspit, while Hans' work was cut out for him—ever to row back and forth for more supplies of booze.

Then Whisky Bob and Nicky the Greek arrived, sober, indignant, outraged in that their fellow pirates had raised their plant. French Frank, aided by John Barleycorn, orated hypocritically about virtue and honesty, and, despite his fifty years, got Whisky Bob out on the sand and proceeded to lick him. When Nicky the Greek jumped in with a short-handled shovel to Whisky Bob's assistance, short work was made of him by Hans. And of course, when the bleeding remnants of Bob and Nicky were sent packing in their skiff, the event must needs be celebrated in further carousal.

By this time, our visitors being numerous, we were a large crowd compounded of many nationalities and diverse temperaments, all aroused by John Barleycorn, all restraints cast off. Old quarrels revived, ancient hates flared up. Fight was in the air. And whenever a longshoreman remembered something against a scow-schooner sailor, or vice versa, or an oyster pirate remembered or was remembered, a fist shot out and another fight was on. And every fight was made up in more rounds of drinks, wherein the combatants, aided and abetted by the rest of us, embraced each other and pledged undying friendship.

And, of all times, Soup Kennedy selected this time to come and retrieve an old shirt of his, left aboard the *Reindeer* from the trip he sailed with Clam. He had espoused Clam's side of the quarrel with Nelson. Also, he had been drinking in the St. Louis House, so that it was John Barleycorn who led him to the sandspit in quest of his old shirt. Few words started the fray. He locked with Nelson in the cockpit of the *Reindeer*, and in the mix-up barely escaped being brained by an iron bar wielded by irate French Frank—irate because a two-handed man had attacked a one-handed man. (If the *Reindeer* still floats, the dent of the iron bar remains in the hard-wood rail of her cockpit.)

But Nelson pulled his bandaged hand, bullet-perforated, out of its sling, and, held by us, wept and roared his Berserker belief that he could lick Soup Kennedy one-handed. And we let them loose on the sand. Once, when it looked as if Nelson were getting the worst of it, French Frank and John Barleycorn sprang unfairly into the fight. Scotty protested and reached for French Frank, who whirled upon him and fell on top of him in a pummelling clinch after a sprawl of twenty feet across the sand. In the course of separating these two, half a dozen fights started amongst the rest of us. These fights were finished, one way or the other, or we separated them with drinks, while all the time Nelson and Soup Kennedy fought on. Occasionally we returned to them and gave advice, such as, when they lay exhausted in the sand, unable to strike a blow, "Throw sand in his eyes." And they threw sand in each other's eyes, recuperated, and fought on to successive exhaustions.

And now, of all this that is squalid, and ridiculous, and bestial, try to think what it meant to me, a youth not yet sixteen, burning with the spirit of adventure, fancy-filled with tales of buccaneers and sea-rovers, sacks of cities and conflicts of armed men, and imagination-maddened by the stuff I had drunk. It was life raw and naked, wild and free—the only life of that sort which my birth in time and space permitted me to attain. And more than that. It carried a promise. It was the beginning. From the sandspit the way led out through the Golden Gate to the vastness of adventure of all the world, where battles would be fought, not for old shirts and over stolen salmon boats, but for high purposes and romantic ends.

And because I told Scotty what I thought of his letting an old man like French Frank get away with him, we, too, brawled and added to the festivity of the sandspit. And Scotty threw up his job as crew, and departed in the night with a pair of blankets belonging to me. During the night, while the oyster pirates lay stupefied in their bunks, the schooner and the *Reindeer* floated on the high water and swung about to their anchors. The salmon boat, still filled with rocks and water, rested on the bottom.

In the morning, early, I heard wild cries from the *Reindeer*, and tumbled out in the chill grey to see a spectacle that made the waterfront laugh for days. The beautiful salmon boat lay on the hard sand, squashed flat as a pancake, while on it were perched French Frank's schooner and the *Reindeer*. Unfortunately two of the *Reindeer*'s planks had been crushed in by the stout oak stem of the salmon boat. The rising tide had flowed through the hole, and just awakened Nelson by getting into his bunk with him. I lent a hand, and we pumped the *Reindeer* out and repaired the damage.

Then Nelson cooked breakfast, and while we ate we considered the situation. He was broke. So was I. The fifty dollars reward would never be paid for that pitiful mess of splinters on the sand beneath us. He had a wounded hand and no crew. I had a burned main sail and no crew.

"What d'ye say, you and me?" Nelson queried. "I'll go you," was my answer. And thus I became partners with "Young Scratch" Nelson, the wildest, maddest of them all. We borrowed the money for an outfit of grub from Johnny Heinhold, filled our water-barrels, and sailed away that day for the oyster-beds.

* * *

Nor have I ever regretted those months of mad devilry I put in with Nelson. He COULD sail, even if he did frighten every man that sailed with him. To steer to miss destruction by an inch or an instant was his joy. To do what everybody else did not dare attempt to do, was his pride. Never to reef down was his mania, and in all the time I spent with him, blow high or low, the *Reindeer* was never reefed. Nor was she ever dry. We strained her open and sailed her open and sailed her open continually. And we abandoned the Oakland water-front and went wider afield for our adventures.

The world was opening up to me. Already I knew several hundred miles of the water-ways of it, and of the towns and cities and fishing hamlets on the shores. Came the whisper to range farther. I had not found it yet. There was more behind. But even this much of the world was too wide for Nelson. He wearied for his beloved Oakland water-front, and when he elected to return to it we separated in all friendliness.

I now made the old town of Benicia, on the Carquinez Straits, my headquarters. In a cluster of fishermen's arks, moored in the tules on the water-front, dwelt a congenial crowd of drinkers and vagabonds, and I joined them. I had longer spells ashore, between fooling with salmon fishing and making raids up and down bay and rivers as a deputy fish patrolman, and I drank more and learned more about drinking. I held my own with any one, drink for drink; and often drank more than my share to show the strength of my manhood. When, on a morning, my unconscious carcass was disentangled from the nets on the drying-frames, whither I had stupidly, blindly crawled the night before; and when the water-front talked it over with many a giggle and laugh and another drink, I was proud indeed. It was an exploit.

And when I never drew a sober breath, on one stretch, for three solid weeks, I was certain I had reached the top. Surely, in that direction, one could go no farther. It was time for me to move on. For always, drunk or sober, at the back of my consciousness something whispered that this carousing and bay-adventuring was not all of life. This whisper was my good fortune. I happened to be so made that I could hear it calling, always calling, out and away over the world. It was not canniness on my part. It was curiosity, desire to know, an unrest and a seeking for things wonderful that I seemed somehow to have glimpsed or guessed. What was this life for, I demanded, if this were all? No; there was something more, away and beyond. (And, in relation to my much later development as a drinker, this whisper, this promise of the things at the back of life, must be noted, for it was destined to play a dire part in my more recent wrestlings with John Barleycorn.)

But what gave immediacy to my decision to move on was a trick John Barleycorn played me—a monstrous, incredible trick that showed abysses of intoxication hitherto undreamed. At one o'clock in the morning, after a prodigious drunk, I was tottering aboard a sloop at the end of the wharf, intending to go to sleep. The tides sweep through Carquinez Straits as in a mill-race, and the full ebb was on when I stumbled overboard. There was nobody on the wharf, nobody on the sloop. I was borne away by the current. I was not startled. I thought the misadventure delightful. I was a good swimmer, and in my inflamed condition the contact of the water with my skin soothed me like cool linen.

And then John Barleycorn played me his maniacal trick. Some maundering fancy of going out with the tide suddenly obsessed me. I had never been morbid. Thoughts of suicide had never entered my head. And now that they entered, I thought it fine, a splendid culminating, a perfect rounding off of my short but exciting career. I, who had never known girl's love, nor woman's love, nor the love of children; who had never played in the wide joy-fields of art, nor climbed the star-cool heights of philosophy, nor seen with my eyes more than a pin-point's surface of the gorgeous world; I decided that this was all, that I had seen all, lived all, been all, that was worth while, and that now was the time to cease. This was the trick of John Barleycorn, laying me by the heels of my imagination and in a drug-dream dragging me to death.

Oh, he was convincing. I had really experienced all of life, and it didn't amount to much. The swinish drunkenness in which I had lived for months (this was accompanied by the sense of degradation and the old feeling of conviction of sin) was the last and best, and I could see for myself what it was worth. There were all the broken-down old bums and loafers I had bought drinks for. That was what remained of life. Did I want to become like them? A thousand times no; and I wept tears of sweet sadness over my glorious youth going out with the tide. (And who has not seen the weeping drunk, the melancholic drunk? They are to be found in all the bar-rooms, if they can find no other listener telling their sorrows to the barkeeper, who is paid to listen.)

The water was delicious. It was a man's way to die. John Barleycorn changed the tune he played in my drink-maddened brain. Away with tears and regret. It was a hero's death, and by the hero's own hand and will. So I struck up my death-chant and was singing it lustily, when the gurgle and splash of the current-riffles in my ears reminded me of my more immediate situation.

Below the town of Benicia, where the Solano wharf projects, the Straits widen out into what bay-farers call the "Bight of Turner's Shipyard." I was in the shore-tide that swept under the Solano wharf and on into the bight. I knew of old the power of the suck which developed when the tide swung around the end of Dead Man's Island and drove straight for the wharf. I didn't want to go through those piles. It wouldn't be nice, and I might lose an hour in the bight on my way out with the tide.

I undressed in the water and struck out with a strong, single-overhand stroke, crossing the current at right-angles. Nor did I cease until, by the wharf lights, I knew I was safe to sweep by the end. Then I turned over and rested. The stroke had been a telling one, and I was a little time in recovering my breath.

I was elated, for I had succeeded in avoiding the suck. I started to raise my death-chant again—a purely extemporised farrago of a drug-crazed youth. "Don't sing—yet," whispered John Barleycorn. "The Solano runs all night. There are railroad men on the wharf. They will hear you, and come out in a boat and rescue you, and you don't want to be rescued." I certainly didn't. What? Be robbed of my hero's death? Never. And I lay on my back in the starlight, watching the familiar wharf-lights go by, red and green and white, and bidding sad sentimental farewell to them, each and all.

When I was well clear, in mid-channel, I sang again. Sometimes I swam a few strokes, but in the main I contented myself with floating and dreaming long drunken dreams. Before daylight, the chill of the water and the passage of the hours had sobered me sufficiently to make me wonder what portion of the Straits I was in, and also to wonder if the turn of the tide wouldn't catch me and take me back ere I had drifted out into San Pablo Bay.

Next I discovered that I was very weary and very cold, and quite sober, and that I didn't in the least want to be drowned. I could make out the Selby Smelter on the Contra Costa shore and the Mare Island lighthouse. I started to swim for the Solano shore, but was too weak and chilled, and made so little headway, and at the cost of such painful effort, that I gave it up and contented myself with floating, now and then giving a stroke to keep my balance in the tide-rips which were increasing their commotion on the surface of the water. And I knew fear. I was sober now, and I didn't want to die. I discovered scores of reasons for living. And the more reasons I discovered, the more liable it seemed that I was going to drown anyway.

Daylight, after I had been four hours in the water, found me in a parlous condition in the tide-rips off Mare Island light, where the swift ebbs from Vallejo Straits and Carquinez Straits were fighting with each other, and where, at that particular moment, they were fighting the flood tide setting up against them from San Pablo Bay. A stiff breeze had sprung up, and the crisp little waves were persistently lapping into my mouth, and I was beginning to swallow salt water. With my swimmer's knowledge, I knew the end was near. And then the boat came—a Greek fisherman running in for Vallejo; and again I had been saved from John Barleycorn by my constitution and physical vigour.

And, in passing, let me note that this maniacal trick John Barleycorn played me is nothing uncommon. An absolute statistic of the percentage of suicides due to John Barleycorn would be appalling. In my case, healthy, normal, young, full of the joy of life, the suggestion to kill myself was unusual; but it must be taken into account that it came on the heels of a long carouse, when my nerves and brain were fearfully poisoned, and that the dramatic, romantic side of my imagination, drink-maddened to lunacy, was delighted with the suggestion. And yet, the older, more morbid drinkers, more jaded with life and more disillusioned, who kill themselves, do so usually after a long debauch, when their nerves and brains are thoroughly poison-soaked.

* * *

So I left Benicia, where John Barleycorn had nearly got me, and ranged wider afield in pursuit of the whisper from the back of life to come and find. And wherever I ranged, the way lay along alcohol-drenched roads. Men still congregated in saloons. They were the poor-man's clubs, and they were the only clubs to which I had access. I could get acquainted in saloons. I could go into a saloon and talk with any man. In the strange towns and cities I wandered through, the only place for me to go was the saloon. I was no longer a stranger in any town the moment I had entered a saloon.

And right here let me break in with experiences no later than last year. I harnessed four horses to a light trap, took Charmian along, and drove for three months and a half over the wildest mountain parts of California and Oregon. Each morning I did my regular day's work of writing fiction. That completed, I drove on through the middle of the day and the afternoon to the next stop. But the irregularity of occurrence of stopping-places, coupled with widely varying road conditions, made it necessary to plan, the day before, each day's drive and my work. I must know when I was to start driving in order to start writing in time to finish my day's output. Thus, on occasion, when the drive was to be long, I would be up and at my writing by five in the morning. On easier driving days I might not start writing till nine o'clock.

But how to plan? As soon as I arrived in a town, and put the horses up, on the way from the stable to the hotel I dropped into the saloons. First thing, a drink—oh, I wanted the drink, but also it must not be forgotten that, because of wanting to know things, it was in this very way I had learned to want a drink. Well, the first thing, a drink. "Have something yourself," to the barkeeper. And then, as we drink, my opening query about roads and stopping-places on ahead.

"Let me see," the barkeeper will say, "there's the road across Tarwater Divide. That used to be good. I was over it three years ago. But it was blocked this spring. Say, I'll tell you what. I'll ask Jerry——" And the barkeeper turns and addresses some man sitting at a table or leaning against the bar farther along, and who may be Jerry, or Tom, or Bill. "Say, Jerry, how about the Tarwater road? You was down to Wilkins last week."

And while Bill or Jerry or Tom is beginning to unlimber his thinking and speaking apparatus, I suggest that he join us in the drink. Then discussions arise about the advisability of this road or that, what the best stopping-places may be, what running time I may expect to make, where the best trout streams are, and so forth, in which other men join, and which are punctuated with more drinks.

Two or three more saloons, and I accumulate a warm jingle and come pretty close to knowing everybody in town, all about the town, and a fair deal about the surrounding country. I know the lawyers, editors, business men, local politicians, and the visiting ranchers, hunters, and miners, so that by evening, when Charmian and I stroll down the main street and back, she is astounded by the number of my acquaintances in that totally strange town.

And thus is demonstrated a service John Barleycorn renders, a service by which he increases his power over men. And over the world, wherever I have gone, during all the years, it has been the same. It may be a cabaret in the Latin Quarter, a cafe in some obscure Italian village, a boozing ken in sailor-town, and it may be up at the club over Scotch and soda; but always it will be where John Barleycorn makes fellowship that I get immediately in touch, and meet, and know. And in the good days coming, when John Barleycorn will have been banished out of existence along with the other barbarisms, some other institution than the saloon will have to obtain, some other congregating place of men where strange men and stranger men may get in touch, and meet, and know.

But to return to my narrative. When I turned my back on Benicia, my way led through saloons. I had developed no moral theories against drinking, and I disliked as much as ever the taste of the stuff. But I had grown respectfully suspicious of John Barleycorn. I could not forget that trick he had played on me—on me who did not want to die. So I continued to drink, and to keep a sharp eye on John Barleycorn, resolved to resist all future suggestions of self-destruction.

In strange towns I made immediate acquaintances in the saloons. When I hoboed, and hadn't the price of a bed, a saloon was the only place that would receive me and give me a chair by the fire. I could go into a saloon and wash up, brush my clothes, and comb my hair. And saloons were always so damnably convenient. They were everywhere in my western country.

And here is another complaint I bring against John Barleycorn. It is these good fellows that he gets—the fellows with the fire and the go in them, who have bigness, and warmness, and the best of the human weaknesses. And John Barleycorn puts out the fire, and soddens the agility, and, when he does not more immediately kill them or make maniacs of them, he coarsens and grossens them, twists and malforms them out of the original goodness and fineness of their natures.

Always I encountered the camaraderie of drink. I might be walking down the track to the water-tank to lie in wait for a passing freight-train, when I would chance upon a bunch of "alki-stiffs." An alki-stiff is a tramp who drinks druggist's alcohol. Immediately, with greeting and salutation, I am taken into the fellowship. The alcohol, shrewdly blended with water, is handed to me, and soon I am caught up in the revelry, with maggots crawling in my brain and John Barleycorn whispering to me that life is big, and that we are all brave and fine—free spirits sprawling like careless gods upon the turf and telling the two-by-four, cut-and-dried, conventional world to go hang.

* * *

Back in Oakland from my wanderings, I returned to the water-front and renewed my comradeship with Nelson, who was now on shore all the time and living more madly than before. I, too, spent my time on shore with him, only occasionally going for cruises of several days on the bay to help out on short-handed scow-schooners.

The result was that I was no longer reinvigorated by periods of open-air abstinence and healthy toil. I drank every day, and whenever opportunity offered I drank to excess; for I still laboured under the misconception that the secret of John Barleycorn lay in drinking to bestiality and unconsciousness. I became pretty thoroughly alcohol-soaked during this period. I practically lived in saloons; became a bar-room loafer, and worse.

I had a few months still to run before I was seventeen; I scorned the thought of a steady job at anything; I felt myself a pretty tough individual in a group of pretty tough men; and I drank because these men drank and because I had to make good with them. I had never had a real boyhood, and in this, my precocious manhood, I was very hard and woefully wise. Though I had never known girl's love even, I had crawled through such depths that I was convinced absolutely that I knew the last word about love and life. And it wasn't a pretty knowledge. Without being pessimistic, I was quite satisfied that life was a rather cheap and ordinary affair.

It was during the early winter of 1892 that I resolved to go to sea. I still drank and frequented saloons—practically lived in saloons. Whisky was dangerous, in my opinion, but not wrong. Whisky was dangerous like other dangerous things in the natural world. Men died of whisky; but then, too, fishermen were capsized and drowned, hoboes fell under trains and were cut to pieces. To cope with winds and waves, railroad trains, and bar-rooms, one must use judgment. To get drunk after the manner of men was all right, but one must do it with discretion. No more quarts of whisky for me.

On the 12th of January, 1893, I was seventeen, and the 20th of January I signed before the shipping commissioner the articles of the Sophie Sutherland, a three topmast sealing schooner bound on a voyage to the coast of Japan. And of course we had to drink on it. Joe Vigy cashed my advance note, and Pete Holt treated, and I treated, and Joe Vigy treated, and other hunters treated. Well, it was the way of men, and who was I, just turned seventeen, that I should decline the way of life of these fine, chesty, man-grown men?

* * *

There was nothing to drink on the *Sophie Sutherland*, and we had fifty-one days of glorious sailing, taking the southern passage in the north-east trades to Bonin Islands. This isolated group, belonging to Japan, had been selected as the rendezvous of the Canadian and American sealing fleets. Here they filled their water-barrels and made repairs before starting on the hundred days' harrying of the seal-herd along the northern coasts of Japan to Behring Sea.

Those fifty-one days of fine sailing and intense sobriety had put me in splendid fettle. The alcohol had been worked out of my system, and from the moment the voyage began I had not known the desire for a drink. I doubt if I even thought once about a drink. Often, of course, the talk in the forecastle turned on drink, and the men told of their more exciting or humorous drunks, remembering such passages more keenly, with greater delight, than all the other passages of their adventurous lives.

In the forecastle, the oldest man, fat and fifty, was Louis. He was a broken skipper. John Barleycorn had thrown him, and he was winding up his career where he had begun it, in the forecastle. His case made quite an impression on me. John Barleycorn did other things beside kill a man. He hadn't killed Louis. He had done much worse. He had robbed him of power and place and comfort, crucified his pride, and condemned him to the hardship of the common sailor that would last as long as his healthy breath lasted, which promised to be for a long time.

We completed our run across the Pacific, lifted the volcanic peaks, jungle-clad, of the Bonin Islands, sailed in among the reefs to the land-locked harbour, and let our anchor rumble down where lay a score or more of sea-gypsies like ourselves. The scents of strange vegetation blew off the tropic land. Aborigines, in queer outrigger canoes, and Japanese, in queerer sampans, paddled about the bay and came aboard. It was my first foreign land; I had won to the other side of the world, and I would see all I had read in the books come true. I was wild to get ashore.

Victor and Axel, a Swede and a Norwegian, and I planned to keep together. (And so well did we, that for the rest of the cruise we were known as the "Three Sports.") Victor pointed out a pathway that disappeared up a wild canyon, emerged on a steep bare lava slope, and thereafter appeared and disappeared, ever climbing, among the palms and flowers. We would go over that path, he said, and we agreed, and we would see beautiful scenery, and strange native villages, and find, Heaven alone knew, what adventure at the end. And Axel was keen to go fishing. The three of us agreed to that, too. We would get a sampan, and a couple of Japanese fishermen who knew the fishing grounds, and we would have great sport. As for me, I was keen for anything.

And then, our plans made, we rowed ashore over the banks of living coral and pulled our boat up the white beach of coral sand. We walked across the fringe of beach under the cocoanut-palms and into the little town, and found several hundred riotous seamen from all the world, drinking prodigiously, singing prodigiously, dancing prodigiously—and all on the main street to the scandal of a helpless handful of Japanese police.

Victor and Axel said that we'd have a drink before we started on our long walk. Could I decline to drink with these two chesty shipmates? Drinking together, glass in hand, put the seal on comradeship. It was the way of life. Our teetotaler owner-captain was laughed at, and sneered at, by all of us because of his teetotalism. I didn't in the least want a drink, but I did want to be a good fellow and a good comrade. Nor did Louis' case deter me, as I poured the biting, scorching stuff down my throat. John Barleycorn had thrown Louis to a nasty fall, but I was young. My blood ran full and red; I had a constitution of iron; and—well, youth ever grins scornfully at the wreckage of age.

Queer, fierce, alcoholic stuff it was that we drank. There was no telling where or how it had been manufactured—some native concoction most likely. But it was hot as fire, pale as water, and quick as death with its kick. It had been filled into empty "square-face" bottles which had once contained Holland gin, and which still bore the fitting legend "Anchor Brand." It certainly anchored us. We never got out of the town. We never went fishing in the sampan. And though we were there ten days, we never trod that wild path along the lava cliffs and among the flowers.

We met old acquaintances from other schooners, fellows we had met in the saloons of San Francisco before we sailed. And each meeting meant a drink; and there was much to talk about; and more drinks; and songs to be sung; and pranks and antics to be performed, until the maggots of imagination began to crawl, and it all seemed great and wonderful to me, these lusty hard-bitten sea-rovers, of whom I made one, gathered in wassail on a coral strand. Old lines about knights at table in the great banquet halls, and of those above the salt and below the salt, and of Vikings feasting fresh from sea and ripe for battle, came to me; and I knew that the old times were not dead and that we belonged to that selfsame ancient breed.

By mid-afternoon Victor went mad with drink, and wanted to fight everybody and everything. I have since seen lunatics in the violent wards of asylums that seemed to behave in no wise different from Victor's way, save that perhaps he was more violent. Axel and I interfered as peacemakers, were roughed and jostled in the mix-ups, and finally, with infinite precaution and intoxicated cunning, succeeded in inveigling our chum down to the boat and in rowing him aboard our schooner.

But no sooner did Victor's feet touch the deck than he began to clean up the ship. He had the strength of several men, and he ran amuck with it. I remember especially one man whom he got into the chain-boxes but failed to damage through inability to hit him. The man dodged and ducked, and Victor broke all the knuckles of both his fists against the huge links of the anchor chain. By the time we dragged him out of that, his madness had shifted to the belief that he was a great swimmer, and the next moment he was overboard and demonstrating his ability by floundering like a sick porpoise and swallowing much salt water.

We rescued him, and by the time we got him below, undressed, and into his bunk, we were wrecks ourselves. But Axel and I wanted to see more of shore, and away we went, leaving Victor snoring. It was curious, the judgment passed on Victor by his shipmates, drinkers themselves. They shook their heads disapprovingly and muttered: "A man like that oughtn't to drink." Now Victor was the smartest sailor and best-tempered shipmate in the forecastle. He was an all-round splendid type of seaman; his mates recognised his worth, and respected him and liked him. Yet John Barleycorn metamorphosed him into a violent lunatic. And that was the very point these drinkers made. They knew that drink—and drink with a sailor is always excessive—made them mad, but only mildly mad. Violent madness was objectionable because it spoiled the fun of others and often culminated in tragedy. From their standpoint, mild madness was all right. But from the standpoint of the whole human race, is not all madness objectionable? And is there a greater maker of madness of all sorts than John Barleycorn?

But to return. Ashore, snugly ensconced in a Japanese house of entertainment, Axel and I compared bruises, and over a comfortable drink talked of the afternoon's happenings. We liked the quietness of that drink and took another. A shipmate dropped in, several shipmates dropped in, and we had more quiet drinks. Finally, just as we had engaged a Japanese orchestra, and as the first strains of the samisens and taikos were rising, through the paper-walls came a wild howl from the street. We recognised it. Still howling, disdaining doorways, with blood-shot eyes and wildly waving muscular arms, Victor burst upon us through the fragile walls. The old amuck rage was on him, and he wanted blood, anybody's blood. The orchestra fled; so did we. We went through doorways, and we went through paper-walls—anything to get away.

And after the place was half wrecked, and we had agreed to pay the damage, leaving Victor partly subdued and showing symptoms of lapsing into a comatose state, Axel and I wandered away in quest of a quieter drinking-place. The main street was a madness. Hundreds of sailors rollicked up and down. Because the chief of police with his small force was helpless, the governor of the colony had issued orders to the captains to have all their men on board by sunset.

What! To be treated in such fashion! As the news spread among the schooners, they were emptied. Everybody came ashore. Men who had had no intention of coming ashore climbed into the boats. The unfortunate governor's ukase had precipitated a general debauch for all hands. It was hours after sunset, and the men wanted to see anybody try to put them on board. They went around inviting the authorities to try to put them on board. In front of the governor's house they were gathered thickest, bawling sea-songs, circulating square faces, and dancing uproarious Virginia reels and old-country dances. The police, including the reserves, stood in little forlorn groups, waiting for the command the governor was too wise to issue. And I thought this saturnalia was great. It was like the old days of the Spanish Main come back. It was license; it was adventure. And I was part of it, a chesty sea-rover along with all these other chesty sea-rovers among the paper houses of Japan.

The governor never issued the order to clear the streets, and Axel and I wandered on from drink to drink. After a time, in some of the antics, getting hazy myself, I lost him. I drifted along, making new acquaintances, downing more drinks, getting hazier and hazier. I remember, somewhere, sitting in a circle with Japanese fishermen, Kanaka boat-steerers from our own vessels, and a young Danish sailor fresh from cowboying in the Argentine and with a penchant for native customs and ceremonials. And with due and proper and most intricate Japanese ceremonial we of the circle drank saki, pale, mild, and lukewarm, from tiny porcelain bowls.

And, later, I remember the runaway apprentices—boys of eighteen and twenty, of middle class English families, who had jumped their ships and apprenticeships in various ports of the world and drifted into the forecastles of the sealing schooners. They were healthy, smooth-skinned, clear-eyed, and they were young—youths like me, learning the way of their feet in the world of men. And they WERE men. No mild saki for them, but square faces illicitly refilled with corrosive fire that flamed through their veins and burst into conflagrations in their heads. I remember a melting song they sang, the refrain of which was:

'Tis but a little golden ring,
I give it to thee with pride,
Wear it for your mother's sake
When you are on the tide.

They wept over it as they sang it, the graceless young scamps who had all broken their mothers' prides, and I sang with them, and wept with them, and luxuriated in the pathos and the tragedy of it, and struggled to make glimmering inebriated generalisations on life and romance. And one last picture I have, standing out very clear and bright in the midst of vagueness before and blackness afterward. We—the apprentices and I—are swaying and clinging to one another under the stars. We are singing a rollicking sea song, all save one who sits on the ground and weeps; and we are marking the rhythm with waving square faces. From up and down the street come far choruses of sea-voices similarly singing, and life is great, and beautiful and romantic, and magnificently mad.

And next, after the blackness, I open my eyes in the early dawn to see a Japanese woman, solicitously anxious, bending over me. She is the port pilot's wife and I am lying in her doorway. I am chilled and shivering, sick with the after-sickness of debauch. And I feel lightly clad. Those rascals of runaway apprentices! They have acquired the habit of running away. They have run away with my possessions. My watch is gone. My few dollars are gone. My coat is gone. So is my belt. And yes, my shoes.

And the foregoing is a sample of the ten days I spent in the Bonin Islands. Victor got over his lunacy, rejoined Axel and me, and after that we caroused somewhat more discreetly. And we never climbed that lava path among the flowers. The town and the square faces were all we saw.

* * *

North we raced from the Bonin Islands to pick up the seal-herd, and north we hunted it for a hundred days into frosty, mitten weather and into and through vast fogs which hid the sun from us for a week at a time. It was wild and heavy work, without a drink or thought of drink. Then we sailed south to Yokohama, with a big catch of skins in our salt and a heavy pay-day coming.

I was eager to be ashore and see Japan, but the first day was devoted to ship's work, and not until evening did we sailors land. And here, by the very system of things, by the way life was organised and men transacted affairs, John Barleycorn reached out and tucked my arm in his. The captain had given money for us to the hunters, and the hunters were waiting in a certain Japanese public house for us to come and get it. We rode to the place in rickshaws. Our own crowd had taken possession of it. Drink was flowing. Everybody had money, and everybody was treating. After the hundred days of hard toil and absolute abstinence, in the pink of physical condition, bulging with health, over-spilling with spirits that had long been pent by discipline and circumstance, of course we would have a drink or two. And after that we would see the town.

It was the old story. There were so many drinks to be drunk, and as the warm magic poured through our veins and mellowed our voices and affections we knew it was no time to make invidious distinctions—to drink with this shipmate and to decline to drink with that shipmate. We were all shipmates who had been through stress and storm together, who had pulled and hauled on the same sheets and tackles, relieved one another's wheels, laid out side by side on the same jib-boom when she was plunging into it and looked to see who was missing when she cleared and lifted. So we drank with all, and all treated, and our voices rose, and we remembered a myriad kindly acts of comradeship, and forgot our fights and wordy squabbles, and knew one another for the best fellows in the world.

Well, the night was young when we arrived in that public house, and for all of that first night that public house was what I saw of Japan—a drinking-place which was very like a drinking-place at home or anywhere else over the world.

We lay in Yokohama harbour for two weeks, and about all we saw of Japan was its drinking-places where sailors congregated. Occasionally, some one of us varied the monotony with a more exciting drunk. In such fashion I managed a real exploit by swimming off to the schooner one dark midnight and going soundly to sleep while the water-police searched the harbour for my body and brought my clothes out for identification.

We hove up anchor to a jolly chanty, and sailed out of Yokohama harbour for San Francisco. We took the northern passage, and with the stout west wind at our back made the run across the Pacific in thirty-seven days of brave sailing. We still had a big pay-day coming to us, and for thirty-seven days, without a drink to addle our mental processes, we incessantly planned the spending of our money.

As we sailed up the San Francisco water-front, the moment the port doctors passed us, the boarding-house runners were alongside in whitehall boats. They swarmed on board, each drumming for his own boarding-house, and each with a bottle of free whisky inside his shirt. But we waved them grandly and blasphemously away. We wanted none of their boarding-houses and none of their whisky. We were sober, thrifty sailormen, with better use for our money.

Came the paying off before the shipping commissioner. We emerged upon the sidewalk, each with a pocketful of money. About us, like buzzards, clustered the sharks and harpies. And we looked at each other. We had been seven months together, and our paths were separating. One last farewell rite of comradeship remained. (Oh, it was the way, the custom.) "Come on, boys," said our sailing master. There stood the inevitable adjacent saloon. There were a dozen saloons all around. And when we had followed the sailing master into the one of his choice, the sharks were thick on the sidewalk outside. Some of them even ventured inside, but we would have nothing to do with them.

There we stood at the long bar—the sailing master, the mate, the six hunters, the six boat-steerers, and the five boat-pullers. There were only five of the last, for one of our number had been dropped overboard, with a sack of coal at his feet, between two snow squalls in a driving gale off Cape Jerimo. There were nineteen of us and it was to be our last drink together. With seven months of men's work in the world, blow high, blow low, behind us, we were looking on each other for the last time. We knew it, for sailors' ways go wide. And the nineteen of us drank the sailing master's treat. Then the mate looked at us with eloquent eyes and called another round. We liked the mate just as well as the sailing master, and we liked them both. Could we drink with one, and not the other?

And Pete Holt, my own hunter (lost next year in the Mary Thomas, with all hands), called a round. The time passed, the drinks continued to come on the bar, our voices rose, and the maggots began to crawl. There were six hunters, and each insisted, in the sacred name of comradeship, that all hands drink with him just once. There were six boat-steerers and five boat-pullers and the same logic held with them. There was money in all our pockets, and our money was as good as any man's, and our hearts were as free and generous.

Nineteen rounds of drinks. What more would John Barleycorn ask in order to have his will with men? They were ripe to forget their dearly cherished plans. They rolled out of the saloon and into the arms of the sharks and harpies. They didn't last long. From two days to a week saw the end of their money and saw them being carted by the boarding-house masters on board outward-bound ships. Victor was a fine body of a man, and through a lucky friendship managed to get into the life-saving service. He never saw the dancing-school nor placed his advertisement for a room in a working-class family. Nor did Long John win to navigation school. By the end of the week he was a transient lumper on a river steamboat. Red John and Axel did not send their pay-days home to the old country. Instead, and along with the rest, they were scattered on board sailing ships bound for the four quarters of the globe, where they had been placed by the boarding-house masters, and where they were working out advance money which they had neither seen nor spent.

What saved me was that I had a home and people to go to. I crossed the bay to Oakland, and, among other things, took a look at the death-road. Nelson was gone—shot to death while drunk and resisting the officers. His partner in that affair was lying in prison. Whisky Bob was gone. Old Cole, Old Smoudge, and Bob Smith were gone. Another Smith, he of the belted guns and the *Annie*, was drowned. French Frank, they said, was lurking up river, afraid to come down because of something he had done. Others were wearing the stripes in San Quentin or Folsom. Big Alec, the King of the Greeks, whom I had known well in the old Benicia days, and with whom I had drunk whole nights through, had killed two men and fled to foreign parts. Fitzsimmons, with whom I had sailed on the Fish Patrol, had been stabbed in the lung through the back and had died a lingering death complicated with tuberculosis. And so it went, a very lively and well-patronised road, and, from what I knew of all of them, John Barleycorn was responsible, with the sole exception of Smith of the *Annie*.

* * *

My infatuation for the Oakland water-front was quite dead. I didn't like the looks of it, nor the life. I didn't care for the drinking, nor the vagrancy of it, and I wandered back to the Oakland Free Library and read the books with greater understanding. Then, too, my mother said I had sown my wild oats and it was time I settled down to a regular job. Also, the family needed the money. So I got a job at the jute mills—a ten-hour day at ten cents an hour. Despite my increase in strength and general efficiency, I was receiving no more than when I worked in the cannery several years before. But, then, there was a promise of a rise to a dollar and a quarter a day after a few months. And here, so far as John Barleycorn is concerned, began a period of innocence. I did not know what it was to take a drink from month end to month end. Not yet eighteen years old, healthy and with labour-hardened but unhurt muscles, like any young animal I needed diversion, excitement, something beyond the books and the mechanical toil.

I strayed into Young Men's Christian Associations. The life there was healthful and athletic, but too juvenile. For me it was too late. I was not boy, nor youth, despite my paucity of years. I had bucked big with men. I knew mysterious and violent things. I was from the other side of life so far as concerned the young men I encountered in the

Y.M.C.A. I spoke another language, possessed a sadder and more terrible wisdom. (When I come to think it over, I realise now that I have never had a boyhood.) At any rate, the Y.M.C.A. young men were too juvenile for me, too unsophisticated. This I would not have minded, could they have met me and helped me mentally. But I had got more out of the books than they. Their meagre physical experiences, plus their meagre intellectual experiences, made a negative sum so vast that it overbalanced their wholesome morality and healthful sports.

In short, I couldn't play with the pupils of a lower grade. All the clean splendid young life that was theirs was denied me—thanks to my earlier tutelage under John Barleycorn. I knew too much too young. And yet, in the good time coming when alcohol is eliminated from the needs and the institutions of men, it will be the Y.M.C.A., and similar unthinkably better and wiser and more virile congregating-places, that will receive the men who now go to saloons to find themselves and one another. In the meantime, we live to-day, here and now, and we discuss to-day, here and now.

I was working ten hours a day in the jute mills. It was hum-drum machine toil. I wanted life. I wanted to realise myself in other ways than at a machine for ten cents an hour. And yet I had had my fill of saloons. I wanted something new. I was growing up. I was developing unguessed and troubling potencies and proclivities. And at this very stage, fortunately, I met Louis Shattuck and we became chums.

Shattuck, without one vicious trait, was a real innocently devilish young fellow, who was quite convinced that he was a sophisticated town boy. And I wasn't a town boy at all. Louis was handsome, and graceful, and filled with love for the girls. With him it was an exciting and all-absorbing pursuit. I didn't know anything about girls. I had been too busy being a man. This was an entirely new phase of existence which had escaped me. And when I saw Louis say good-bye to me, raise his hat to a girl of his acquaintance, and walk on with her side by side down the sidewalk, I was made excited and envious. I, too, wanted to play this game.

"Well, there's only one thing to do," said Louis, "and that is, you must get a girl."

Which is more difficult than it sounds. Let me show you, at the expense of a slight going aside. Louis did not know girls in their home life. He had the entree to no girl's home. And of course, I, a stranger in this new world, was similarly circumstanced. But, further, Louis and I were unable to go to dancing-schools, or to public dances, which were very good places for getting acquainted. We didn't have the money. He was a blacksmith's apprentice, and was earning but slightly more than I. We both lived at home and paid our way. When we had done this, and bought our cigarettes, and the inevitable clothes and shoes, there remained to each of us, for personal spending, a sum that varied between seventy cents and a dollar for the week. We whacked this up, shared it, and sometimes loaned all of what was left of it when one of us needed it for some more gorgeous girl-adventure, such as car-fare out to Blair's Park and back—twenty cents, bang, just like that; and ice-cream for two—thirty cents; or tamales in a tamale-parlour, which came cheaper and which for two cost only twenty cents.

I did not mind this money meagreness. The disdain I had learned for money from the oyster pirates had never left me. I didn't care over-weeningly for it for personal gratification; and in my philosophy I completed the circle, finding myself as equable with the lack of a ten-cent piece as I was with the squandering of scores of dollars in calling all men and hangers-on up to the bar to drink with me.

But how to get a girl? There was no girl's home to which Louis could take me and where I might be introduced to girls. I knew none. And Louis' several girls he wanted for himself; and anyway, in the very human nature of boys' and girls' ways, he couldn't turn any of them over to me. He did persuade them to bring girl-friends for me; but I found them weak sisters, pale and ineffectual alongside the choice specimens he had.

"You'll have to do like I did," he said finally. "I got these by getting them. You'll have to get one the same way."

And he initiated me. It must be remembered that Louis and I were hard situated. We really had to struggle to pay our board and maintain a decent appearance. We met each other in the evening, after the day's work, on the street corner, or in a little candy store on a side street, our sole frequenting-place. Here we bought our cigarettes, and, occasionally, a nickel's worth of "red-hots." (Oh, yes; Louis and I unblushingly ate candy—all we could get. Neither of us drank. Neither of us ever went into a saloon.)

But the girl. In quite primitive fashion, as Louis advised me, I was to select her and make myself acquainted with her. We strolled the streets in the early evenings. The girls, like us, strolled in pairs. And strolling girls will look at strolling boys who look. (And to this day, in any town, city, or village, in which I, in my middle age, find myself, I look on with the eye trained of old experience, and watch the sweet innocent game played by the strolling boys and girls who just must stroll when the spring and summer evenings call.)

The trouble was that in this Arcadian phase of my history, I, who had come through, case-hardened, from the other side of life, was timid and bashful. Again and again Louis nerved me up. But I didn't know girls. They were strange and wonderful to me after my precocious man's life. I failed of the bold front and the necessary forwardness when the crucial moment came.

Then Louis would show me how—a certain, eloquent glance of eye, a smile, a daring, a lifted hat, a spoken word, hesitancies, giggles, coy nervousnesses—and, behold, Louis acquainted and nodding me up to be introduced. But when we paired off to stroll along boy and girl together, I noted that Louis had invariably picked the good-looker and left to me the little lame sister.

I improved, of course, after experiences too numerous to enter upon, so that there were diverse girls to whom I could lift my hat and who would walk beside me in the early evenings. But girl's love did not immediately come to me. I was excited, interested, and I pursued the quest. And the thought of drink never entered my mind. Some of Louis' and my adventures have since given me serious pause when casting sociological generalisations. But it was all good and innocently youthful, and I learned one generalisation, biological rather than sociological, namely, that the "Colonel's lady and Judy O'Grady are sisters under their skins."

And before long I learned girl's love, all the dear fond deliciousness of it, all the glory and the wonder. I shall call her Haydee. She was between fifteen and sixteen. Her little skirt reached her shoe-tops. We sat side by side in a Salvation Army meeting. She was not a convert, nor was her aunt who sat on the other side of her, and who, visiting from the country where at that time the Salvation Army was not, had dropped in to the meeting for half an hour out of curiosity. And Louis sat beside me and observed—I do believe he did no more than observe, because Haydee was not his style of girl.

We did not speak, but in that great half-hour we glanced shyly at each other, and shyly avoided or as shyly returned and met each other's glances more than several times. She had a slender oval face. Her brown eyes were beautiful. Her nose was a dream, as was her sweet-lipped, petulant-hinting mouth. She wore a tam-o'-shanter, and I thought her brown hair the prettiest shade of brown I had ever seen. And from that single experience of half an hour I have ever since been convinced of the reality of love at first sight.

All too soon the aunt and Haydee departed. (This is permissible at any stage of a Salvation Army meeting.) I was no longer interested in the meeting, and, after an appropriate interval of a couple of minutes or less, started to leave with Louis. As we passed out, at the back of the hall a woman recognised me with her eyes, arose, and followed me. I shall not describe her. She was of my own kind and friendship of the old time on the water-front. When Nelson was shot, he had died in her arms, and she knew me as his one comrade. And she must tell me how Nelson had died, and I did want to know; so I went with her across the width of life from dawning boy's love for a brown-haired girl in a tam-o'-shanter back to the old sad savagery I had known.

And when I had heard the tale, I hurried away to find Louis, fearing that I had lost my first love with the first glimpse of her. But Louis was dependable. Her name was—Haydee. He knew where she lived. Each day she passed the blacksmith's shop where he worked, going to or from the Lafayette School. Further, he had seen her on occasion with Ruth, another schoolgirl, and, still further, Nita, who sold us red-hots at the candy store, was a friend of Ruth. The thing to do was to go around to the candy store and see if we could get Nita to give a note to Ruth to give to Haydee. If this could be arranged, all I had to do was write the note.

And it so happened. And in stolen half-hours of meeting I came to know all the sweet madness of boy's love and girl's love. So far as it goes it is not the biggest love in the world, but I do dare to assert that it is the sweetest. Oh, as I look back on it! Never did girl have more innocent boy-lover than I who had been so wicked-wise and violent beyond my years. I didn't know the first thing about girls. I, who had been hailed Prince of the Oyster Pirates, who could go anywhere in the world as a man amongst men; who could sail boats, lay aloft in black and storm, or go into the toughest hang-outs in sailor town and play my part in any rough-house that started or call all hands to the bar—I didn't know the first thing I might say or do with this slender little chit of a girl-woman whose scant skirt just reached her shoe-tops and who was as abysmally ignorant of life as I was, or thought I was, profoundly wise.

I remember we sat on a bench in the starlight. There was fully a foot of space between us. We slightly faced each other, our near elbows on the back of the bench; and once or twice our elbows just touched. And all the time, deliriously happy, talking in the gentlest and most delicate terms that might not offend her sensitive ears, I was cudgelling my brains in an effort to divine what I was expected to do. What did girls expect of boys, sitting on a bench and tentatively striving to find out what love was? What did she expect me to do? Was I expected to kiss her? Did she expect me to try? And if she did expect me, and I didn't what would she think of me?

Ah, she was wiser than I—I know it now—the little innocent girl-woman in her shoe-top skirt. She had known boys all her life. She encouraged me in the ways a girl may. Her gloves were off and in one hand, and I remember, lightly and daringly, in mock reproof for something I had said, how she tapped my lips with a tiny flirt of those gloves. I was like to swoon with delight. It was the most wonderful thing that had ever happened to me. And I remember yet the faint scent that clung to those gloves and that I breathed in the moment they touched my lips.

Then came the agony of apprehension and doubt. Should I imprison in my hand that little hand with the dangling, scented gloves which had just tapped my lips? Should I dare to kiss her there and then, or slip my arm around her waist? Or dared I even sit closer?

Well, I didn't dare. I did nothing. I merely continued to sit there and love with all my soul. And when we parted that evening I had not kissed her. I do remember the first time I kissed her, on another evening, at parting—a mighty moment, when I took all my heart of courage and dared. We never succeeded in managing more than a dozen stolen meetings, and we kissed perhaps a dozen times—as boys and girls kiss, briefly and innocently, and wonderingly. We never went anywhere—not even to a matinee. We once shared together five cents worth of red-hots. But I have always fondly believed that she loved me. I know I loved her; and I dreamed day-dreams of her for a year and more, and the memory of her is very dear.

* * *

The jute mills failed of its agreement to increase my pay to a dollar and a quarter a day, and I, a free-born American boy whose direct ancestors had fought in all the wars from the old pre-Revolutionary Indian wars down, exercised my sovereign right of free contract by quitting the job.

I was still resolved to settle down, and I looked about me. One thing was clear. Unskilled labour didn't pay. I must learn a trade, and I decided on electricity. The need for electricians was constantly growing. But how to become an electrician? I hadn't the money to go to a technical school or university; besides, I didn't think much of schools. I was a practical man in a practical world. Also, I still believed in the old myths which were the heritage of the American boy when I was a boy.

A canal boy could become a President. Any boy who took employment with any firm could, by thrift, energy, and sobriety, learn the business and rise from position to position until he was taken in as a junior partner. After that the senior partnership was only a matter of time. Very often—so ran the myth—the boy, by reason of his steadiness and application, married his employer's daughter. By this time I had been encouraged to such faith in myself in the matter of girls that I was quite certain I would marry my employer's daughter. There wasn't a doubt of it. All the little boys in the myths did it as soon as they were old enough.

So I bade farewell for ever to the adventure-path, and went out to the power plant of one of our Oakland street railways. I saw the superintendent himself, in a private office so fine that it almost stunned me. But I talked straight up. I told him I wanted to become a practical electrician, that I was unafraid of work, that I was used to hard work, and that all he had to do was look at me to see I was fit and strong. I told him that I wanted to begin right at the bottom and work up, that I wanted to devote my life to this one occupation and this one employment.

The superintendent beamed as he listened. He told me that I was the right stuff for success, and that he believed in encouraging American youth that wanted to rise. Why, employers were always on the lookout for young fellows like me, and alas, they found them all too rarely. My ambition was fine and worthy, and he would see to it that I got my chance. (And as I listened with swelling heart, I wondered if it was his daughter I was to marry.)

"Before you can go out on the road and learn the more complicated and higher details of the profession," he said, "you will, of course, have to work in the car-house with the men who install and repair the motors. (By this time I was sure that it was his daughter, and I was wondering how much stock he might own in the company.)

"But," he said, "as you yourself so plainly see, you couldn't expect to begin as a helper to the car-house electricians. That will come when you have worked up to it. You will really begin at the bottom. In the car-house your first employment will be sweeping up, washing the windows, keeping things clean. And after you have shown yourself satisfactory at that, then you may become a helper to the car-house electricians."

I didn't see how sweeping and scrubbing a building was any preparation for the trade of electrician; but I did know that in the books all the boys started with the most menial tasks and by making good ultimately won to the ownership of the whole concern.

"When shall I come to work?" I asked, eager to launch on this dazzling career.

"But," said the superintendent, "as you and I have already agreed, you must begin at the bottom. Not immediately can you in any capacity enter the car-house. Before that you must pass through the engine-room as an oiler."

My heart went down slightly and for the moment as I saw the road lengthen between his daughter and me; then it rose again. I would be a better electrician with knowledge of steam engines. As an oiler in the great engine-room I was confident that few things concerning steam would escape me. Heavens! My career shone more dazzling than ever.

"When shall I come to work?" I asked gratefully.

"But," said the superintendent, "you could not expect to enter immediately into the engine-room. There must be preparation for that. And through the fire-room, of course. Come, you see the matter clearly, I know. And you will see that even the mere handling of coal is a scientific matter and not to be sneered at. Do you know that we weigh every pound of coal we burn? Thus, we learn the value of the coal we buy; we know to a tee the last penny of cost of every item of production, and we learn which firemen are the most wasteful, which firemen, out of stupidity or carelessness, get the least out of the coal they fire." The superintendent beamed again. "You see how very important the little matter of coal is, and by as much as you learn of this little matter you will become that much better a workman—more valuable to us, more valuable to yourself. Now, are you prepared to begin?"

"Any time," I said valiantly. "The sooner the better."

"Very well," he answered. "You will come to-morrow morning at seven o'clock."

I was taken out and shown my duties. Also, I was told the terms of my employment—a ten-hour day, every day in the month including Sundays and holidays, with one day off each month, with a salary of thirty dollars a month. It wasn't exciting. Years before, at the cannery, I had earned a dollar a day for a ten-hour day. I consoled myself with the thought that the reason my earning capacity had not increased with my years and strength was because I had remained an unskilled labourer. But it was different now. I was beginning to work for skill, for a trade, for career and fortune, and the superintendent's daughter.

I was beginning in the right way—right at the beginning. That was the thing. I was passing coal to the firemen, who shovelled it into the furnaces, where its energy was transformed into steam, which, in the engine-room, was transformed into the electricity with which the electricians worked. This passing coal was surely the very beginning-unless the superintendent should take it into his head to send me to work in the mines from which the coal came in order to get a completer understanding of the genesis of electricity for street railways.

Work! I, who had worked with men, found that I didn't know the first thing about real work. A ten-hour day! I had to pass coal for the day and night shifts, and, despite working through the noon-hour, I never finished my task before eight at night. I was working a twelve-to thirteen-hour day, and I wasn't being paid overtime as in the cannery.

I might as well give the secret away right here. I was doing the work of two men. Before me, one mature able-bodied labourer had done the day shift and another equally mature able-bodied labourer had done the night-shift. They had received forty dollars a month each. The superintendent, bent on an economical administration, had persuaded me to do the work of both men for thirty dollars a month. I thought he was making an electrician of me. In truth and fact, he was saving fifty dollars a month operating expenses to the company.

But I didn't know I was displacing two men. Nobody told me. On the contrary, the superintendent warned everybody not to tell me. How valiantly I went at it that first day. I worked at top speed, filling the iron wheelbarrow with coal, running it on the scales and weighing the load, then trundling it into the fire-room and dumping it on the plates before the fires.

Work! I did more than the two men whom I had displaced. They had merely wheeled in the coal and dumped it on the plates. But while I did this for the day coal, the night coal I had to pile against the wall of the fire-room. Now the fire-room was small. It had been planned for a night coal-passer. So I had to pile the night coal higher and higher, buttressing up the heap with stout planks. Toward the top of the heap I had to handle the coal a second time, tossing it up with a shovel.

I dripped with sweat, but I never ceased from my stride, though I could feel exhaustion coming on. By ten o'clock in the morning, so much of my body's energy had I consumed, I felt hungry and snatched a thick double-slice of bread and butter from my dinner pail. This I devoured, standing, grimed with coal-dust, my knees trembling under me. By eleven o'clock, in this fashion I had consumed my whole lunch. But what of it? I realised that it would enable me to continue working through the noon hour. And I worked all the afternoon. Darkness came on, and I worked under the electric lights. The day fireman went off and the night fireman came on. I plugged away.

At half-past eight, famished, tottering, I washed up, changed my clothes, and dragged my weary body to the car. It was three miles to where I lived, and I had received a pass with the stipulation that I could sit down as long as there were no paying passengers in need of a seat. As I sank into a corner outside seat I prayed that no passenger might require my seat. But the car filled up, and, half-way in, a woman came on board, and there was no seat for her. I started to get up, and to my astonishment found that I could not. With the chill wind blowing on me, my spent body had stiffened into the seat. It took me the rest of the run in to unkink my complaining joints and muscles and get into a standing position on the lower step. And when the car stopped at my corner I nearly fell to the ground when I stepped off.

I hobbled two blocks to the house and limped into the kitchen. While my mother started to cook, I plunged into bread and butter; but before my appetite was appeased, or the steak fried, I was sound asleep. In vain my mother strove to shake me awake enough to eat the meat. Failing in this, with the assistance of my father she managed to get me to my room, where I collapsed dead asleep on the bed. They undressed me and covered me up. In the morning came the agony of being awakened. I was terribly sore, and, worst of all, my wrists were swelling. But I made up for my lost supper, eating an enormous breakfast, and when I hobbled to catch my car I carried a lunch twice as big as the one the day before.

Work! Let any youth just turned eighteen try to out-shovel two man-grown coal-shovellers. Work! Long before midday I had eaten the last scrap of my huge lunch. But I was resolved to show them what a husky young fellow determined to rise could do. The worst of it was that my wrists were swelling and going back on me. There are few who do not know the pain of walking on a sprained ankle. Then imagine the pain of shovelling coal and trundling a loaded wheelbarrow with two sprained wrists.

Work! More than once I sank down on the coal where no one could see me, and cried with rage, and mortification, and exhaustion, and despair. That second day was my hardest, and all that enabled me to survive it and get in the last of the night coal at the end of thirteen hours was the day fireman, who bound both my wrists with broad leather straps. So tightly were they buckled that they were like slightly flexible plaster casts. They took the stresses and pressures which hitherto had been borne by my wrists, and they were so tight that there was no room for the inflammation to rise in the sprains.

And in this fashion I continued to learn to be an electrician. Night after night I limped home, fell asleep before I could eat my supper, and was helped into bed and undressed. Morning after morning, always with huger lunches in my dinner pail, I limped out of the house on my way to work.

I no longer read my library books. I made no dates with the girls. I was a proper work beast. I worked, and ate, and slept, while my mind slept all the time. The whole thing was a nightmare. I worked every day, including Sunday, and I looked far ahead to my one day off at the end of a month, resolved to lie abed all that day and just sleep and rest up.

The strangest part of this experience was that I never took a drink nor thought of taking a drink. Yet I knew that men under hard pressure almost invariably drank. I had seen them do it, and in the past had often done it myself. But so sheerly non-alcoholic was I that it never entered my mind that a drink might be good for me. I instance this to show how entirely lacking from my make-up was any predisposition toward alcohol. And the point of this instance is that later on, after more years had passed, contact with John Barleycorn at last did induce in me the alcoholic desire.

I had often noticed the day fireman staring at me in a curious way. At last, one day, he spoke. He began by swearing me to secrecy. He had been warned by the superintendent not to tell me, and in telling me he was risking his job. He told me of the day coal-passer and the night coal-passer, and of the wages they had received. I was doing for thirty dollars a month what they had received eighty dollars for doing. He would have told me sooner, the fireman said, had he not been so certain that I would break down under the work and quit. As it was, I was killing myself, and all to no good purpose. I was merely cheapening the price of labour, he argued, and keeping two men out of a job.

Being an American boy, and a proud American boy, I did not immediately quit. This was foolish of me, I know; but I resolved to continue the work long enough to prove to the superintendent that I could do it without breaking down. Then I would quit, and he would realise what a fine young fellow he had lost.

All of which I faithfully and foolishly did. I worked on until the time came when I got in the last of the night coal by six o'clock. Then I quit the job of learning electricity by doing more than two men's work for a boy's wages, went home, and proceeded to sleep the clock around.

Fortunately, I had not stayed by the job long enough to injure myself—though I was compelled to wear straps on my wrists for a year afterward. But the effect of this work orgy in which I had indulged was to sicken me with work. I just wouldn't work. The thought of work was repulsive. I didn't care if I never settled down. Learning a trade could go hang. It was a whole lot better to royster and frolic over the world in the way I had previously done. So I headed out on the adventure-path again, starting to tramp East by beating my way on the railroads.

* * *

But behold! As soon as I went out on the adventure-path I met John Barleycorn again. I moved through a world of strangers, and the act of drinking together made one acquainted with men and opened the way to adventures. It might be in a saloon with jingled townsmen, or with a genial railroad man well lighted up and armed with pocket flasks, or with a bunch of alki stiffs in a hang-out. Yes; and it might be in a prohibition state, such as Iowa was in 1894, when I wandered up the main street of Des Moines and was variously invited by strangers into various blind pigs—I remember drinking in barber-shops, plumbing establishments, and furniture stores.

Always it was John Barleycorn. Even a tramp, in those halcyon days, could get most frequently drunk. I remember, inside the prison at Buffalo, how some of us got magnificently jingled, and how, on the streets of Buffalo after our release, another jingle was financed with pennies begged on the main-drag.

I had no call for alcohol, but when I was with those who drank, I drank with them. I insisted on travelling or loafing with the livest, keenest men, and it was just these live, keen ones that did most of the drinking. They were the more comradely men, the more venturous, the more individual. Perhaps it was too much temperament that made them turn from the commonplace and humdrum to find relief in the lying and fantastic sureties of John Barleycorn. Be that as it may, the men I liked best, desired most to be with, were invariably to be found in John Barleycorn's company.

In the course of my tramping over the United States I achieved a new concept. As a tramp, I was behind the scenes of society—aye, and down in the cellar. I could watch the machinery work. I saw the wheels of the social machine go around, and I learned that the dignity of manual labour wasn't what I had been told it was by the teachers, preachers, and politicians. The men without trades were helpless cattle. If one learned a trade, he was compelled to belong to a union in order to work at his trade. And his union was compelled to bully and slug the employers' unions in order to hold up wages or hold down hours. The employers' unions like-wise bullied and slugged. I couldn't see any dignity at all. And when a workman got old, or had an accident, he was thrown into the scrap-heap like any worn-out machine. I saw too many of this sort who were making anything but dignified ends of life.

So my new concept was that manual labour was undignified, and that it didn't pay. No trade for me, was my decision, and no superintendent's daughters. And no criminality, I also decided. That would be almost as disastrous as to be a labourer. Brains paid, not brawn, and I resolved never again to offer my muscles for sale in the brawn market. Brain, and brain only, would I sell.

I returned to California with the firm intention of developing my brain. This meant school education. I had gone through the grammar school long ago, so I entered the Oakland High School. To pay my way I worked as a janitor. My sister helped me, too; and I was not above mowing anybody's lawn or taking up and beating carpets when I had half a day to spare. I was working to get away from work, and I buckled down to it with a grim realisation of the paradox.

Boy and girl love was left behind, and, along with it, Haydee and Louis Shattuck, and the early evening strolls. I hadn't the time. I joined the Henry Clay Debating Society. I was received into the homes of some of the members, where I met nice girls whose skirts reached the ground. I dallied with little home clubs wherein we discussed poetry and art and the nuances of grammar. I joined the socialist local where we studied and orated political economy, philosophy, and politics. I kept half a dozen membership cards working in the free library and did an immense amount of collateral reading.

And for a year and a half on end I never took a drink, nor thought of taking a drink. I hadn't the time, and I certainly did not have the inclination. Between my janitor-work, my studies, and innocent amusements such as chess, I hadn't a moment to spare. I was discovering a new world, and such was the passion of my exploration that the old world of John Barleycorn held no inducements for me.

Come to think of it, I did enter a saloon. I went to see Johnny Heinhold in the Last Chance, and I went to borrow money. And right here is another phase of John Barleycorn. Saloon-keepers are notoriously good fellows. On an average they perform vastly greater generosities than do business men. When I simply had to have ten dollars, desperate, with no place to turn, I went to Johnny Heinhold. Several years had passed since I had been in his place or spent a cent across his bar. And when I went to borrow the ten dollars I didn't buy a drink, either. And Johnny Heinhold let me have the ten dollars without security or interest.

More than once, in the brief days of my struggle for an education, I went to Johnny Heinhold to borrow money. When I entered the university, I borrowed forty dollars from him, without interest, without security, without buying a drink. And yet—and here is the point, the custom, and the code—in the days of my prosperity, after the lapse of years, I have gone out of my way by many a long block to spend across Johnny Heinhold's bar deferred interest on the various loans. Not that Johnny Heinhold asked me to do it, or expected me to do it. I did it, as I have said, in obedience to the code I had learned along with all the other things connected with John Barleycorn. In distress, when a man has no other place to turn, when he hasn't the slightest bit of security which a savage-hearted pawn-broker would consider, he can go to some saloon-keeper he knows. Gratitude is inherently human. When the man so helped has money again, depend upon it that a portion will be spent across the bar of the saloon-keeper who befriended him.

Why, I recollect the early days of my writing career, when the small sums of money I earned from the magazines came with tragic irregularity, while at the same time I was staggering along with a growing family—a wife, children, a mother, a nephew, and my

Mammy Jennie and her old husband fallen on evil days. There were two places at which I could borrow money; a barber shop and a saloon. The barber charged me five per cent. per month in advance. That is to say, when I borrowed one hundred dollars, he handed me ninety-five. The other five dollars he retained as advance interest for the first month. And on the second month I paid him five dollars more, and continued so to do each month until I made a ten strike with the editors and lifted the loan.

The other place to which I came in trouble was the saloon. This saloon-keeper I had known by sight for a couple of years. I had never spent my money in his saloon, and even when I borrowed from him I didn't spend any money. Yet never did he refuse me any sum I asked of him. Unfortunately, before I became prosperous, he moved away to another city. And to this day I regret that he is gone. It is the code I have learned. The right thing to do, and the thing I'd do right now did I know where he is, would be to drop in on occasion and spend a few dollars across his bar for old sake's sake and gratitude.

* * *

Three years was the time required to go through the high school. I grew impatient. Also, my schooling was becoming financially impossible. At such rate I could not last out, and I did greatly want to go to the state university. When I had done a year of high school, I decided to attempt a short cut. I borrowed the money and paid to enter the senior class of a "cramming joint" or academy. I was scheduled to graduate right into the university at the end of four months, thus saving two years.

And how I did cram! I had two years' new work to do in a third of a year. For five weeks I crammed, until simultaneous quadratic equations and chemical formulas fairly oozed from my ears. And then the master of the academy took me aside. He was very sorry, but he was compelled to give me back my tuition fee and to ask me to leave the school. It wasn't a matter of scholarship. I stood well in my classes, and did he graduate me into the university he was confident that in that institution I would continue to stand well. The trouble was that tongues were gossiping about my case. What! In four months accomplished two years' work! It would be a scandal, and the universities were becoming severer in their treatment of accredited prep schools. He couldn't afford such a scandal, therefore I must gracefully depart.

I did. And I paid back the borrowed money, and gritted my teeth, and started to cram by myself. There were three months yet before the university entrance examinations. Without laboratories, without coaching, sitting in my bedroom, I proceeded to compress that two years' work into three months and to keep reviewed on the previous year's work.

Nineteen hours a day I studied. For three months I kept this pace, only breaking it on several occasions. My body grew weary, my mind grew weary, but I stayed with it. My eyes grew weary and began to twitch, but they did not break down. Perhaps, toward the last, I got a bit dotty. I know that at the time I was confident I had discovered the formula for squaring the circle; but I resolutely deferred the working of it out until after the examinations. Then I would show them.

Came the several days of the examinations, during which time I scarcely closed my eyes in sleep, devoting every moment to cramming and reviewing. And when I turned in my last examination paper I was in full possession of a splendid case of brain-fag. I didn't want to see a book. I didn't want to think or to lay eyes on anybody who was liable to think.

There was but one prescription for such a condition, and I gave it to myself—the adventure-path. I didn't wait to learn the result of my examinations. I stowed a roll of blankets and some cold food into a borrowed whitehall boat and set sail. Out of the Oakland Estuary I drifted on the last of an early morning ebb, caught the first of the flood up bay, and raced along with a spanking breeze. San Pablo Bay was smoking, and the Carquinez Straits off the Selby Smelter were smoking, as I picked up ahead and left astern the old landmarks I had first learned with Nelson in the unreefer *Reindeer.*

Benicia showed before me. I opened the bight of Turner's Shipyard, rounded the Solano wharf, and surged along abreast of the patch of tules and the clustering fishermen's arks where in the old days I had lived and drunk deep.

And right here something happened to me, the gravity of which I never dreamed for many a long year to come. I had had no intention of stopping at Benicia. The tide favoured, the wind was fair and howling—glorious sailing for a sailor. Bull Head and Army Points showed ahead, marking the entrance to Suisun Bay which I knew was smoking. And yet, when I laid eyes on those fishing arks lying in the water-front tules, without debate, on the instant, I put down my tiller, came in on the sheet, and headed for the shore. On the instant, out of the profound of my brain-fag, I knew what I wanted. I wanted to drink. I wanted to get drunk.

The call was imperative. There was no uncertainty about it. More than anything else in the world, my frayed and frazzled mind wanted surcease from weariness in the way it knew surcease would come. And right here is the point. For the first time in my life I consciously, deliberately, desired to get drunk. It was a new, a totally different manifestation of John Barleycorn's power. It was not a body need for alcohol. It was a mental desire. My over-worked and jaded mind wanted to forget.

And here the point is drawn to its sharpest. Granted my prodigious brain-fag, nevertheless, had I never drunk in the past, the thought would never have entered my mind to get drunk now. Beginning with physical intolerance for alcohol, for years drinking only for the sake of comradeship and because alcohol was everywhere on the adventure-path, I had now reached the stage where my brain cried out, not merely for a drink, but for a drunk. And had I not been so long used to alcohol, my brain would not have so cried out. I should have sailed on past Bull Head, and in the smoking white of Suisun Bay, and in the wine of wind that filled my sail and poured through me, I should have forgotten my weary brain and rested and refreshed it.

So I sailed in to shore, made all fast, and hurried up among the arks. Charley Le Grant fell on my neck. His wife, Lizzie, folded me to her capacious breast. Billy Murphy, and Joe Lloyd, and all the survivors of the old guard, got around me and their arms around me. Charley seized the can and started for Jorgensen's saloon across the railroad tracks. That meant beer. I wanted whisky, so I called after him to bring a flask.

Many times that flask journeyed across the railroad tracks and back. More old friends of the old free and easy times dropped in, fishermen, Greeks, and Russians, and French. They took turns in treating, and treated all around in turn again. They came and went, but I stayed on and drank with all. I guzzled. I swilled. I ran the liquor down and joyed as the maggots mounted in my brain.

And Clam came in, Nelson's partner before me, handsome as ever, but more reckless, half insane, burning himself out with whisky. He had just had a quarrel with his partner on the sloop *Gazelle*, and knives had been drawn, and blows struck, and he was bent on maddening the fever of the memory with more whisky. And while we downed it, we remembered Nelson and that he had stretched out his great shoulders for the last long sleep in this very town of Benicia; and we wept over the memory of him, and remembered only the good things of him, and sent out the flask to be filled and drank again.

They wanted me to stay over, but through the open door I could see the brave wind on the water, and my ears were filled with the roar of it. And while I forgot that I had plunged into the books nineteen hours a day for three solid months, Charley Le Grant shifted my outfit into a big Columbia River salmon boat. He added charcoal and a fisherman's brazier, a coffee pot and frying pan, and the coffee and the meat, and a black bass fresh from the water that day.

They had to help me down the rickety wharf and into the salmon boat. Likewise they stretched my boom and sprit until the sail set like a board. Some feared to set the sprit; but I insisted, and Charley had no doubts. He knew me of old, and knew that I could sail as long as I could see. They cast off my painter. I put the tiller up, filled away before it, and with dizzy eyes checked and steadied the boat on her course and waved farewell.

The tide had turned, and the fierce ebb, running in the teeth of a fiercer wind, kicked up a stiff, upstanding sea. Suisun Bay was white with wrath and sea-lump. But a salmon boat can sail, and I knew how to sail a salmon boat. So I drove her into it, and through it, and across, and maundered aloud and chanted my disdain for all the books and schools. Cresting seas filled me a foot or so with water, but I laughed at it sloshing about my feet, and chanted my disdain for the wind and the water. I hailed myself a master of life, riding on the back of the unleashed elements, and John Barleycorn rode with me. Amid dissertations on mathematics and philosophy and spoutings and quotations, I sang all the old songs learned in the days when I went from the cannery to the oyster boats to be a pirate—such songs as: "Black Lulu," "Flying Cloud," "Treat my Daughter Kindly," "The Boston Burglar," "Come all you Rambling, Gambling Men," "I Wisht I was a Little Bird," "Shenandoah," and "Ranzo, Boys, Ranzo."

Hours afterward, in the fires of sunset, where the Sacramento and the San Joaquin tumble their muddy floods together, I took the New York Cut-Off, skimmed across the smooth land-locked water past Black Diamond, on into the San Joaquin, and on to Antioch, where, somewhat sobered and magnificently hungry, I laid alongside a big potato sloop that had a familiar rig. Here were old friends aboard, who fried my black bass in olive oil. Then, too, there was a meaty fisherman's stew, delicious with garlic, and crusty Italian bread without butter, and all washed down with pint mugs of thick and heady claret.

My salmon boat was a-soak, but in the snug cabin of the sloop dry blankets and a dry bunk were mine; and we lay and smoked and yarned of old days, while overhead the wind screamed through the rigging and taut halyards drummed against the mast.

* * *

My cruise in the salmon boat lasted a week, and I returned ready to enter the university. During the week's cruise I did not drink again. To accomplish this I was compelled to avoid looking up old friends, for as ever the adventure-path was beset with John Barleycorn. I had wanted the drink that first day, and in the days that followed I did not want it. My tired brain had recuperated. I had no moral scruples in the matter. I was not ashamed nor sorry because of that first day's orgy at Benicia, and I thought no more about it, returning gladly to my books and studies.

Long years were to pass ere I looked back upon that day and realised its significance. At the time, and for a long time afterward, I was to think of it only as a frolic. But still later, in the slough of brain-fag and intellectual weariness, I was to remember and know the craving for the anodyne that resides in alcohol.

In the meantime, after this one relapse at Benicia, I went on with my abstemiousness, primarily because I didn't want to drink. And next, I was abstemious because my way led among books and students where no drinking was. Had I been out on the adventure-path, I should as a matter of course have been drinking. For that is the pity of the adventure-path, which is one of John Barleycorn's favourite stamping grounds.

I completed the first half of my freshman year, and in January of 1897 took up my courses for the second half. But the pressure from lack of money, plus a conviction that the university was not giving me all that I wanted in the time I could spare for it, forced me to leave. I was not very disappointed. For two years I had studied, and in those two years, what was far more valuable, I had done a prodigious amount of reading. Then, too, my grammar had improved. It is true, I had not yet learned that I must say "It is I"; but I no longer was guilty of a double negative in writing, though still prone to that error in excited speech.

I decided immediately to embark on my career. I had four preferences: first, music; second, poetry; third, the writing of philosophic, economic, and political essays; and, fourth, and last, and least, fiction writing. I resolutely cut out music as impossible, settled down in my bedroom, and tackled my second, third, and fourth choices simultaneously. Heavens, how I wrote! Never was there a creative fever such as mine from which the patient escaped fatal results. The way I worked was enough to soften my brain and send me to a mad-house. I wrote, I wrote everything—ponderous essays, scientific and sociological short stories, humorous verse, verse of all sorts from triolets and sonnets to blank verse tragedy and elephantine epics in Spenserian stanzas. On occasion I composed steadily, day after day, for fifteen hours a day. At times I forgot to eat, or refused to tear myself away from my passionate outpouring in order to eat.

And then there was the matter of typewriting. My brother-in-law owned a machine which he used in the day-time. In the night I was free to use it. That machine was a wonder. I could weep now as I recollect my wrestlings with it. It must have been a first model in the year one of the typewriter era. Its alphabet was all capitals. It was informed with an evil spirit. It obeyed no known laws of physics, and overthrew the hoary axiom that like things performed to like things produce like results. I'll swear that machine never did the same thing in the same way twice. Again and again it demonstrated that unlike actions produce like results.

How my back used to ache with it! Prior to that experience, my back had been good for every violent strain put upon it in a none too gentle career. But that typewriter proved to me that I had a pipe-stem for a back. Also, it made me doubt my shoulders. They ached as with rheumatism after every bout. The keys of that machine had to be hit so hard that to one outside the house it sounded like distant thunder or someone breaking up the furniture. I had to hit the keys so hard that I strained my first fingers to the elbows, while the ends of my fingers were blisters burst and blistered again. Had it been my machine I'd have operated it with a carpenter's hammer.

The worst of it was that I was actually typing my manuscripts at the same time I was trying to master that machine. It was a feat of physical endurance and a brain storm combined to type a thousand words, and I was composing thousands of words every day which just had to be typed for the waiting editors.

Oh, between the writing and the typewriting I was well a-weary. I had brain and nerve fag, and body fag as well, and yet the thought of drink never suggested itself. I was living too high to stand in need of an anodyne. All my waking hours, except those with that infernal typewriter, were spent in a creative heaven. And along with this I had no desire for drink because I still believed in many things—in the love of all men and women in the matter of man and woman love; in fatherhood; in human justice; in art—in the whole host of fond illusions that keep the world turning around.

But the waiting editors elected to keep on waiting. My manuscripts made amazing round-trip records between the Pacific and the Atlantic. It might have been the weirdness of the typewriting that prevented the editors from accepting at least one little offering of mine. I don't know, and goodness knows the stuff I wrote was as weird as its typing. I sold my hard-bought school books for ridiculous sums to second-hand bookmen. I borrowed small sums of money wherever I could, and suffered my old father to feed me with the meagre returns of his failing strength.

It didn't last long, only a few weeks, when I had to surrender and go to work. Yet I was unaware of any need for the drink anodyne. I was not disappointed. My career was retarded, that was all. Perhaps I did need further preparation. I had learned enough from the books to realise that I had only touched the hem of knowledge's garment. I still lived on the heights. My waking hours, and most of the hours I should have used for sleep, were spent with the books.

* * *

My sister and her husband grubstaked me into the Klondike. It was the first gold rush into that region, the early fall rush of 1897. I was twenty-one years old, and in splendid physical condition. I remember, at the end of the twenty-eight-mile portage across Chilcoot from Dyea Beach to Lake Linderman, I was packing up with the Indians and out-packing many an Indian. The last pack into Linderman was three miles. I back-tripped it four times a day, and on each forward trip carried one hundred and fifty pounds. This means that over the worst trails I daily travelled twenty-four miles, twelve of which were under a burden of one hundred and fifty pounds.

Yes, I had let career go hang, and was on the adventure-path again in quest of fortune. And of course, on the adventure-path, I met John Barleycorn. Here were the chesty men again, rovers and adventurers, and while they didn't mind a grub famine, whisky they could not do without. Whisky went over the trail, while the flour lay cached and untouched by the trail-side.

As good fortune would have it, the three men in my party were not drinkers. Therefore I didn't drink save on rare occasions and disgracefully when with other men. In my personal medicine chest was a quart of whisky. I never drew the cork till six months afterward, in a lonely camp, where, without anaesthetics, a doctor was compelled to operate on a man. The doctor and the patient emptied my bottle between them and then proceeded to the operation.

Back in California a year later, recovering from scurvy, I found that my father was dead and that I was the head and the sole breadwinner of a household. When I state that I had passed coal on a steamship from Behring Sea to British Columbia, and travelled in the steerage from there to San Francisco, it will be understood that I brought nothing back from the Klondike but my scurvy.

Times were hard. Work of any sort was difficult to get. And work of any sort was what I had to take, for I was still an unskilled labourer. I had no thought of career. That was over and done with. I had to find food for two mouths beside my own and keep a roof over our heads—yes, and buy a winter suit, my one suit being decidedly summery. I had to get some sort of work immediately. After that, when I had caught my breath, I might think about my future.

Unskilled labour is the first to feel the slackness of hard times, and I had no trades save those of sailor and laundryman. With my new responsibilities I didn't dare go to sea, and I failed to find a job at laundrying. I failed to find a job at anything. I had my name down in five employment bureaux. I advertised in three newspapers. I sought out the few friends I knew who might be able to get me work; but they were either uninterested or unable to find anything for me.

The situation was desperate. I pawned my watch, my bicycle, and a mackintosh of which my father had been very proud and which he had left to me. It was and is my sole legacy in this world. It had cost fifteen dollars, and the pawnbroker let me have two dollars on it. And—oh, yes—a water-front comrade of earlier years drifted along one day with a dress suit wrapped in newspapers. He could give no adequate explanation of how he had come to possess it, nor did I press for an explanation. I wanted the suit myself. No; not to wear. I traded him a lot of rubbish which, being unpawnable, was useless to me. He peddled the rubbish for several dollars, while I pledged the dress-suit with my pawnbroker for five dollars. And for all I know the pawnbroker still has the suit. I had never intended to redeem it.

But I couldn't get any work. Yet I was a bargain in the labour market. I was twenty-two years old, weighed one hundred and sixty-five pounds stripped, every pound of which was excellent for toil;

and the last traces of my scurvy were vanishing before a treatment of potatoes chewed raw. I tackled every opening for employment. I tried to become a studio model, but there were too many fine-bodied young fellows out of jobs. I answered advertisements of elderly invalids in need of companions. And I almost became a sewing machine agent, on commission, without salary. But poor people don't buy sewing machines in hard times, so I was forced to forgo that employment.

Of course, it must be remembered that along with such frivolous occupations I was trying to get work as wop, lumper, and roustabout. But winter was coming on, and the surplus labour army was pouring into the cities. Also I, who had romped along carelessly through the countries of the world and the kingdom of the mind, was not a member of any union.

I sought odd jobs. I worked days, and half-days, at anything I could get. I mowed lawns, trimmed hedges, took up carpets, beat them, and laid them again. Further, I took the civil service examinations for mail carrier and passed first. But alas! there was no vacancy, and I must wait. And while I waited, and in between the odd jobs I managed to procure, I started to earn ten dollars by writing a newspaper account of a voyage I had made, in an open boat down the Yukon, of nineteen hundred miles in nineteen days. I didn't know the first thing about the newspaper game, but I was confident I'd get ten dollars for my article.

But I didn't. The first San Francisco newspaper to which I mailed it never acknowledged receipt of the manuscript, but held on to it. The longer it held on to it the more certain I was that the thing was accepted.

And here is the funny thing. Some are born to fortune, and some have fortune thrust upon them. But in my case I was clubbed into fortune, and bitter necessity wielded the club. I had long since abandoned all thought of writing as a career. My honest intention in writing that article was to earn ten dollars. And that was the limit of my intention. It would help to tide me along until I got steady employment. Had a vacancy occurred in the post office at that time, I should have jumped at it.

But the vacancy did not occur, nor did a steady job; and I employed the time between odd jobs with writing a twenty-one-thousand-word serial for the "Youth's Companion." I turned it out and typed it in seven days. I fancy that was what was the matter with it, for it came back.

It took some time for it to go and come, and in the meantime I tried my hand at short stories. I sold one to the "Overland Monthly" for five dollars. The "Black Cat" gave me forty dollars for another. The "Overland Monthly" offered me seven dollars and a half, pay on publication, for all the stories I should deliver. I got my bicycle, my watch, and my father's mackintosh out of pawn and rented a typewriter. Also, I paid up the bills I owed to the several groceries that allowed me a small credit. I recall the Portuguese groceryman who never permitted my bill to go beyond four dollars. Hopkins, another grocer, could not be budged beyond five dollars.

And just then came the call from the post office to go to work. It placed me in a most trying predicament. The sixty-five dollars I could earn regularly every month was a terrible temptation. I couldn't decide what to do. And I'll never be able to forgive the postmaster of Oakland. I answered the call, and I talked to him like a man. I frankly told him the situation. It looked as if I might win out at writing. The chance was good, but not certain. Now, if he would pass me by and select the next man on the eligible list and give me a call at the next vacancy—

But he shut me off with: "Then you don't want the position?"

"But I do," I protested. "Don't you see, if you will pass me over this time—"

"If you want it you will take it," he said coldly.

Happily for me, the cursed brutality of the man made me angry.

"Very well," I said. "I won't take it."

* * *

Having burned my ship, I plunged into writing. I am afraid I always was an extremist. Early and late I was at it—writing, typing, studying grammar, studying writing and all the forms of writing, and studying the writers who succeeded in order to find out how they succeeded. I managed on five hours' sleep in the twenty-four, and came pretty close to working the nineteen waking hours left to me. My light burned till two and three in the morning, which led a good neighbour woman into a bit of sentimental Sherlock-Holmes deduction. Never seeing me in the day-time, she concluded that I was a gambler, and that the light in my window was placed there by my mother to guide her erring son home.

The trouble with the beginner at the writing game is the long, dry spells, when there is never an editor's cheque and everything pawnable is pawned. I wore my summer suit pretty well through that winter, and the following summer experienced the longest, dryest spell of all, in the period when salaried men are gone on vacation and manuscripts lie in editorial offices until vacation is over.

My difficulty was that I had no one to advise me. I didn't know a soul who had written or who had ever tried to write. I didn't even know one reporter. Also, to succeed at the writing game, I found I had to unlearn about everything the teachers and professors of literature of the high school and university had taught me. I was very indignant about this at the time; though now I can understand it. They did not know the trick of successful writing in the years 1895 and 1896. They knew all about "Snow Bound" and "Sartor Resartus"; but the American editors of 1899 did not want such truck. They wanted the 1899 truck, and offered to pay so well for it that the teachers and professors of literature would have quit their jobs could they have supplied it.

I struggled along, stood off the butcher and the grocer, pawned my watch and bicycle and my father's mackintosh, and I worked. I really did work, and went on short commons of sleep. Critics have complained about the swift education one of my characters, Martin Eden, achieved. In three years, from a sailor with a common school education, I made a successful writer of him. The critics say this is impossible. Yet I was Martin Eden. At the end of three working years, two of which were spent in high school and the university and one spent at writing, and all three in studying immensely and intensely, I was publishing stories in magazines such as the "Atlantic Monthly," was correcting proofs of my first book (issued by Houghton, Mifflin Co.), was selling sociological articles to "Cosmopolitan" and "McClure's," had declined an associate editorship proffered me by telegraph from New York City, and was getting ready to marry.

Now the foregoing means work, especially the last year of it, when I was learning my trade as a writer. And in that year, running short on sleep and tasking my brain to its limit, I neither drank nor cared to drink. So far as I was concerned, alcohol did not exist. I did suffer from brain-fag on occasion, but alcohol never suggested itself as an ameliorative. Heavens! Editorial acceptances and cheques were all the amelioratives I needed. A thin envelope from an editor in the morning's mail was more stimulating than half a dozen cocktails. And if a cheque of decent amount came out of the envelope, such incident in itself was a whole drunk.

Furthermore, at that time in my life I did not know what a cocktail was. I remember, when my first book was published, several Alaskans, who were members of the Bohemian Club, entertained me one evening at the club in San Francisco. We sat in most wonderful leather chairs, and drinks were ordered. Never had I heard such an ordering of liqueurs and of highballs of particular brands of Scotch. I didn't know what a liqueur or a highball was, and I didn't know that "Scotch" meant whisky. I knew only poor men's drinks, the drinks of the frontier and of sailor-town—cheap beer and cheaper whisky that was just called whisky and nothing else. I was embarrassed to make a choice, and the steward nearly collapsed when I ordered claret as an after-dinner drink.

* * *

As I succeeded with my writing, my standard of living rose and my horizon broadened. I confined myself to writing and typing a thousand words a day, including Sundays and holidays; and I still studied hard, but not so hard as formerly. I allowed myself five and one-half hours of actual sleep. I added this half-hour because I was compelled. Financial success permitted me more time for exercise.

I rode my wheel more, chiefly because it was permanently out of pawn; and I boxed and fenced, walked on my hands, jumped high and broad, put the shot and tossed the caber, and went swimming. And I learned that more sleep is required for physical exercise than for mental exercise. There were tired nights, bodily, when I slept six hours; and on occasion of very severe exercise I actually slept seven hours. But such sleep orgies were not frequent. There was so much to learn, so much to be done, that I felt wicked when I slept seven hours. And I blessed the man who invented alarm clocks.

And still no desire to drink. I possessed too many fine faiths, was living at too keen a pitch. I was a socialist, intent on saving the world, and alcohol could not give me the fervours that were mine from my ideas and ideals. My voice, on account of my successful writing, had added weight, or so I thought. At any rate, my reputation as a writer drew me audiences that my reputation as a speaker never could have drawn. I was invited before clubs and organisations of all sorts to deliver my message. I fought the good fight, and went on studying and writing, and was very busy.

Up to this time I had had a very restricted circle of friends. But now I began to go about. I was invited out, especially to dinner, and I made many friends and acquaintances whose economic lives were easier than mine had been. And many of them drank. In their own houses they drank and offered me drink. They were not drunkards any of them. They just drank temperately, and I drank temperately with them as an act of comradeship and accepted hospitality. I did not care for it, neither wanted it nor did not want it, and so small was the impression made by it that I do not remember my first cocktail nor my first Scotch highball.

Well, I had a house. When one is asked into other houses, he naturally asks others into his house. Behold the rising standard of living. Having been given drink in other houses, I could expect nothing else of myself than to give drink in my own house. So I laid in a supply of beer and whisky and table claret. Never since that has my house not been well supplied.

When out at dinner I noticed the kindly, genial glow of the preliminary cocktail. It seemed a very fitting and gracious thing. Yet so little did I stand in need of it, with my own high intensity and vitality, that I never thought it worth while to have a cocktail before my own meal when I ate alone.

On the other hand, I well remember a very brilliant man, somewhat older than I, who occasionally visited me. He liked whisky, and I recall sitting whole afternoons in my den, drinking steadily with him, drink for drink, until he was mildly lighted up and I was slightly aware that I had drunk some whisky. Now why did I do this? I don't know, save that the old schooling held, the training of the old days and nights glass in hand with men, the drinking ways of drink and drinkers.

Besides, I no longer feared John Barleycorn. Mine was that most dangerous stage when a man believes himself John Barleycorn's master. I had proved it to my satisfaction in the long years of work and study. I could drink when I wanted, refrain when I wanted, drink without getting drunk, and to cap everything I was thoroughly conscious that I had no liking for the stuff. During this period I drank precisely for the same reason I had drunk with Scotty and the harpooner and with the oyster pirates—because it was an act that men performed with whom I wanted to behave as a man. These brilliant ones, these adventurers of the mind, drank. Very well. There was no reason I should not drink with them—I who knew so confidently that I had nothing to fear from John Barleycorn.

And the foregoing was my attitude of mind for years. Occasionally I got well jingled, but such occasions were rare. It interfered with my work, and I permitted nothing to interfere with my work. I remember, when spending several months in the East End of London, during which time I wrote a book and adventured much amongst the worst of the slum classes, that I got drunk several times and was mightily wroth with myself because it interfered with my writing. Yet these very times were because I was out on the adventure-path where John Barleycorn is always to be found.

Then, too, with the certitude of long training and unholy intimacy, there were occasions when I engaged in drinking bouts with men. Of course, this was on the adventure-path in various parts of the world, and it was a matter of pride. It is a queer man-pride that leads one to drink with men in order to show as strong a head as they. But this queer man-pride is no theory. It is a fact.

For instance, a wild band of young revolutionists invited me as the guest of honour to a beer bust. It is the only technical beer bust I ever attended. I did not know the true inwardness of the affair when I accepted. I imagined that the talk would be wild and high, that some of them might drink more than they ought, and that I would drink discreetly. But it seemed these beer busts were a diversion of these high-spirited young fellows whereby they whiled away the tedium of existence by making fools of their betters. As I learned afterward, they had got their previous guest of honour, a brilliant young radical, unskilled in drinking, quite pipped.

When I found myself with them, and the situation dawned on me, up rose my queer man-pride. I'd show them, the young rascals. I'd show them who was husky and chesty, who had the vitality and the constitution, the stomach and the head, who could make most of a swine of himself and show it least. These unlicked cubs who thought they could out-drink ME!

You see, it was an endurance test, and no man likes to give another best. Faugh! it was steam beer. I had learned more expensive brews. Not for years had I drunk steam beer; but when I had, I had drunk with men, and I guessed I could show these youngsters some ability in beer-guzzling. And the drinking began, and I had to drink with the best of them. Some of them might lag, but the guest of honour was not permitted to lag.

And all my austere nights of midnight oil, all the books I had read, all the wisdom I had gathered, went glimmering before the ape and tiger in me that crawled up from the abysm of my heredity, atavistic, competitive and brutal, lustful with strength and desire to outswine the swine.

And when the session broke up I was still on my feet, and I walked, erect, unswaying—which was more than can be said of some of my hosts. I recall one of them in indignant tears on the street corner, weeping as he pointed out my sober condition. Little he dreamed the iron clutch, born of old training, with which I held to my consciousness in my swimming brain, kept control of my muscles and my qualms, kept my voice unbroken and easy and my thoughts consecutive and logical. Yes, and mixed up with it all I was privily a-grin. They hadn't made a fool of me in that drinking bout. And I was proud of myself for the achievement. Darn it, I am still proud, so strangely is man compounded.

But I didn't write my thousand words next morning. I was sick, poisoned. It was a day of wretchedness. In the afternoon I had to give a public speech. I gave it, and I am confident it was as bad as I felt. Some of my hosts were there in the front rows to mark any signs on me of the night before. I don't know what signs they marked, but I marked signs on them and took consolation in the knowledge that they were just as sick as I.

Never again, I swore. And I have never been inveigled into another beer bust. For that matter, that was my last drinking bout of any sort. Oh, I have drunk ever since, but with more wisdom, more discretion, and never in a competitive spirit. It is thus that the seasoned drinker grows seasoned.

* * *

I drank when others drank and I was with them. But, imperceptibly, my need for alcohol took form and began to grow. It was not a body need. I boxed, swam, sailed, rode horses, lived in the open an arrantly healthful life, and passed life insurance examinations with flying colours. In its inception, now that I look back upon it, this need for alcohol was a mental need, a nerve need, a good-spirits need. How can I explain?

It was something like this. Physiologically, from the standpoint of palate and stomach, alcohol was, as it had always been, repulsive. It tasted no better than beer did when I was five, than bitter claret did when I was seven. When I was alone, writing or studying, I had no need for it. But—I was growing old, or wise, or both, or senile as an alternative. When I was in company I was less pleased, less excited, with the things said and done. Erstwhile worthwhile fun and stunts seemed no longer worthwhile; and it was a torment to listen to the insipidities and stupidities of women, to the pompous, arrogant sayings of the little half-baked men. It is the penalty one pays for reading the books too much, or for being oneself a fool. In my case it does not matter which was my trouble. The trouble itself was the fact. The condition of the fact was mine. For me the life, and light, and sparkle of human intercourse were dwindling.

I had climbed too high among the stars, or, maybe, I had slept too hard. Yet I was not hysterical nor in any way overwrought. My pulse was normal. My heart was an amazement of excellence to the insurance doctors. My lungs threw the said doctors into ecstasies. I wrote a thousand words every day. I was punctiliously exact in dealing with all the affairs of life that fell to my lot. I exercised in joy and gladness. I slept at night like a babe. But—

Well, as soon as I got out in the company of others I was driven to melancholy and spiritual tears. I could neither laugh with nor at the solemn utterances of men I esteemed ponderous asses; nor could I laugh, nor engage in my old-time lightsome persiflage,

with the silly superficial chatterings of women, who, underneath all their silliness and softness, were as primitive, direct, and deadly in their pursuit of biological destiny as the monkeys women were before they shed their furry coats and replaced them with the furs of other animals.

And I was not pessimistic. I swear I was not pessimistic. I was merely bored. I had seen the same show too often, listened too often to the same songs and the same jokes. I knew too much about the box office receipts. I knew the cogs of the machinery behind the scenes so well that the posing on the stage, and the laughter and the song, could not drown the creaking of the wheels behind.

It doesn't pay to go behind the scenes and see the angel-voiced tenor beat his wife. Well, I'd been behind, and I was paying for it. Or else I was a fool. It is immaterial which was my situation. The situation is what counts, and the situation was that social intercourse for me was getting painful and difficult. On the other hand, it must be stated that on rare occasions, on very rare occasions, I did meet rare souls, or fools like me, with whom I could spend magnificent hours among the stars, or in the paradise of fools. I was married to a rare soul, or a fool, who never bored me and who was always a source of new and unending surprise and delight. But I could not spend all my hours solely in her company.

Nor would it have been fair, nor wise, to compel her to spend all her hours in my company. Besides, I had written a string of successful books, and society demands some portion of the recreative hours of a fellow that writes books. And any normal man, of himself and his needs, demands some hours of his fellow men.

And now we begin to come to it. How to face the social intercourse game with the glamour gone? John Barleycorn. The ever patient one had waited a quarter of a century and more for me to reach my hand out in need of him. His thousand tricks had failed, thanks to my constitution and good luck, but he had more tricks in his bag. A cocktail or two, or several, I found, cheered me up for the foolishness of foolish people. A cocktail, or several, before dinner, enabled me to laugh whole-heartedly at things which had long since ceased being laughable. The cocktail was a prod, a spur, a kick, to my jaded mind and bored spirits. It recrudesced the laughter and the song, and put a lilt into my own imagination so that I could laugh and sing and say foolish things with the liveliest of them, or platitudes with verve and intensity to the satisfaction of the pompous mediocre ones who knew no other way to talk.

A poor companion without a cocktail, I became a very good companion with one. I achieved a false exhilaration, drugged myself to merriment. And the thing began so imperceptibly that I, old intimate of John Barleycorn, never dreamed whither it was leading me. I was beginning to call for music and wine; soon I should be calling for madder music and more wine.

It was at this time I became aware of waiting with expectancy for the pre-dinner cocktail. I WANTED it, and I was CONSCIOUS that I wanted it. I remember, while war-corresponding in the Far East, of being irresistibly attracted to a certain home. Besides accepting all invitations to dinner, I made a point of dropping in almost every afternoon. Now, the hostess was a charming woman, but it was not for her sake that I was under her roof so frequently. It happened that she made by far the finest cocktail procurable in that large city where drink-mixing on the part of the foreign population was indeed an art. Up at the club, down at the hotels, and in other private houses, no such cocktails were created. Her cocktails were subtle. They were masterpieces. They were the least repulsive to the palate and carried the most "kick." And yet, I desired her cocktails only for sociability's sake, to key myself to sociable moods. When I rode away from that city, across hundreds of miles of rice-fields and mountains, and through months of campaigning, and on with the victorious Japanese into Manchuria, I did not drink. Several bottles of whisky were always to be found on the backs of my pack-horses. Yet I never broached a bottle for myself, never took a drink by myself, and never knew a desire to take such a drink. Oh, if a white man came into my camp, I opened a bottle and we drank together according to the way of men, just as he would open a bottle and drink with me if I came into his camp. I carried that whisky for social purposes, and I so charged it up in my expense account to the newspaper for which I worked.

Only in retrospect can I mark the almost imperceptible growth of my desire. There were little hints then that I did not take, little straws in the wind that I did not see, little incidents the gravity of which I did not realise.

For instance, for some years it had been my practice each winter to cruise for six or eight weeks on San Francisco Bay. My stout sloop yacht, the *Spray*, had a comfortable cabin and a coal stove. A Korean boy did the cooking, and I usually took a friend or so along to share the joys of the cruise. Also, I took my machine along and did my thousand words a day. On the particular trip I have in mind, Cloudesley and Toddy came along. This was Toddy's first trip. On previous trips Cloudesley had elected to drink beer; so I had kept the yacht supplied with beer and had drunk beer with him.

But on this cruise the situation was different. Toddy was so nicknamed because of his diabolical cleverness in concocting toddies. So I brought whisky along—a couple of gallons. Alas! Many another gallon I bought, for Cloudesley and I got into the habit of drinking a certain hot toddy that actually tasted delicious going down and that carried the most exhilarating kick imaginable.

I liked those toddies. I grew to look forward to the making of them. We drank them regularly, one before breakfast, one before dinner, one before supper, and a final one when we went to bed. We never got drunk. But I will say that four times a day we were very genial. And when, in the middle of the cruise, Toddy was called back to San Francisco on business, Cloudesley and I saw to it that the Korean boy mixed toddies regularly for us according to formula.

But that was only on the boat. Back on the land, in my house, I took no before breakfast eye-opener, no bed-going nightcap. And I haven't drunk hot toddies since, and that was many a year ago. But the point is, I LIKED those toddies. The geniality of which they were provocative was marvellous. They were eloquent proselyters for John Barleycorn in their own small insidious way. They were tickles of the something destined to grow into daily and deadly desire.

* * *

Part of the process of recovering from my long sickness was to find delight in little things, in things unconnected with books and problems, in play, in games of tag in the swimming pool, in flying kites, in fooling with horses, in working out mechanical puzzles. As a result, I grew tired of the city. On the ranch, in the Valley of the Moon, I found my paradise. I gave up living in cities. All the cities held for me were music, the theatre, and Turkish baths.

And all went well with me. I worked hard, played hard, and was very happy. I read more fiction and less fact. I did not study a tithe as much as I had studied in the past. I still took an interest in the fundamental problems of existence, but it was a very cautious interest; for I had burned my fingers that time I clutched at the veils of Truth and wrested them from her. There was a bit of lie in this attitude of mine, a bit of hypocrisy; but the lie and the hypocrisy were those of a man desiring to live. I deliberately blinded myself to what I took to be the savage interpretation of biological fact. After all, I was merely forswearing a bad habit, forgoing a bad frame of mind. And I repeat, I was very happy. And I add, that in all my days, measuring them with cold, considerative judgment, this was, far and away beyond all other periods, the happiest period of my life.

But the time was at hand, rhymeless and reasonless so far as I can see, when I was to begin to pay for my score of years of dallying with John Barleycorn. Occasionally guests journeyed to the ranch and remained a few days. Some did not drink. But to those who did drink, the absence of all alcohol on the ranch was a hardship. I could not violate my sense of hospitality by compelling them to endure this hardship. I ordered in a stock—for my guests.

I was never interested enough in cocktails to know how they were made. So I got a bar-keeper in Oakland to make them in bulk and ship them to me. When I had no guests I didn't drink. But I began to notice, when I finished my morning's work, that I was glad if there were a guest, for then I could drink a cocktail with him.

Now I was so clean of alcohol that even a single cocktail was provocative of pitch. A single cocktail would glow the mind and tickle a laugh for the few minutes prior to sitting down to table and starting the delightful process of eating. On the other hand, such was the strength of my stomach, of my alcoholic resistance, that the single cocktail was only the glimmer of a glow, the faintest tickle of a laugh. One day, a friend frankly and shamelessly suggested a second cocktail. I drank the second one with him. The glow was appreciably longer and warmer, the laughter deeper and more resonant. One does not forget such experiences. Sometimes I almost think that it was because I was so very happy that I started on my real drinking.

I remember one day Charmian and I took a long ride over the mountains on our horses. The servants had been dismissed for the day, and we returned late at night to a jolly chafing-dish supper. Oh, it was good to be alive that night while the supper was preparing, the two of us alone in the kitchen. I, personally, was at the top of life. Such things as the books and ultimate truth did not exist. My body was gloriously healthy, and healthily tired from the long ride. It had been a splendid day. The night was splendid. I was with the woman who was my mate, picnicking in gleeful abandon. I had no troubles. The bills were all paid, and a surplus of money was rolling in on me. The future ever-widened before me. And right there, in the kitchen, delicious things bubbled in the chafing-dish, our laughter bubbled, and my stomach was keen with a most delicious edge of appetite.

I felt so good, that somehow, somewhere, in me arose an insatiable greed to feel better. I was so happy that I wanted to pitch my happiness even higher. And I knew the way. Ten thousand contacts with John Barleycorn had taught me. Several times I wandered out of the kitchen to the cocktail bottle, and each time I left it diminished by one man's size cocktail. The result was splendid. I wasn't jingled, I wasn't lighted up; but I was warmed, I glowed, my happiness was pyramided. Munificent as life was to me, I added to that munificence. It was a great hour—one of my greatest. But I paid for it, long afterwards, as you will see. One does not forget such experiences, and, in human stupidity, cannot be brought to realise that there is no immutable law which decrees that same things shall produce same results. For they don't, else would the thousandth pipe of opium be provocative of similar delights to the first, else would one cocktail, instead of several, produce an equivalent glow after a year of cocktails.

One day, just before I ate midday dinner, after my morning's writing was done, when I had no guest, I took a cocktail by myself. Thereafter, when there were no guests, I took this daily pre-dinner cocktail. And right there John Barleycorn had me. I was beginning to drink regularly. I was beginning to drink alone. And I was beginning to drink, not for hospitality's sake, not for the sake of the taste, but for the effect of the drink.

I WANTED that daily pre-dinner cocktail. And it never crossed my mind that there was any reason I should not have it. I paid for it. I could pay for a thousand cocktails each day if I wanted. And what was a cocktail—one cocktail—to me who on so many occasions for so many years had drunk inordinate quantities of stiffer stuff and been unharmed?

The programme of my ranch life was as follows: Each morning, at eight-thirty, having been reading or correcting proofs in bed since four or five, I went to my desk. Odds and ends of correspondence and notes occupied me till nine, and at nine sharp, invariably, I began my writing. By eleven, sometimes a few minutes earlier or later, my thousand words were finished. Another half-hour at cleaning up my desk, and my day's work was done, so that at eleven-thirty I got into a hammock under the trees with my mail-bag and the morning newspaper. At twelve-thirty I ate dinner and in the afternoon I swam and rode.

One morning, at eleven-thirty, before I got into the hammock, I took a cocktail. I repeated this on subsequent mornings, of course, taking another cocktail just before I ate at twelve-thirty. Soon I found myself, seated at my desk in the midst of my thousand words, looking forward to that eleven-thirty cocktail.

*   *   *

But the same stimulus to the human organism will not continue to produce the same response. By and by I discovered there was no kick at all in one cocktail. One cocktail left me dead. There was no glow, no laughter tickle. Two or three cocktails were required to produce the original effect of one. And I wanted that effect. I drank my first cocktail at eleven-thirty when I took the morning's mail into the hammock, and I drank my second cocktail an hour later just before I ate. I got into the habit of crawling out of the hammock ten minutes earlier so as to find time and decency for two more cocktails ere I ate. This became schedule—three cocktails in the hour that intervened between my desk and dinner.

I was always willing to drink when any one was around. I drank by myself when no one was around. Then I made another step. When I had for guest a man of limited drinking calibre, I took two drinks to his one—one drink with him, the other drink without him and of which he did not know. I STOLE that other drink, and, worse than that, I began the habit of drinking alone when there was a guest, a man, a comrade, with whom I could have drunk. But John Barleycorn furnished the extenuation. It was a wrong thing to trip a guest up with excess of hospitality and get him drunk. If I persuaded him, with his limited calibre, into drinking up with me, I'd surely get him drunk. What could I do but steal that every second drink, or else deny myself the kick equivalent to what he got out of half the number?

Please remember, as I recite this development of my drinking, that I am no fool, no weakling. As the world measures such things, I am a success—I dare to say a success more conspicuous than the success of the average successful man, and a success that required a pretty fair amount of brains and will power. My body is a strong body. It has survived where weaklings died like flies. And yet these things which I am relating happened to my body and to me. I am a fact. My drinking is a fact. My drinking is a thing that has happened, and is no theory nor speculation; and, as I see it, it but lays the emphasis on the power of John Barleycorn—a savagery that we still permit to exist, a deadly institution that lingers from the mad old brutal days and that takes its heavy toll of youth and strength, and high spirit, and of very much of all of the best we breed.

To return. After a boisterous afternoon in the swimming pool, followed by a glorious ride on horseback over the mountains or up or down the Valley of the Moon, I found myself so keyed and splendid that I desired to be more highly keyed, to feel more splendid. I knew the way. A cocktail before supper was not the way. Two or three, at the very least, was what was needed. I took them. Why not? It was living. I had always dearly loved to live. This also became part of the daily schedule.

Then, too, I was perpetually finding excuses for extra cocktails. It might be the assembling of a particularly jolly crowd; a touch of anger against my architect or against a thieving stone-mason working on my barn; the death of my favourite horse in a barbed wire fence; or news of good fortune in the morning mail from my dealings with editors and publishers. It was immaterial what the excuse might be, once the desire had germinated in me. The thing was: I WANTED alcohol. At last, after a score and more of years of dallying and of not wanting, now I wanted it. And my strength was my weakness. I required two, three, or four drinks to get an effect commensurate with the effect the average man got out of one drink.

One rule I observed. I never took a drink until my day's work of writing a thousand words was done. And, when done, the cocktails reared a wall of inhibition in my brain between the day's work done and the rest of the day of fun to come. My work ceased from my consciousness. No thought of it flickered in my brain till next morning at nine o'clock when I sat at my desk and began my next thousand words. This was a desirable condition of mind to achieve. I conserved my energy by means of this alcoholic inhibition. John Barleycorn was not so black as he was painted. He did a fellow many a good turn, and this was one of them.

And I turned out work that was healthful, and wholesome, and sincere. It was never pessimistic. The way to life I had learned in my long sickness. I knew the illusions were right, and I exalted the illusions. Oh, I still turn out the same sort of work, stuff that is clean, alive, optimistic, and that makes toward life. And I am always assured by the critics of my super-abundant and abounding vitality, and of how thoroughly I am deluded by these very illusions I exploit.

And while on this digression, let me repeat the question I have repeated to myself ten thousand times. WHY DID I DRINK? What need was there for it? I was happy. Was it because I was too happy? I was strong. Was it because I was too strong? Did I possess too much vitality? I don't know why I drank. I cannot answer, though I can voice the suspicion that ever grows in me. I had been in too-familiar contact with John Barleycorn through too many years. A left-handed man, by long practice, can become a right-handed man. Had I, a non-alcoholic, by long practice become an alcoholic?

I was so happy. I had won through my long sickness to the satisfying love of woman. I earned more money with less endeavour. I glowed with health. I slept like a babe. I continued to write successful books, and in sociological controversy I saw my opponents confuted with the facts of the times that daily reared new buttresses to my intellectual position. From day's end to day's end I never knew sorrow, disappointment, nor regret. I was happy all the time. Life was one unending song. I begrudged the very hours of blessed sleep because by that much was I robbed of the joy that would have been mine had I remained awake. And yet I drank. And John Barleycorn, all unguessed by me, was setting the stage for a sickness all his own.

The more I drank the more I was required to drink to get an equivalent effect. When I left the Valley of the Moon, and went to the city, and dined out, a cocktail served at table was a wan and worthless thing. There was no pre-dinner kick in it. On my way to dinner I was compelled to accumulate the kick—two cocktails, three, and, if I met some fellows, four or five, or six, it didn't matter within several. Once, I was in a rush. I had no time decently to accumulate the several drinks. A brilliant idea came to me. I told the barkeeper to mix me a double cocktail. Thereafter, whenever I was in a hurry, I ordered double cocktails. It saved time.

* * *

When the *Snark* sailed on her long cruise from San Francisco there was nothing to drink on board. Or, rather, we were all of us unaware that there was anything to drink, nor did we discover it for many a month. This sailing with a "dry" boat was malice aforethought on my part. I had played John Barleycorn a trick. And it showed that I was listening ever so slightly to the faint warnings that were beginning to arise in my consciousness.

Of course, I veiled the situation to myself and excused myself to John Barleycorn. And I was very scientific about it. I said that I would drink only while in ports. During the dry sea-stretches my system would be cleansed of the alcohol that soaked it, so that when I reached a port I should be in shape to enjoy John Barleycorn more thoroughly. His bite would be sharper, his kick keener and more delicious.

We were twenty-seven days on the traverse between San Francisco and Honolulu. After the first day out, the thought of a drink never troubled me. This I take to show how intrinsically I am not an alcoholic. Sometimes, during the traverse, looking ahead and anticipating the delightful lanai luncheons and dinners of Hawaii (I had been there a couple of times before), I thought, naturally, of the drinks that would precede those meals. I did not think of those drinks with any yearning, with any irk at the length of the voyage. I merely thought they would be nice and jolly, part of the atmosphere of a proper meal.

Thus, once again I proved to my complete satisfaction that I was John Barleycorn's master. I could drink when I wanted, refrain when I wanted. Therefore I would continue to drink when I wanted.

Some five months were spent in the various islands of the Hawaiian group. Being ashore, I drank. I even drank a bit more than I had been accustomed to drink in California prior to the voyage. The people in Hawaii seemed to drink a bit more, on the average, than the people in more temperate latitudes. I do not intend the pun, and can awkwardly revise the statement to "latitudes more remote from the equator." Yet Hawaii is only sub-tropical. The deeper I got into the tropics, the deeper I found men drank, the deeper I drank myself.

From Hawaii we sailed for the Marquesas. The traverse occupied sixty days. For sixty days we never raised land, a sail, nor a steamer smoke. But early in those sixty days the cook, giving an overhauling to the galley, made a find. Down in the bottom of a deep locker he found a dozen bottles of angelica and muscatel. These had come down from the kitchen cellar of the ranch along with the home-preserved fruits and jellies. Six months in the galley heat had effected some sort of a change in the thick sweet wine—branded it, I imagine.

I took a taste. Delicious! And thereafter, once each day, at twelve o'clock, after our observations were worked up and the *Snark*'s position charted, I drank half a tumbler of the stuff. It had a rare kick to it. It warmed the cockles of my geniality and put a fairer face on the truly fair face of the sea. Each morning, below, sweating out my thousand words, I found myself looking forward to that twelve o'clock event of the day.

The trouble was I had to share the stuff, and the length of the traverse was doubtful. I regretted that there were not more than a dozen bottles. And when they were gone I even regretted that I had shared any of it. I was thirsty for the alcohol, and eager to arrive in the Marquesas.

So it was that I reached the Marquesas the possessor of a real man's size thirst. And in the Marquesas were several white men, a lot of sickly natives, much magnificent scenery, plenty of trade rum, an immense quantity of absinthe, but neither whisky nor gin. The trade rum scorched the skin off one's mouth. I know, because I tried it. But I had ever been plastic, and I accepted the absinthe. The trouble with the stuff was that I had to take such inordinate quantities in order to feel the slightest effect.

From the Marquesas I sailed with sufficient absinthe in ballast to last me to Tahiti, where I outfitted with Scotch and American whisky, and thereafter there were no dry stretches between ports. But please do not misunderstand. There was no drunkenness, as drunkenness is ordinarily understood—no staggering and rolling around, no befuddlement of the senses. The skilled and seasoned drinker, with a strong constitution, never descends to anything like that. He drinks to feel good, to get a pleasant jingle, and no more than that. The things he carefully avoids are the nausea of over-drinking, the after-effect of over-drinking, the helplessness and loss of pride of over-drinking.

What the skilled and seasoned drinker achieves is a discreet and canny semi-intoxication. And he does it by the twelve-month around without any apparent penalty. There are hundreds of thousands of men of this sort in the United States to-day, in clubs, hotels, and in their own homes—men who are never drunk, and who, though most of them will indignantly deny it, are rarely sober. And all of them fondly believe, as I fondly believed, that they are beating the game.

On the sea-stretches I was fairly abstemious; but ashore I drank more. I seemed to need more, anyway, in the tropics. This is a common experience, for the excessive consumption of alcohol in the tropics by white men is a notorious fact. The tropics is no place for white-skinned men. Their skin-pigment does not protect them against the excessive white light of the sun. The ultra-violet rays, and other high-velocity and invisible rays from the upper end of the spectrum, rip and tear through their tissues, just as the X-ray ripped and tore through the tissues of so many experimenters before they learned the danger.

White men in the tropics undergo radical changes of nature. They become savage, merciless. They commit monstrous acts of cruelty that they would never dream of committing in their original temperate climate. They become nervous, irritable, and less moral. And they drink as they never drank before. Drinking is one form of the many forms of degeneration that set in when white men are exposed too long to too much white light. The increase of alcoholic consumption is automatic. The tropics is no place for a long sojourn. They seem doomed to die anyway, and the heavy drinking expedites the process. They don't reason about it. They just do it.

The sun sickness got me, despite the fact that I had been in the tropics only a couple of years. I drank heavily during this time, but right here I wish to forestall misunderstanding. The drinking was not the cause of the sickness, nor of the abandonment of the voyage. I was strong as a bull, and for many months I fought the sun sickness that was ripping and tearing my surface and nervous tissues to pieces. All through the New Hebrides and the Solomons and up among the atolls on the Line, during this period under a tropic sun, rotten with malaria, and suffering from a few minor afflictions such as Biblical leprosy with the silvery skin, I did the work of five men.

To navigate a vessel through the reefs and shoals and passages and unlighted coasts of the coral seas is a man's work in itself. I was the only navigator on board. There was no one to check me up on the working out of my observations, nor with whom I could advise in the ticklish darkness among uncharted reefs and shoals. And I stood all watches. There was no sea-man on board whom I could trust to stand a mate's watch. I was mate as well as captain. Twenty-four hours a day were the watches I stood at sea, catching cat-naps when I might. Third, I was doctor. And let me say right here that the doctor's job on the *Snark* at that time was a man's job. All on board suffered from malaria—the real, tropical malaria that can kill in three months. All on board suffered from perforating ulcers and from the maddening itch of ngari-ngari. A Japanese cook went insane from his too numerous afflictions. One of my

Polynesian sailors lay at death's door with blackwater fever. Oh, yes, it was a full man's job, and I dosed and doctored, and pulled teeth, and dragged my patients through mild little things like ptomaine poisoning.

Fourth, I was a writer. I sweated out my thousand words a day, every day, except when the shock of fever smote me, or a couple of nasty squalls smote the *Snark*, in the morning. Fifth, I was a traveller and a writer, eager to see things and to gather material into my note-books. And, sixth, I was master and owner of the craft that was visiting strange places where visitors are rare and where visitors are made much of. So here I had to hold up the social end, entertain on board, be entertained ashore by planters, traders, governors, captains of war vessels, kinky-headed cannibal kings, and prime ministers sometimes fortunate enough to be clad in cotton shifts.

Of course I drank. I drank with my guests and hosts. Also, I drank by myself. Doing the work of five men, I thought, entitled me to drink. Alcohol was good for a man who over-worked. I noted its effect on my small crew, when, breaking their backs and hearts at heaving up anchor in forty fathoms, they knocked off gasping and trembling at the end of half an hour and had new life put into them by stiff jolts of rum. They caught their breaths, wiped their mouths, and went to it again with a will. And when we careened the *Snark* and had to work in the water to our necks between shocks of fever, I noted how raw trade rum helped the work along.

* * *

I went to Australia to go into hospital and get tinkered up, after which I planned to go on with the voyage. And during the long weeks I lay in hospital, from the first day I never missed alcohol. I never thought about it. I knew I should have it again when I was on my feet. But when I regained my feet I was not cured of my major afflictions. Naaman's silvery skin was still mine. The mysterious sun-sickness, which the experts of Australia could not fathom, still ripped and tore my tissues. Malaria still festered in me and put me on my back in shivering delirium at the most unexpected moments, compelling me to cancel a double lecture tour which had been arranged.

So I abandoned the *Snark* voyage and sought a cooler climate. The day I came out of hospital I took up drinking again as a matter of course. I drank wine at meals. I drank cocktails before meals. I drank Scotch highballs when anybody I chanced to be with was drinking them. I was so thoroughly the master of John Barleycorn I could take up with him or let go of him whenever I pleased, just as I had done all my life.

After a time, for cooler climate, I went down to southermost Tasmania in forty-three South. And I found myself in a place where there was nothing to drink. It didn't mean anything. I didn't drink. It was no hardship. I soaked in the cool air, rode horseback, and did my thousand words a day save when the fever shock came in the morning.

And for fear that the idea may still lurk in some minds that my preceding years of drinking were the cause of my disabilities, I here point out that my Japanese cabin boy, Nakata, still with me, was rotten with fever, as was Charmian, who in addition was in the slough of a tropical neurasthenia that required several years of temperate climates to cure, and that neither she nor Nakata drank or ever had drunk.

When I returned to Hobart Town, where drink was obtainable, I drank as of old. The same when I arrived back in Australia. On the contrary, when I sailed from Australia on a tramp steamer commanded by an abstemious captain, I took no drink along, and had no drink for the forty-three days' passage. Arrived in Ecuador, squarely under the equatorial sun, where the humans were dying

of yellow fever, smallpox, and the plague, I promptly drank again—every drink of every sort that had a kick in it. I caught none of these diseases. Neither did Charmian nor Nakata who did not drink.

Enamoured of the tropics, despite the damage done me, I stopped in various places, and was a long while getting back to the splendid, temperate climate of California. I did my thousand words a day, travelling or stopping over, suffered my last faint fever shock, saw my silvery skin vanish and my sun-torn tissues healthily knit again, and drank as a broad-shouldered chesty man may drink.

*   *   *

Back on the ranch, in the Valley of the Moon, I resumed my steady drinking. My programme was no drink in the morning; first drink-time came with the completion of my thousand words. Then, between that and the midday meal, were drinks numerous enough to develop a pleasant jingle. Again, in the hour preceding the evening meal, I developed another pleasant jingle. Nobody ever saw me drunk, for the simple reason that I never was drunk. But I did get a jingle twice each day; and the amount of alcohol I consumed every day, if loosed in the system of one unaccustomed to drink, would have put such a one on his back and out.

It was the old proposition. The more I drank, the more I was compelled to drink in order to get an effect. The time came when cocktails were inadequate. I had neither the time in which to drink them nor the space to accommodate them. Whisky had a more powerful jolt. It gave quicker action with less quantity. Bourbon or rye, or cunningly aged blends, constituted the pre-midday drinking. In the late afternoon it was Scotch and soda.

My sleep, always excellent, now became not quite so excellent. I had been accustomed to read myself back asleep when I chanced to awake. But now this began to fail me. When I had read two or three of the small hours away and was as wide awake as ever, I found that a drink furnished the soporific effect. Sometimes two or three drinks were required.

So short a period of sleep then intervened before early morning rising that my system did not have time to work off the alcohol. As a result I awoke with mouth parched and dry, with a slight heaviness of head, and with a mild nervous palpitation in the stomach. In fact I did not feel good. I was suffering from the morning sickness of the steady, heavy drinker. What I needed was a pick-me-up, a bracer. Trust John Barleycorn, once he has broken down a man's defences! So it was a drink before breakfast to put me right for breakfast—the old poison of the snake that has bitten one! Another custom begun at this time was that of the pitcher of water by the bedside to furnish relief to my scorched and sizzling membranes.

I achieved a condition in which my body was never free from alcohol. Nor did I permit myself to be away from alcohol. If I travelled to out-of-the-way places, I declined to run the risk of finding them dry. I took a quart, or several quarts, along in my grip. In the past I had been amazed by other men guilty of this practice. Now I did it myself unblushingly. And when I got out with the fellows, I cast all rules by the board. I drank when they drank, what they drank, and in the same way they drank.

I was carrying a beautiful alcoholic conflagration around with me. The thing fed on its own heat and flamed the fiercer. There was no time, in all my waking time, that I didn't want a drink. I began to anticipate the completion of my daily thousand words by taking a drink when only five hundred words were written. It was not long until I prefaced the beginning of the thousand words with a drink.

The gravity of this I realised too well. I made new rules. Resolutely I would refrain from drinking until my work was done. But a new and most diabolical complication arose. The work refused to be done without drinking. It just couldn't be done. I had to drink in order to do it. I was beginning to fight now. I had the craving at last, and it was mastering me. I would sit at my desk and dally with pad and pen, but words refused to flow. My brain could not think the proper thoughts because continually it was obsessed with the one thought that across the room in the liquor cabinet stood John

Barleycorn. When, in despair, I took my drink, at once my brain loosened up and began to roll off the thousand words.

In my town house, in Oakland, I finished the stock of liquor and wilfully refused to purchase more. It was no use, because, unfortunately, there remained in the bottom of the liquor cabinet a case of beer. In vain I tried to write. Now beer is a poor substitute for strong waters: besides, I didn't like beer, yet all I could think of was that beer so singularly accessible in the bottom of the cabinet. Not until I had drunk a pint of it did the words begin to reel off, and the thousand were reeled off to the tune of numerous pints. The worst of it was that the beer caused me severe heart-burn; but despite the discomfort I soon finished off the case.

The liquor cabinet was now bare. I did not replenish it. By truly heroic perseverance I finally forced myself to write the daily thousand words without the spur of John Barleycorn. But all the time I wrote I was keenly aware of the craving for a drink. And as soon as the morning's work was done, I was out of the house and away down-town to get my first drink. Merciful goodness!—if John Barleycorn could get such sway over me, a non-alcoholic, what must be the sufferings of the true alcoholic, battling against the organic demands of his chemistry while those closest to him sympathise little, understand less, and despise and deride him!

* * *

Of course, no personal tale is complete without bringing the narrative of the person down to the last moment. But mine is no tale of a reformed drunkard. I was never a drunkard, and I have not reformed.

It chanced, some time ago, that I made a voyage of one hundred and forty-eight days in a windjammer around the Horn. I took no private supply of alcohol along, and, though there was no day of those one hundred and forty-eight days that I could not have got a drink from the captain, I did not take a drink. I did not take a drink because I did not desire a drink. No one else drank on board. The atmosphere for drinking was not present, and in my system there was no organic need for alcohol. My chemistry did not demand alcohol.

So there arose before me a problem, a clear and simple problem: THIS IS SO EASY, WHY NOT KEEP IT UP WHEN YOU GET BACK ON LAND? I weighed this problem carefully. I weighed it for five months, in a state of absolute non-contact with alcohol. And out of the data of past experience, I reached certain conclusions.

In the first place, I am convinced that not one man in ten thousand or in a hundred thousand is a genuine, chemical dipsomaniac. Drinking, as I deem it, is practically entirely a habit of mind. It is unlike tobacco, or cocaine, or morphine, or all the rest of the long list of drugs. The desire for alcohol is quite peculiarly mental in its origin. It is a matter of mental training and growth, and it is cultivated in social soil. Not one drinker in a million began drinking alone. All drinkers begin socially, and this drinking is accompanied by a thousand social connotations such as I have described out of my own experience in the first part of this narrative. These social connotations are the stuff of which the drink habit is largely composed. The part that alcohol itself plays is inconsiderable when compared with the part played by the social atmosphere in which it is drunk. The human is rarely born these days, who, without long training in the social associations of drinking, feels the irresistible chemical propulsion of his system toward alcohol. I do assume that such rare individuals are born, but I have never encountered one.

On this long, five-months' voyage, I found that among all my bodily needs not the slightest shred of a bodily need for alcohol existed. But this I did find: my need was mental and social. When I thought of alcohol, the connotation was fellowship. When I thought of fellowship, the connotation was alcohol. Fellowship and alcohol were Siamese twins. They always occurred linked together.

Thus, when reading in my deck chair or when talking with others, practically any mention of any part of the world I knew instantly aroused the connotation of drinking and good fellows. Big nights and days and moments, all purple passages and freedoms, thronged my memory. "Venice" stares at me from the printed page, and I remember the cafe tables on the sidewalks. "The Battle of Santiago," someone says, and I answer, "Yes, I've been over the ground." But I do not see the ground, nor Kettle Hill, nor the Peace Tree. What I see is the Cafe Venus, on the plaza of Santiago, where one hot night I drank and talked with a dying consumptive.

The East End of London, I read, or someone says; and first of all, under my eyelids, leap the visions of the shining pubs, and in my ears echo the calls for "two of bitter" and "three of Scotch." The Latin Quarter—at once I am in the student cabarets, bright faces and keen spirits around me, sipping cool, well-dripped absinthe while our voices mount and soar in Latin fashion as we settle God and art and democracy and the rest of the simple problems of existence.

In a pampero off the River Plate we speculate, if we are disabled, of running in to Buenos Ayres, the "Paris of America," and I have visions of bright congregating places of men, of the jollity of raised glasses, and of song and cheer and the hum of genial voices. When we have picked up the North-east Trades in the Pacific we try to persuade our dying captain to run for Honolulu, and while I persuade I see myself again drinking cocktails on the cool lanais and fizzes out at Waikiki where the surf rolls in. Someone mentions the way wild ducks are cooked in the restaurants of San Francisco, and at once I am transported to the light and clatter of many tables, where I gaze at old friends across the golden brims of long-stemmed Rhine-wine glasses.

And so I pondered my problem. I should not care to revisit all these fair places of the world except in the fashion I visited them before. GLASS IN HAND! There is a magic in the phrase. It means more than all the words in the dictionary can be made to mean. It is a habit of mind to which I have been trained all my life. It is now part of the stuff that composes me. I like the bubbling play of wit, the chesty laughs, the resonant voices of men, when, glass in hand, they shut the grey world outside and prod their brains with the fun and folly of an accelerated pulse.

No, I decided; I shall take my drink on occasion. With all the books on my shelves, with all the thoughts of the thinkers shaded by my particular temperament, I decided coolly and deliberately that I should continue to do what I had been trained to want to do. I would drink—but oh, more skilfully, more discreetly, than ever before.

Books from Skyhorse Publishing

To see our complete catalog or to order online, please visit www.skyhorsepublishing.com.

An Autobiography of Davy Crockett
Edited by *Stephen Brennan* (6 x 9, 320 pages, hardcover, $12.95)

An Autobiography of Theodore Roosevelt
Edited by *Stephen Brennan* (6 x 9, 400 pages, hardcover, $12.95)

An Autobiography of General Custer
by *Stephen Brennan* (6 x 9, 256 pages, hardcover, $12.95)